Jim Summers also

2020

Julia Kristeva (1941–) is a p
novelist, and professor whose wo
interdisciplinary thought. Born
dedicated to Darwin and a father devoted to Orthodox Christianity, she began her education in a French Catholic primary school. Her state education was supplemented with afternoons at the Alliance Française, which is where her voracious appetite for (French) literature first took hold. At university, she joined a small circle of talented dissident writers in Sofia, making a name for herself in print by the age of 24. In 1965, she was awarded a French government scholarship to study in Paris. Working with Lucien Goldmann and Roland Barthes, she discovered the journal *Tel Quel*, where she met her future husband, Philippe Sollers. Kristeva became known in the 1960s and 1970s for her work on how the unconscious impacts the production of desire and language, and in the 1980s and 1990s addressed multiple forms of marginal subjectivity as well as the question of how to revolt. Her six novels, published from 1990 to 2015, explore many of the same themes as her theoretical work, but while "traveling through herself." Her books on "women's genius" in the 2000s and on religion in the 2010s have changed the international conversation about how to (re)think the 21st century in an increasingly hyperconnected, violent world.

Alice Jardine is a professor at Harvard University, where she teaches 20th- and 21st-century French/Francophone literature, poststructuralist and feminist theory, and Studies of Women, Gender, and Sexuality. Her *Gynesis: Configurations of Woman and Modernity* (1985), co-translation of Kristeva's *Desire in Language* (1980), and several co-edited volumes (e.g. *The Future of Difference, Men in Feminism, Shifting Scenes, Living Attention*) reflect her deep investment in understanding how issues of women, gender, and sexuality are integral to the analysis of politics, culture, and society.

Mari Ruti (PhD, Harvard University) is Distinguished Professor of Critical Theory and of Gender and Sexuality Studies at the University of Toronto, Canada. She is the author of thirteen books, including *Between Levinas and Lacan: Self, Other, Ethics* (Bloomsbury Press, 2015) and *Distillations: Theory, Ethics, Affect* (Bloomsbury Press, 2018).

Psychoanalytic Horizons

Psychoanalysis is unique in being at once a theory and a therapy, a method of critical thinking and a form of clinical practice. Now in its second century, this fusion of science and humanism derived from Freud has outlived all predictions of its demise. **Psychoanalytic Horizons** evokes the idea of a convergence between realms as well as the outer limits of a vision. Books in the series test disciplinary boundaries and will appeal to scholars and therapists who are passionate not only about the theory of literature, culture, media, and philosophy but also, above all, about the real life of ideas in the world.

Volumes in the Series:

At the Risk of Thinking

An Intellectual Biography of Julia Kristeva

Alice Jardine

Edited by Mari Ruti

BLOOMSBURY ACADEMIC
NEW YORK · LONDON · OXFORD · NEW DELHI · SYDNEY

BLOOMSBURY ACADEMIC
Bloomsbury Publishing Inc
1385 Broadway, New York, NY 10018, USA
50 Bedford Square, London, WC1B 3DP, UK

BLOOMSBURY, BLOOMSBURY ACADEMIC and the Diana logo are trademarks of
Bloomsbury Publishing Plc

First published in the United States of America 2020

For legal purposes the Acknowledgments on p. xi constitute an extension of
this copyright page.

Cover design by Alice Marwick
Cover photographs from top: Recent portrait © Sophie Zhang;
© Julia Kristeva; © Julia Kristeva

Bloomsbury Publishing Inc does not have any control over, or responsibility for, any
third-party websites referred to or in this book. All internet addresses given in this book
were correct at the time of going to press. The author and publisher regret any
inconvenience caused if addresses have changed or sites have ceased to
exist, but can accept no responsibility for any such changes.

Library of Congress Cataloging-in-Publication Data
Names: Jardine, Alice, author. | Ruti, Mari, editor.
Title: At the risk of thinking: an intellectual biography of Julia
Kristeva / Alice Jardine; edited by Mari Ruti.
Description: New York: Bloomsbury Academic, 2020. | Series: Psychoanalytic
horizons | Includes bibliographical references and index. | Summary:
"The first biography of Julia Kristeva-one of the most important
intellectuals of the last 100 years. It connects her personal journey
with the history of her ideas, clarifies her legacy within the context
of postwar European thought, and demonstrates her crucial importance for
the future of interdisciplinary thought"– Provided by publisher.
Identifiers: LCCN 2019028646 (print) | LCCN 2019028647 (ebook) | ISBN
9781501341342 (hb) | ISBN 9781501341335 (pb) | ISBN 9781501341359
(ebook) | ISBN 9781501341366 (epdf)
Subjects: LCSH: Kristeva, Julia, 1941–
Classification: LCC B2430.K7544 J37 2020 (print) | LCC B2430.K7544
(ebook) | DDC 194 [B]–dc23
LC record available at https://lccn.loc.gov/2019028646
LC ebook record available at https://lccn.loc.gov/2019028647

ISBN: HB: 978-1-5013-4-1342
PB: 978-1-5013-4-1335
ePDF: 978-1-5013-4-1366
eBook: 978-1-5013-4-1359

Series: Psychoanalytic Horizons
D.30

Typeset by Deanta Global Publishing Services, Chennai, India
Printed and bound in the United States of America

To find out more about our authors and books visit www.bloomsbury.com and
sign up for our newsletters.

For all those who are able
to revolt
and to begin again.

Contents

Acknowledgments

There are a handful of people without whom this book simply would not exist. First and foremost, of course, I am deeply grateful to Julia Kristeva for her generous attention and time, as well as for her patience with my endless questions. I also want to thank Nancy K. Miller who first suggested that I undertake this project and who has remained available whenever I needed good advice. I am forever grateful to Mari Ruti, who—beyond her normal responsibilities as one of the coeditors of Bloomsbury Academic's Psychoanalytic Horizons Series—put her life and work on hold for several weeks at the end of this project in order to undertake a detailed editing of this entire volume. A world-class editor, Mari was my graduate student decades ago and, in a strange bit of role reversal, has turned out to be my most important writing mentor as I have returned to my writing desk after years of institutional activism.

I do not know how to thank enough my two talented and generous research and editorial assistants, David Francis and Emma Zitzow-Childs, who brought their acute intelligence and diligent editorial acumen to this manuscript. I also want to thank Philip Sayers for his meticulous attention to detail at the final stages of this project. Thanks also to Amy Martin and Leela Ulaganathan for their graceful responses to my countless queries during the production process. A special thanks to Loren Wolfe—co-interviewer and co-producer of the "biography tapes"—and a totally unflappable *compagnon de route*, whether driving remote Île de Ré roads or trying to read menus in Cyrillic.

I also want to thank very sincerely Haaris Naqvi, Editorial Director of Bloomsbury Academic in New York. I had forgotten what it is like to have a great publisher in one's corner. I also owe much gratitude to the Ruth Landes Memorial Research Fund and to Mr. David Latham, Programs Director of the Reed Foundation, for believing in this project from the very beginning and for funding the sabbatical which allowed me to begin it. I am also indebted to many other sources of support both near and far: in Cambridge, MA—especially Dean Robin Kelsey and the Faculty Publication Fund, the Chairs and staff of Romance Languages and Literatures and of Studies of Women, Gender, and Sexuality—and in Sofia, Bulgaria—especially the dedicated research librarians at the National Library. I have been immensely helped by Kristeva's assistant in Paris, Guillaume Leplâtre, and the wonderful photographers/videographers in France: Georgi Galabov, Sophie Zhang, and Alain Monclin.

I also want to thank the many friends and colleagues who have in one way or another supported this project from its inception: warm thanks to Miglena Nikolchina and Iskra Angelova who generously guided me not only through the streets of Sofia but also through the mysteries of communist and post-communist Bulgarian history and culture. I want to thank Kelly Oliver, Rebecca Tuvel, and the Kristeva Circle for their welcoming reception at Vanderbilt where I first presented some of this book's material. Thanks are due as well to Patsy Baudoin who translated several of Kristeva's journalistic responses on short notice in the midst of the media frenzy around the Sabina dossier in 2018 and to Susan Suleiman who helped me understand better the Eastern European contextual complexities of the dossier. I also owe a debt of gratitude to two excellent translators/transliterators from Bulgarian to English: Margarita Teneva, a young intellectual in Sofia with a Master's Degree from the English and American Studies Department, University of Sofia, and Maria Vassileva, translator and doctoral candidate in the Department of Slavic Languages and Literatures, Harvard University.

Finally, I want to thank my family and friends everywhere for their patience and support during this extended writing project. Gratitude is especially due to my close Boston circle of friends who never lost faith in me and listened 24/7 to my complaints: among many, special thanks to Janet Beizer, Afsaneh Najmabadi, Kathy Richman, Nancy Salzer, and Hope Steele. Last, but far from least, I want to thank my daughter, Anna, for everything from her expertise in photography and digital magic to her willingness to take scary moonlit walks over the salt marshes of the Île de Ré. Thank you, Anna, for your unwavering belief in me.

Author's Note

For the convenience of English-speaking readers, the titles of Kristeva's books, articles, and talks are provided in English in the text. However, because the chronological sequence of publications and public appearances is important in an intellectual biography such as this one, the date that accompanies each title refers to the original French date of publication or presentation. Complete French references, along with complete references to English translations, are provided in the endnotes. Where no official English translation exists, the translation is mine, and in such cases, given that no English publication information exists, only the French reference is provided in the notes.

In order to avoid unnecessary repetition in the endnotes, in most instances complete references to Kristeva's books are given when these books are examined in detail rather than at the first (allusive) mention. The Table of Contents—which lists Kristeva's books—guides readers to sections of the text where complete citations are provided. For the sake of specialist readers, Appendix 2 contains a chronological list of Kristeva's books in French.

All quotations not otherwise attributed are from my private taped interviews with Kristeva. Likewise, all translations of quotations not otherwise attributed are mine.

Portions of the Introduction and Part I have been published in *New Forms of Revolt: Essays on Kristeva's Intimate Politics*, ed. Sarah K. Hansen and Rebecca Tuvel (Albany: SUNY Press, 2017) and *Being Contemporary: French Literature, Culture, and Politics Today*, ed. Lia Brozgal and Sara Kippur (Liverpool: Liverpool University Press, 2016). Images not attributed are in the public domain or are posted on Julia Kristeva's website: http://www.kristeva.fr. I have captured some of them as screen shots from the documentary, *Histoires d'amour et de passerelles* (2011), written and directed by Teri Wehn-Damisch. The complete documentary is available on Kristeva's website.

To listen to the unconscious means that one is at once in the story/in history . . . because people come with stories . . . they tell stories . . . and at the same time, you are surveying . . . you enter the depths of this verticality . . . it is a very specific temporality.

The question is unavoidable: if we are not on the side of those whom society wastes in order to reproduce itself, where are we?

Julia Kristeva

Introduction:
At the Risk of Thinking

Julia Kristeva is the first to admit that she is quite at a loss to know who Julia Kristeva is. It was the very first thing she said during the first of my many interviews with her: "It's very difficult. Sometimes I do not recognize myself in the demands people make of me to talk about Julia Kristeva. Because I am not entirely sure who this woman is. There is an image, there is a received idea, there is even sometimes a cult."

Kristeva asks: Who is this woman, Julia Kristeva? She travels around the world, accepting honors and speaking to huge audiences wherever she goes—often to her genuine astonishment. She knows, as a practicing psychoanalyst, that autobiography is a "false genre." On top of that, she has been psychoanalyzed, which is a process that, in her opinion, leads to a complete "transvaluation of the self." As she puts it: "Julia Kristeva, that's a lot of people: psychoanalyst, linguist, teacher, writer, mother, wife."

But what about biography? What about someone else taking on the role of biographer? Why should someone else care about "who Julia Kristeva is"? Why should I care? Who am I to care?

The Question of the Intellectual—Again

I care in large part because in our still early part of the twenty-first century, there is in my opinion no more urgent matter than developing through dialogue, debate, and practice a new model of the intellectual. I imagine this new model as flexible, contingent, but powerful, yet hopefully beyond the careerist and/or media models that I see in the American university. And one thing is clear: Julia Kristeva has never stopped thinking not only about what it means to be an intellectual but also, more precisely, about how to live a thinking life.

In the epistemological, political, and artistic situation today, what does it mean for me to engage in what might be called a "strong autobiographical reading" of Kristeva's work in order to help sort through the chaos of how to live, think, and work as an intellectual in the twenty-first century?[1] Does this kind of reading as a search for how to work as an intellectual amount to narcissism at a moment when intellectuals might need to adopt perhaps a more historically familiar "committed" model of labor? Is it possible to engage in strong auto-bio-graphical reading without allowing oneself to get in the way of the biographical project, without occupying all the space?

I open with these questions because although this book is technically an "intellectual biography," it does not follow the genre in a loyal way. Rather, I offer an "essay" in the French tradition, a reading of Kristeva's life and work as part of my own search for a new model of the intellectual. My founding question for this book has been quite simply: What constitutes Kristeva's originality and authority for the twenty-first century? Through her emphasis on the need for an urgent revival of the humanities, does a new model of the intellectual emerge that is viable for the twenty-first century as we are living it? I think it does. Is it a compelling model? I think it is. *The contestatory intellectual*: that is what Kristeva calls it.

In the Face of Resistance

There is no doubt that Kristeva is one of the most important writers of the twentieth and early twenty-first centuries. She is the author of some fifty well-known books, written across several disciplinary fields including philosophy, psychoanalysis, anthropology, linguistics, semiotics, and theology, and translated across the entire world. As her international reputation as an influential intellectual has expanded, she has received many high honors: she was the first Laureate of the international Holberg Prize created in 2004 by the Norwegian government; she was awarded the Hannah Arendt Prize for Political Thought in 2006; she was named Commander in the Legion of Honor in 2015; and she received the prestigious Prix Saint-Simon in 2017. She taught for many years at the University of Paris 7, where she founded a well-respected Humanities Institute, as well as at several North American universities, including Columbia University and the University of Toronto. She has also been celebrated for her creation of the international Simone de Beauvoir Prize, awarded to extraordinary women intellectuals, writers, artists, and activists.

In spite of all this accomplishment and acclaim, Kristeva's work is also attacked, marginalized, and even ridiculed both in the media and in certain parts of the academy, particularly in the United States, on the right as well as the left. Some have said that this is because she is a woman, because she is following in the footsteps of the very few major women intellectuals of the twentieth century, especially Simone de Beauvoir.[2] Indeed, it is impossible not to see how similar the negative reactions have been to their very different work, undertaken at very different historical moments. To the extent that mine is an explicitly feminist biographical project, I do attempt to show what is unique about Kristeva as a woman intellectual, a "female genius," including what is revealing in that regard about the attacks on her work.[3] But truthfully, I have never fully understood the resistance she encounters—although sometimes I think I do.

What I know for sure is that since I first started reading Kristeva in the mid-1970s, I have remained fascinated by her loyal defense of the creative, psychic process at the heart of the literary and artistic humanities as well as by her ability to maintain this defense across mind-numbing historical change. Do I still read Kristeva today because of this defense? Or is it because of my fascination with her status as a "migrant female intellectual"? Or is it because of her identity as an intellectual and writer who is also a mother? Or is it because of her advocacy for those who are marginalized in frightening new ways in an increasingly technologically flattened-out world? Or is it because of my attraction to risk: to the risk of thinking, to the idea of putting at risk my sense of who I am while embracing Julia Kristeva's call for all of us to take the risk of thinking. *Period*.

The title of my volume, *At the Risk of Thinking*, is a play on Kristeva's 2001 *At the Risk of Thought*[4]—a collection of her interviews with the journalist Marie-Christine Navarro—in part because this book was the first time that Julia Kristeva exercised her formidable powers of thinking while also making herself personally vulnerable in public. My choice to echo the title of her 2001 book—to entitle my own volume just slightly differently with a gerund as noun—is not only due to the fact that *thinking* is the active core of Kristeva's life/ work. It also reflects my belief that it has been through her increasing willingness to reveal her own vulnerabilities *while still thinking* that Kristeva has more rapidly connected with millions of readers worldwide.

Sometimes I wonder whether the strong resistance to Kristeva's thought, particularly on the American left, is an allergy to thinking— *period*. Kristeva thinks all the time. For her, like for Hannah Arendt, thinking is living. Life is thinking. Moreover, like Arendt, she believes that the incapacity to think—especially when thinking is uncomfortable, challenging, or even dangerous—inevitably leads to totalitarianism, to monologism, of one sort or another. The resistance to re-thinking, to remembering—the loss of historical memory—is what leads to the banality of evil. Even today. Perhaps most especially today.

Whatever the reasons for the resistance to Kristeva's work, the critiques are serious, loud, and often difficult to answer. There is the familiar accusation of elitism, most often accompanied by an allusion to the difficulty of her prose; there are the accusations of Eurocentrism;[5] there is the often virulent critique of her persistent interest in religion; and there are, of course, the complaints about her allegiance to psychoanalysis with all of its nineteenth-century echoes of the heteronormative bourgeoisie and its twentieth-century emphases on the individual psyche as opposed to social and political forces.[6] For example, I could not believe the angry hullabaloo in the 2000s about her psychoanalytic focus on male adolescence, on the adolescent's need to believe in ideals, and on how the shattering of these ideals can lead to nihilism, indeed to crisis, in the context of which Kristeva made reference not only to Western male adolescents but also to young men of Middle Eastern and North African descent being pulled into nihilistic extremism. Her critics seemed to believe that she was saying that there are no other reasons for terrorism besides teenage angst—which is far from being the case.[7]

Although I do not directly engage with Kristeva's most fervent critics in what follows, I do try to highlight what in Kristeva's thought both invites and repels these critiques. Implicitly at least, and in some cases even somewhat forcefully, I address dismissals of Kristeva's work that seem to be based on her "person" and a series of received ideas—almost mythologies—about Kristeva that need dispelling, or at least nuancing. That is, as with most celebrated intellectuals in France, there is an aura of notoriety that surrounds Kristeva, but in a way that is different from what happens to male celebrity intellectuals, given that most often hers is a notoriety that has little to do with her published work. There are, for example, accusations that she is rich (she is not); that she is elitist (no, not in any simple way); that she is relentlessly ambitious (not at all). I can hear the objections: "She wears designer clothes and lives in the 6th arrondissement of Paris and has property on a beautiful French island. Besides, she lets her husband be awful to her . . ." I hope that what follows relieves the popular pressure of these mythologies and reveals them to be profoundly gendered if not misogynist.

By far the longest, loudest, most frequent—and snarkiest—complaint about Kristeva, particularly on the part of feminists, is her long, loyal, passionate, and very public love affair with Philippe Sollers—from their earliest days to now:

Figure 1.1. Kristeva and Sollers as a young couple. The Julia Kristeva Archive.

Figure 1.2. Kristeva and Sollers as an older couple. Photo by Sophie Zhang.

In Sollers's words: "What is a *coup de foudre*? A *coup de foudre* is a very common expression. It seems that it actually happens from time to time . . . There are attractions . . . But what is a *coup de foudre* that endures? That, well, that's something else. It's complex. It necessarily has to do with the very complex individuals who can eventually reignite each other from time to time."[8]

My *Coup de Foudre*

What is a *coup de foudre* that endures over time?

I must ask *myself* this question, since I had one of those for Julia Kristeva in my youth, at least on the intellectual level. And it has endured in the sense that I remain fascinated by Kristeva's work in an unresolved way. I confess that I am, in part at least, writing an intellectual biography of her in order to help my readers to fully engage with the above-mentioned critiques of a body of work that I myself continue to admire and find vitally important. However, I am also searching for an etiology that is not an origin, but rather a start to figuring out what it means to be an *intellectual* in the twenty-first century. Not an aesthete. Not an expert. Not a politician. Not even a scholar. Rather, what Kristeva calls a contestatory intellectual. That is what I try to be, but it is hard. I have not succeeded yet as I write these words.

I first met Julia Kristeva in 1976 when I was twenty-five years old, a naïve woman in my second year of graduate work at Columbia. I was on work-study, and the then chair of the Department of French, Michael Riffaterre, asked me if I wanted to be Kristeva's research assistant. The Kristeva I met then—only ten years my senior—was mesmerizing to me in every way. I was particularly struck by the fact that even as a relatively young intellectual, she could, without batting an eye, withstand being viciously attacked by Marxist graduate students and right-wing faculty alike! She did not care. She was too busy devouring Mallarmé.

What I remember most acutely about Kristeva from that time was the impressive amalgamation of her intellectual brilliance and her devotion to her baby son, David, born in 1975. Over the years, I have stayed attached to David, first babysitting him when he was small, singing "Twinkle, Twinkle, Little Star" with him over and over and over again.

In part, it was the way Kristeva looked at David that most fascinated me.

Over the years, it has never entered my mind to ask Kristeva about David's developmental and cognitive delays and disabilities. He was—and is—gorgeous. He is always just himself—just David. And he is adored by both of his parents who have done everything humanly possible to make space for his exquisite singularity.

Figure 1.3. David with his parents, Île de Ré, 1990. The Julia Kristeva Archive.

One of the most mysterious things for Kristeva about "Julia Kristeva" is how detached the image of the academic celebrity is from the everyday struggles of a mother of a handicapped child, a loving wife, an overworked professor, a practicing psychoanalyst, and, of course, someone who thinks, reads, and writes in every spare minute she has. David shares her bafflement at the circulation of the idealized image of "Julia Kristeva" that has very little to do with their daily lives. "I do not know Julia Kristeva," he says with an ironic smile.

Figure 1.4. Summer home on Île de Ré. *Histoires d'amour et de passerelles* (2011), dir. Teri Wehn-Damisch @Cinétévé]

In the summer of 2012, I spent some time on the Île de Ré with David, listening to him recite La Rochefoucauld by heart. The island, located off the western coast of France near La Rochelle and known for its salt marshes, is usually overrun with tourists in the summer. But that summer, it was relatively quiet and I was able to stay long enough to conduct a series of intensive interviews with Kristeva about her life. Yes, I decided to take the risk of figuring out who Julia Kristeva is for me today. I decided to take seriously one of the most significant things I have learned from Kristeva: the importance of the intimate. I am following my desire to better understand how she connects her *vie intime* with the thought processes that she makes public through her constant writing. That is something I want to learn to do better myself.

But I also want to implicitly engage the pesky critiques I have mentioned. Kristeva has described herself as an "energetic pessimist"—which also describes me exactly. Indeed, the world that we are living in right now feeds my energetic pessimism so acutely that I have come to be certain that while I do not always agree with my subject-object, I deeply admire Kristeva's personal and intellectual courage.

Why Now? The Contestatory Intellectual

As Simone de Beauvoir states in the preface to the second volume of her autobiography, *The Prime of Life*, "I must warn [my readers] that I have no intention of telling them everything."[9] That is, there is a specific shape to what follows. While in no way is this book a hagiography (Kristeva is no saint), I am nevertheless not neutral here and want to be clear about where I am coming from. I believe that

*The world we are living in needs Kristeva's strong ethical drive as a cosmopolitan and contestatory intellectual;

*It needs her insistence on thinking not about identity, but about how to achieve and value what she calls universal singularity;

*It needs her strong insistence on secularism and a new, renewed form of humanism, a transvaluation of classical religion, with the infinite Chain of Being coming to us through books rather than through God and religion;

*It needs her valuing of the arts and literature as unique forms of thought, as when she emphasized recently in China, agreeing with a colleague, that "the only way to confront totalitarian thought is to learn and to ensure that new generations are taught the plurality of languages, literatures, and mentalities of the world, and how to problematize and analyze them";[10]

*It needs her ability to embrace, indeed embody, marginalization and vulnerability. It needs her insistence on all the edges of subjectivity: mental illness, delinquency, mysticism, maternity. And it needs her ideas on disability as not a lack to be fixed through charity but rather an opportunity, not a deprivation but rather an irreducible singularity;

*It needs Kristeva's reflection on "new forms of revolt," given that revolt seems to be the order of the day on a global scale.

Regarding revolt, Kristeva asks: "Is it in the process of waking up digital humanity from its hyperconnected dream? Or is it rather just another ruse of the culture of spectacle that requires more and more ruses in order to endure?"[11] Kristeva argues first and foremost that to truly be alive, one must have a living psychic space and that in the contemporary world, one has to make a strong effort to keep it alive, for example through psychoanalysis, through an artistic practice of some kind, or through the rediscovery of past religious experience—even if one is an atheist. She calls for a new "discourse on life" because the need to believe—to have an immovable certitude about something—is in crisis today, in large part because of the suffocation of psychic space. According to Kristeva, this state of affairs leads to "new maladies of the soul"—to violence, addiction, criminality, nihilism, and somatic suffering.

Kristeva's work toward understanding what Arendt called "extreme evil" has led her to emphasize the necessity of revolt against new forms and practices of biopolitics, including new global strategies for managing subjectivity through technologies such as social media. For Kristeva, psychic death is about the death of the imaginary—a death from which only a culture of revolt can save us. But how can we revolt in our hypermodern world? How can we revolt when there are obstacles to our psychic life wherever we turn? And how can we revolt against what is perceived as a power vacuum that lacks the kind of central figure—such as a king—that older models of revolution opposed? Kristeva has issued strong warnings about new forms of fascism for our time, warnings increasingly echoed from many other corners as I write these words.

In short, Kristeva urges resistance to mediatization and mechanization, pushing back against an increasingly digitalized, commodified, and neoliberal technocracy that is taking over human psychic space. For this reason, we need her reflections on biopolitics in late capitalism, particularly as an "update" to Foucauldian ideas of disciplinary regimes.[12] This is especially so at a time in history when the complex dance between what she calls "the need to believe" and "the desire to know" is being replaced by a trudging obsession with how one might fit into the marketplace, where everything and everyone can be bought and sold—preferably in English.

I emphasize all of these things in this intellectual biography, in dialogue with the difficulties of the times in which we are living, and for the sake of my own intellectual narrative. But equally importantly, I insist upon, and therefore highlight in my text, the fact that at the heart of Kristeva's strong thinking over the last fifty years, there is an intimately experiential shape.

Born in Sliven, Bulgaria in 1941, Kristeva arrived in Paris in 1965 very much a young woman educated in the Eastern European communist bloc, a foreigner, an immigrant, a bit traumatized by such a radical change, and searching for a way to be part of all the exciting intellectual and artistic innovation of that time. She found that life-changing experience in Paris. She also found friendship and camaraderie through the group *Tel Quel* and eventually love (and citizenship) with her husband, Philippe Sollers. Soon thereafter she discovered what can only be described as *jouissance*, pure joy/bliss, through becoming mother to her son. During those years, Kristeva remained intensely loyal to the prevailing poststructuralist currents being developed by the pretty much exclusively male intelligentsia in Paris. During the 1960s and 1970s, she was at her most theoretical, developing her abstract vocabularies with breathless rapidity. The major insights of her first publications, such as her 1969 *Semiotike*, 1974 *Revolution in Poetic Language*, and 1977 *Polylogue*, were buried in scientifically driven narrative prose. In retrospect, it is easy to see that this vulnerable yet tough young woman's intense desire for her work to be taken seriously is inscribed on every page.

What is most striking to me about the texts of these years is their lack of autobiographical inscription.[13] The Kristeva of the 1960s and 1970s was faithful mostly to the very abstract. She was also primarily focused on male subjectivity. While her status as a woman occasionally breaks through (as it does, for example, in the 1974 *About Chinese Women*), she was careful to distance herself from—when she was not outright critiquing—feminism. When she focused on nationality, she looked to the United States or China rather than Eastern Europe. Her status as a mother was mostly hidden from public view. Any conceivable autobiographical voice that there might have been at that point was buried under some very heavy prose, perhaps out of caution given how women's writing has for centuries been dismissed as "only autobiographical." Kristeva's work in the 1980s and 1990s shifted radically toward a more forthright consideration of what she saw as a serious crisis at the heart of Western civilization, a crisis brought on in large part by the assault of technology and the media on human subjectivity. Her books of this time period insist upon our state of "permanent crisis": her 1980 *Powers of Horror* analyzes the horror of the abject at the heart of Judeo-Christianity; her 1983 *Tales of Love* focuses on the breakdown of love; her 1987 *Black Sun* examines the prevalence and dangers of melancholia and depression; her 1988 *Strangers to Ourselves* discusses the dilemmas of strangeness and foreignness; and her 1993 *New Maladies of the Soul* emphasizes the importance of psychoanalytic theory for thinking about the social. After this important series of theoretical books, Kristeva finally arrived at fiction. It was almost as if Kristeva got to a point where trying to communicate the "deep logics" of Western civilization and their consequences today in theoretical language became too frustrating; it was as if only the language of fiction could capture what she was getting at. Kristeva thus became a novelist, publishing *The Samurai* in 1990, *The Old Man and the Wolves* in 1991, and *Possessions* in 1996.

Kristeva also began to speak out in the 1990s on the pressing issues that she saw as haunting the West, issues seemingly unable to attract the attention of the Western world's increasingly conservative intellectual class—most centrally, the issues of migration/immigration and of religious belief systems (and their demise). She returned with foreboding to the question of the body in the human sciences as well as to the crises of human subjectivity leading to a retreat into religious extremism and violence against those who are different from oneself. This is when she began to write about the importance of revolt, even small, localized, "intimate" revolt in the West, about a continuous revolt against allowing one's inner life—whether one calls it soul or psyche—

to be colonized by the technocratic world of media spectacle, capitalist consumption, and information overload. She also turned explicitly to the question of women and genius with the first volume of her trilogy of intellectual biographies, the 1999 *Hannah Arendt.*

Since 2000, Kristeva has continued the call she began in the 1990s for new, complex, flexible, and hybrid subjectivities, as well as for the sociopolitical acceptance of otherness in Europe and around the world. However, she has left behind the scientifically abstract, theoretical prose of the first two decades of her work as well as the crisis-driven, predictive prose of the following twenty years, and returned explicitly to her own experiential beginnings. She writes more personally for a larger public about the body politic, particularly "foreignness," including her worries about the shocks and echoes of the end of the Cold War and their effects on the formerly communist world, especially Eastern Europe: *Crisis of the European Subject* (2000); *Micropolitics* (2001); *Chronicles of a Sensitive Time* (2003); *Hatred and Forgiveness* (2005); and *Passions of Our Time* (2013). She explores more openly female genius, femininity, women, and motherhood: *Melanie Klein* (2000); *Colette* (2002); *Alone, a Woman* (2007); *Beauvoir Presents/In the Present* (2016). And she questions world religions, atheism, and current relationships to the sacred: *This Incredible Need to Believe* (2007) and *Teresa, My Love* (2008).

Kristeva moreover acts publicly on behalf of the vulnerable: for example, she has created the National Council for the Handicapped, largely because of her personal experience of raising a handicapped child, chronicled in the 2011 *Their Look Pierces Our Shadows.* She has likewise worked to focus public consciousness on the plight of the ill and elderly in France and across Europe, largely because of the way she experienced the tragic—indeed criminal—death of her father in a Bulgarian hospital. Her fourth novel, *Murder in Byzantium* (2004), explores all of these topics via a female detective who—as Kristeva puts it—"travels through herself." Kristeva also explicitly defends and celebrates her long marriage to Philippe Sollers in their 2015 *Marriage as a Fine Art*, and has begun to expose her private life to her vast public readership through an autobiographical collection of interviews with Samuel Dock: *Traveling Through Myself* (2016).

It is the determined movement forward of Kristeva's work through the postwar twentieth century as well as her thoughtful return in the early twenty-first century to her earlier life experiences that I examine most deeply in what follows. I explore for myself and for my reader the shape of Kristeva's experiential, intellectual, and political trajectory with the goal of illuminating new possibilities for the cosmopolitan and contestatory intellectual in the twenty-first century. I try to elucidate Kristeva's status as an outsider who defends the interpretive and creative process at the heart of global interdisciplinarity, making a special effort to render visible how she does this through an increasingly brave, explicit, and strong insistence on the value of her life experience.

Kristeva has reflected at some length on the fact that she has never planned her life. She has never had a program or a strategy. She never thought about leaving Bulgaria before she actually left. She never thought: "I will go to France." She explains that she swims through life, traveling through herself, living for the most part in a "vertical present tense" close to the logic of the unconscious: "Je me voyage." For her, what is important is to move along in life and writing, pulled by pure curiosity, just seeing where it all leads:

> Even though I think of myself as very Cartesian, rational, etc., I don't follow a program. I don't say: I will do this and I will do that, and then that. I don't follow a trajectory fixed in advance. I do things a bit as they come to me, as if I were swimming. I let myself be carried by the waves. I swim, but there is also the movement of the waves. I never thought I would leave Bulgaria—never! But it's true that in a way all of my studies have been escapes, a way of taking distance from my parents while staying close, distancing myself but at the same time transcending where they were.

Kristeva has talked to me a lot about how she has always just tried to construct herself as she swims through the waves of the world and history, hovering in vertical time. My attention really perks up here, for that is the way I have lived as well, with way less illustrious results I am afraid. But the same lack of a plan characterizes my life as well. So what can I learn from my slightly senior contemporary, my friend, right now, about how to live, how to work, how to be, how to contest? One thing I know is that over the past few years, Kristeva and I have come to share a deep concern about the world of our children and students, a world where there is no room for vulnerability, a world where everyone is becoming so commodified, mechanized, and programmed that they are never present to themselves. As Kristeva puts it, "Humanity is so caught up in a frantic race for a so-called 'happiness'—a well-being made up of enjoyment, performance, brilliance—that all vulnerability is considered to be an intolerable, unthinkable menace. This is a vision of humanity that is commercialized and mechanical."[14]

Kristeva believes that this kind of programming runs entirely counter-current to the kind of self-making that relies on curiosity and ethical passion:

> I try to construct myself through the waves of the world and history . . . There's a lot of chance involved, a lot of necessity too, but I do not think that I have a destiny. And I've had a lot of deaths and resurrections in my life. When one leaves one's language, one's country, one's childhood, one loses a lot of things . . . and a lot of things are erased just as one erases writing in the sand . . . but there are always re-beginnings and it has been living through these tests, these deaths and resurrections, that I have achieved satisfactions in life that would have been unimaginable to me beforehand.[15]

Whomever history ultimately determines Julia Kristeva to have been, can we embrace the fact that such a cosmopolitan and contestatory intellectual is living life so in the moment, so caught in the waves of curiosity? And how can her utter lack of strategy help me—her autobiographically inclined biographer—find my way forward with integrity?

In speaking of her life, Kristeva often quotes Colette: "To be reborn has never been too much for me."[16] Indeed, these are the words that Kristeva would like inscribed on her tombstone. Perhaps it is time for me—for us?—to contemplate some re-birth, or at least some re-self-invention: perhaps it is time to nurture the capacity to begin again.

Figure 1.5. Kristeva walking on wall on Île de Ré. *Histoires d'amour et de passerelles* (2011), dir. Teri Wehn-Damisch @Cinétévé.

Taking on the challenge of strong thinking, traveling through oneself, constructing oneself, walking the tightrope between intellect and revolt, between the intimate and the public, between work and play, with no plan, no program, no strategy or directive—that is the kind of contestatory intellectual I want to be henceforth—for whatever time I have left on this earth. And you? It's worth the risk, don't you think?

Notes on the Biography

There are three relationships that I want to address with regard to the writing of this intellectual biography.

First, there is the question of *my* relationship to the biography, a question of the kind of distance and tone I have adopted. Yes, I am a great admirer of Julia Kristeva's work and I consider her to be an important personal friend. But—as I have already said—this is not a hagiography. This is not an adoring book. What follows is not the product of the kind of starry-eyed reverence that characterizes many texts written about Kristeva, a reverence almost always fixated on her beauty, her charm, or her intelligence—all three of which she has in abundance. Both men and women seem to indulge in this reverence. Most recently, Dock opens *Traveling Through Myself* by evoking Kristeva's large smile, and two erudite female professors who interviewed Kristeva in 2009 begin their interview by describing her warmth.[17] These kinds of descriptions are undoubtedly accurate. But in what follows, I attempt only to provide the ground, the background, and the glue holding together this beautiful and brilliant—and imposing—personal and textual presence.

Second, there is the question of *Julia Kristeva's* relationship to this biography. Kristeva is still, thankfully, very much alive. This biography is in some ways premature. It is hybrid, tentative, and only a first attempt at sharing publicly the details of this remarkable woman's life. *Traveling Through Myself* was also a tentative effort by Kristeva herself to begin to consolidate and protect her legacy—and it has been an important source for my work here. But both of these efforts are just the beginning.

Kristeva still has a lot of living to do. She is likely to write many more books—she is currently writing one on Dostoevsky—and many more books will be written about her. After her death, archives will be opened, her papers and letters will be published, and so on. Michel de Certeau, a masterful historian, once made a distinction between "reconstitution" and "reminiscence."[18] The hybridity of what follows is largely due to my reconstitution of Kristeva's reminiscences as, for example, they were shared with me through long, very alive and lively interview sessions. These interviews are not by any means the only sources for what follows, but they are important sources.

The hybridity of my text is also due to the fact that Kristeva does not live in linear, biographical—chronological—time. Given Kristeva's aforementioned tendency to live in "vertical time," the reconstitution of her story has at times been a genuine challenge. Kristeva floats through time. She swims and catches each wave a bit *par hasard*. Her memories are gathered into complex rhythms that most often have very little to do with linear experience. As a result, it has been hard to reconstitute what-happened-when in Kristeva's life. Indeed, often her memories and my memories surge together to the surface somewhat willy-nilly. I have nevertheless tried to reconstitute her reminiscences as best I can, while carefully respecting the fact that she is still alive and hopefully will be so for a considerable time to come. I have, for instance, limited my sources to scholars, students, friends, and family members who are eager to speak on the record now, during Kristeva's lifetime. I have not pursued intimate sources. That is, I have protected most of Kristeva's closest intimacies—an unusual procedure for a genre that cries out in our time for "tell-all" transparency. I decided upon starting this project that someone else will have to reveal the content of Kristeva's intimate correspondence and the names of her lovers "after her death," as Kristeva prefers. The tone of this biography is personal but not completely intimate, with my own unconscious, perhaps transferential connections to Kristeva and her writing surfacing more often than is usual for the genre.

Third, there is the question of *the reader's* relationship to what follows. From my perspective, that is the clearest of the three relationships. I have written for the interested, non-specialist reader who might be intrigued by Kristeva's life and work. For me, such a reader might or might not have read Kristeva's work directly. Those who have read at least some of Kristeva might have done so with passionate and informed interest and comprehension. Or they might have found her texts too demanding. Either way is fine. This book is written for the sophisticated, the uninformed, and everyone in between. That is, I have assumed my readers' interest in Kristeva and her work but not necessarily their expertise. I in fact hope that my book will help readers tackle Kristeva's books. At the very least, I hope that what follows will make them *want* to try to tackle them, if they have not already.

Finally, I want to say something about the time of the writing of this intellectual biography.

Over the past decade of my intense engagement with Kristeva's life and work, much has changed in the world, often in ways that have shaken me to my core. My own "energetic pessimism" has increased tenfold since I started this project. I have been shocked by the spiraling crisis in the viability of democratic philosophy, the dangerous expansion of an often surreal atmosphere of post-factuality, the enthusiastic embrace by millions of populist ideologies that frequently include appeals to violent extremism, the escalation of authoritarian nationalism and identity paranoia with its attendant racism, sexism, and homophobia, and the truly head-spinning election of Donald Trump—not to mention the global emergency, and delusional denial, of ecological collapse and climate chaos. Closer to home, as someone who has labored at the heart of the academy for decades, I have been appalled by attacks from multiple special interest perspectives on progressive intellectuals, on the arts and humanities and, indeed, on all ethical pursuits of knowledge that are not immediately marketable. My concurrent loss of faith in the capacity of progressive academics to change the university from within has brought me face to face with my now truly outlived idealism. How indeed is it possible to be a contestatory intellectual in the twenty-first century?

In the middle of all this, in early 2018 Kristeva was suddenly accused of having been an agent of the murderous Secret Services of the proto-Stalinist government of Bulgaria in the early 1970s (see Part III). This out-of-nowhere assault on one of the most respected, progressive, and ethical intellectuals in the world was mind-boggling to me. Indeed, in the context of grappling with this assault, as I came to understand better the history and lived experience of Eastern Europeans from the Second World War until now, many of the more recent historical shocks listed above have been amplified for me as if from within an uncanny echo chamber. I want my reader to know that I believe Kristeva when she says that she has never been an agent for anyone, least of all for the totalitarian state she ran away from in 1965. And I want my reader to know that given everything that I have come to understand about Kristeva, as well as about the particularities of the totalitarianism from which she escaped, I have made an active decision to continue telling her story in the way that she has lived it. What follows is the story of Julia Kristeva's life as I believe it has been lived.

Part I

Bulgaria, My Suffering (1941–1965)

Julia Kristeva would be the first to say that one is not—cannot be—determined by one's childhood. Nor does she see her country of birth as constituting her identity or origin, identity for her being a constant state of questioning. In fact, she sees exile as her permanent condition and goes so far as to say that each person's truth resides not in their belonging to an origin but in their capacity to exile themselves, to take some distance from their origins:[1]

> Many things from my childhood resonate with what I am doing today. But if I am Freudian, it is because I believe, like Freud, that we are not explained, we are not determined by our childhood—contrary to what many people think about Freudianism. Our childhood provides us with the seeds of personality, but what one rediscovers in analysis is that one has reconstructed one's childhood. Something is given to us, but we have rebuilt it. Therefore, one never finds the exact, current situation in the past. Lots of people who entertain this idea are disappointed by analysis. They complain: But I can never find the memory that explains who I am now ... I can't find the delicate flower ... the love ... the enigma ... That's why I say that memories are not deterministic; they are invitations to travel.[2]

And yet . . .

A Production of History

Kristeva was born at home in Sliven, Bulgaria, at 8 a.m. on June 24, 1941, two days after World War II became a daily reality in that part of the

Figure 2.1. Map of Bulgaria. University of Texas Libraries.

world with the German invasion of the Soviet Union and the bombing of Kiev on June 22, 1941. Her mother, a brilliant scientist who gave up her career to dedicate herself to her family, was especially delighted to have a daughter, although she was distressed that she could not nurse her because of an infection. Her father, a brilliant theologian and writer, and Yordana, her caretaker, fed her sheep's milk from a bottle (initiating a life-long intolerance for any kind of milk). Both of her parents as well as Yordana doted on her continually, setting in play a life-long loving loyalty to family and friends no matter what.

Sliven is an industrial town in east-central Bulgaria. It lies in the southern foothills of the eastern Balkan Mountains at the confluence of the Novoselska and Asenovska rivers close to the Black Sea. Kristeva frequently evokes, especially in her novels, young childhood memories of running free in her maternal grandmother's flower gardens, flowers in her hair, when her family visited her mother's native city of Yambol not far from Sliven. Sometimes she even links her relationship to time itself to her observations of plants and flowers in her grandmother's gardens, echoing the rhapsodic love of nature of Rousseau and Colette. She also has fond memories of playing in the sand by the sea during childhood trips to the Black Sea. Two towns in particular stand out in her memory: Sozopol and Nessebar, located near the two larger Black Sea cities of Varna and Burgas. Nessebar—originally a Thracian settlement, a Greek colony beginning in the sixth century BC, then part of the Byzantine Empire, captured by the Turks until the nineteenth century, and a sleepy village of Greek fishermen in the early twentieth century—is described vividly in *Murder in Byzantium*.

The historical layers of Nessebar deeply impressed the young Kristeva. She vividly remembers the town as a magnificent place that had not yet been spoiled by the postwar tourist industry. In particular, she recalls the hundreds of beautiful and historic church ruins from the ninth to the twelfth centuries. Whether built during the Byzantine, Ottoman, or Bulgarian rule of the city, the churches of Nessebar represent the rich architectural heritage of the Eastern Orthodox world and provided many of Kristeva's earliest sensorial pleasures. In *At the Risk of Thought*, Kristeva also evokes with affection the larger Bulgarian countryside, especially the gorgeous "valley of roses": "Bulgaria is the country of roses, for between two mountains, a valley is planted with roses from east to west and reputable refineries extract a magnificent essence. A scented country then, but also a country with an extraordinary cultural memory."³

Kristeva lived in Sliven until the family relocated to Sofia after the war in 1946, first to 4 Saint Sophia Street and then to 31 A. Kanchev Street. Her only sibling, a sister named Ivanka, was born in January 1945, just before the family moved.

Today these streets are small, winding reminders of the charm of this part of the city, not far from the Saint Nedelya Church, and relatively quiet compared to the rest of the city. During a trip to Sofia in 2014 when I accompanied Kristeva to her childhood haunts, I was struck by how central her family's apartments were, how close they were to the church where her father sang in his free time. I was also struck by how well Kristeva remembered her way around the streets, as if she had been walking in these neighborhoods her entire life.

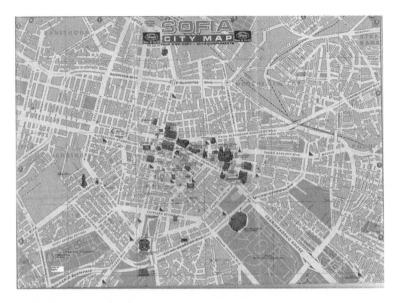

Figure 2.2. Map of Sofia.

Figure 2.3. The Saint Nedelya Church. Photo by Alice Jardine.

Figure 2.4. Kristeva ringing the bell at 4 Saint Sophia Street, 2014. Photo by Alice Jardine.

Kristeva's parents could not but have felt that she was a glimpse of bright joy in the midst of the darkness of war and, indeed, they smothered their baby girl with love. Kristeva has described herself as a "royal baby," born into the chaos of war. She recalls:

> There was a song that we sang during my childhood—a Russian song—that goes like this [Kristeva sings the song with clear delight]:

> Dvadtsat' vtorogo iyunya,
> Rovno v chetyre chasa,
> Kiev bombili, nam ob"yavili,
> Chto nachalasya voyna.

> The 22nd of June,
> At 4 o'clock precisely,
> They bombed Kiev and announced,
> The war has started.

It was the 22nd of June 1941 . . . Kiev was bombed and we were at war . . . I was born two days after. Sometimes when I hear this song, I imagine how dramatic it must have all been for my parents. Bulgaria was entering the war and, very quickly, it was the German presence that made itself felt since Bulgaria and Germany were allies. To give birth to a child in those circumstances was no doubt a great joy, but also at the same time a huge uncertainty. What was going to happen?

The stories dominating Kristeva's earliest memories of her childhood were shaped by the two devastating totalitarian invasions—the first undertaken by the Nazis and the second by the Soviets—that Bulgaria experienced during the twentieth century. At the beginning of the Second World War, in 1939–41, Bulgaria remained neutral. It entered the war in March 1941 as a member of the Axis Powers. However, it quickly took its distance from the Nazis. Operating as a constitutional monarchy during most of the war (Boris III was Tsar 1918–43), the government managed to fend off the Nazis' strongest demands. For example, Bulgaria declined to participate in Operation Barbarossa, the Nazi plan to enslave Slavs beginning with the Axis invasion of the Soviet Union; it did not declare war on the Soviets; and it actively saved its Jewish population from deportation to concentration camps.

Antisemitism was not rampant in Bulgaria at the time and there was a highly assimilated Jewish minority of about 50,000 people living in the country at the beginning of the war. What distinguishes Bulgaria from many of its European neighbors is the ferocity with which it resisted the Nazis' orders: it was one of the few Nazi-occupied countries in Europe not to do the Nazis' bidding when it came to Jews; the Bulgarian government stood mostly firm on its policy of not deporting Jews, even as members of the communist resistance, especially the Fatherland Front, accused the government of collaboration.[4]

As the war turned against Germany, Bulgaria also did not fully comply with Soviet demands to expel German forces from its territory. By the summer of 1944, the Soviet army was approaching Bulgaria through Romania (which had already left the Axis powers and declared war on Germany). Bulgaria tried to claim neutrality, but on

September 5, the Soviet Union declared war on Bulgaria and the Red Army invaded three days later (the communists entered Sofia the night of September 8–9, 1944). Bulgaria was forced to give up its neutrality. The communist-dominated Fatherland Front took power, and Bulgaria formally joined the Allies until the war ended. The left-wing uprisings of September 1944 (called a coup by some) led to the abolition of the monarchy, but it was not until 1946 that a single-party people's republic was established. The Tsar went into exile and Bulgaria became part of the Soviet sphere of influence under the leadership of Georgi Dimitrov (1946–49) who, in spite of his protection of Bulgarian Jews, laid the foundations for a repressive Stalinist state that executed thousands of dissidents during its long postwar rule.[5]

This complicated history means that from her birth to the age of five or six, Kristeva's earliest childhood memories, earliest stories and photos, earliest psychic inscriptions and echoes, are infused with what she calls the great "Bulgarian Ambiguity." This land where Greek myth, Christianity, Judaism, and Islam meet; where first there were Nazi boots on the ground, then Soviet boots; where the monarchical government aligned itself with the Nazis but adamantly refused to deport Jews; where Russians took over but where Stalinism arrived slowly and relatively late in the game—this was the historical cauldron in which Julia Kristeva was formed. It is the foundation of what she sees as the overdetermined formation of her psycho-social identity by history. Calling herself a product of history, and citing Bulgaria as an important crossroads of history, Kristeva literally sees herself as a *production* of history:

> My Hegelian-Marxist education, which subordinates the individual to the collective, leads me to say that I am a product of history: the Second World War, the Yalta Conference, the partition of our continent into two Europes—a Europe of the East and of the West; the dream of General de Gaulle, who already saw Europe as stretching from the Atlantic to the Ural Mountains and so gave doctoral fellowships to young students from the East who spoke French; then May of 1968; the fall of the Berlin Wall; Perestroika; Glasnost; the awakening of

China and other emerging powers; structuralism; poststructuralism; Freudianism; the clash of religions; hyperconnectivity; the financial-economic-political-social-metaphysical-existential crisis . . . and many more.[6]

One of Kristeva's earliest memories is of sneaking down with her parents to the basement of their home in Sliven to listen to Radio London. This was done with extreme caution because the building Kristeva's family lived in had both communist teachers—resisters—and Germans. Kristeva has described with emotion how her family watched, through the slim line of windows at the very top of the basement wall, first Nazi boots but then Stalinist boots marching in unison along the sidewalk outside her building. Safety was inside, down below, in the basement, with Europe, with family: "My parents and I went down to the basement to listen to Radio London . . . so that no one could hear . . . I vaguely remember seeing soldiers in German uniform pass by . . . And I can still hear the sound . . . dun dun dun da . . . the signal of Radio London."

However, when Kristeva evokes the Bulgaria of her childhood, it is the intimacy of family she remembers best. She was surrounded by affection and her earliest memories swim in the love that her parents showered upon her as a small child. It is perhaps because of this constant affection that her memories of the period are fluid, filled with sensations of curiosity and discovery: "When I speak of and think about Bulgaria, or about Sofia—both of which abound with memories— these memories, every time I evoke them, there is nothing fixed or determinant about them. What matters in my experience of memory is the voyage toward and through it . . . it's a perpetual questioning."[7]

Stoyan Kristev

Kristeva's father, Stoyan Kristev (Kristev: literally "of the cross"), lost his parents as a child. He did not know his father, who was an officer in the Bulgarian Army and died at the front during the Balkan Wars of 1912–13. His mother, Mithra, died shortly thereafter in childbirth.

He was raised by a peasant woman named Yordana who also took care of Kristeva as a very young girl, passing away when Kristeva was three years old. Yordana did not legally adopt Stoyan but raised him as her own child in the countryside and then doted, along with Kristeva's parents, on the "royal baby" born in the midst of the war. Kristeva called her "grandmother" and was told that her own first name, Julia, was a modern version of "Yordana," a name whose etymology in turn harkens back to the Biblical Jordan River.

Kristeva describes herself as having been a true *fille à papa* (daddy's girl): she looked like her father; her father adored her; he was a father in love. The feeling was mutual, for Kristeva adored him as well. She has often spoken of how being held by such a loving father psychically imprinted her. In fact, to this day she attributes her inability to be jealous of anyone to the intensity of her father's love, noting that she "can never seem to envy anyone." She explains that even when there has been conflict in her life, the legacy of having been certain of her father's love as a child is that she has never wavered in her sense that she is right and that the other person is wrong. Kristeva recognizes that her mother and father's "parental madness"—their idealization of their first daughter in the midst of a world war—could have led her to develop a classically insolent egotism. Instead, she believes that it gave her an energetic self-confidence that she values to this day.

Because Kristeva's father was an orphan, he had only two choices in life: he could join the military or he could become a priest. He decided to join the seminary, later studying at the Theology Faculty of Sofia. He was a practicing Orthodox Christian, but he had a sharp, critical, and restless mind. He took young Julia constantly to concerts, the theater, the opera, etc. He was also an athlete and pushed Julia toward sports, especially basketball and gymnastics. She became a swimmer.[8] Her parents saw all this activity-in-pleasure as a form of lightness, of resistance to the heavy conformity of communist era social norms. For this reason, they were for their time and place an unusually open and complex couple.

Figure 2.5. Kristeva with her father and sister, c. 1948. The Julia Kristeva Archive.

Kristeva's father was especially enthusiastic about languages and literature, particularly Russian literature: Dostoevsky, Gogol, and Tolstoy. He spoke many different languages—Russian was obligatory—and this was what he wanted for his daughters too. He repeatedly told his daughters that he wanted two things for them: to learn languages and to be financially independent. He introduced Kristeva to literature and poetry from a very young age. The other thing he loved was music, and Kristeva remembers well his beautiful voice booming through the Saint Nedelya Church.[9] But she is always quick to point out that he passed on his musical talent to her sister Ivanka rather than to her.

According to Kristeva, it was unquestionably Ivanka who was musically talented, Kristeva never having been able to carry a tune. Music was at the heart of their family universe and Ivanka took center stage in this regard from an early age. She was a talented child musician with a "perfect ear." She played the piano and the violin, giving concerts to family and friends, and she attended the prestigious Music High

Figure 2.6. Kristeva's sister, Ivanka, in a recent photo. Music Without Limits.

School in Sofia.[10] She carried the name of the girls' maternal grandfather (Ivan) and was also much loved and supported by her parents. But like many younger siblings, Ivanka vied for her parents' attention and got angry with Julia when Julia captured academic praise. The sisters often ended up fighting. It seems that Kristeva was frequently the more (sometimes literally) injured of the two, but her father always found her to be the guilty one, guilty of causing the fray or at least of not stopping it, which he said she should have been able to do because she was the eldest. Kristeva describes her childhood relationship with her sister as close—Ivanka having taught her "to admire the talents of another woman"—but their father was often exasperated with their sibling rivalry as he struggled in the public realm with some of the urgent political problems of their time and place.

During the early part of the war, under Nazi occupation, Kristeva's father was part of the resistance to the deportation of Jews (much like the one in Holland), belonging to a brave group of intellectuals who went straight to the Tsar with their demand that the deportations not take place. (Kristeva has often praised the "fraternity" of intellectuals

and religious leaders who fought the deportations.) At the end of
the war, with the Russians in charge and the passage to communism,
Kristeva's father left the seminary (Kristeva took her last communion
at the age of seven). Although her father was very religious and had
a degree in theology, he decided to study medicine because of the
communist regime's intense crackdown on religion in Bulgaria.[11] He
told some that he left the seminary because he wanted to marry, but
Kristeva has said that this is unlikely given that priests were able to
marry at that time. It is more likely that he thought that his future in
communist Bulgaria was going to be more viable as a doctor. However,
this changed when he found out that—as was the law after September
9, 1944, the official date of the liberation of Bulgaria from fascism (and
as would later be the case in Maoist China)—he was going to have to
go to the countryside as a "barefoot doctor" to treat the poor with no
help or supplies.

Because Stoyan Kristev wanted, above all else, for his daughters to
have a good education in Sofia, he ended up deciding against medicine
and never practiced as a doctor. Instead, in order to stay in Sofia with
his family, he became a bureaucrat in the Orthodox Church while at the
same time detaching himself from a (potentially dangerous) visible-
to-the-government religious practice of his own. In considering this
seemingly contradictory situation, one must keep in mind the complex
status of Orthodox Christianity in communist Bulgaria: on the one
hand, religion was restrained by the communist regime but, on the
other, the Orthodox Church continued to function due to the need
to appease the population. The church never regained the influence it
had held under the monarchy and most of the high roles within it were
assumed by communist functionaries. Kristeva's father, though not a
communist, joined such functionaries at the Holy Synod, which in the
Orthodox Church is the permanent council at the top of the religious
hierarchy. At what was, in the end, a Soviet-style Ministry of Religion,
he patiently administrated and interpreted while keeping himself sane
by writing fascinating stories and essays, both under his own name
and as a ghost writer, on Christian Orthodoxy for Christians trying to

carry on with their lives in the young communist state—for example, essays on the place of the Virgin in Orthodox Christianity or on such and such a Bulgarian saint who had struggled against the Turkish occupation.[12]

All My Childhood Was Bathed in This

It was not until I accompanied Kristeva to Sofia in 2014 that I began to truly understand her complicated relationship to Orthodox Christianity, which has a great deal to do with her father's passionate experience with it, right down to his insistence that his name, Kristev, had originated during the Crusades.

During our visit with the Christian Orthodox Patriarch in Sofia and our visit to the Rila Monastery close to Sofia, I watched Kristeva speak urgently and at great length with senior members of the clergy about the problems facing Eastern Europe and indeed the world. She

Figure 2.7. Kristeva with the Patriarch Neophyte of Bulgaria, head of the Bulgarian Orthodox Church, and associates, 2014. Photo by Alice Jardine.

Figure 2.8. Outside Rila Monastery, 2014. Photo by Alice Jardine.

Figure 2.9. Fresco of angels and devils, Rila Monastery, 2014. Photo by Alice Jardine.

seemed as at ease in the private suites of the Patriarch as in her Parisian classrooms.

The frescos and murals surrounding us on the walls of the monastery made me realize that these images must have haunted Kristeva's childhood imagination alongside the realist views of the communist state. It is, then, no wonder that the blues of the Madonnas, the cruel frenzy embedded in images of Biblical hell, and other religious allusions can be found in her writing decades later. Looking back, one can also see that her notorious fascination with the preverbal is something that she associates with the liturgy of the Orthodox Church. As she states in relation to this liturgy, "All my childhood was bathed in this."[13]

Kristeva has often stated that she experienced the Orthodox faith of her father as dissident—as secretive and associated with the unknown—and that it was this experience that kept her from completely identifying with the Bulgarian communist identity of the time. She has spoken of a force of resistance sleeping within Orthodox faith, absorbed by her along with the incense and flowers of the church where her father sang. This spiritual climate had something of the forbidden about it: the importance of the story about how, when they were very young, Stoyan Kristev took Kristeva and her sister to communion only in the earliest and darkest morning hours so as to avoid being seen cannot be overestimated when thinking about the overall shape of Kristeva's work and about the centrality of religion to this work.

Kristeva's worries about Eastern Orthodoxy falling into historical irrelevance are already visible in her 1995 article, "Bulgaria, My Suffering."[14] But she sums up her concerns most concisely in *At the Risk of Thought*, where she compares Orthodox Christianity to Western theology. Whereas the latter, in her view, has combined its faith with reason since the Greeks, she sees the former as having sacrificed thinking for praying, for having opted for mysticism rather than comprehension, dependence on the raptures of the spirit rather than the independence of the mind. Her worries overall about post-communist Bulgaria are very much rooted in what she sees as the failures of the Orthodox Church: "Today I have the feeling—and that's why I suffer for

Bulgaria—that people hesitate between nihilistic resignation (people are overwhelmed by what is happening to them, by marketplace liberalism, by banks, by productivism, and they are unhappy, depressed, they cry, they blame the West, etc.) and the brutality of the mafias. It seems to me that one has perhaps not sufficiently interrogated the weight of faith and religious tradition in the current context."[15] Witnessing her father's strong faith, his devotion to the church and its music, while also seeing how he and the entire family suffered in communist Bulgaria because of that faith, could not help but leave a deep impression on the young Julia and perhaps leave behind for the adult Kristeva a certain nostalgia for the magic of the Orthodox faith as presented to her by her adored and respected father. In *The Old Man and the Wolves*, where we see one of Kristeva's first *cris du cœur* in response to her father's cruel death in a Bulgarian hospital in 1989, she also indulges in thinly veiled descriptions of the Bulgarian people of today as lost, hardened, and deeply challenged in their quest to belong to Europe. Nonetheless, she is always quick to recognize with pride the unique history of Bulgaria where Judaism, Islam, and Christianity have managed to co-exist for such a long time.

Kristina Kristeva

Kristeva's mother, Kristina Kristeva (maiden name: Paskova) came from a more bourgeois background than her father: Kristeva's maternal grandfather was a shopkeeper. Kristeva has some ancestors from Spain on the maternal side of her family. Her mother's family also goes back two generations into what Kristeva calls the "religious polyphony" of the Balkans. There one finds her grandmother Nevena (maiden name Zhekova, a version of Jacob) genealogically traced to dissident Jews who are in turn linked to the celebrated seventeenth-century Balkan Jewish mystic, Sabbatai Zevi. Zevi is famous for having converted to Islam and founded a sect awaiting the Second Coming—with Zevi as the Messiah. This sect still has followers today, especially in Turkey.[16]

Kristeva's family, however, turned toward Orthodox Christianity in the eighteenth century.

Kristeva has written—for example in *Murder in Byzantium* (where Byzantium is in part a metaphor for today's Bulgaria)—about the links between Judaism, Islam, and Christianity in Eastern Europe, Greece, and Turkey as well as about the schism between Rome and Byzantium. The Schism of 1054 is called either "The Grand Oriental Schism" or "The Orthodox Schism" (from a Western point of view) or "The Schism of Rome" or "The Latin Schism" or "The Catholic Schism" (from the Eastern Orthodox point of view). It was the outcome of numerous decades of conflicts and reconciliations between the two churches. Whatever one calls it, because of this schism, the mystic descendants of Bulgarian Christian Orthodoxy—whose multilingual, panspiritual history extends to Kristeva's family's religious history—remain largely invisible to the Western world. In speaking of this mystical heritage, Kristeva is quick to point out that there is no direct correspondence between her life and her work, emphasizing that her mother was *both* the result of the religious polyphony of the Balkans *and* an atheist. Yet she hastens to add that, as with everyone, the stories she inherited are what matter for her life's work. Her father's stories based on his love of languages, of Russian literature, and her mother's stories about the religious polyphony of the Balkans—as they were shared with the young, impressionable Kristeva—provide a rich bio-psycho-graphical background to her later published work.

In spite of her hybridized spiritual history, Kristeva's mother was not at all religious. She was completely secular, she and her brother having been raised in a humanist and secular atmosphere. She was a scientist, excellent at math, had studied biology, and was a follower of Darwin. But she was also an artist, and in particular was very good at drawing. For Kristeva, drawing is where there is no distance between thought and hand; it is thinking in action. She attributes her fascination with drawing to her mother: "A face, a countryside, an animal, a flower, an object—they all unexpectedly lived again at the tip of her pencil, with a precision all the more surprising because it came so naturally to her:

without forcing it, without thinking about it, as if it were nothing, my mother drew as others breathe or embroider."[17]

In *The Severed Head*, Kristeva writes of a drawing by her mother that influenced her greatly. During an intense, snowy Balkan winter, warming herself by the coal stove, young Kristeva was listening to a children's radio show announce a contest: whoever could answer—and draw the answer—to a question could win a prize. The question was, "What is the fastest mode of transport in the world?" Kristeva's younger sister yelled, "An airplane!" Kristeva corrected her, "Sputnik!" Their mother answered last: "I think, rather, that it's thought." Kristeva retorted, not without insolence, "Maybe, but one can't draw a thought. It's invisible." Her mother responded, "You'll see!" Kristeva remarks that she can still see the postcard her mother then drew, under Kristeva's name. It was a drawing that won the radio contest for her. On the card, her mother had drawn a large snowman, melting and tipping to his left, his head falling off as if cut off by the invisible guillotine that was a ray of the sun. To the right of the snowman was the earth (and Sputnik in all of its orbital glory) that the snowman was imagining, even as it was perishing. The young Kristeva was deeply impressed by this vision of mortality, by this vision of how ideas survive after death. The body dies, but Sputnik continues. One cannot help but wonder whether this maternal inspiration might not be in part behind Kristeva's non-stop production of ideas for over fifty years!

The young Julia Kristeva was caught—almost every night—in the middle of good-humored but passionate debates at dinner, where her religious father was "the dinosaur" and her scientific, Darwinian mother the "progenitor of monkeys":

> My mother never disputed papa's ideas, but one could sense that she went to church only to please him, that she herself did not believe. She had studied biology and so her ideas were the opposite of my father's. At the dinner table, we would tease my father. We called him a dinosaur and we would say that, as Darwin had argued, we descended from monkeys. My mother was a strong Darwinian. And papa would get furious! He would yell, "Yes, of course you are both descendants of

monkeys" (because my sister would follow me in my teasing of him). "Yes, yes, it's very easy to see! One just has to take a look at you to see that you descend from the monkeys!"

In speaking of her mother, Kristeva often evokes her clear maternal role and the ways in which her mother came to represent for her one pole of a strict choice for women of that time. On the one hand, there was her mother, a brilliant woman who sacrificed her career and devoted all of herself to her children.[18] On the other hand, there was someone like the Bulgarian poetess, Blaga Dimitrova—whom Kristeva has called her "symbolic mother"—who only late in life, after many trips to Vietnam as a journalist during the Vietnam War, adopted a little Vietnamese girl in 1967 and became the vice president of Bulgaria in 1992. Kristeva often criticized her mother to her face for her lack of ambition—"you are letting yourself be crushed!"—but at the same time, Kristeva deeply admired her and freely admits that she owes a lot of her early academic success to her because her mother was very hands-on about tutoring her in math and science.

Kristeva's father more or less fulfilled the normative expectations of paternity at the time. He was Kristeva's explicit intellectual guiding star, full of love and affection, but also very strict. He was always telling her to stand up straight (in the name of rightness and justice) and, unlike her mother, he was a severe disciplinarian. Kristeva tells stories about how he would, perhaps because of his religious fervor, punish her by making her kneel with a very straight back in a corner for hours (maybe this is where she got her backbone from). Because young Kristeva was spirited, strong-minded, and at times insolent, her father insisted that she needed to learn humility. She spent so much time in the corner that she came to feel that everything was always her fault. There is no doubt in my mind that this experience helped set up Kristeva's life-long passion for justice (or at least for psychoanalysis).

Kristeva admits that she believes that her mother was, in some ways, more intelligent than her father. His intelligence was literary, imaginative. Her mother was more rational, reasonable, and pragmatic. But she had learned to be silent, to never put herself out front—to the point where some thought that she was depressed. It was her father who put himself in the lead, a bit hysterically, especially given his strong temper. However, Kristeva acknowledges that it was her mother who secretly approved of Kristeva's outspoken resistance to her father and later openly approved of Kristeva's choice to live as "a free woman" in Paris.

It is clear that Kristeva was deeply imprinted by the complexity of her parents, especially with regard to the tension in the parental couple surrounding religion and science. This is a tension that has persevered in Kristeva's work to this day. Kristeva spent her childhood resisting her father's religiosity. She was much closer to her mother's scientific mind, becoming the family spokesperson for Darwin. She says that it took her a long time to take religion seriously and that she has only recently come to embrace its foundational importance for understanding human behavior. Kristeva has in fact been reflecting a great deal on the struggles in the twenty-first century between religion and science, suggesting that we may have as much to learn from what the dinosaurs have had to say historically as from what the monkeys are saying today.

One Spoonful at a Time

Kristeva was a very independent young girl in the young communist state. She remembers it as a time of having everything she needed but not what she wanted. She emphasizes that she did not suffer under communism. However, although she did not experience directly the brutality of communist rule, the fear-inducing stories of terrible things associated with this rule did pervade her young consciousness. She overheard visitors to the house speak of hangings and tortures. She was especially haunted by stories of drownings in bathtubs filled with waste. One night, she was scared when loudspeakers in the streets of her maternal grandmother's town warned of impending executions and she and her mother ran all the way home, pushing the baby carriage with her sister in it frantically before them, with the baby even falling out at one point.

Living under communist rule meant for Kristeva and her family that life was constrained. You had to eat whatever was put on the table. There were long lines. The apartment in Sofia was considerably smaller than the one she had been used to in Sliven. But it was not without its charm. During my visit with Kristeva to Sofia in 2014, I was struck by how Kristeva's world as a small child was closely bordered by the family apartment, the Saint Nedelya Church, and her school.

As a kind of parable for life under communist rule, Kristeva tells the story of being forced to leave her house in Sliven when her sister was being born. She talks about going next door and seeing Anne, who lived there, being fed water one spoonful at a time.[19] This felt like the libidinal economy of those communist times—spoonful by spoonful, drop by drop, one got what one needed but only that. For Kristeva, this was an imaginary relationship to the real conditions of existence: the pervasive sensation of parsimony, of surveillance. She admits that this memory might have more to do with what is normally experienced by children as an increase in discipline because of the arrival of a new sibling than with any Soviet psycho-economics. In any case, she rebelled against that economy, preferring instead to run wild in her grandmother's garden among the flowers, or among the beautiful old Byzantine churches by the sea. These are very physical memories for her. But, of course, she was also always a very good student.

There was a widely accepted saying in communist Bulgaria at the time, namely that the Bulgarian people were caught "in the intestines of hell." Kristeva's father felt that the only way out—the only ticket out of hell—was through gaining cultural capital: music for Ivanka and foreign languages and literatures for Julia. However, both Kristeva's formal and informal education—her choices of schools to attend, her eligibility for scholarships and honors—were deeply impacted because her father was not a member of the Communist Party; many options were denied to children whose parents were not members of the Party. Although Kristeva was always "the best student," she was consistently disappointed by not being able to carry the school flag.

At first—when Kristeva was six or seven—her parents enrolled her in the French "maternal school" where she was taught by French Catholic—Dominican—nuns.[20] For a couple of years, she absorbed languages, especially French, like a sponge and was taught to memorize songs and French literary texts, with the nuns teaching her fables by La Fontaine, poems by Hugo, and stories by Colette.[21] She remembers plays in French with lots of bright costumes. She learned "La Marseillaise" before she learned the Bulgarian National Anthem, recited the fables of La Fontaine before she learned to recite the poems of the nineteenth-century Bulgarian National Poet, Hristo Botev.[22] She even prayed in French.

Figure 2.10. Kristeva in traditional costume, 1944. The Julia Kristeva Archive.

Kristeva loved her Dominican Nun teachers and was devastated when they were arrested, condemned as spies, and chased out of the country, to be replaced in her life by the Alliance Française. She was incredibly lucky to have such an opportunity: the Sofia office of the Alliance Française, founded in 1904, was able to continue its basic activities throughout World War II and was considered a space of open dialogue and calm in the midst of violence and political turmoil. Kristeva has reflected a great deal on the beautiful fragility of the poetic imagination, particularly on the importance of the French poetic tradition. This emphasis becomes less mysterious when we realize that whatever else she was up to as a child, French literature was at the center of her young life.

Like most excellent students, Kristeva longed for symbolic recognition. In relation to this longing, there are two stories that she wants everyone to know about her Bulgarian childhood. She has in fact written about both many times. First, Bulgaria holds a Festival of the Alphabet every spring, and from the age of seven she was an avid participant in the festival, often receiving a Prix d'Excellence.

Kristeva has evoked this unique, annual May 24 celebration so many times, both in writing and in interviews, that anyone familiar with her work has to notice that she never tires of explaining the ritual's intellectual significance:

> Bulgaria gave birth to two inventors of the Slavic alphabet, the brothers Cyril and Methodius. In the 9th century, these monks created the alphabet that not only permitted the progression of Christianity into Slavic territories, but also allowed the foundation of a State that would be very significant in the Middle Ages . . . Bulgaria is the only country in the world celebrating a national festival of culture, moreover, a festival of the alphabet, honoring its two learned saints. This commemoration consists of a procession in the squares of towns and villages (I lived in the capital, Sofia), processions in which school children participated (I wore my top student ribbon and also a letter to personify this alphabet), but also those who work in the domain of culture: artists, journalists, professors, writers, etc. On this occasion, the entire population celebrates the verbal and the written.

This moment is of capital symbolic importance, because it shows how deeply culture is rooted in the Bulgarian people. Throughout its entire history, this cultural rooting, at once very physical and very spiritual, has been lived as a major form of resistance against various forms of occupation, notably that of the Turks, which lasted five centuries.[23]

Whenever Kristeva evokes this celebration of language, culture, and the unique contribution of her native country to world culture, her pride and admiration shine through. And it is easy to see how this festival influenced the young intellectual whose strong belief in the power of the imaginary and the symbolic to shape what we call reality through language has never faltered. In her 2012 article, "My Alphabet; or, How I Am a Letter,"[24] Kristeva is explicit about her relationship to the Festival of the Alphabet, to her native Bulgarian, and to her fully

Figure 2.11. Kristeva at the Festival of the Alphabet. The Julia Kristeva Archive.

internalized French. She explains how definitional her relationship to language is, how her existence as a foreigner in France and her life as a writer are intrinsically bound together through her love of language—and how it all started in Bulgaria. In reference to her multilingualism, she goes so far as to say that "to speak another language is quite simply the first and minimal condition necessary for being alive."[25]

Second, Kristeva wants everyone to know that Georgi Dimitrov, the leader of the Communist Party in Bulgaria who had once been accused by the Nazis of setting the Reichstag on fire, and who some claim helped stop Bulgarian Jews from being deported during the Nazi occupation, was brilliant—and persuasive—in the delivery of his anti-Nazi speeches. Following Moscow's lead, Dimitrov helped make it possible for many Jews to emigrate to Israel after the war (Dimitrov's wife was Jewish, and to this day Kristeva has cousins in Israel). Kristeva wants us to know that it is not her in any of the official pictures presenting bouquets of flowers to Dimitrov. It should have been her—first in her class—doing so. But she was so nervous that she got sick and could not go. She still gets sick when she gets very nervous—like before meeting the Pope.

I Didn't Want to Take Care of All That

Then there are two stories from Kristeva's Bulgarian childhood that *I* really want you to know. One has to do with Kristeva's love of books and her impatience with anything that smacked of girlish destiny. She especially did not like any kind of dolls, although they were continually thrust upon her. (She only ever owned one, given to her at the age of four and relegated to a drawer by the age of seven.) She remembers her intense disappointment at receiving a dollhouse as a gift:

> I remember that I once received the gift of a dollhouse: a representation of a house, where there's a doll, a bathroom, a kitchen, a dining room, etc. And then there's the little girl who's supposed to take care of all that! Me? I was really disappointed because I didn't want to take care of all that! I never played with it much. It's still pretty much all in

one piece. It stayed in a cupboard. I thought it was ridiculous for little girls to push strollers. Me? I had my books. They might have been kept in a drawer, but I really used them, and they ended up completely torn apart through use. So this gift of a dollhouse disappointed me a little. On the other hand, in that package of things that little girls were supposed to have—the bathroom, the kitchen, etc.—there was that little dollhouse doll which could sit up in order to be bathed because there was a hole in its buttocks . . . a hole in order to be able to sit her up on a little peg . . . I found it all so absolutely stupid. In all of that, the only thing that interested me was to see what was inside of the hole! My mother said I would be a doctor.

Kristeva was only interested in what was inside of the little dollhouse doll.

The other story I want to share about Kristeva's Bulgarian childhood is that she almost never cried. She was often disappointed—disappointed that she could not carry the flag at parades because of her father not joining the Communist Party, disappointed that her long-awaited gift was a dollhouse, and so on—but she did not cry when she was disappointed, or even when she was sick or hurt. In fact, this "keep calm and carry on" posture is integral to her character. This became clear to me during what I call the "running story": Kristeva as a child did not walk, she ran! Ran and ran as fast as she could, until she would fall down! And when her mother—tearful and worried—caught up with her, Kristeva would touch her mother's cheek and say: "Don't cry, Mama, I will take care of you":

> It's something that's just part of my character: not to cry. My mother used to tell me about it. As soon as I could walk, I wouldn't walk but would, rather, run. And I ran very, very fast! So I started running . . . and there's a park in Sofia called the Park of Roses where I would run and run until I would fall . . . and Mama would yell, "But stop! Stop!" And I would fall and she would catch up with me. I would stand up, with my knees all bloody and my mother would plead with me, "Please stop! Your knees are all bloody!" And I would reply: "Listen mama, don't be upset. Let me comfort you." And then I would take off running . . .

Kristeva explains that she takes care of herself by taking care of others. She admits that family for her is about complex caring rather than comfort.

As in many countries in the former Soviet bloc, the elites of the Bulgarian Communist Party wanted their children to attend elite schools in capital cities. Kristeva's parents would have liked her to be able to continue her education in one of the Russian, French, English, or even American schools in Sofia—the schools where the children of the red nomenklatura were sent. But, again, she could not, mostly because her father was not a communist. For elementary and high school, she therefore attended public school. I was able to visit Kristeva's elementary school, Patriarkh Evtimiy, Asparukh Street, and I was told that it looks much as it did when she was there and still looks like just about any public elementary school in Eastern Europe: the classrooms contain orderly wooden desks in rows with each student's notebooks and pencils neatly arranged on top.

Figure 2.12. Kristeva's public elementary school in Sofia, 2014. Photo by Alice Jardine.

Kristeva attended High School #33, but most important in her memory about her years in public school is her "extra time" at the Alliance Française. There, two to three afternoons a week, she continued her linguistic and literary studies begun at the French maternal school. She strengthened her command of French and eventually learned Russian and English. Kristeva has consistently spoken of French as her language of freedom, a language that has allowed her to ask questions and to develop a singular voice. She has spoken of "traveling through herself," most often in French, as a way (unconsciously) to transcend her childhood situation.

Literature was Kristeva's other avenue of escape. She devoured "the classics": Dostoevsky, Pushkin, Chekhov, Gorky, but also Molière and Hugo, through Proust and Sartre, to Ionesco and Beckett. She credits a professor of French at the Alliance Française, Kiril Bogoyavlenski, with forming her taste in literature as well as her desire for everything French. She has spoken often of her admiration for the French literary imagination, which often allows for a fruitful encounter between reason (especially science) and the comic (when not the absurd). For her, the ultimate escape was that of the imagination, away from any form of predictable, one-dimensional thought. As a child at her maternal grandmother's house, she would hide high in the trees in order to read Hugo or Colette without interruption. Reading was a great adventure in an overly pragmatic world for this self-described romantic.

Though solitary and stubborn—as well as a bit of a dreamer—Kristeva was also a sociable child. She remembers a couple of good friends in elementary and high school: Emiliya (who became a doctor) and Lydiya (who became a translator at the United Nations in Geneva). At university, there were Anastasia and Elena (whom I met during a televised interview in Sofia).[26]

At one point, Kristeva thought that she would become a doctor. At university she took the medical exam mostly to please her parents. But she also took the exam in French literature. Although she succeeded at both, in fact scoring higher in letters than in science, at first she decided to follow her parents' wishes by pursuing medicine. However, during the very first class in medicine, the professor took the students to the local morgue. Kristeva stepped up to the plate, determined as always, and successfully dissected a human body. Then, as she was leaving, she promptly fainted. She decided to go back to literature!

It was apparent that literature was her genuine passion and also, as she has emphasized, a way to contest the realist ideology of communist Bulgaria where the drumbeat was about the necessity to represent—always and everywhere—the reproduction of the class struggle. She devoured French literature as an antidote to this emphasis on communist realism. For her, French literature was the "flesh of French mentality"—a cherished vehicle of eighteenth-century French Enlightenment. It was in many ways how she consoled herself. She also likes to say that it was how she found out about love.

As for her own experiences of love, in elementary school, there was a boy named Simeon who was a little in love with her, but she could run faster than him. Kristeva describes it as "love by competition." In high school—and while studying French together at the Alliance Française— there was a more serious love: Anton. Anton was brilliant. He studied to be an engineer and eventually, much to the young Kristeva's chagrin, left for a secret scientific facility in Siberia. When she saw him again years later when she was teaching in Paris, she was struck by how fearful he was of a Cold-War atomic conflict. In 2014, when Kristeva and I were in Sofia, a man about her age came up to her after her wildly applauded lecture at the university and handed her a picture of herself at sixteen years old. When she asked him how and where he got it, he replied, "I'm Anton." Kristeva was understandably overcome with emotion. When Anton was interviewed for a recent Bulgarian documentary about Kristeva, he said that, still today, "I am in love with a goddess."[27]

The Journalist

Early in her life, Kristeva took up journalism. Even when she was as young as thirteen and fourteen, she constantly wrote stories for high school papers such as *The High School Banner*. Later, she wrote for

Figure 2.13. Photo of Kristeva's article on Radevski. The Bulgarian National Library. Photo by Alice Jardine.

Popular Youth as well as other newspapers, getting paid enough to become relatively independent. (In fact, while working for her doctorate, Kristeva was completely independent financially.) The young Kristeva wrote about some of the best-known writers of the day: for example, Khristo Radevski.

Radevski seems like an understandable choice for the young journalist at that time. He was a celebrated Bulgarian poet who was loyal to the Communist Party and who denounced the bourgeois social order and adhered closely to the standard techniques of socialist realism, mixing these with strong anti-modernist rhetoric. As both a poet and party bureaucrat, Radevski painted an optimistic picture of socialist reality and the development of the communist revolution. He was best known for his poetic development of the motifs derived from socialist reality that appear in his works written after 1951. He also translated classic Russian poetry.

However, not all the writers that Kristeva chose to write about were predictable. For example, she also wrote about her "symbolic mother,"

Blaga Dimitrova, who was also very much admired by Kristeva's father and eventually became a close friend.[28] This is especially fascinating since Dimitrova, outside of her name appearing as an author of poetry, only appears once in the English language to this day: as a character named Vera Glavanakova in John Updike's famous story, "The Bulgarian Poetess."[29] As is the case in most of Updike's stories, the woman only exists as a mysterious object of fascination for Updike's alter-ego writer hero, Bech, who moves from one woman to another during his tour of Eastern Europe: "But I have nothing to say to [Glavanakova]. I'm just curious about such an intense conjunction of good looks and brains. I mean, what does a soul do with it all?"[30] This Updike trope echoes strangely the kinds of things I have heard many men say about Kristeva over the years.

When Kristeva was twenty-one, she became widely known for an article she published in *Septemvri*, the journal of a small group of forward-looking and fairly open-minded young elite intellectuals, the Union of Writers. *Septemvri* brandished a certain liberty of tone and insisted upon allowing conversation and debate even though each "open" article was accompanied by an article loyal to the communist party line that categorically refuted its argument.

A Bulgarian communist—but increasingly dissident—journalist named Albert Koen (no relationship to the fiction writer) had published a collection of essays on the Soviet Thaw: the period of de-Stalinization in the Soviet Union and its satellite countries during the Khrushchev era. In 1956, Khrushchev had proclaimed the doctrine of "peaceful coexistence" with the West and Stalin as a Soviet hero was becoming less visible by the early 1960s even as the Berlin Wall (1961) and the rest of the Soviet Cold-War ideology was at full tilt. Koen's 1962 book, *Roads and Stops*, which was essentially a travelogue of his time spent in Western Europe, was written in the spirit of this so-called *perestroika*. No one at *Septemvri*—or anyone else in the communist bloc media— was willing to review Koen's book. The brave (or perhaps naïve) Kristeva was the notable exception.

Kristeva appreciated Koen's book. In her short review, "Western Europe Through the Eyes of a Journalist,"[31] she carefully utilized codes of "openness" to praise Koen's ways of observing Western cities while simultaneously adding a heavy vocabulary of communist cliché to judge what he saw there. Her review is an accomplished exercise in "doublespeak," in the kind of palimpsestic (multilayered, often purposefully opaque) prose used by dissident intellectuals on the communist side of the Iron Curtain.[32] In Part II of this book, I will discuss in greater detail the significance of this type of writing for Kristeva's intellectual formation. Here it suffices to note that, in her review of Koen's collection of essays, Kristeva walked a fine line between adhering to the communist party line and pushing the boundaries of that line, writing, "Koen's articles are marked by well-grounded analysis, broad perspective, communist passion, and a vivid journalistic style." She went on to admire his "keen sense for colors, shapes, and volume," which, "with a luscious brush, lays before our eyes a rich range of colors: from the bright and lively hues of the Swiss lakes and mountains to the grey patina of the homes in Paris and the dried mud on the Spanish village huts." But the astute young reviewer specified that Koen did not get carried away, for he also wanted to "show the back of the coin":

> Then it turns out that in Paris the pre-Christmas fuss conceals the false philanthropy of the rich and the careful frugality of the poor: will the money suffice?; that the myths of the "new" are simply a mask of conformism and of the cult of various "stars"; that there is nothing romantic in returning after a vacation because it means an increase in prices. Thus the class divisions, the casts, the political maneuvers are revealed . . . [The book] juxtaposes our reality with the capitalist one . . . His voice is not the voice of someone who criticizes with *partis pris*, who has come with a definite goal—to see and reject. Koen contemplates patiently, he tries to understand and only then, soberly and civilly, without any loud-mouthedness and journalistic straining, puts everyone in his place, depicts the capitalist world in its shameful nakedness, and reasons as a communist-publicist.

While this may seem like dated, fairly innocuous prose to an American reader today, Kristeva's words set off loud alarms in communist Bulgaria. The day after the review was published, there appeared on the front page of the communist newspaper, *Rabotnichesko Delo*, a violent article denouncing Kristeva as a cosmopolitan agent of the capitalist hyena. She was called a spy, a Zionist. Her father was deeply worried, hiding the newspaper headlines so as not to alarm Kristeva's mother and sister. He took Kristeva out of the city to a café near a monastery in the mountains where he asked repeatedly, clearly distraught, what they were going to do. He feared that they would be thrown into one of the labor camps that were said to exist on the banks of the Danube. For months, Kristeva's family listened for noises in their building, especially in the early morning hours when people were usually "taken away." Radio Free Europe, the anti-communist, American-controlled radio station broadcasting from West Berlin, said all kinds of nice things about Kristeva's review, which only made her situation worse. Was she a "Zionist hyena" (according to the Bulgarian government) or a "liberating heroine" (according to the Americans)? She had no idea. In the end, no one came to their home at dawn. Kristeva has speculated that this was in part because she was not a known activist and in part because she was serving as a translator in both French and Russian for important visitors to Bulgaria such as Waldeck Rochet, a French communist politician, and Yuri Gagarin, the Soviet cosmonaut.

Little did Kristeva know at the time that she would bump into Albert Koen upon her arrival in Paris three years later and that it would be he who would help make her stay in France possible. However, it would be impossible to exaggerate the effect that this episode with "dissidence" had on her. She became acutely aware, in part because of the Soviet Thaw in the early 1960s, of the work of many dissidents in the Soviet bloc—an attitude much applauded by her forward-looking parents and evident later as inspiration for her controversial 1977 article, "A New Type of Intellectual: The Dissident."[33]

Pure Oxygen

Kristeva was eventually able to finish with great accolades her studies in Sofia, in part through a correspondence course in French, and in part through becoming a successful, full-time, well-paid journalist focusing on education, culture, and the arts. Due to her studies in French language and literature, she received a degree in Romance Philology from the University of Sofia in 1963 and wrote her doctoral thesis on the French New Novel while working toward her 1964 doctorate in Comparative Literature at the Academy of Sciences, Sofia.

Kristeva's professor of Comparative Literature, Emil Georgiev, liked her even though he did not know much about French literature. What he did know was that it was important to get this brilliant young woman out of Cold-War Bulgaria and, taking advantage of the absence of the communist director of the department on vacation in Moscow, he whisked her off to the French Embassy where she promptly impressed the French cultural attaché with her excellent spoken French, her knowledge of French culture, history, and literature, and especially her intention to write her doctoral thesis on the very, very new French New Novel.[34]

The attaché was shocked that Kristeva had even heard of the New Novelists, particularly Alain Robbe-Grillet and Nathalie Sarraute, in France. Kristeva explained that through the government's Communist Youth Program, she had been encouraged to correspond with young communist women in France and that she had become particularly friendly with one of them, Mireille Bourdeur in Lyon.[35] Kristeva had told Mireille that she was interested in literature, and Mireille had answered that if she loved literature, she should read *Les Lettres françaises*, a French literary magazine that had been founded in 1941 by Jacques Decour and Jean Paulhan, had been crucially active in the French Resistance, and had been taken over by the famous French communist writer, Louis Aragon, in 1953.[36] In Sofia, Kristeva only had access to certain issues of the magazine—never to ones criticizing Stalin, for example—but she devoured the articles Aragon published on Picasso and Lautréamont, Sartre and Robbe-Grillet, Sarraute and Butor, and Claude Simon. Kristeva and her friends threw themselves onto these issues of *Les Lettres françaises* and, occasionally, another communist journal called *Clarté*.[37]

Kristeva became very good at imagining the larger context of the fictions, articles, and debates she was encountering, especially after Mireille gave her the Paris address of the director of *Les Lettres françaises*, Pierre Daix, who worked with Aragon and who began to send some of the more controversial issues of the journal directly to Kristeva in Sofia. Even though Daix was younger and much less well known than Aragon, Kristeva—from a distance—was thrilled to tell everyone that she was a "correspondent" with the famous "untouchable, inaccessible Pierre Daix! At my age!"

Mireille also sent Kristeva some books: for example, several novels by Vercors (a pseudonym used by a writer named Jean Bruller to protect himself from the Nazis during the Occupation). Vercors had written several popular wartime resistance novellas, such as *The Silence of the Sea*, which was a huge (literally) underground hit credited with moving to tears millions of readers agonized by the Nazi occupation.[38] Vercors was one of the many French writers Kristeva wrote about before leaving Sofia. However, there was a long list of French writers she had come to know well: Blanchot, Camus, Sartre, and even a little Roland Barthes. She had always read and written about literature, especially French literature, with great pleasure—from her six-year-old self at the Alliance Française to her twenty-two-year-old self writing newspaper literary reviews.

In addition, because Kristeva took some French literature courses by correspondence, she occasionally had to attend class in order to perform in front of her peers and professors. She remembers well three oral exposés she had to give. One was on "The Red Lily" by Anatole France. (She did not impress herself with that one.) But the second one, on Camus's *The Pest* and *The Rebel*, still makes her proud today. In that exposé, she used Hegel to argue that freedom, indeed independence, is a conscious necessity for all human beings. She also threw in a few vague psychoanalytic notions about desire. Her father had hidden behind a bookshelf a copy of Freud's *Introductory Lectures on Psychoanalysis* (a 1947 edition in French and one of the only copies of any text by Freud in all of Bulgaria), and Kristeva had devoured it. Her third exposé was on Vercors's *The Silence of the Sea*. Daix in fact put Kristeva directly in touch with Vercors by correspondence. The young Bulgarian was ecstatic.

It is important to remember that books from the West were sneaked into Eastern Europe at great risk to their carriers. Vladimir Kostov, who directed a student newspaper and served as a correspondent for the Bulgarian communist newspaper in Paris, was quite impressed by Kristeva and brought her many books that were being talked about in Paris: Barthes's 1953 *Writing Degree Zero*, Blanchot's 1955 *The Space of Literature*, and the very first (1964) issue of the magazine *Le Nouvel Observateur*. Kostov did all he could to encourage the young Kristeva's growing love of French literature and culture.

For Kristeva, these winks at liberty were narrow windows through the Iron Curtain to an exciting world on the other side. Her essays impressed her professors who struggled to open further for her some windows into a communism that could at times be dissident. Meanwhile she was relatively safe to explore these dissident ideas in public under the protective umbrella of "French Letters." Marginal but tolerated, she was increasingly allowed to talk about Vercors or Camus in print and it thrilled her to do so. She has often explained that literature was for her, from the beginning, a heritage from her parents, an important vehicle for the human imagination, and a way to resist.

The bits and pieces of French culture that Kristeva was exposed to in Sofia had passed through the French Enlightenment. But they had also passed through the Second World War, the Shoah, the Occupation, and the French Resistance, and therefore exhibited a hope for change that was dependent on Marxist thought at the same time as it bathed in Greek and German philosophy so that Marxism could ultimately be critiqued. For the young Kristeva, literature—and increasingly Hegel, Lukács, and Freud—became the air she breathed, the waters in which she swam. She increasingly saw Eastern Europe as a prison that kept her from reading, from thinking, from living, even as Western Europe became more and more visible to her and her friends through the cracks in the Iron Curtain as they worked in the margins, in secret, but for real. There were only about ten to twenty young intellectuals in Sofia who had this kind of access to Western ideas, and for them, these stolen texts were pure oxygen.[39]

The Writer

What is perhaps most striking about Kristeva's late teens and early twenties in Sofia is her emergent relationship to writing. It is as if she was ravished by the compulsion to write from a very young age. And she energetically, from the beginning of her intellectual life, surrounded herself by other writers, whether journalists, critics, or poets. Writing started in those early years, before she even dreamed of going to Paris, to occupy the center of her life. Today, when one asks her how she has ended up writing so much, she does not quite know what to say. She usually stares at the person asking the question as if they were speaking a language she does not understand. I would go so far as to say that she has this reaction because writing for her is like breathing.

As a young journalist, Kristeva needed to write constantly. In Sofia, before Paris, the incredible speed with which she wrote and the large volume of her journalistic and critical writing impressed everyone around her, especially her teachers. The Bulgarian theorist and critic, Miglena Nikolchina, has recently brought to light that Kristeva, to the amazement of most Western scholars, published her first book—*Characteristic Trends in 20th-Century Western Literature*[40]—in Bulgarian at the age of twenty-three. As Nikolchina explains:

> In this book the twenty-three-year-old author discusses the "characteristic trends" in a manner characteristic of the time and place: on the surface, this is a critique of decadent Western literature and philosophy; in effect, this is a smart and seductive presentation of authors and books otherwise unavailable because of censorship. The book is slim and encyclopedically concise and yet striking in terms of both erudition and analytic incisiveness. It shares a lot of common ground with a number of contemporaneous Bulgarian authors, including earlier and later writing by Tzvetan Stoyanov.[41]

Tzvetan Stoyanov was Kristeva's boyfriend—a topic I will get to shortly. At this juncture, it is important to note that many of Kristeva's later intellectual interests were already apparent in her early choices of texts to focus on as well as in her emergent conviction that there was something to life beyond party and national loyalty. For instance, her interest in resistant writers and poets—an interest that she took with her to Paris—resonates with her later emphasis on the need to move beyond nationalism and to embrace "foreignness." The passion she showed for dissidence as a young intellectual is also aligned with her later reflections upon her own situation as a major foreign woman writer and theorist in France.

Long after Kristeva's arrival in Paris, the ambiguity of her position as a Bulgarian living in France and her attempt to speak as a cosmopolitan intellectual weighed upon her both personally and intellectually even as she admitted that "it is beneficial to be a cosmopolitan when one comes from a small country such as Bulgaria."[42] As has often been the case with her, she theorized the problem she found herself living by writing a book about it. I am referring to her 1988 *Strangers to Ourselves*, which examines the condition of foreignness. In this book, she states with regard to her use of Freud to understand nationalism and xenophobia: "Delicately, analytically, Freud does not speak of foreigners: he teaches us how to detect foreignness in ourselves. That is perhaps the only way not to hound it outside of us."[43]

One could argue that quite a few of Kristeva's early theoretical emphases in Paris—such as her celebration of polyphony after Bakhtin—are rooted in her personal experiences of estrangement. For Kristeva, polyphony, both literally and figuratively, is a precondition of creativity, an antidote to the automatization of the human, whether in its communist or capitalist form. Indeed, although it has taken a while, Kristeva has come to increasingly value her estrangement—her foreignness—publicly. She has come to embrace foreignness and even nomadism as a prerequisite of the ability to resist totalizing logic and language of all kinds, especially when they are political. In 2009, more than forty years after leaving communist Bulgaria, she looked back and embraced her budding polyphonic dissonance and dissidence on her eve of departure from Sofia as well as their manifestations in her life and work ever since:

Nietzsche affirmed, in *The Antichrist* (1895), that our preoccupation should be to put "a large question mark" after "that which is most serious." My own crossing of frontiers . . . has led me to interrogate dogmas, confinements, disciplines, to question identity, the multiplicity of identities. And even if, at the present moment, the answers to all these questions are still uncertain, they are a source of respiration and an antidote to the automatization of the species which—via technology, the media, and religious fanaticism—is a new form of totalitarianism . . . And even if the "polyphonic individual" is badly accepted or badly understood, he causes disturbance, he troubles order . . . I am convinced that this continuous uprooting is a kind of election, a source of good fortune, for it offers the possibility of psychic rebirth—that the bet on openness to the other is a cultural advantage. Lots of effort, lots of anguish, and sometimes suffering accompany this transformation— that's inevitable—but which I, for my part, try to translate into work, into sublimation, into creation.[44]

Sputnik or the New Novel

Looking back at Kristeva's years in Bulgaria, the critical importance of one event in her intellectual journey cannot be overestimated. As Kristeva was finishing her studies, she was also contemplating her future realistically. Indeed, almost in spite of her literary interests, there came a time in Kristeva's academic journey to make big, mostly practical decisions about her future. She was excellent at math and science, and while in high school had often—with her mother's help—won the Mathematical Olympics. This was also the time of Sputnik. Kristeva spoke Russian. And she was deeply inspired by the first two Soviet cosmonauts, one of whom was a woman. Kristeva in fact spent some time with both the cosmonauts, accompanying them as their interpreter.[45] Her goal therefore became to be an astronomer or an astrophysicist. She and her family decided that she should go off to a Cold-War military facility such as the Dubno Air Base in the Soviet Union to study (and probably to develop new Cold-War weapons for the young Soviet state). She applied for a fellowship she clearly should have won. But once again, because her father was not a member of the Communist Party, she was not chosen. The envelope arrived:

> One day I saw an envelope addressed to my father in the mailbox and I understood immediately what it was: the response to my application. I opened it, thinking to myself that maybe I had been accepted . . . but . . . no. They told my father that his daughter perhaps had all the necessary qualities for acceptance, but that they only accepted the children of those who were members of the Communist Party and that since that wasn't the case with him . . . With that, my father completely broke down in tears. But not me. I didn't cry. I pursued my studies of the humanities.

At the bad news, Kristeva's father cried but she did not. She did not yet know that by the time she would finish her studies in the humanities, the French government would be offering a scholarship to a top Bulgarian student to study the human sciences in Paris. By the mid-1960s, enthralled by the idea of a Europe stretching from the Atlantic to the Urals, Charles de Gaulle's government had begun sponsoring scholarships for young French-speaking Eastern Europeans. These scholarships were usually co-opted by the Bulgarian government because the country did not want its young people staying on the other side of the Iron Curtain: the scholarships were given to older Bulgarians who did not speak French and were therefore not allowed to leave. The Iron Curtain was very real: very few ever left Bulgaria to study in France. Kristeva's was an exceptional but not unique case. Kristeva always says that she went to France because of de Gaulle's for that time grandiose idea of "One Europe."[46]

Kristeva was able to bypass normal procedures in 1965 because, as I have already mentioned, the French cultural attaché in Sofia was deeply impressed by her knowledge of twentieth-century French literature.

He awarded her the nine-month scholarship without hesitation. Both determined and fragile, she decided to leave for Paris. The French Embassy told her that she could leave right away (it was mid-December) but that her scholarship would not start until the end of January.

She left right away.

Endings, Beginnings

Little did Kristeva know what awaited her in Paris. Could she even have imagined? It was especially hard to say goodbye to her parents, and years later, after their deaths, she would repeatedly come back to that moment of initial separation. Part of what she could not have imagined was that both of her parents' deaths would take place close to her rare visits to Sofia. Indeed, in person and in writing, Kristeva today ponders the timing of her parents' deaths with deep melancholia.

In January 1989, Kristeva traveled to Bulgaria as part of the French President François Mitterrand's delegation. She had only been back to Sofia once before, in 1983–84, and was quite overwhelmed to be there. She also had the sense that something earth-shaking was about to happen. She was right. The Berlin Wall was about to come down. And she was about to lose her father.

During the visit, Mitterrand's delegation went to the grand Nevsky Cathedral in Sofia, descending into the crypt to see an exhibition of medieval icons. Afterward, there was a concert in which her father performed, his booming voice traveling across the great expanse of the cathedral. He smiled and waved at his daughter and Mitterrand asked who he was. "It's my father," Kristeva answered simply. A few moments later, Roland Dumas, the French Minister of Foreign Affairs, led Kristeva and Mitterrand around the security guards so that Stoyan Kristev and François Mitterrand could shake hands. It would be hard to say who—father or daughter—was more proud at that moment. By September 1989, Kristeva's father would die from a botched operation, which Kristeva does not hesitate to call murder by the state.

The year that Kristeva lost her mother, 2002, she was also invited to Sofia, this time to have a documentary—*Strange Foreigner*—made about her and to receive an honorary doctorate from the University of Sofia. What was meant to be a joyous, celebratory trip ended tragically with the death of Kristeva's mother from a serious case of meningitis.

As Kristeva left for Paris just before Christmas 1965, there was no way for her to grasp the weightiness of what she was doing. It was an epochal turning point for her and, it turns out, for her current and future readers worldwide. Not to overwork a cliché, "The rest is literature."

Figure 2.14. Photos of Kristeva's parents during a memorial for them at the Nedelya Church, 2014. Photo by Alice Jardine.

Part II

The Crazy Truth of It (1965–1979)

I vividly remember my first impression of Julia Kristeva. It was the fall of 1976. I was beginning my second year of graduate studies in Comparative Literature at Columbia. Kristeva was standing at an old, beat-up wooden desk in Philosophy Hall, the home of the French Department and normally a rather scary place for students. She was wearing a long, blue denim dress, her hair a bit awry. On her right shoulder was her baby son, David—about ten months old with curly hair and a cherubic face. He was not asleep, but was content and quiet, probably because Kristeva was rhythmically moving back and forth, in that swaying motion that babies tend to love. She was holding him tightly with her right arm, glancing down at him every once in a while. Balanced on Kristeva's left shoulder was the office telephone receiver, attached awkwardly to one of those old, clunky desk phones via a curly cord that was too short to let one do anything besides cradle the large receiver over one's ear and mouth for as long as one could keep one's shoulder raised to one's ear in a steady way. Most remarkable to me was the fact that at the same time, Kristeva was using her left hand to turn the pages of a book that I had brought from the library. It almost seemed as if she were actually reading, but I remember thinking that she could not possibly be doing anything except juggling her baby, talking to her interlocutor (I later discovered that she was talking to her editor in Paris), and flipping through her book. What I did not know yet was that this was and still is Kristeva in a nutshell: an insatiably curious intellectual, generously in dialogue with others, and always lovingly attentive to those she cares about.

This is who she was when she got on the plane from Sofia to Paris on December 15, 1965, and this is who she continued to be even as she quickly faced the difficulties of abrupt exile and radical change in a deeply patriarchal 1960s France. Here is how she describes her younger self just before she got on the plane to Paris:

> The [good] student had become a young twenty-something woman, rather seductive and courted by her student friends, journalists, and professors . . . and no less preoccupied by her future, her freedom, her emancipation as a reader of *The Second Sex*. In between romantic passions and disappointments and in the effervescence of generously watered nights danced away (this was very fashionable in Moscow, Prague, Warsaw, and Sofia), the journalism but also the teaching my French degree was preparing me for were nothing but a bit of effervescent foam. Was my [intense] desire to understand, my scientific or spiritual avidity, inherited from my parents—or was it simply an enthusiastic jumpstart to protect myself from a latent depression? Not clear. But what is clear is that I became passionate about philosophy, literary theory, linguistic research—so many pathways that converged for me, in clarification, through fiction.[1]

Early Exile

There are a handful of personal stories that Kristeva has told many times in interviews, films, essays, and fiction. None is as often told and retold as the story of her arrival in Paris on a cold wintry night in December 1965, all by herself, with no place to go, and with very little money.[2] It is clearly one of her favorites. It would be impossible not to hear the slightly romantic tone with which Kristeva conjures up the image of a twenty-four-year-old Eastern European woman arriving at Le Bourget (Orly) airport with five dollars in her pocket. Because she had to leave Bulgaria so quickly, there had been little time to prepare and her father had only been able to procure five American dollars (Eastern European money had no value in the West at the time). It turns out, though, that she did have a few more items in her suitcase besides the famous five dollars: a toothbrush, she says with a smile, but also two books by Hegel, the *Phenomenology of Spirit* and the *Science of Logic*.[3]

Alas, the "friend of a friend" who was supposed to meet her at the airport with more money to tide her over did not show up. She was frightened because she knew that her scholarship would not become available until the end of January and she had no return ticket home. A woman on the plane from Sofia who worked for the Bulgarian embassy in Paris tried to reassure her and suggested that she might find her missing friend at the embassy.[4] Off they went in dreary, gray, sleet-soaked weather, which was disappointing to Kristeva given her idealized image of Paris as "the city of lights." And she was ill-prepared for the wet snow, realizing very soon that her thin coat and inappropriate shoes were sopping wet. But when Kristeva arrived at the embassy, she was reminded of home in a surprising way.

All of a sudden, the woman from the plane was introducing Kristeva to a man whose face, upon hearing her name, brightened in delight. He was Albert Koen, the Bulgarian writer whose collection of essays Kristeva had reviewed a few years earlier. In 1965, Koen was serving as a correspondent for a communist newspaper in Washington, DC, and was passing through Paris on his way back to Sofia. He knew the young woman's name well—very well. He was just surprised that she was so young. He had assumed that "Julia Kristeva" was a mature, experienced, and fearless journalist.

On that snowy evening, Koen had the wherewithal to know that he owed this young woman a great deal. They sat for a while in the dull waiting room of the Bulgarian embassy while he listened to Kristeva's story of abandonment at the airport. She actually started to cry—very atypical of her. And then, quickly and kindly, Koen took her out to dinner. After dinner, he took her straight to the home of his colleague, Mira Todorova, who lived on rue de Passy in the 16th arrondissement of Paris and who was also a correspondent for the same communist newspaper, but in Paris. Both Koen and Todorova were extremely hospitable and generous with the young Bulgarian. They were partisan communists who had fought against the Nazis, but they were also open-minded in the spirit of the post-Stalinist thaw, sharing in the desire to dismantle Stalinism and democratize communism.

Kristeva stayed at Todorova's house for several months and was not only lodged but also fed by Todorova until she could get her feet on the ground. Kristeva also looked up some Jewish cousins by marriage, Shabtai Haimov and his wife Nelly, Israeli students studying in Paris, who welcomed her to their apartment at Les Gobelins and eventually found her a maid's room not far from them. Her cousins and her first French friends—Geneviève Blaise, Claude Nouzeilles, Catherine Lwoff, and Yves Bastide—made her feel at home in the pubs, cafés, and Chinese restaurants of the Latin Quarter. She remembers fondly the long nights they sat up talking and arguing about their lives, painting, music, film, and, of course, literature.

Two primary narratives about Kristeva's earliest days in her new surroundings emerge in her autobiographical essays and fiction. First, there are her mixed descriptions of Paris and its inhabitants. It was undoubtedly strange for Kristeva, who had never been outside of communist Bulgaria, to find herself in the capital of de Gaulle's Fifth Republic where Gaullism had reigned since 1959, conservative Georges Pompidou was Prime Minister, and the French public was still processing the fallout from the horrors of the French-Algerian War. Kristeva was vaguely aware of the disconnect between image and reality:

> During Christmas '65, in a bleak and rainy Paris, I would have been completely disappointed with the "city of lights" had I not attended midnight mass at Notre-Dame, the ultimate meeting place for tourists. When I arrived in the French capital, I met people who were rather poor, whereas the elegant little restaurants and the chic little boutiques seemed to me to belong to a prewar movie. Between the technical brilliance of America and the leveling radicalisms of Eastern European societies (which embodied, for me, two aspects of "modernity"), France seemed stuck in a pleasant archaicness, attractive and unreal. However, the social discontent that was brewing reached me through

newspapers and conversations I overheard—even among people who seemed to be well off. I then realized that this country of shopkeepers wished to become the most developed of East European countries, as if its occult, unspoken goal was transforming itself into a society such as the one I had just left, a society that was criticized in Paris, only in fascinated, hushed tones.[5]

Kristeva described Parisians in the streets as seeming unselfconscious, brightly wrapped Christmas presents—"very beautiful, but very confusing."[6] However, among her new, mostly left-wing acquaintances, Kristeva was hearing lively and informed social discontent, with generational discord becoming a constant topic of conversation among young intellectuals in Paris at the time. All of this discontent would of course explode in the "revolution of 1968" just a few years later. Meanwhile, intertwined with Kristeva's observations of Paris and its different kinds of citizens, there quickly surfaced her second and more sustained primary narrative: her determined, even frenzied quest to find and be welcomed into what was for her at times a vaguely familiar but also a shockingly uninhibited intellectual community of pre-1968 Paris. In retrospect, this is an impressive narrative, and much has been made of Kristeva's rapid succession of successful encounters with luminaries such as Lucien Goldmann, Louis Aragon, Roland Barthes, Jacques Lacan, and even the young male upstarts of the journal *Tel Quel*—including her soon-to-be husband, Philippe Sollers.

Almost as if Kristeva were hopping from stone to stone in a river, or climbing steps on a ladder, every so often she encountered a brilliant, published, and well-known man who recognized in her a fellow traveler without making her conscious of her status as a beautiful young woman (except, of course, her future husband, Philippe Sollers, who never tires of recounting how gorgeous he found her to be). For a number of years, these exclusively male scholars and writers, Sollers included, guided her through and across all kinds of institutional and intellectual territories that were completely foreign to her. And they did so without ever making her feel undervalued.[7]

Kristeva has often said that while she may at times have felt marginalized during her first years in Paris, she never felt discriminated against, manipulated by those with power, or pressured for favors as a woman or as a foreigner. This is hard to imagine today when one thinks about those times in the French Fifth Republic. But, thankfully, it is clear that Kristeva never felt explicitly cornered, academically trapped, or professionally limited by any of her mentors. I suspect that even if she was casually objectified, Kristeva probably did not notice because she was both naïve and focused on her work. What was obvious to everyone was that she was on a determined and single-minded quest to understand the world she was living in. She has emphasized in talking about her younger self that it was not ambition or even "projects" or "goals" that served as the motor for her energetic pursuit of new people and unfamiliar pathways: she was just propelled along. She traveled "through herself," as she puts it, wherever her curiosity—and her mentors—led her.

Kristeva's rapid integration into the edgiest circles of the Parisian intelligentsia soon after her arrival in Paris has served as fodder mostly to her critics and detractors. It has been foregrounded as evidence of her supposedly oversized and unattractive ambition—presented as a desire to attach herself to powerful men—as well as of her supposed subservience to patriarchal norms, exemplified by her almost instantaneous romance with Sollers. Soon after her arrival in Paris, there was even a right-wing account of her in the magazine *Minute*, which speculated that her integration into the Parisian intelligentsia was due to her being a zealous communist spy covertly infiltrating France. Kristeva was astonished by these rumors.

The Lost Territory

I believe that there was more to Kristeva's rapid inclusion in Parisian avant-garde intellectual circles in the mid-1960s than sheer historical coincidence and active personal effort. I think that it had to do with

Kristeva's overwhelming—both conscious and unconscious—desire to recreate what she had left behind as a young adult in Sofia: a vibrant, activist community of journalists and other writers with whom she felt solidarity and affection. Two aspects of her relationship to what and whom she had left behind in Sofia (beyond her immediate family) strike me as compellingly relevant to the intellectual she became— and remains even today—in France: 1) her passionate relationship to the intellectual conversation and complex writing undertaken by her Bulgarian community of dissidence and revolt; and 2) her romantic relationship with a particularly brilliant dissident Bulgarian writer— Tzvetan Stoyanov.

Some have argued that Kristeva has placed an excessive emphasis on her exile and foreignness in France in her autobiographical writings. After all, she moved from an Eastern to a Western but still European country; she was not a refugee or a migrant forced into exile out of sheer misery. While I understand the validity of this line of reasoning, it seems to me to ignore the hidden experience of the still young and impressionable Bulgarian Kristeva that the emergent French intellectual Kristeva tried—unsuccessfully, I would argue—to abandon when she left her country; it ignores the far-reaching psychic as well as political power of the Iron Curtain. Miglena Nikolchina, in her fascinating book *Lost Unicorns of the Velvet Revolutions* goes so far as to propose that pre-1965 Bulgaria is always present in Kristeva's work as a mysterious lost territory or as a lost motherland:

> In the course of twenty-five years or so—in fact, until the collapse of the Eastern bloc system—Bulgaria is hardly ever mentioned in her writing. One notable exception is the painful—and rather unusual for her—confessional tone of "The Novel as Polylogue," in which she states that she speaks "in French and about literature because of Yalta." . . . And yet, it would be more accurate to say that the Bulgarian shadow has passed into its own regime of discretion.[8]

It seems reasonable to suggest that, on some level at least, Kristeva's discretion about Bulgaria functions to conceal the torment of rapid personal transformation. Recall that primary to Kristeva's young adult experience was writing in Bulgarian. Her descriptions of permanently switching from Bulgarian to French are some of the few instances I know of in her writing where genuine trauma radiates from her prose, the other two subjects being her son David's lifelong disabilities and illnesses and her father's death. She has in recent years become more aware of, and more willing to acknowledge, the perhaps incomplete transformation of her consciousness from the East to the West and her resultant linguistic strangeness to her readers—a strangeness that still persists today:

> At the crossroads of two languages and two durations at least, I fossilize an idiom that seeks clarity, excavating pathos-filled allusions. Beneath the smooth appearance of those French words, polished like stone holy-water fonts, the dark gilding of orthodox icons is revealed. Giant or dwarf, the monster who emerges takes pleasure in never being content, while exasperating the natives: those of the country of origin as well as those of the host country.[9]

What can get lost in Kristeva's acknowledgments of the conceptual hybridity lurking within her perfect command of French is the record of the genuine suffering she went through as she changed so dramatically in her twenties:

> I remember my first two articles [written in French]—"Bakhtin, The Word, Dialogue, and the Novel" and "For a Semiology of Paragrammes." I had a cold, like today, it was winter, I was seeing my own hand write and I had the impression that I was writing in a dead language and that someone inside me was also dead. In fact, something else was dying inside me: the Bulgarian language.[10]

Bulgarian—or Bulgaria—may have been dying inside Kristeva, but traces of it have arguably survived. Nikolchina in fact proposes that although Kristeva hardly ever mentions Bulgaria in her best-known theoretical work, her connection to her motherland has reappeared bit by bit, slowly but surely, in her fiction: it is almost as if her fiction was her theory in reverse, an undoing of her theory, capturing what came before it.

Another thing that survived Kristeva's transition to French was the palimpsestic doublespeak that I mentioned in Part I, where I suggested that Kristeva's relationship to writing in Bulgarian was complicated by her status as a free-thinking intellectual and dissident journalist, by the necessity to communicate implicitly what one was not able to write explicitly. Nikolchina describes Kristeva's French writing as a theoretical hurricane that utilizes the techniques that she had used in Bulgaria as a cloaking device to shield herself from the authorities, a hurricane "characterized by a broad interdisciplinarity, a taste for the exact sciences, a penchant for neologisms, and . . . a profusion of newly formed or refunctionalized terms."[11] Noting that this type of conceptual "thickness"—this "tough terminological machinery"—was characteristic of Kristeva's generation in Bulgaria, Nikolchina proposes that Kristeva carried the practice to France.[12] More specifically, she suggests that the linguistic voracity that is discernible in Kristeva's youthful Bulgarian book is replicated "in *Semeiotiké* (still considered by many Bulgarian scholars to be her best book) and *Revolution in Poetic Language* (both books are as yet not translated in their totality in English, precisely, I guess, because of their too-muchness)."[13]

I agree with Nikolchina that the famous density—or for some, unreadability—of Kristeva's work, particularly of her early work, is due in part to her early practice of eluding censorship through linguistic camouflage.[14] In this context, it is important to add that Kristeva was extremely devoted to journalism as an art and as a form of revolt. Indeed, her commitment—which she shared with the Bulgarian community of her youth—to this genre of writing has recently resurfaced in her defense of newspaper journalism in the context of her critique of contemporary Western media culture. Although the latter is less a situation of overt censorship than of hyperconnective numbness, Kristeva recognizes the authoritarian parallels: "The media empire invaded today by NTIC (New Information and Communication Technologies) has replaced totalitarianism, for better and worse, and its powers have a formidable efficiency."[15] For this reason, on the occasion of being appointed Editor-in-Chief for one day of the left Parisian newspaper, *L'Humanité,* on March 7, 2014, she praised the newspaper form and its crucial importance to democracy: "I am betting on the genius of journalism. Impossible? [Journalism] is the intimate laboratory of democracy. It is a question of preserving and updating a political experience within the reach of individual, singular—men and women—readers."[16]

Kristeva could have written this powerful defense of principled journalism in Bulgaria in the early 1960s, when she was writing frantically day after day with a sense of mission shared by her closest friends within a whirlwind of intellectual labor where multilayered density was a survival mechanism and where one careless linguistic step could lead to the (literal) death of the author. As Nikolchina explains, the young rebels seized Bakhtin's ideas of polyphony and dialogism "as an oblique form of dissent from totalitarian monologism," thereby creating a "theoretical dome" that was vertical because there was nowhere to go horizontally.[17] It is not widely known in the West that it was such early dissident intellectual efforts that eventually led to the debates of "The Seminar": the passionate conversations that took place among intellectuals, writers, and artists in the Soviet bloc during the 1980s just before the demise of the Soviet Union and its Eastern European satellites. Kristeva herself has argued that it was the thinking and writing of intellectuals in Eastern Europe in the 1960s that helped bring about the 1980s downfall of Soviet-style communism:

> When did the Berlin Wall come down? However much this event took us by surprise in the autumn of 1989—indeed, no one foresaw either its rapidity or its consequences—I believe the fissures in the Wall began to be clearly felt in the early 1960s. A few unknown scholars—thinkers expressing disturbing ideas in hermetic idioms—were regrouping, like a colony of ants, to carry out subversive labors. Too complex for the nascent media culture, their work was, of course, invisible from Paris or New York; but the masters of the Kremlin were not unaware of its undermining effects.[18]

The kind of complex thinking and writing required on the part of intellectuals in communist Bulgaria during the 1960s is difficult to describe today, but it had a deep impact on the young Kristeva. She and her friends knew that authoritarian reactions to some forms of dissident behavior were predictable. For instance, Bulgarian intellectuals and artists were fascinated by Western hippie culture, music, and protest marches, and the reaction of the communist authorities was swift and sometimes verging on the ridiculous: "The police raided cafes and pubs that were known to be youth haunts and proceeded systematically to cut off long hair, rip off blue jeans, and stamp on the thighs of young women in miniskirts."[19] The official reaction to intellectual debates was more subtle, and therefore even more dangerous. It took the Bulgarian State Secret Services a while to figure out the strategies of its targets. But figure them out it did.

Due to Bulgarian archives declassified in 2007, the tragic extent of the murderous plots of the Bulgarian State Secret Services—the Darzhavna Sigurnost (the DS)—has now finally been revealed for historians to document. The First Department of the Sixth Directorate (usually called the Sixth Department) of the DS targeted—sometimes silently, sometimes loudly and murderously—domestic intellectuals, writers, and artists. As part of the Committee for State Security, and tutored by the Soviet KGB, it attacked both resident and émigré dissidents from the early 1960s through the 1980s. The expanded DS—especially in the form of the First Directorate for International Intelligence—controlled Bulgarian emigration, kidnapped and assassinated opponents of the regime, and developed extensive covert operations against Bulgarians living in Britain, Denmark, Ethiopia, France, Italy, Sweden, Switzerland, Turkey, and West Germany.

The most famous of their "targets for eradication" was Georgi Markov, prolific dissident author, playwright, broadcaster, and respected intellectual, who was murdered in London on September 7, 1978. Markov had left Sofia in 1969 to work for the BBC World Service and the American-funded Radio Free Europe in London where he became a widely followed, mordantly sarcastic critic of the Bulgarian communist state. He was well known in Kristeva's Sofia circles and was a personal friend of her friend and romantic partner, Tzvetan Stoyanov.

Markov was standing at a bus stop in London when he was pricked by the poisonous tip of a large umbrella. His death was painful and prolonged. The perpetrators were never caught, although efforts are still underway today to find out the details of the "hit" right down to tracing the ricin produced by complicit pharmaceutical companies. What is now known for certain is that these kinds of murders, especially of dissident intellectuals, were not unusual. In fact, another intellectual expatriate, Vladimir Kostov, was targeted ten days before Markov.

We now know that Kostov was a former officer of the Bulgarian military intelligence unit who served as an undercover agent in Paris until 1977 when he defected to the West. Kostov was also, of course, a correspondent for the Bulgarian communist newspaper in Paris. Recall that he was the person who brought books to Kristeva in Sofia before she left for Paris. He was also the one who had arranged for a friend to meet her at Le Bourget airport. As a defector, Kostov was pricked by a poisoned umbrella while waiting for the metro in Paris in August 1978. He was hospitalized immediately and because the poison pellet did not contain enough ricin (so the theory goes), he eventually recovered.[20]

In Kristeva's autobiographical novel, *The Samurai*, there is a scene where Olga's ("Kristeva's") Bulgarian boyfriend (almost fiancé) Dan comes to Paris toward the end of her study-abroad year to try to convince her to return to Sofia. Dan is clearly modeled on Kristeva's serious boyfriend in Sofia, Tzvetan Stoyanov, but Stoyanov did not actually travel to Paris to convince Kristeva to return to Sofia. He only went a few years later with his wife, Antoaneta Voynikova, meeting up with Kristeva who was already married to Sollers.[21] (Both Voynikova and Kristeva remember this meeting of the two couples.) It seems, however, that Stoyanov did indeed travel somewhere to "bring someone back": it seems that he was hired by the DS to travel to London in January 1971 to convince Markov to return to Sofia. He obviously failed in that mission and died under mysterious circumstances in July 1971 at the very young age of forty-one. He was an accomplished—and complicated— man. He and Kristeva have frequently been compared because of their prolific, dense writing as well as because of their passionate devotion to thinking and writing as a form of activism—their shared belief in writing as a martial art.

Tzvetan Stoyanov

Figure 3.1. Tzvetan Stoyanov. The Julia Kristeva Archive.

Figure 3.2. Tzvetan Stoyanov's dedication of his photo to Kristeva. The Julia Kristeva Archive.

The back of the photograph says:

Доспат [Dospat]
и [and]
Green Fields
Орфей е много близо! [Orpheus is very close!]
A memory for times immemorial
1964
Jim[22]

It is impossible to know how much Kristeva loved Stoyanov. (And I have not asked her.) But what is clear is *why* she would have been deeply attracted to him as an intellectual. He is today recognized as one of Bulgaria's most influential twentieth-century thinkers.

Stoyanov was born on January 28, 1930, in Sofia (so he was eleven years older than Kristeva). His mother was a respected teacher. His father owned a textbook publishing house. He graduated from the Sofia University Law School in 1952, obtained a degree in journalism in 1954, and went to work for the Bulgarian News Agency (BTA). He was the editor of the famous *Septemvri* magazine for which Kristeva wrote her review of Koen's collection of essays. He was also a literary historian and critic, philosopher, translator, and fiction writer. He translated the works of classic Western writers such as Shakespeare, Swift, Byron, Shaw, Shelley, Whitman, Coleridge, Kipling, Steinbeck, Robert Burns, Harper Lee, Emily Dickinson, and Edgar Allen Poe ("Annabel Lee")— as well as Goethe. He was particularly well known for his translation of Dickens's *Bleak House*. He published fifteen books of his own (four books of fiction, one of theory, one on popular science, and several on literature) as well as important critical articles in multiple newspapers and journals. He is also remembered as a brilliant conversationalist who wrote several significant essays on the importance of communication. The premature loss of such an influential intellectual in Bulgaria in the early 1970s was keenly felt. His voice may not have been heard very well during his lifetime because of censorship and threats to his safety, but the posthumous publication of most of his work fed "The Seminar" conversations of the 1980s as well as the ideas held by many leading intellectuals right before the fall of the Berlin Wall. In recent years, his voice has continued to gain ground in Europe as his books have been translated.[23]

Kristeva does not give Stoyanov much space either in *The Samurai* or in *Traveling Through Myself*. But Kristeva scholars often write about him not only because of the influence she acknowledges that he had on her personally but also because of the striking similarities between them— similarities that have to do with their coming of age when and where they did. They shared a moment in Bulgarian history when literary and artistic culture was being held up as one of humanity's most important assets, and neither of them ever lost their belief in culture writ large. As Marie Vrinat states regarding Stoyanov: "He saw in culture a unifying power, the highest possible expression of the cosmopolitan essence of humanity, the most efficacious remedy for human alienation and hostility."[24]

Kristeva is not shy about acknowledging what she learned from Stoyanov. Her fictional Olga praises Dan as brilliant, linguistically gifted, and fired by an endless appetite for reading: "Their love had been one of lips and eyes: they read the same books in the same bed, talked about them, kissed, discussed, and sometimes, almost without noticing, they would go all the way, as the saying goes. Then they'd turn back to their books."[25] My first reaction when I read this passage for the first time was: "Ouch." Was this just an instance of a European fluidity between intellectual and sexual pleasure, or was it a hint at a lackluster sexual relationship? Either way, it strikes me that Kristeva might mean it when she says that her deepest truths can be found in her fiction. Be this as it may, the comments she makes in interviews regarding her indebtedness to Stoyanov are invariably generous, even if she normally omits comments about their physical relationship.[26]

Harder to elucidate are the non-personal, more politico-historical connections between their intellectual and writing selves. Here I will only mention the ones that seem especially pertinent going forward.

Most importantly, there is their theoretical "excessiveness": the aforementioned hurricane, or voracity, of writing that they saw as necessary for truly powerful thought, for a form of thinking that does not invite censorship in part because of the bewilderment it creates. To describe this genre, Nikolchina turns to one of Stoyanov's novels, *The Extraordinary Biography of Budi Budev*, and invokes what would be "the ultimate book" as imagined by the Candide-like character in the novel, Budi Budev. And Budi Budev's ultimate, imaginary book, I would argue, could very well serve as a parody of the way some critics see Kristeva's own more ambitious volumes. Here is how Budi Budev describes "the ultimate book":

A book that would gather into a focus the whole of our century, and that would be both a summing-up and a prognosis for the future. It would comprise philosophy, history, geography, economics, all of the spheres of the humanities, even poetry, because it wouldn't be written dryly, it would be written with passion and emotion! And most importantly, it would be a polemic against the communists from the highest possible vantage point, with all the complexity and knowledge of the opponent![27]

Even as they and their friends argued about utopianism and Marxism, about whether the point of their work should be enlightenment or revolution, what Stoyanov and Kristeva agreed upon was their belief in the material power of thought and the "martial art" of writing. As the narrator puts it in *The Samurai*, perhaps the samurai understood that "there was no better way of acting—before, in, and after death—than joining together the art of war and the art of writing."[28] "Enlightenment or revolution, the patient labor of the intellectual or the explosive self-sacrifice of the rebel?"[29]—this was the question that they both insisted on asking in their youthful writing and that Kristeva in some ways is still asking today. Kristeva's transparent alter-ego Olga especially emphasizes and recognizes their shared belief in writing as a transformative force. In *The Samurai*, Dan in fact becomes angry with Olga when he realizes that he has lost her to the West. He accuses her of losing sight of the real battle which can only take place back home.[30]

Stoyanov stayed in Sofia. Kristeva stayed in Paris. This was the crossroads at which their sameness uncoupled and their destinies diverged. Stoyanov continued to write in a context where just about the only strategy was to "manipulate the manipulator." This is what he thought he was doing when he agreed to travel to London to convince Markov to return to Bulgaria. He believed that the work of dissident intellectuals was in their own country. He therefore wanted to convince Markov to return for *his* reasons, not for the reasons of the Secret Service. As Nikolchina explains, some dissidents working under authoritarian surveillance have called this strategy the work of "non-coinciding coincidence."[31] That is, Stoyanov's efforts to persuade Markov to return to Bulgaria coincided with the regime's demand, but there was in actuality no coincidence because Stoyanov was asking Markov to return home for completely different reasons: to continue the good fight. It was a dangerous game, as he well knew. Indeed, his last, unfinished book on Dostoevsky, written during the last six months of his life and published posthumously, explores exactly the necessity to "manipulate the manipulator" via the process of "non-coinciding coincidence." It does so through a study of the relationship between Dostoevsky and his famous mentor (and censor), Konstantin Pobedonostsev.[32] Stoyanov argues that all intellectuals, in whatever circumstance, must proceed with extreme imagination, just like Dostoevsky.[33]

Stoyanov never finished his brilliant parable of his own life via Dostoevsky's because he died in a hospital where he was ostensibly having a very simple appendectomy (some commentators have mentioned peritonitis as well). Most intellectuals in Bulgaria are very careful with their language when discussing Stoyanov's unexpected death from what was by all accounts a routine operation. Nikolchina writes that—after traveling to London on his mission to convince Markov to return—Stoyanov returned to Bulgaria and "six months later he was dead in a manner which, in accordance with his darkest forebodings . . . denied him even the aura of self-sacrifice," adding that some of his friends find his death suspicious.[34] In a short piece recently written by a close friend of Stoyanov (and the husband of Blaga Dimitrova), Yordan Vassilev, and personally communicated to me by Nikolchina, the feelings of most Bulgarian intellectuals are expressed movingly—and as explicitly as possible:

> There are many oddities in this mysterious death. There are hardly more experienced surgeons than the ones in Pirogov. And for them to lose the big, young, and strong Tzvetan during the simplest of interventions! It does not seem likely to me. When travelling abroad, high-level delegations sometimes took Tzvetan with them as an interpreter. He knew a lot of secrets, and at the same time, he was seen as inconvenient by the rulers, due to his texts. There was also another strange death. Not a year had passed when the surgeon who

had operated on Tzvetan also died an untimely death. He used to live
at Slaveikov Square, in the same co-op where the *Septemvri* magazine
was housed.[35]

In the end, Stoyanov stands as an intellectual hero to younger
generations of Bulgarian intellectuals.[36] And it is impossible to ignore
the following parallel between Stoyanov and Kristeva's father (whose
first name was Stoyanov): both were dignified, brave men who found
ways to stand up to the powers that be through the sheer power of
their intellects and both were assassinated in hospitals by the Bulgarian
communist regime. Another thing that the two men shared—and that I
would argue also characterizes Kristeva's husband, Philippe Sollers—is
a passionate dislike of "the ordinary." Kristeva mentions this detail in
a fictional context when she, in *The Old Man and the Wolves*, sounds
her cry of rage about her father's death by depicting the senseless
assassination of the character Septicius Clarus. It also resounds in her
loud and persistent insistence over the decades on maintaining a spirit
of revolt.

Kristeva acknowledges that one of the most important things she
learned from Stoyanov was that to be an intellectual, one must contest
and revolt, because if one does not, one risks becoming an aesthete or
an expert and this must be avoided at all cost. What must have been at
the forefront of Kristeva's mind upon arriving in France in 1965 was
that revolt is the ultimate goal of all truly great intellectuals, including
the ones Kristeva so earnestly sought out in Paris.

Mentors and a Doctorate

One of the first intellectuals Kristeva looked up in Paris was Pierre Daix,
the director of *Les Lettres françaises*, with whom she had corresponded
from Sofia.[37] Daix welcomed her warmly and immediately invited her
to lunch, which she took as a great compliment. He introduced her right
away to Louis Aragon, the great French poet and novelist, who was a
leading voice of the French Surrealist Movement (he co-founded the

surrealist review, *Littérature*) and a staunch member of the Communist Party.[38] Kristeva explained to both of them that she was writing her doctoral thesis in Sofia on the French New Novel, had been working on it since her arrival in Paris, but was thoroughly discouraged. She could not figure out how to write a serious critical volume about the New Novel when the whole concept of "the novel" itself remained so mysterious. She could not possibly write on the New Novel without thoroughly understanding the old novel. She had realized that in order to write about the French New Novel—with its bare-bones narrative, invisible characters, lack of psychology, etc.—she first had to understand why it had emerged in the first place: Was the novel form in crisis? If so, why? How was the literary form of the novel constructed, how had it evolved? Where to start? She was spending hours at the library trying to understand the roots of the novel but getting nowhere.

Kristeva asked Daix how she might work on the origins of the novel. She explained that she knew that she should probably start with the sixteenth-century French writer Rabelais, but doing so seemed way too complicated, and thus overwhelming, to her.[39] Daix told her to talk to Aragon ("who knew everything") about an author from before Rabelais he was looking at: the fifteenth-century French writer, Antoine de la Sale, who, in 1456, at the age of seventy, wrote a text entitled *Little John of Saintré*. Kristeva literally ran to the library to begin her research on what would become her doctoral thesis (*doctorat de 3ème cycle*), the basis of one of her most famous articles, and eventually her third book published in France: *The Text of the Novel: A Semiological Approach to Discursive Structure*.[40]

Kristeva also contacted her compatriot Tzvetan Todorov. Todorov was also born in Sofia (two years before Kristeva), had studied literature and philology, and had also managed to get permission to study in Paris for a year. Under the guidance of Roland Barthes, he was able to stay and complete his doctorate in 1966.[41] Because he had arrived in Paris before Kristeva, he was ready and willing to give her advice and was in fact very helpful and protective when she first arrived. However, once Kristeva became more involved with the journal *Tel Quel*—and its editor, Philippe Sollers—Todorov became more distant and critical. Framing his advice to Kristeva was his assumption that, unlike him, she would eventually have to return to Bulgaria. Consequently, although he believed that she should study structuralism, he told her that instead of going to hear Roland Barthes or Jacques Lacan, she should study the topic from a Marxist perspective under the tutelage of Lucien Goldmann.[42] She did attend the seminars of Barthes and Lacan, but it was Goldmann who became her academic adviser because of Todorov's guidance. She telephoned Goldmann right away after speaking with Todorov. He told her to come see him at his apartment on rue de Rennes in two days. Kristeva was again thrilled by her good fortune.

Goldmann was an eccentric—and by many accounts often egocentric—yet brilliantly unforgettable Jewish and Marxist Romanian for whom Kristeva retains to this day a deep fondness even though their relationship in later years was not easy.[43] He was a large man, a true *bon vivant*, and very charming. Her favorite adjective for him even today is "adorable," although that probably was not the first word that came to her mind the day she visited him:

> Adorable . . . really nice . . . a bit flirty . . . blurting out, "Well, yes, of course we are going to work together! Come see me the day after tomorrow, before vacation." After the catastrophe of my arrival and the Parisian snow and my bad shoes . . . suddenly someone like Lucien Goldmann invites me to his house!? I ran!! But he was walking down his staircase as I was walking up. He had forgotten our appointment.

Goldmann insisted that him having forgotten the appointment was not a problem and suggested that they could go to a tea salon nearby. She ordered what he suggested: lots of cakes and cookies. Kristeva recalls:

> It was obvious that what I was saying didn't interest him. He wanted to speak only about himself. I was fascinated. I didn't eat anything. All of a sudden, he had to leave. "But you are great, I can see that. I will be your thesis director. We will work well together. The New Novel interests me a lot." He had already studied the New Novel through

the lens of reification, via Lukács and the theory of the object . . . the
becoming merchandise of the world . . . "After vacation, come see me.
You go get enrolled and I will be your director. We will get your stay in
France extended. Let's go."

As they were leaving the tea salon, Goldmann turned around and
saw all their cookies still sitting on their table. He said, "Oh no, we
mustn't leave anything to the capitalists!" and promptly devoured all of
them on the way out.

Even as Kristeva was working hard at the library on the origins of
the novel and meeting with Goldmann, she was attending seminars
in Paris, especially those of Émile Benveniste, Roland Barthes,
and Jacques Lacan. Todorov also told her about a young group of
experimental writers organized around a literary journal called *Tel
Quel*. But it was Barthes's seminar at l'École des Hautes Études that she
found particularly compelling. She remembers the warm ambiance
of the seminar, filled with foreign students like herself listening with
rapt attention to the seemingly magic words of the famous instructor.
She, too, was mesmerized. She was especially intrigued by the strange
and new mixture of references to thinkers and writers like Freud and
Mallarmé, and to the field of semiotics, that Barthes offered.[44] She
knew a lot about the Russian formalists,[45] but not so much about
semiotics, and almost nothing about psychoanalysis except what
she had been able to glean from the hidden volume of Freud in her
childhood home.

As she was writing her thesis on Antoine de la Sale, she was running
from seminar to seminar, exhilarated by the discoveries she was making.
She also met many interesting young intellectuals, especially in Barthes's
seminar. Yet even as she listened and discovered, she focused on the
ways in which la Sale's text, *Little John of Saintré*—and by extension,
the origins of the novel—could be illuminated by the theoretical work
of the Russian post-formalist, Mikhail Bakhtin.[46] She was beginning
to see the connections between Bakhtin's idea of the "carnivalesque,"
the scientific chronicles of the fourteenth century, and what she would

eventually name "intertextuality": the ways in which texts talk to each other, repeat each other, and form a palimpsestic history of both their time of writing and their time of reading. She came to believe that although the famous "structuralism" that she was hearing about in the seminars of Barthes and Goldmann was a fascinating and elegant system of thought, it had forgotten two things vital to both literature and life: the speaking subject and history.[47]

Kristeva began to tell others, including Barthes, about her work on Bakhtin. She explained that in Eastern Europe, the focus was more and more on Russian post-formalism, especially Bakhtin, and that the Western European emphasis on structuralism was behind the times, was really just about finding a way to do formalism. Moreover, she thought that structuralism was a way of doing formalism without what she and her compatriots had been discovering, via Bakhtin, to be essential to any meaningful analysis of the human imagination, namely the speaking subject and history.[48]

Barthes was impressed. He did not know anything about Bakhtin and promptly invited Kristeva to give a lecture on Bakhtin in his seminar. This was monumental for her. Everyone in the seminar had been very excited most recently about a talk on Mallarmé by Philippe Sollers and about a psychoanalytic reading of Kafka by Marthe Robert. These were hard acts to follow. But Kristeva did—and she was a smash hit. René Girard, the respected French philosopher who was teaching at Johns Hopkins in Baltimore, was so impressed that he immediately began trying to recruit Kristeva to Johns Hopkins. Gérard Genette, the well-known French theorist of narratology, was so impressed that he insisted that she meet the writers of *Tel Quel* so that she could move on to the "*new* New Novel."

The talk that Kristeva gave on Bakhtin in that 1966 seminar at 44 rue de Rennes launched her reputation as a mind to be reckoned with in the heady Parisian intellectual circles and later became the best known of the articles that constituted her first book, *Semiotike*, published in 1969.[49] It contained many of her core ideas about the need for literary theoretical insights to mirror those of the literary text being examined, about the polyphonic logic of novels from Rabelais and Swift to Dostoevsky and Joyce, about how the human subject and its history can be "done and undone" by the complex linguistic theater that we call the novel, and even about how perhaps it is only Freud (about whom she knew little at the time) who can open the novel up to an exploration of nothing less than history's unconscious. Kristeva's references to literary authors are dizzying: Rabelais, Cervantes, Swift, Sade, Balzac, Dostoevsky, Lautréamont, Joyce, Proust, and Kafka. Coming from Bulgarian intellectual circles, she knew more about an international array of authors and disciplines than her more classically trained French classmates and professors. Fortunately, they wanted to know more. Most of all, they wanted to know more about this young, beautiful Eastern European woman who spoke perfect French.

Especially Roland Barthes. Kristeva and Barthes came to genuinely love each other. It was an affectionate love between teacher and student—their roles in the dyad often alternating—rooted in admiration and gratitude. One only has to read their texts about each other—his published in 1970, hers in 2015—to see the extent to which this is true. Barthes's 1970 article, "Julia Kristeva, the Stranger," already speaks of *owing* this young foreigner because of the sheer force of her work: "Julia Kristeva changes the place of things; she destroys the latest prejudice . . . what she displaces is the already-said . . . what she subverts is authority."[50] Kristeva responds with the same measure of affection and respect forty-five years later in her "Roland Barthes, the Stranger."[51]

Kristeva was thinking about the future even as she was finishing her doctorate. She asked Goldmann if she should accept Girard's invitation to move to the United States to teach at Johns Hopkins. Goldmann said, "Why not?" Kristeva answered, "Because of Vietnam of course!" To which Goldmann replied, "Listen. Capitalism? You have to take it from the inside!" In spite of this encouragement, Kristeva stayed in Paris and finished her thesis. Her dissertation jury consisted of Goldmann (as her director), Barthes, and Jean Dubois, a well-known French linguist, grammarian, and lexicographer. This was a formidable committee, but even more formidable was the fact that her dissertation defense took place in June 1968, directly in the wake of the student and worker uprisings of May 1968. Gatherings in the halls of university buildings were not allowed. Only the defenses of foreign students who had to return to their native countries were allowed to take place. For this reason, Kristeva's committee was allowed to proceed without drama from without. However, there was plenty of drama from *within* the committee to go around.

Goldmann had been aware for a while that Kristeva was increasingly taking her distance from Marxism in her thesis, that she was moving toward linguistics and psychoanalysis as reservoirs of analytic tools for her study of the novelistic form. Kristeva was discovering that even Bakhtin's "speaking subject" was very meagre, even narrow, and this dissatisfaction was being reinforced by her conversations with other intellectuals, and especially by what she was hearing in Lacan's seminar. She was profoundly intrigued by the Freudian unconscious and compelled by some of Lacan's basic teachings, such as the idea that we are all manipulated by linguistic logic in ways that we may not be conscious of. She dug deeply into psychoanalytic theory and in her thesis on the origins of the novel, wrote explicitly about sexuality, about desire, indeed about the sexual romance between Little John of Saintré and the Lady of the Fair Cousins—about the libidinal side of courtly love.

This was all very new at the time. At the beginning of the defense, Goldmann praised Kristeva's work as truly original and deserving of its high grade (*mention très bien avec félicitations*, roughly equivalent to High Honors with Special Congratulations from the Jury). *But*, said Goldmann, why are you so interested in sex? Why are you not interested in the belly? In food? It seems that everyone in the room looked at each other awkwardly. It was fairly clear that Goldmann wanted his star student to return to his form of Marxist literary analysis. But all Kristeva could think of was the cakes and cookies he had devoured at their first meeting, and for the first (and last) time in her life, she lost her temper with a teacher.

In a sudden outburst of temper, Kristeva raised her voice and addressed her teacher informally, using his first name (as he had allowed): "Listen here, Lucien." But she continued in the formal form of *vous*, thereby taking her distance. Goldmann was surprised. He had maintained a very informal atmosphere in his classrooms and with his graduate students, which was very unusual at the time and for which his students adored him. But it also created space for contestation, and perhaps in part because of the already contestatory atmosphere of Paris 1968, Kristeva stepped into that space quite forcefully. She continued formally but with emotion. She insisted that she would not return to the repetitive and simplistic discourses of "the human condition" or representations of "pity for those without enough food." She called that approach "archaic" and no longer done by those serious about literature. She chided him for talking about the belly, which was merely a matter of talking about himself, and blamed him for not engaging at all with the subject of her thesis. Tears rolled down Goldmann's cheeks. He and Kristeva became friends again eventually, but not like before.[52]

In spite of this drama, Kristeva did receive her *doctorat de 3ème cycle* in French Literature (Semiotics) in 1968 for her thesis: *The Text of the Novel*. It was the culmination of two and a half years of exhilarating discovery and difficult challenge. From her arrival in Paris in December 1965 until her thesis defense in June 1968, she had never stopped writing. She wrote constantly, frequently falling ill from sheer exhaustion. Essay after essay was published, many of them eventually ending up in *Semiotike*. Over her first two and a half years in Paris, Kristeva also went to every course she could find. She made many mostly foreign friends, remembering fondly, for example, her early friendship with Marian Hobson (a student from England who would become a recognized scholar of Diderot and a member of the British Academy). It was in fact with Hobson and a few other friends that she made one of the biggest discoveries of her life—a discovery that would give shape to the rest of her life: Philippe Sollers.

Philippe Sollers

It was in early 1966 that something—or rather, someone—managed to stop the hard-working Kristeva in her tracks, at least briefly: a large photo of Philippe Sollers (accompanying an interview with him) that she discovered with her friends in an issue of the communist journal *Clarté*. She found Sollers very handsome and thought that his text was brilliant—in the spirit of the Surrealists, of the Futurists, of the newest of new novels, and even more radical than all of them! Sollers seemed to express in his (to her) very French way the same kinds of convictions as many of the avant-gardists she had read in Sofia, namely that one's political life is deeply rooted in one's interior psychic life and especially in one's experience of language. Kristeva wrote a letter to Sollers, asking to meet with him, and he gave her an appointment. She was excited: she was going to meet Philippe Sollers—already known as the Pope of St. Germain—only five months after her arrival in Paris, in May 1966.

Kristeva and Sollers met in the tiny office of Sollers's journal, *Tel Quel*, at the Éditions du Seuil on rue Jacob . . . and they have not left each other's side since then. Kristeva remembers:

> He was very handsome, with a fantastic profile: a very good-looking boy! He said that literature is indispensable to revolution—a bit of a surrealist idea, really. He argued that one can't change society without changing the way of thinking, and that literature does that . . . by changing form and all that.[53] So I said to myself: that's the New Novel. I must meet him! As usual, I felt like I didn't dare, but everyone, especially Genette and Barthes, encouraged me: "You must meet him, it's all exactly meant for you." He was so handsome *and* he believed that one must change the form and not just the content of something in order to be revolutionary! It was a combination that was irresistible . . . I told him that he didn't look like an intellectual, but more like a football player. He was flattered! He started fiddling with my neck in the subway . . . He has said that I looked at him in a very intense way, not in a scattered way like most of the girls . . . that I showed interest! It was immediately both an intellectual and a physical fascination.

In the wake of their 2015 book on (their) marriage—*Marriage as a Fine Art*[54]—Sollers has also spoken in the media of his first encounter with Kristeva:

> This ravishing young woman landed in my small *Tel Quel* review office. We were living during a very cornered, blocked time . . . Our little avant-garde review was preparing the terrain for the explosion that would come a little later [1968] . . . When Julia Kristeva arrived, I was expecting to welcome a university academic—with all the characteristics of the dusty and disoriented university of that period— who was going to ask me all the usual questions. But not at all! In remarkable French, it was she who brought to me really considerable new information from far away. It was she who genuinely explained to me what Russian Futurism was and exactly how it had been wiped out by Stalinism. How could she have all this information?[55]

Who was this handsome, brilliant, erudite, and cocky, but also distracted, shy, and even reclusive poetic young man in 1966? The man Kristeva was about to fall madly in love with? It is hard to say.

Figure 3.3. The *Tel Quel* Board with Kristeva and Sollers (l–r: Denis Roche, Jean Ricardou, Pierre Rotenberg, Marcelin Pleynet, Julia Kristeva, Jean-Louis Baudry, Philippe Sollers).

Sollers is known for his flippant, ironic, and self-parodic style, for an acute playfulness that is especially present when he is talking about himself. His public persona is consequently very difficult to pin down. I am reminded of Marcel Duchamp's famous dictum: "I force myself to contradict myself in order to avoid conforming to my own taste." Over the decades, so many literary critics and historians have complained about this difficulty regarding Sollers (as well as about the fact that his novels are not "real novels") that in 2007, Sollers published *Un vrai roman—A Real Novel*—about "himself" and "his life." On one page, in one paragraph, about halfway through the book, he is perhaps at his most honest as he sums up his life as follows:

> At 10 years old, deep in the garden, I am dazzled by the simple fact of being there (and not about being me), in the unlimited-limit of space. At 20, huge temptation to commit suicide; it is minus two, but my encounter with Dominique saves me. At 30, relapse and a keen desire to get it over with, but my encounter with Julia saves me. At 40, the abyss: my son's health problems, Paradis impossible, New York drama, leaden years in France. At 50, "fight," that's all there is to say. At 60 years old, I begin to see the synthesis, and at 70, the big picture, with a talisman from Nietzsche: Luck, a wide and slow staircase.[56]

A more mundane summary of Sollers's life reveals one that has been very full—mostly of writing. Sollers was born Philippe Joyaux in Bordeaux in 1936. He was raised there, in the conservative Gironde region of southwestern France, by a very Catholic family that owned and ran a factory for the galvanization of metals. After economic studies in high school, he was sent off to study with the Jesuits, at the school of Sainte-Geneviève in Versailles. He was supposed to be preparing for elite graduate studies in economics (at L'École des Hautes Études Commerciales) so that he could take over running his father's factory.[57] But Sollers did not want to run the factory, and in any case, he was expelled by the Jesuits in 1953 for reading Sade and Bataille—and for spitting on the Tomb of the Unknown Soldier after one of his best friends was killed in Algeria.

In 1957, at the age of twenty-one, he published his first novel, *A Strange Solitude*,[58] under the pen name, Sollers: sollus (unbroken) + ars (arts—also clever and tricky). The young Philippe invented the name when he was fifteen or sixteen so as not to embarrass his parents by his publications. He was quickly discovered, celebrated, and mentored: by the deeply conservative French writer François Mauriac; by the upstart left-wing "poet of things," Francis Ponge; by Aragon; and soon by Barthes. In 1958, at the age of twenty-two, he fell madly in love with the Belgian writer Dominique Rolin, who was forty-five at the time, and who—unbeknownst to most of Kristeva's English-speaking readers— remained Sollers's "other" great love for over half a century, until her death in 2012.

Soon after meeting Rolin, Sollers founded *Tel Quel* in 1960, received the coveted Prix Médicis in 1961 for his novel, *The Park*, and simply did not stop writing after that: *Event* (1965), *Numbers* (1966) . . . These early publications eventually led to some thirty novels and some thirty volumes of essays.[59] And in the midst of this rapidly unfolding brilliant career and complicated private life, in 1966 (at the age of thirty), there, suddenly, was Julia Kristeva (who was twenty-five).

Neither Kristeva nor Sollers was having an easy time when they began their story together in the spring of 1966. Kristeva thought that she was going to have to return to Sofia at the end of the summer of 1966 and was working insanely hard, writing constantly, and making the most of every last minute of her time in Paris. She kept getting sick, so much so that she ended up at the Cochin Hospital with a bad case of viral hepatitis which, in retrospect, she thinks may have been in part at least the result of a psychological shakeup. This episode in her life reminds her of Colette arriving in turn-of-the-century Paris with her husband, Willy, and coming down with a terrible, probably psychosomatic, illness from the sheer shock of Parisian life. But in Kristeva's case, the illness was real and serious, treated in those days with constant doses of corticosteroids (in due course replaced with lots of lemonade).[60]

Both the French Embassy and Sollers had to intervene in order for her to get a room in the famous Parisian hospital. Because she was from a communist country—and had been in the news as a "probable spy"—she was initially denied care. It was in fact one of Sollers's rivals at *Tel Quel*, Jean-Edern Hallier, who had written the article for the right-wing *Minute* claiming that it was clear that she was a Russian spy given how many writers she had met since her arrival: Goldmann, Barthes, Daix, Aragon . . . and, after all, she had written to Sarraute and Butor and Robbe-Grillet!: "Like a diplomat, Madame, you do a lot of letter-writing!"

Tel Quel

Sollers in turn was working non-stop as the director of *Tel Quel*. He was already a published, well-connected author of the "new-New-Novel" who was getting considerable attention and enjoyed the protection of Mauriac and Aragon. His life was never dull. Both of these more senior mentors were outspoken stylistic innovators, constantly saying new, often unexpected things, in public. Even the conservative Mauriac, in spite of his right-wing politics, was quite visionary and therefore inevitably controversial for his time, for example, around issues of postcolonialism. Aragon was a countercultural force to be reckoned with, a breaker of molds, never well-behaved, a convinced communist, and—especially after the death of his wife Elsa—an out-of-the-closet homosexual. The early 1960s were inherently turbulent times, and Sollers was particularly caught up in the political and artistic dramas that these better-known intellectuals seemed to both produce and attract. Even within the confines of Sollers's own journal, there was intense rivalry—a bit like with the Surrealists earlier in the century, albeit with even more venom. It was a situation reminiscent of the ethos of clan versus clan.

For example, there was the intense rivalry between Hallier and Sollers. Hallier came from a Vichy-friendly family associated with

L'Action française, the notorious right-wing nationalist movement and journal. Sollers's family was Gaullist, conservative, and Catholic, but open-minded. One issue at the time caused a great deal of trouble. Francis Ponge had intervened on behalf of Sollers with André Malraux, the Minister of Culture, so that Sollers could be relieved of his duty to serve in the military during the Algerian War. He consequently worked in several psychiatric hospitals with schizophrenic patients while his childhood friends went off to a war where many were killed, much to the horror of the young Sollers. At one point, Sollers was told that Hallier's father, a military general, wanted to send Sollers to the front lines of the Algerian War so that his son could take over the directorship of *Tel Quel*. Whether this was true or not was unclear. All these years later, it is still unclear. But it is indicative of the kinds of drama that Kristeva suddenly found herself involved in as early as May 1966.

Sollers had founded the journal *Tel Quel* in 1960 with the help of Marcelin Pleynet. It was, in Sollers's words, dedicated to questions at the intersection of knowledge (epistemology) and society (politics). The journal was published by Seuil until 1982 when Sollers renamed it *L'Infini*, after which it was published first by Denoël and then by Gallimard. The journal was and still is a lightning rod for controversy, but in its earliest days, it was mostly a source of great discovery and intellectual excitement.[61] In the spring of 1966, the editorial board was publishing its 25th issue. The young men at the helm of this ambitious enterprise at that moment—Sollers, Jean-Louis Baudry, Michel Maxence, Marcelin Pleynet, Jean Ricardou, and Jean Thibaudeau— were very sure of themselves and very much into their bad-boy image.

In a 1963 television interview at the Seuil offices on rue Jacob entitled "The Future Is Theirs!," these young men offer visually a strange combination of the deepest seriousness and smirking self-confidence.[62] "What do you detest?" asks the interviewer. "Pretenders . . . those who present themselves as being on the side of literature but are really just journalists in disguise." "What do you love?" Out pours a litany of names: Borges, Swift, Bataille, Ponge, avant-garde artists like Braque and Picasso . . . the New Novel. Sollers talks a bit about his challenging

book published that year in the *Tel Quel* collection—*The Intermediary*—
which consists of essays and poetry intermediate between dream and
reality.[63] There is little in the interview to suggest how wildly influential
these young men's journal will be for more than half a century.

And it was a journal only of men at the time. This is clear from a
quick survey of those who published in the journal in 1966: Denis
Hollier, Jacques Derrida, Hubert Damisch, John Ashbery, William
Burroughs, Roland Barthes, and Jean Genet, just to name some of
the better-known personalities. It was only in the spring of 1967 that
a woman's name—Kristeva's name—appeared: *Tel Quel* published her
influential "Towards a Semiology of Paragrams." Placed right alongside
an article by the great Russian Formalist, Roman Jakobson, it is one of
Kristeva's best-known articles (even if the writer and editor Bernard
Pingaud at the time called it "the most unreadable article ever published
in French").[64]

Kristeva and Jacqueline Risset, the poet and Dante scholar, would in
fact be the only two women ever closely affiliated with *Tel Quel*. Risset
joined the editorial board in 1967, Kristeva in 1968. Both were avid
participants in the weekly meetings of the theoretical group organized
around *Tel Quel* at 44 rue de Rennes, in late-night discussions at the
Falstaff Restaurant (42 rue de Montparnasse), or at Jacques Derrida's
house in the Parisian suburb of Ris-Orangis. How did Kristeva
experience all of this?

Kristeva has often spoken publicly about her discovery of *Tel Quel*
and her dedication to it, and in some ways, the overall trajectory of her
work of the 1960s and 1970s can be closely linked to that of the journal.[65]
Her fascination was both abstractly intellectual and concretely personal.
She has argued that, in retrospect, the cultural and political excitement
of those years in Paris before and after the cultural revolution of 1968
was hopelessly intellectually contagious for her.[66] Even as she swam well
in the familiar Marxist, linguistic, and avant-garde waters of the still
young *Tel Quel*, Kristeva found the intellectual enthusiasm and textual
ambitions of her friends peculiarly French—just as she did when it came
to the political uprisings of 1968. When asked in 2006 whether France

in 1968 had not been a little behind other national efforts at cultural and political renewal, her enthusiasm rang clear: "But what imaginary fervor, what a curiosity for the unusual, what a capacity for moving the violence of the body and its pleasures into discourse so precisely!"[67]

Kristeva's attraction to the young men of *Tel Quel* was not only intellectual. It also had to do with the fact that they accepted her, welcoming her without hesitation into the conversations that she felt most passionately about. And she did not experience this openness due to her relationship with Sollers; rather, it was due to the fact that she had so much to bring to the conversation. In the French documentary, *A Foreigner, Citizen of the World*,[68] Kristeva focuses on her affinities with the group: they were talking about the New and the post-New Novel; they were focusing on complex forms of language and thought; they were rethinking society's relationship to the political; they were fighting vulgarization. This was all compelling enough. But what was irresistible to Kristeva, I think, was the humor and playfulness and passion and intelligence at the heart of their conversations.

Like her father, Kristeva saw herself as having a critical spirit that craved freedom. But she also liked to play. She reveled in the long nights of drinking and laughter amid political debate and literary invention. She was inspired by the iconoclasm, the irreverences, and the feverishness of the group thinking together. She loved it when narratives were dislocated, time was mixed up, and the sentence never ended. For her, what mattered was perpetual conflict and smart play, that their conversations felt alive and that the stakes—the main one being no less than the future role of the intellectual—felt life-and-death serious. I would venture to suggest that all of this reminded her of Sofia. But it was not Sofia and she was still a foreigner. Nevertheless, while she never felt completely part of the group, and occasionally even felt marginalized, she never felt rejected as a foreigner—or as a woman.[69] Even before she met Sollers and his closest friends, such as Marcelin Pleynet and Jean-Louis Baudry, the intellectuals and their interminable conversations in Paris felt alive to her. Even more established figures such as Barthes opened their hearts and minds to her with great warmth.[70] The young rebels with a cause of *Tel Quel* did the same.

Resurrections

In one of our interviews, I asked Kristeva how it felt to be around all these men, about whether she was conscious of what she was doing at the time, and about whether it was part of her ambition to be accepted by the avant-garde of the male avant-garde elite. Once again, counter to the usual image of Kristeva as a rising star in the 1960s Paris, she returned to the theme of swimming through life, and admitted having experienced more sadness and loneliness at the time than most of her readers know about:

> They weren't macho. There was a sort of psychic bisexuality that led them to the feminine . . . and, after all, I was capable of having a good conversation so I was "a bit of a boy" as well.[71] And France was coming out of the Algerian War a bit turned in on itself and terrified. In contrast, the intellectuals at the time were fascinated by everything coming from the East, especially from Russia and China . . . I was actually in an extreme state of solitude, even of suffering, and at the same time, from the outside, extremely well received, welcomed, a great example of successful integration.

Along related lines, in a 2011 book co-authored with the Catholic philanthropist Jean Vanier, Kristeva wrote of her depression, of her deep experience of mortality during her first couple of years in Paris.[72] She goes back to the feelings she had when writing in French, her impression that she was confronting a death within herself. She experienced it as a death of her Bulgarian self, but with another self slowly coming into view.

This suffering was not always consciously lived. But at times it was. For example, Kristeva would catch herself feeling at war with time. She would stare at her mother's handwriting in the letters mailed to her:

it was the handwriting of a woman no longer young. She missed her parents deeply. She felt the passage of time acutely, felt like she herself was passing. She has described this suffering as incisive and painful but invisible to others. But she did not allow it to take over her spirit. She decided to think it, to live it, and to move beyond it, because that effort provided her with a kind of happiness, a beyond. She came to value her solitude, a pleasure she has always shared with Sollers in their "complicity of solitudes."

Kristeva decided to resurrect herself, to reincarnate herself in French. She experienced then and still does today an intense joy of discovery when writing in French, which is one reason she has never stopped doing so. In the early days, though, she was also hanging onto her work, to her writing, looking for ever-renewed languages with which to continue swimming. There were "befores" and "afters," and she searched for what would get her through the tough parts in between. She remembers those first few years in Paris as a time of going beyond herself, of experiencing exile as an exile of/from the self.[73]

In counterpoint to her spiritual suffering, and no doubt connected to it, there were her newly discovered corporeal pleasures:

> At the same time, I was a fairly pretty young woman who had been much courted in Bulgaria, but [with the exception of Tzvetan Stoyanov], it was mostly all about flirting. In any case, I didn't really have a fully developed sexual life . . . and had landed in the Paris of 1968. It was the time of sexual liberation and it was Philippe who showed me that side of life! Plus I was having fun with all the new ideas because, down deep, I was a really good student, quite impressive really. I really wasn't inhibited . . . but I also wasn't part of that 1968 world. I felt divided between the values that I had been taught—fidelity, a certain serenity—and the crazy Parisian life I was suddenly living, a kind of Kama Sutra, a real bordel, with riots to boot!

What remained especially strange to Kristeva was how much success she was having: a foreign woman with a French doctorate at twenty-seven? And she received her state doctorate at thirty-three, which was unheard of! Yet she still felt like a foreigner, like she would never really be French. She spoke French better than most immigrants, but she knew that she still had an accent and, besides, there were the small ways in which the French let you know that you were "not one of theirs," "atypical," or a "curiosity." This feeling has only hardened over the decades:

> It was only later—when the extreme right, Le Pen, etc. began to make gains in France [in the 1980s]—I began to experience all this as a genuine rejection. In intellectual circles, that was not the form the reaction took of course. There, it was a rejection of the theoretical language I embraced, a rejection of intellectualism. When I started to write novels [in the 1990s], it was said that I wanted to redo Beauvoir whereas I really did not want to do that at all! Or when I wrote about the death of my father [in *The Old Man and the Wolves*], it was said that it was "too dark"—and that "writing like that isn't French." I did take all of this as a rejection of my deepest self, of all my complexity. It was a rejection of my emotions, of me as a foreigner, as an immigrant who never really integrated (except that I have a salary). It felt like I would never stick . . . to the point where when I was so well received in Canada and the United States, I was very tempted to go. But it was too complicated, especially for David and Philippe. So I gave up . . . I decided I must simply make the best of myself, do what pleases me . . . what pleases me in the sense of exile from the self, going beyond oneself. In that early period, certain tickets presented themselves for choosing a direction to take. Because there always is a direction, there always is conduct after all. *Que sera sera* . . . except one does do something nonetheless! . . . one doesn't do just whatever . . . What were the two things I did to find my direction, to coincide with my preferred state of "going beyond," of "exceeding"? Psychoanalysis and maternity.

Sit Down! Sit Down!

But first there was marriage. Sollers and Kristeva were married right down the street from their apartment on the boulevard de Port-Royal, in the town hall of the 5th arrondissement, on August 2, 1967. It was a small ceremony: her sister, Ivanka, came from Sofia; Marcelin Pleynet and Jean-Louis Baudry from the editorial board of *Tel Quel* were their witnesses. No parents were there. Afterward, they went to La Bûcherie Restaurant across from the Notre-Dame where, completely by accident, they found themselves seated next to Louis Aragon and Elsa Triolet.[74]

This is the story that Kristeva most often tells about the day of her marriage to Sollers, perhaps because the encounter was awkward, weirdly coincidental, for more reasons than one. Most simply, it was awkward because Kristeva and Sollers had not invited the other couple to the wedding ceremony because of political tensions between the two couples: Kristeva and Sollers were moving away from the Communist Party, becoming what in French is termed "gauchistes," or simply "leftists." But more complexly, and more importantly I think, it was weirdly coincidental because Kristeva and Sollers were already trying to forge a new model of "marriage," a new philosophy of "multiverses" that they could inhabit loyally together but also happily apart, and not only publicly but also privately. In the midst of this struggle, they were feeling resistant to the "couple image" being forced upon them in public—mostly due to Kristeva's Bulgarian passport—as not so much the new "Beauvoir-Sartre," but rather the new "Aragon-Triolet." In addition, there was the fact that Sollers did not like Triolet very much. It seems that she had once written a dedication to him and that he had hated this, finding it intolerably maternalistic. He did not need her praises and refused to see her any more than was necessary.

This was difficult for Kristeva because she admired Triolet, who seemed to know everyone (and had, for example, introduced Mayakovsky to Aragon). In addition, Kristeva had always felt warmly welcomed by Triolet. Pierre Daix had introduced them, and they had become what is sometimes called circumstantial friends, Triolet often confiding her deep unhappiness to Kristeva. Triolet felt misunderstood—publicly as a communist but also privately as the wife of a man reputed to be gay—and this led to a kind of abrupt coldness with others on her part. Kristeva sometimes contrasts this type of cold self-protectiveness of creative women with the warm, if clueless, narcissism of creative men:

One day, talking with Triolet about Eastern Europe, I asked her if she was still a communist. She responded dryly: Why do you ask me that question? Why not ask me if I'm a cook? Aragon, on the other hand, was narcissistic (a little like Goldmann, except that at least Goldmann knew I was there when he was talking). Whenever I would tell Aragon that I was interested in a writer—from Antoine de la Sale to Raymond Roussel—he would simply read that writer's texts to me for hours.

There is no doubt that Kristeva and Sollers were very much in love in 1966, but it would not be untrue to say that their legal marriage ceremony was largely a practical matter. When Sollers is asked why he got married, he almost always evokes Kristeva's practical situation: the poor girl with a communist passport, five dollars in her pocket, accused of being a spy, sick with jaundice, unable to get a hospital room, and her visa expiring—she needed papers! Kristeva admits that she did need practical help: she did not want to go back to Bulgaria. But she has also over time been more willing to talk about how in love she was with Sollers, as well as about how quickly she came to love Sollers's parents and their home on the Île de Ré.

Sollers's parents, Octave and Marcelle Joyaux, found their son's marriage to Kristeva a shock for at least three reasons. First, they were surprised that Sollers was getting married at all! They had not thought that their writerly son would ever marry. They had built a little house for Sollers next to their own larger house because they had assumed that he would live there like a monk in order to write his books. (Their larger house was supposed to go to his sisters.) Second, if their son was to marry, they had assumed that it would be to a "well-placed" French woman, not to a Bulgarian without a penny to her name. Third, Kristeva and Sollers did not have a religious ceremony. As conservative Catholics, the Joyaux were upset that there was no wedding in a church.

The first time Kristeva and Sollers visited the Île de Ré, Marcelle Joyaux did not allow them to stay at the house because they were not married. Sollers was furious, had a terrible fight with his mother, and he and Kristeva returned to La Rochelle, the closest city on the mainland, for the night. The next day, after his parents had gone out, the young couple returned to the house on Sollers's insistence that it was his house too. But after they were married, Sollers's mother called Kristeva to tell her that she had heard Roland Barthes say wonderful things about her on the radio, exclaiming, "You are amazing, Julia!" She went on and on about how wonderful Kristeva's accomplishments were and asked if she liked white diamonds. Marcelle then sent Kristeva a diamond ring she had reset. Kristeva still has it.[75]

Slowly but surely, Marcelle warmed to Kristeva, always showing her both affection and respect. She said that her son needed someone exactly like Kristeva because she understood him, whereas, they—his parents—did not. Sollers's father was also very fond of Kristeva. Once Kristeva's visa was renewed (because of her marriage) and her scholarship was renewed (so that she could accept a position at the French National Center for Scientific Research[76]), Octave teased Kristeva: "Aha, you have a salary now . . . not exactly a dowry . . . actually, better than a dowry and just fine by us!" And he was always ready to help. When she was learning to drive and was out with her American friend, Geneviève Blaise, she took a corner too fast—much like when, as a child, she ran too fast in the park or when, as a young student, she decided too quickly to cut open a cadaver—and crashed their car into a ravine. Thankfully, they survived, Geneviève with some cuts and Kristeva with a couple of cracked ribs. It was Octave who hurried to get them, and have them cared for and taken home safe and sound. Whatever hesitation there had been at the beginning in the Joyaux family to accept Kristeva quickly disappeared and she was welcomed wholeheartedly into the family.

While she is careful not to caricature, Kristeva has agreed with the characterization of French culture as generally, at least initially, quite hard to break into. It takes some persistence but it is worth it since, as she often puts it, "Nowhere is one more foreign than in France; and nowhere is it better to be foreign than in France."[77] Kristeva has said that the Joyaux family was fairly atypical when it comes to French families because her acceptance came quite quickly and was complete and unquestioning once in place. She attributes this in part to her mother-in-law's very particular culture, a culture of some genuine if limited freedom for women.

One of the greatest gifts the Joyaux family gave to Kristeva was a real home in France, a space she has loved for decades now, a place where she does her best writing, where she goes to relax, swim, and play with her family and, increasingly, to regroup after demanding travel and appearances. It is where she wants to be buried: on their small plot of land located on the narrowest section of the Île de Ré called Le Martray, in Ars-en-Ré, off the west coast of France. Wild but elegant, it is a charming landscape of sea salt fields (complete with trousered donkeys helping to harvest the salt for the tourists), lovely white sand beaches, and quaint old village squares with enticing restaurants and lively cafés. But it is mostly residential, and the Joyaux property is hidden behind walls of towering *sanguenite* flowers (sea wormwood or *artemisia maritima*)—the favorite flowers of Artemis, both a remedy and a poison—that grow profusely in the salty earth of Ré. Behind the walls of flowers, one finds three separate, modest-size homes: the main house (where Kristeva writes), a small house for Sollers (every room filled floor to ceiling with books), and a small residence for their son David (where he loves to retreat to read or look at his photographs). Surrounding the three small houses are colorful gardens, bordered by a stone wall separating the property from the sea.

Kristeva has often reflected on the mysterious trajectory of her life path: she went from one end of Europe to the other, from the extreme eastern boundary of Europe (the Black Sea) to its extreme western boundary (the Atlantic Ocean). The fact that she is so connected with these two bodies of water pleases her, supports her sensation of living-with-waves as a form of Tao, yin and yang in harmony with nature. But she always adds that her freedom to play in the waters of Ré brings to her sensations of life, whereas the communism of her youth at the Black Sea brought to her mostly feelings of death. Kristeva's love of swimming in the Atlantic was apparent to me as she fearlessly dove (quite naked) into the (to me, at least) quite frigid waters of mid-August Atlantic waves.

When she describes the Île de Ré publicly, she is quite historical:

The notarial act of this domicile is signed by Louis XVI. A great-great-uncle of Philippe, a navigator, had rendered service to the crown. Photos from the beginning of the 20th century show a solid farmhouse turning its back to the sea and surrounded by walls, protecting tropical trees . . . The farmhouse was torn down by the Germans who built bunkers to protect against a feared allied invasion from La Rochelle. My parents-in-law were compensated by reconstruction plans [after the war], the new buildings being rather ordinary, but the views of the Ars bell tower and the sunsets are magnificent. I love to share the peace here with my loyal visitor for years, the white swan I named Leibniz in [my novel] *The Enchanted Clock*, because the white curve of his neck folds the infinity of the sky into the infinity of the water.[78]

Privately, Kristeva tends to focus more on the comic strangeness of a penniless girl from Bulgaria ending up in the lap of the French bourgeoisie. One of the stories Kristeva has told me several times, always laughing while doing so, has to do with the cultural theater she had to learn during her earliest days of visiting the Île de Ré: the discreet habits of the Bordeaux bourgeoisie—so very foreign to her. Basically, in the traditional bourgeois Bordelaise family, the "mistress of the house" must never get up from the table during a meal. When Sollers's family was still there, whenever Kristeva or Marcelle Joyaux got up to help bring something to the table, or carry away empty plates, all hell broke loose. Everyone would yell, "Sit down, sit down!" This bourgeois habit has remained with Sollers and has been inculcated in their son, David, with the result that now that it is just the three of them at the Île de Ré, they have with them a helper, Annie (a refugee from Georgia whose family was killed in the 2008 Russo-Georgian war). Annie serves the family meals and creates at least the illusion that they are a moneyed home. Kristeva always laughs at this image. "I work hard for our money," she notes. She also insists that she feels a bit enslaved by the bourgeois rules. She and Annie are in fact fairly inseparable, always plotting together to make life fun and unpredictable on the Île de Ré as part of Kristeva's overall efforts to resist the role of the "wife."

It is actually hard for me to think of Julia Kristeva as anyone's wife, perhaps especially as Sollers's wife. In fact, the number one question journalists have asked Kristeva over the years is, "How can you be married to Philippe Sollers?" This question has been amplified by the 2015 publication of Kristeva and Sollers's book, *Marriage as a Fine Art*. It has also gathered urgency since the publication of the first two volumes of Sollers's and Dominique Rolin's love letters: Sollers's letters to Rolin, his mistress of more than a half century—*Letters to Dominique Rolin 1958–1980*—were published in 2017; and Rolin's letters to Sollers, her truest love for more than a half century—*Letters to Philippe Sollers 1958–1980*—were published in 2018.[79]

Dominique Rolin

Dominique Rolin, born in 1913, was a widely read and much praised Belgian novelist (with Jewish ancestors from Poland, as Sollers always hastens to add), who published some thirty novels and essays before her death in 2012. Her career was launched by Jean Cocteau and Jean Paulhan; she won the Femina Prize in 1952; and she was greatly honored by her election to the Belgian Royal Academy. At the center of her novels after 1958 was a young man named Jim—a nod to James Joyce and a thinly veiled autobiographical nod to the love of her life, Philippe Sollers. Because Rolin described the character Jim in detail, the fifty-year love story of Rolin and Sollers was an open secret but it was never talked about publicly. Only a handful of close friends and, of course, Kristeva, had certain knowledge of it.

But by now there are many recountings of how Rolin and Sollers met in 1958, and all of them agree on the basic facts. Chief among the most

Figure 3.4. Dominique Rolin. Photo by Emmanuel Chaume.

frequently repeated details—evidently the most fascinating detail—is that Rolin was forty-five when they met:

> He was not yet 22 and his first novel, *A Strange Solitude*, was making waves. His editor wanted this young man to become well known and had organized to that end a literary lunch. Dominique Rolin, at the height of her beauty at 45 [and already a well-known novelist], was seated next to him. She confided to him that since the death of her husband, the sculptor Bernard Milleret, she couldn't write. He responded: "Are you sure?" Later he wrote to her. [Her response?] "He wants to see me again, he says he doesn't like unfinished things. I please him. He pleases me. After all, why not?"[80]

Thus began an affair that was grounded in a deep love of language, a passionate practice of writing, and a hunger for pleasure that took the couple from St. Germain cafés to private escapes in Barcelona (in the early days) and to sensuous vacations in Venice (every summer for decades). It was only in 2000 that all of this became known publicly, transparently:

> It is then the 24th of March, 2000. On the television set [of the French television personality Bernard Pivot] are several invited guests. Among them: Dominique Rolin for the publication of her book, *The Love Diary*, Philippe Sollers for the publication of his book, *Fixed Passion*, and Michel Onfray for his essay, *Theory of the Body in Love*. Bernard Pivot has his coup well prepared. The cameramen know exactly what they are to do. During Dominique Rolin's admirable discussion, the director regularly frames the face of Philippe Sollers who is listening, smiling, and relaxed. And then, near the end of the first sequence: "*the trap*." And the indiscretion: "The man that you have loved for 40 years . . . it's Jim . . . and Jim is Philippe Sollers." Dominique tries to dodge, and then in her sovereign manner, continues . . . At the end, she insists: we are after all talking about a novel. ("Life is a novel.") Sollers then intervenes calmly to "reframe" Bernard Pivot. Praise of discretion. Praise of love as anti-social act, immediately and necessarily clandestine. It's the theme of all of his novels. And notably of *Fixed Passion*. "How would I have held on and lived without Dora? Impossible to foresee," writes Sollers in the novel. It's almost surprising that Bernard Pivot doesn't ask who Dora is, who is the heroine of the book. But that would probably have been *too much*.[81]

The proverbial cat was out of the proverbial bag: never again was the affair clandestine. Recently Sollers has undertaken the project of publishing all of his and Rolin's love letters. Sometimes there were three letters a day. On March 20, 2014, the Foundation of King Baudouin in Belgium announced that all of their correspondence, more than 10,000 letters from 1958 to 2008, has been donated to the Royal Library of Belgium: "Fifty years of love between two great names of Francophone literature and also a witnessing of an entire era," the newspapers of France and Belgium announced loudly. Moreover, not only are the love letters open to the public, but so are thirty-five volumes of Rolin's private diaries. In addition, the first two volumes of their letters (1958–80) are the talk of Paris and will be followed by the second volume of his letters to her, and, finally, by the last volume of her letters to him.[82] Neither Sollers nor Kristeva talk directly about Rolin in interviews very often even now, although they have gone out of their way over the past few years to both talk and write about their theory and practice of marriage, at least of *their* marriage.

Sollers loves to project an image of himself as a Don Juan and he also loves to talk about how he plays with the media in this regard. This has been true from the beginning of his public life but he has become even more provocative of late. He has explained himself by writing about how his relationship to the media involves a series of deliberate tactics "in order to be left alone": "As I am unable to obtain the approbation of my time period (especially because of my too-libertine novels), I think it necessary to utilize at least its reprobation . . . I remain an outsider, that's my role."[83] He invites critique with glee and utter seriousness at the same time: he announces that it is women who have saved him (along with Nietzsche of course), but at the same time, he does not want to enter into the social, necessarily paranoid constructions of identity that bind men and women into strict social roles. With regard to his very public affair with Rolin since 2000 and his very public marriage with Kristeva, he does not see a problem— there is no contradiction for him. Rolin is his Artemis. Kristeva is his Athena. He needs both.[84]

In Sollers's longest interview to date on his relationship with Rolin, he resists interpretation, especially the psychoanalytic one that Rolin was a maternal figure for him. He also resists talking about the co-existence of the two women so important to his life. When asked directly, he diverts to a conversation about how he seems to be attracted over and over again to foreign women (and about the lamentable situation of masculinity today).[85] But he has addressed his choices in a collection of essays he published in 2013, shortly after Rolin's death: *Portraits of Women*. In this book, he dedicates a great deal of space to Rolin, but an equally adoring amount of space to Kristeva—whose love, he says, is his unshakable rock.

But what about the feelings of the unshakable rock in all this? Overall, Kristeva is fiercely protective of what she refers to as her "intimacy," and I have had to accept this as a given in undertaking this biography. She has kept a diary for many years and has collected mountains of letters, but she insists that the most intimate matters of her life are already in her novels and that the rest—the details—must come out after her death. She admits that we still live in a patriarchal world that judges the intimacies of women much more harshly than those of men who engage in the same behavior:[86]

> It was clear [at the beginning] that I too could have as many intense relationships with men as I wanted, although I didn't overly allow myself to do so given that I was very much wrapped up in the value of fidelity. But given [Sollers's] way of putting himself on exhibit, even when not true, living a free life, I said to myself: perhaps that's not so bad, perhaps I should try it myself. But it's also not symmetrical. A man can allow himself . . . but for a woman to preserve her authority, her dignity . . . she can and should do whatever she wants, but I'm afraid it's still better not to talk about it.

At the same time, Kristeva will not even begin to talk about jealousy. For her, given the bisexuality of the psyche, in order to be jealous in a heterosexual situation, one has to love the same sex more than the opposite sex—and she does not. In addition, as I have already mentioned, she claims that she has never felt jealousy, sexual or otherwise, because her father loved her so much that when she feels that someone does not love her enough, that is their problem! In short, Kristeva tends in these matters either to move toward abstraction—to theorize, mostly psychoanalytically—or to talk about Sollers rather than about herself: "One can't be jealous of a violinist who has his virtuosity. I read [Sollers's] novels as morsels of virtuosity as he writes them. He needs complicity more than I do. His Rabelaisian image is constructed. He gives the impression of being frivolous, whereas he is serious and even, at the end of the day, rather dramatic."[87]

When Kristeva is asked in *Traveling Through Myself* whether it was hard to live with the Rolin affair for four decades, she replies:

Why? A fixed passion that had been built long before we met, with a woman of a generation before me. I had the impression that he was confronting the primary, maternal love object. This relationship had more to do with Sollers's mother than with me. I was never jealous of my mother, convinced as I was that my father preferred me to her and to everyone else for that matter. It's my symptom to believe it, certainly, unless it's my strength … [Sollers's love for Rolin was] an essential dependence, a relationship of influence, with the first object of attachment from which it was impossible for him to detach. Sollers owes her a lot for what he is today. He accompanied Dominique Rolin with fidelity and dignity right up until her death … As I've said before, in our life together, we are married-lovers: I am the wife-mistress; he is the lover-husband. I was the intruder, the anomaly, the troublemaker in that scene of libertinage. The situation made my foreignness [even more] exceptional and irremediable. "Irremediable" means neither condemned nor constrained. Rather I felt myself to be delivered from the chains of the moral superego, delivered over to my own singularity. And my isolation proved to be a source of liberty.[88]

Kristeva seems to be almost grateful to Rolin for all that she did for Sollers. She felt deep compassion for Rolin in her later years as she suffered from Alzheimer's and deep sadness for Sollers when Rolin died. Kristeva emphasized to me how much Rolin helped Sollers when he was working at the hospital in Paris instead of going off to war. She referred in depth to Melanie Klein's theory of the good and bad mother and explained that for Sollers, his biological mother was the "bad mother" because she did not want him to write in his way. She wanted him to take over his father's factory. She even asked Mauriac to tell him to give up the writing. Rolin, in contrast, was the "good mother" who told him how great his writing was. One of Sollers's qualities that Kristeva most admires is the intensity of his "psychic bisexuality" and how he is drawn to women who "can think through their masculinity."

He is drawn to women with whom he can share ideas, who will agree with him, critiquing when necessary but not too much, encouraging him without being condescending. Kristeva is grateful that Sollers had that support from Rolin. It helped him a lot. And in some ways, it was a help to Kristeva as well. She told me several times that she "was lucky to have fallen for someone like Sollers."

The idea that Kristeva feels lucky to have fallen for Sollers most likely strikes the general reading public in France as self-sabotaging if not ludicrous. And that reaction is not surprising given the way the media has hyped Sollers's Don Juan/Casanova image rather than exploring in depth the fascinating ways in which both Kristeva and Sollers have written and spoken about their relationship and about marriage in general. Having read about and listened to their ideas about their relationship and marriage for some time, I myself have frequently wondered whether perhaps Sollers's "women"—for example, as presented in his famous novel *Women*—might not have been fantasies for the most part. It is true that he has always had a lot of close women friends, especially journalists and intellectuals working in the publishing and culture industry. He emphasizes over and over again in his writings how important women are to him and how much he respects and admires them.

When the media responds with his image as Casanova, Sollers does not object, does not clarify. I think that this is because his image as a "man about town" has given him the visibility he craves. He plays with the Don Juan image in part because he is fascinated by images and how false they are. I myself have come to see these images as a smoke screen behind which Sollers hides in order to do his serious intellectual work. I see him basically as a very private person, almost a recluse, completely dedicated to full-time reading and writing. I mostly think that whatever the reality of his relationships with all of his "women," over the decades he could not abide the idea of being publicly displayed as caught between Kristeva and Rolin, with the result that he invented a tsunami of female companions. I could be wrong. I have not asked him. But whatever the truth, his utter dedication to the two great loves of his life cannot be in doubt. And Kristeva's rock-solid love for Sollers is unmistakable. Bottom line: for both of them, writing is like breathing. And they breathe together.[89]

Multiverses

There are a few basic ideas that Kristeva and Sollers have shared about why their relationship has stayed so strong for so long and in the face of so many challenges. I have narrowed them down to four.

First, very simply, both Kristeva and Sollers have insisted in multiple interviews that the most important necessity for a sustained relationship is financial independence. To stay together, both people in the relationship must be financially autonomous as individuals. Otherwise, at least eventually, power struggles will prevail over all else.

Second, and more complexly, both Kristeva and Sollers are constantly saying in different ways that their love is not about "fusion." They entirely reject the modern, sentimental model of love and marriage. There can be no "monotheism" of love, no "absolutism," and certainly no "hystericization." Nor can there be even "exceptional models"—hence both Kristeva's and Sollers's strong resistance to being compared to Sartre/Beauvoir, Aragon/Triolet, Mitterrand/Danielle.[90] (And they do not want to serve as a model either.) Rather, they have both insisted that a love that endures must be about the embrace and maintenance over time of a shared "multiverse," a kaleidoscopic view of two people together and apart, a genuine meeting of two "strangers/foreigners," and most importantly, of the children they once were and indeed still are deep within themselves if they are adults still capable of playfulness. At minimum, the two people in any important relationship (they both hate the word "couple") must remain at least four, each both male and female, ultimately absolutely *singular* and strange—if not foreign—to each other and to the world (think in terms of Bordeaux *and* Bulgaria, Catholicism *and* atheism, with Sollers remaining as strange/foreign vis-à-vis the French language as Kristeva, etc.).[91]

It is probably the word *singularity* that captures what is most important for Kristeva—both for herself and the other(s)—in any relationship:

> [Singular: by that I mean] no community, no clan, no belonging-to, no image: it's pointless . . . [In the Paris of the early sixties] we were all similar in that way. Girondian Sollers, and me the Byzantine . . . Roland Barthes: informulable affinities, giving new, enlarged meaning to *stranger/foreigner*, to *strangeness/foreignness*: which one? His? That of writing [?] . . . Lucien Goldmann: Lukácsian Marxist, atheist Pascalian, dialectical structuralist. Émile Benveniste: severe linguist and surrealist petitioner. Claude Durand: that free electron of the publishing world . . . An accumulation of paradoxes that moved toward me, and I toward them. Instinctive, intermittent, and efficacious solidarities . . . They responded to a traveling energy that might have been, without them, suicidal. [These solidarities] allowed this [same energy] to evolve, both in France and elsewhere. Toward the atypicals, the unclassifiables, in the margins of their families or their brotherhoods . . . with no "background," rather magnetic attractions that activate and then dissipate, sleep and awaken. Here you have it before you: a foreigner and proud of it, an atypical couple withdrawn from the world, and the multiverse of history as tested through writing.[92]

Part of becoming—and living in—a multiverse involves being open to multiple kinds of relationships. While refusing to satisfy the prurient curiosity of many a journalist and scholar about her own "multiple relationships," Kristeva does not deny that she takes very seriously the need for a multiversal life.

Third, there is the necessity of respecting each other's life's work, whatever that work is, and for Kristeva, her work—writing—is like breathing, is so much a part of her that to not respect it would be to not respect her: "For me, writing is not work. It is respiration itself. It costs me nothing. Writing, correcting proofs, or whatever else is involved with writing, takes no energy. Errands, speaking, teaching, seeing people—now that's work! But the fact of thinking, no." As I have already suggested, Sollers shares this vision and the respect for intellectual and creative work. Their work together has been a continual, respectful conversation—a thinking and writing together-but-separately—embraced enthusiastically by both of them:

> Sollers: You have before you two people who have been discussing ideas for decades, and in an improbable way. The conversation started a long time ago and was augmented by physical passion. And this unceasing conversation is more and more rich and interesting. It continues, but each of us has our own place of work.[93]

> Kristeva: We have always talked a lot, exchanged a lot. We are not into being together as in a cocoon, but rather within a complicity of solitudes. We detest [any form of] reciprocal flattery.[94]

In a culture that still does not always encourage men to respect a woman who thinks and writes, especially if she is well known, Kristeva and Sollers have found their way by occasionally, always playfully, changing places of dominance:

> A lot of men are not capable of living such a situation. Whereas Philippe is not only capable of it, he ridicules it in his own ways . . . When one calls him Monsieur Kristeva, he responds that only Americans could think that way . . . "I know it's me who is on top." That is, even if he is annoyed, he plays with it. And, of course, in France, he is much better known than I am. For example, when I go to the Closerie des Lilas restaurant with American friends, and I say that I have a reservation for Madame Sollers, my American friends ask me, but how can you do that?! It's true that Mme Sollers exists nowhere on paper (our legal name is Joyaux), but for the public that watches television, as in a restaurant . . . it's Madame Sollers.

This can indeed be unsettling for anyone who knows who Kristeva is. However, Kristeva is careful to point out that the one thing that is certain in their relationship is that Sollers has never limited her because she is a woman:

> A woman intellectual is a monster! It was necessary for me to find someone who can put up with a woman who is visible, foreign,

ambitious, and who thinks! Most men can't get there. And so the woman cheats: she allows herself to be "fathered" or she hides. Sollers is the person with whom I am the least forced to cheat. Hannah Arendt used to say that around Karl Jaspers, she had to keep proving that she knew how to count to three. With Sollers, I can count to a million.[95]

Financial independence, multiversal singularity, respect for each other's life work, and fourth and finally: fidelity and care. These words may seem out of place in the context of such an unusual relationship, but they are words that both Kristeva and Sollers use frequently to describe what is at the heart of their love for each other. They advocate the utmost fidelity to taking care of each other. One way to do this is to reject the call for transparency about their sexual choices, refusing its inevitable destructivity—the opposite of the choice made by Beauvoir and Sartre.[96] As Kristeva says in *Traveling Through Myself*, "I figure I am protecting my love and my friendships by not laying them out on the table."[97] Another important way of being loyal, along with living one's choices with discretion, is the promise to take care of each other. Here is how Kristeva puts it:

It seems to me that when a marriage lasts, it assumes there is passion, and love, but also the possibility of moving on from passion to the aptitude for giving care to the other. This aptitude is neither therapeutic nor maternal, even if it can rely on both: it concerns simply the respect of the other. And I want to very much insist on this dimension of care—"I will take care of you"—words today absolutely indispensable to a lasting relationship [especially] between the two sexes.[98]

For me, in the context of Kristeva's and Sollers's lives together, it is impossible not to hear circling around these words—*fidelity, care, protective discretion*—a certain vocabulary, certain values of the Christian faith, especially of Catholicism. And both Kristeva and Sollers have indeed made the link between Kristeva's early exposure to Christianity (through Dominican nuns in elementary school and through her immersion in Orthodox Christianity as a child) and Sollers's lifelong strongly held Catholic faith. I first pondered this idea while listening to one of the most moving tributes to anyone's work I have ever heard: a talk Kristeva gave on June 29, 2010, at the Collège des Bernardins in Paris—at an event in Sollers's honor—in which she gave an introduction to Sollers's lifetime of writing under the rubric "The Childhood and Adolescence of a French Writer." Kristeva's short talk was positively stunning in its articulate and elegant praise of Sollers's life work: he is the most French of writers in his ability to "penser en roman" (think as in/like a novel) and in belonging to a tradition of literature as sacred text, where identity is a question—rather than a basis for nationalism—and where through his long "war of taste" he has been able to hold his childhood close, laughing without pause, always a believer in revolt.[99]

This address by Kristeva was about Sollers's successful singularity as a writer, about respect for his lifetime of labor, about caring for him in the deepest possible way, or at least in the way that matters most to him. What was most stunning to me, though, was that at the end of her talk, as she turned the microphone over to him, he did not thank her for her generosity. He *expected* praise from her. He expected the seriousness of her reading, the exquisite intelligence of her insight into his writing. He simply jumped in with his own remarks. But first, he corrected her because before ending her remarks, while invoking Sollers's birth, she had mistakenly replaced the word "biological" with "biographical." He absorbed her tribute, corrected her, and moved on. While I am sure that their understanding is that she would respond in the same way to him, it is the only time I have ever felt like I was witnessing one of them shortchange the other in public.

Yet I am fairly certain that she was not even fazed. It is part of her character to receive, to absorb, disappointment and critique and then just shake it off and move on. As she puts it, it is not that she is indifferent or impervious to criticism. She may feel attacked, rejected, or even nauseated for a moment (even when it is Sollers doing the hurting? maybe even more so when it is him?), but on she goes, counting only on herself to move forward, just as she was taught to do as a child.[100]

Beneath the Paving Stones

Kristeva has often noted that one of the main reasons she and Sollers were able to imagine and pursue their relationship the way they did was that, when their relationship began, they were experiencing the time right before what is sometimes called the "Other French Revolution": May 1968. It was an "effervescent time" in their words, when all kinds of social, cultural, sexual, emotional, and artistic restraints were being shrugged off when not blatantly rejected, mostly by the young. Not that Kristeva was immediately aware of the extent of the political storm brewing in France and, indeed, around the Western world. She was too busy! She was building her relationship with Sollers while working at an inhuman pace. She was publishing her first several articles. She was finishing her first doctorate and getting ready to start the second. She had accepted a position as an assistant and then primary researcher in Linguistics and French Literature within the Social Anthropology Laboratory run by Claude Lévi-Strauss at the National Center for Scientific Research (affiliated with the Collège de France and the School for Advanced Studies in the Social Sciences).[101] She was teaching at the University of Paris 7. She became General Secretary of the International Association for Semiotic Studies and a member of the editorial board of its journal, *Semiotica*.[102] And she was recruited onto the editorial board of *Tel Quel*. In *The Samurai*, she tells the story of how, in the midst of her furiously productive research and writing, the events of early 1968 were at first a bit mystifying to her fictional self, Olga. As Olga marched with her friends in the streets of Paris, her confusion transformed into annoyed bewilderment when she heard young French students singing, with great fervor, the Communist International.[103]

Kristeva was fascinated by the student demonstrations across the United States and Europe because they were not only against war but seemingly against everything. In Paris, thousands of young idealists thought that under the paving stones, there was . . . a beach.[104] Half a century later, debates about the true nature and legacy of May 1968 still simmer and occasionally burn.[105] The most interesting intellectuals of the

Left Bank in Paris have not left behind their quest to understand why 1968 was so transformational and how its spirit might be sustained today.

Semiotike (1969)

Kristeva's first two books in French appeared in 1969. The first of these was *Semiotike: Research for a Semanalysis*.[106] *Semiotike* is a collection of Kristeva's eleven articles from 1966 to 1969, all of them written in dense, technical prose, requiring of the reader at least some mastery of semiotics, linguistics, and philosophy (not to mention Marxist theory). The three earliest pieces, dating from 1966 and 1967, are the best known and in many ways the most consequential in terms of Kristeva's intellectual legacy. Her 1966-67 "The Bounded Text" was a summary of the doctoral thesis on *Little John of Saintré* that she was busy writing under the direction of Goldmann. Several of Kristeva's main arguments in the article have remained at the heart of her work ever since, especially the idea that it is important to understand the history and ideology of whatever seems to be most transhistorical (or "natural") at any given moment and place.

In brief, Kristeva posits that during the European Middle Ages, the foundation of the production of meaning shifted from the symbol to the sign—the latter being a system of signifiers (words) that become attached to signifieds (images), producing a meaning that may or may not coincide with the referent (the real thing in the world). Mimesis, the practice of copying reality through the construction of sign systems, became the dominant ideology of the Western imagination and resulted in "the novel" as a "signifying practice" that strives above all for verisimilitude.[107] She further argues that the novel's ideology of verisimilitude places "the other" (women) at its center, to be exchanged among "the same" (men), in a plot structure that overwhelms, indeed works hard to hide, all the deep writerly productivity out of which the illusion of a "universal" narrative is created. A bit like Michel Foucault's 1966 argument that the idea of Man only appeared in the Western imagination at the advent of the Renaissance, Kristeva's theoretical fable of the origins of the novel was the beginning of her effort to create both a historical and contemporaneous typology of texts.[108]

Kristeva's second best-known article, "Word, Dialogue, and the Novel," was first published in the prestigious journal *Critique* in 1967, and brought her much-admired Bakhtin to the attention of French intellectuals. In this article, she praises, elaborates on, and extrapolates from Bakhtin's literary analytic tools so powerfully that one of her inventions eventually became one of the most famous terms in semiotics. "Intertextuality"— the idea that any text represents the absorption and transformation of others—along with other key terms such as the "carnivalesque," the "dialogical," and the "ambivalent," became essential to her typology of writing she calls "polyphonic."

Over the next several years, the attentive reader (or the obsessive one, such as my graduate student self) will begin to see two primary typologies of texts emerge, one "good" and one "bad." By good and bad here, I am not speaking about inherent qualities, but about the values that Kristeva attaches to texts in the two Western typologies she isolates: monological texts (epic, historical, and scientific discourses) and dialogical texts (carnivalesque discourses and the polyphonic novel). It is the latter texts that Kristeva celebrates: Dostoevsky over Tolstoy becomes one of her best-known examples of the difference. From this time on, the Kristevian polyphonic literary canon comes into view: from Rabelais, Cervantes, Swift, Sade, and Balzac to Lautréamont, Dostoevsky, Joyce, Kafka, Bataille, Artaud, and, eventually, Philippe Sollers.

I will just mention here that two of the texts in the collection focus at least in part on Sollers's work: 1) "Towards a Semiology of Paragrams," which examines Saussure's anagrams along with Sollers's *Event*,[109] and 2) "Engendering the Formula," which focuses on Sollers's *Numbers*.[110] It is in this latter, the third best-known text in *Semiotike*, that Kristeva begins to invent a new vocabulary to describe what she is getting at. For example, she calls for a new critical practice that she calls *la sémanalyse* ("semanalysis"): a combination of semiotics and psychoanalysis where the critical language of analysis remains carefully isomorphic to the form of the discourse being analyzed. (She has also called it a "critique of meaning," a "materialist gnosology," and a "new philosophy.")

Other examples of Kristeva's new vocabulary include the concept of *signifiance*—the process of creating signification—and the *genotext* and the *phenotext*, with the former indicating the (heretofore invisible) process of generating meaning and the latter referring to the (always visible) phenomenon of that meaning in the text at hand.[111] She argues that what Sollers does textually is to render visible the genotext in the phenotext. That is, what writers like Sollers practice is "paragrammaticism": a process of putting into visible textual play a series of signifying differentials that bring the genotext into the phenotext. James Joyce does this. Other writers that Kristeva analyzes in several of her collected articles as practitioners of this type of writing include some of the most difficult writers in the French language: Raymond Roussel and Mallarmé, among others.

Another important figure that begins to emerge at this time in Kristeva's published essays is Freud, especially his notion of the unconscious. Some have pointed out that there was a shared tendency among the *Tel Quel* authors to bring a Marxist emphasis on materiality into dialogue with the psychoanalytic goal of uncovering the unconscious processes at work behind and through human, historical, as well as textual events (such as the anagrams Saussure discovered woven into narrative storytelling). I agree with this, but I would say that Kristeva's early forays into psychoanalytic theory also contain a cautious but distinctive fascination with the irrational, even the mystical, combined with an explicit effort to discredit the scientific/ rational practice of reducing literary practice to a reflection of social reality (the base/superstructure model of "Soviet semiotics"). For the young Kristeva, there is no way for the poetic spirit to become law.[112]

The appearance of *Semiotike* was heralded as a major publishing event, with Roland Barthes in particular heaping praise on Kristeva's strong analysis and erudition: "Already owing her a lot (and from the beginning), I have just experienced, once again, the force of this work."[113] However, Kristeva did not really take in the praise; instead, she was depressed and fragile and working frantically on new material. As she recalls with the unique acumen that her training as a psychoanalyst—which came much later in her life—gives her:

> This first book in French condenses a period where I was both destabilized and intensely receptive. A state of exile, a "limit state," but without the psychopathological connotations this term has come to have. A crossing of frontiers in every way, with the anguish of rootlessness, itself carried along by the giddiness produced by all the possibilities for going beyond (without suppressing) so many limits, norms, identities, and disciplines . . . Migrants are very exposed [to limit-states]: I was able to see this from the beginnings of my practice as a psychoanalyst at the Hospital of the Cité Universitaire. Exile is a loss of bearings, of identity, and psychosomatic problems can follow. I myself was not sheltered from this: my frequent sore throats, colds, and attacks of the flu right up to the viral hepatitis treated at Cochin right after my arrival, were probably part of this. But culture shock can also generate, thank goodness, [work as] research—the path that I took. The avant-gardes explore, by artistic means, the existential disquiet of modernity, the crossing of limits, in affinity with the identity vertigos of exile, of love . . . a vertigo that philosophy, semiotics, and psychoanalysis can conceptualize and think through. I like to think that my previous education [combined with] my ferocious investment in [my] "desire for France" led me to not separate my body from my head. It was with great passion that I dove into the human sciences and the experience of modern literature. [Here] exile transforms itself not into an integration, but into a solicitation to re-create without end what is already given and already acquired . . . You dare to think starting from this movement that you have [yourself] become. You dare to innovate. Perhaps to discover.[114]

Language, the Unknown (1969)

Kristeva's second book to appear in 1969, *Language, the Unknown*,[115] was signed with Julia Joyaux—that is, with Kristeva's married name—in part, I would speculate, because it was not really a book of Kristevian invention but more a pedagogical survey of what linguistics might/ could/should be. She wrote the book for money, but also to prove to the Scientific Council at the National Center for Scientific Research that she was a serious student of linguistics, semiotics, and psychoanalysis. For this reason, it is a rather remarkable book that, while marketing itself as an accessible, neutral introduction to linguistics, is much more than that, announcing many of Kristeva's long-term emphases on what the standard discipline of linguistics ignores. Kristeva's relationship to this discipline has always been complicated and ambiguous—a fact that she attributes to her love of language as an *unknown* rather than as an *object*.[116]

Kristeva has said that she never actually found the French linguistics that she had come to France looking for. Rather, for her, after Saussure and all those who followed him (Jakobson, Benveniste), the trail ran cold. What she did find was Benveniste (who told Kristeva that the two greatest linguists in France had been Artaud and Mallarmé) and Barthes and Derrida and Foucault and *Tel Quel* and they were much more interesting to her than French linguistics. This was true for her mainly because these new kinds of thinkers understood, quite simply, that writers are not always conscious of what they write. In contrast, she has described the field of linguistics as it has developed in Europe and in the United States as a form of positivism that suppresses altogether the question of subjectivity (and of history), let alone the unconscious mind. In 1969, she was already more interested in elaborating on what traverses language than in "mathematizing" it in order to find its constants. She much preferred Benveniste and Jakobson to strict semioticians, whom she called the "technicians" and "managers" of language. In particular, she critiqued semioticians and linguists working in the United States, whether renowned semioticians like Thomas Sebeok or linguists like Noam Chomsky, for either depoliticizing their discipline or, in Chomsky's case, putting political advocacy on a separate track from linguistic research. For her, there was an epistemological revolution going on in France, whereas what prevailed in the United States was a "calculus of thought" grounded in puritan Protestantism and positivist logic. In her opinion, American linguistics was in the final analysis only interested in utility, in how its practitioners could use language to serve some purpose.[117]

The subtitle of *Language, the Unknown—An Initiation into Linguistics*—marks the book as an "initiation" into linguistics rather than as an introduction to the field of linguistics, and I think that Kristeva's word choice is very conscious. Only the first part of the book—which consists of a concise fifty-page introduction to the vocabulary of linguistics—is called "An Introduction to Linguistics." In the second section, "Language in History," Kristeva's voice comes through loud and clear. She puts history back into linguistics via an emphasis on the Egyptian and Mesopotamian civilizations and on Chinese, Indian, Phoenician, Hebrew, Greek, and Arabic signifying systems. She also tackles European history from medieval speculation to structural linguistics. The third section looks forward to what she believes linguistics should be grappling with going forward: human-subjectivity-in-history via psychoanalysis and semiotics—that is, her very own *semanalysis*. Bottom line: Man has been replaced by language and the field of linguistics should wake up.

Émile Benveniste

During the couple of years after the uprising of 1968 and the appearance of Kristeva's first two books in French, politics was constantly in the air and on her mind. On the national front, Georges Pompidou had taken over the French Presidency (1969–74), a young politician named Mitterrand was rising rapidly through the ranks of political power, Charles de Gaulle died (1970), and Kristeva attended conferences on how to rethink Marxism. One such conference, "Literature and Ideologies," took place at the Cluny Colloquium in April 1970 and the proceedings were published in the official journal of the French Communist Party,

La Nouvelle Critique. Kristeva was clear in her contribution that she wanted to bring the French post-formalists and the Marxists together in order to think about the speaking subject in discourse and ideology. She countered monologism with polyphonic literature. The silence of her audience in response to her call for superdisciplinarity was deafening. After that colloquium, she increasingly turned away from the project of "rethinking Marxism" without ever giving up her emphasis on the materiality of signification. But she became more interested in engaging work that was rethinking how the human subject gets inserted into language and discourse and hence into history. In thinking through this question, her two most important mentors in Paris were the very famous Roman Jakobson and the not-so-famous (but much beloved by Kristeva) Émile Benveniste.

Kristeva met Jakobson in person in Paris in 1968. She of course already knew his work. The great Russian linguist's personal relationships with many of the historical avant-gardists, such as Khlebnikov and Mayakovsky, fascinated her and his love and mastery of poetry astounded her. She also had many affinities with the politics of this Russian Jew, with his understanding of the politics of poetics.[118] Besides Barthes, it was, however, the brilliant linguist Émile Benveniste with whom Kristeva was the closest among her many male mentors. The publication of his *Problems in General Linguistics* in 1966 at the age of sixty-four (the English edition came out in 1971) had propelled Benveniste into the midst of the lively conversations of which Kristeva was such an important part. And it cannot be overstated how much Kristeva admired Benveniste, how much she learned from him, how fond she was of him—and he of her.

Intellectually, Kristeva discovered in Benveniste a fatherly soulmate who was able to provide erudite words for the "life" that she was attuned to in poetic language. Among other things, he helped her to distinguish between the *énoncé* (the statement) and the *énonciation* (the utterance), or more simply put, between the said and the way it is said. This in turn connected with her growing interest in the divided subject (the human subject divided between the conscious and unconscious mind) because it meant that the "I" of the statement is not necessarily the "I" of the utterance, that the "I" is always "other." For Kristeva, Benveniste was the first to elaborate a linguistics focusing on *discourse*, on dialogue, opening up the usual simple and static description of the utterance to the processes of enunciation, subjectivity, and intersubjectivity—in time and in place, in history.

Unlike most of his colleagues in linguistics, Benveniste was deeply interested in psychoanalytic theory (finding Lacan interesting if opaque), especially in the position of femininity—and sexuality—in writing. Where other linguists at the time focused on the conscious intentionality of the Cartesian subject, Benveniste gave Kristeva intellectual permission to pursue her *semanalysis*, gave her an opening toward the unconscious motivations and symbolisms of the literary text. As if in corroboration of his and Kristeva's intellectual affinities, Benveniste's last lectures in 1968–69 focused on the act of writing as graphic representation of what she was calling *signifiance* in the poetic text.[119]

But it was not merely Benveniste's erudition that brought him close to Kristeva. They shared an affective sense not only of the political but also of the epistemological urgency with regard to the times they were living in. As Kristeva explained in hindsight in 2012: "In Warsaw, in Italy, in Czechoslovakia, in the still Soviet-controlled Baltic States, and elsewhere, *la sémiologie* [semiotics] was a synonym for the freedom to think."[120] She articulated the matter even more explicitly in 2016: "It was not the least accomplishment of semiology to constitute in Eastern Europe and in the Baltic States of the URSS, a counterweight to the all-powerful Marxist ideology!"[121]

In part because she had read all of Benveniste's work she could get her hands on and had attended all of his seminars, they became close friends. Kristeva has written of their long conversations at his apartment on rue Monticelli, near the Porte d'Orléans in Paris. She has described how overwhelmed she was by all the books in Benveniste's study and by the way they smelled, how impressed she was by his "sacred" office where all the Indo-European and Iranian secrets of time immemorial seemed to be hidden. And the conversations! He was always asking her intriguing questions out of the blue, such as, "But Madame, don't you think that the future of man is woman?" He was interested in everything: her work, debates in Eastern Europe (especially about Bakhtin), and the experiments of the group meetings of *Tel Quel*. They discussed Raymond Roussel, Chomsky, and obscure Sanskrit texts.[122]

Benveniste was fascinated by how, in the wake of 1968 in France and Eastern Europe, people were beginning to rebel against pure Stalinism and, simultaneously, in the universities, people were beginning to talk about semiology, which—for both Kristeva and Benveniste—offered a vision of society where humans are more shaped by language than by economics. They got in touch with dissidents in Tartu, Estonia, Czechoslovakia, and Poland and, along with Jakobson, Umberto Eco, and Josette Rey-Debove (editor of the *Petit Robert Dictionary*), headed to Warsaw to found the International Association of Semiotics (AIS). On that trip, Kristeva was carrying Artaud's *Letters of Rodez*—a collection of harrowing letters written while Artaud was subjected to electroshock treatments at the Rodez Asylum during World War II—and Benveniste asked if he could borrow the volume.[123] She saw him hide it between the pages of Plato's *Symposium* and read it with a slight smile on his face whenever the conference proceedings bored him. Emboldened by his seeming interest in such a hallucinatory text, Kristeva approached him and mentioned that she was very touched to see him so interested in Artaud, and that she had also been moved to see his signature (alongside those of Artaud, Aragon, Breton, Éluard, Leiris, and others) to the 1925 *Manifesto of Surrealism*. She depicts their exchange as follows:

> Monsieur, what a joy to see your name among the signatories of a surrealist manifesto! "Fâcheuse coïncidence, Madame" ["A regrettable coincidence, Madam"]. His smile had disappeared, his cold and empty look nailed me to the floor, and I collapsed with shame in the presence of the conference attendees all around us. A few hours later, with no witnesses around, the professor whispered in my ear, "Of course

it's me, but you mustn't say so. You see, now I'm at the Collège de France!"[124]

For Kristeva, Benveniste was someone who hid in the university from the more dramatic calls for both political and poetic radicalism, but who nevertheless remained deeply radical in his own way because of his understanding of "the trace of free and creative subjectivity within the duality of signifiance: between the experience without name of 'interior language' and the semantics of the discourse used to communicate and to order [the world]."[125]

Kristeva remembers well her and Benveniste's last real conversation in late 1969, on the telephone. He had just received *Semiotike*, really liked it, and wanted to see her to talk about it. But before they met, she received a different phone call letting her know that Benveniste had had an attack of some kind. He had been on the street without his identification papers or anything to suggest that he had health insurance. For several days, he was with the homeless collected off the streets of Paris. When he was finally admitted to a public hospital, he was aphasic. The cause of his illness was never discovered. Perhaps he had had a reaction to a flu shot that he had just received. Or perhaps he had had a stroke. It turned out that Benveniste had indeed forgotten to enroll in health insurance, with the consequence that he was housed in terrible conditions, without adequate medical or rehabilitative care. Kristeva and several of his students tried to help him, but the bureaucracy was overwhelming. She was overwrought with helpless frustration: "Sometimes I reproach myself for not having tried harder . . . but by what right? I was neither family nor a speech therapist." She did manage to find and engage a famous specialist of aphasia, François Lhermitte, who visited Benveniste and asked him to draw a house. Nothing. But when Julia asked him, it worked.

By the early 1970s, Benveniste was enrolled in a speech rehabilitation program, but progress was slow. Because their emotional closeness seemed to draw him out, Kristeva spent hours and hours with him each week. She was convinced that he was still cognitively and intellectually present. When she brought in one of his books for him to dedicate, he did so by signing his name and correcting the date—correctly—to September 24, 1971. He showed great pleasure when the journal *Langages* dedicated a special issue, edited by Kristeva, to him. He was also overjoyed by the publication of the second volume of his *Problems in General Linguistics*, as well as by a 1975 book Kristeva co-edited in his honor: *Language and Culture: In Honor of Émile Benveniste.*[126] It is with great sadness, and some regret, that Kristeva admits that as those long seven years of his illness continued, when she was writing her state doctoral thesis (defended in 1973) and welcoming her son David (born in 1975) to the world, etc., she went to see him less and less. But one day he asked to see her. It was to be her last visit.

There is one story Kristeva tells often, always with emotion. During one of her last visits with Benveniste, she was standing by his bed at the Créteil Hospital when he asked her to come closer, and with a shy smile, he started tracing letters on her chest with his index finger. She was startled, embarrassed, not sure what to think. But she soon understood that he was trying to say something, so she found a pencil and paper, and he slowly and carefully wrote the letters THEO. What was he trying to say to Kristeva? Was he evoking God (*theos*)? Theory (*theoria*)? Kristeva admits that even all these years later, those four letters traced shakily on her body, over her heart, by this dignified, brilliant, dying man, remain enigmatic. She did however proffer a reading of the event in 2012:

> The chance events of our respective lives placed me on his path, in such a way that he would call forth, before leaving us, a message he wanted to trace on a body: That whatever the "semantics" of our discourse (as we communicate through the dialogues of our temporal existence), the diversity of our languages—and language itself—engenders this "semiotic capacity" (as the unpronounceable graphism YHWH bears witness but which the professor chose to analyze with the tools of Greek onto-theology / THEO / and its scientific follow-ups) in the encounter between the "interior languages" of our subjectivities.[127]

In other words, in Kristevian terms, each of us contains a doubled interior of our "self." On the one hand, there is a complex signifying process that is one of the most important components of history-making through language; each of us, regardless of whether or not we acknowledge it, is part of history just by talking. On the other hand, the core process, the one buried under the empirical dialogues of our material, bodily existence— the "interior languages of our subjectivities"—is mysterious . . . spiritual . . . unknown . . . of *Theo*.

Not long after this reminder from her dear friend and mentor, Kristeva formalized, in her 1973 doctoral thesis, *Revolution in Poetic Language*, her best-known and most often repeated formulation of the process through which meaning is produced: the interaction between the *semiotic* and *symbolic*. For those who know of these terms and their meanings, the resonance between them and the passage on Benveniste quoted above is striking. To Kristeva's immense sadness, Benveniste died on October 3, 1976.

The Text of the Novel (1970)

But we are getting ahead of ourselves. About the time Benveniste was struck with aphasia in 1969, Kristeva was finishing the revisions on her first doctoral thesis (the one directed by Lucien Goldmann on the origins of the novel)—*The Text of the Novel*—which she had defended in 1968, and which was published as a book in 1970.[128] She was already starting to write her thesis for her state doctorate (*doctorat d'État*): *Revolution in Poetic Language*, published in 1974. Moreover, one of the most interesting and influential interviews of that time period was when the philosopher Jacques Derrida interviewed Kristeva.[129] Another landmark moment was an article entitled "The System and the Speaking Subject," which was published directly in English in the *Times Literary Supplement* in 1973.[130] But most importantly, by 1970 Kristeva had made one of the most consequential decisions of her life: she had decided to find a psychoanalyst and to begin an analysis.

Ilse Barande

In 1970, when Kristeva began thinking about undertaking an analysis, she was not yet sure if she would become a practicing analyst. She certainly did not yet know that she would one day be a world-renowned psychoanalyst, nor that psychoanalytic theory would be henceforth at the heart of her thinking about everything: life, love, literature, art, humankind, history, and world politics. At the time, moving to the couch simply felt like the next intellectual pathway to take. As I have already mentioned, she knew almost nothing about Freud before her arrival in Paris. And even in Paris, Kristeva found that Freud was still marginal and slightly worrying to the academic establishment. But she had been reading both Freud and Lacan (at the same time!) with Sollers and others in *Tel Quel*. She had also been attending Lacan's seminars where the church-like mood of those present, hanging on Lacan's every word as sacred, had deeply impacted her. As she read and listened, she began to perceive that she did not yet have access to the experiential core of the psychoanalytic message. She was studying linguistics and

Figure 3.5. Ilse Barande. Photo by Eric Barande.

semiotics in depth. She was writing theoretical essays about the speaking subject. Recognizing that in grammar-based linguistics, there was no room for the experience of drives or passions or even sensations, she had been scanning all of history to find other ways of thinking about language and its human subject. Semiotics had provided some access: the dialogism of Bakhtin. But to read, to listen, to think . . . was not enough. She needed to feel *implicated*. What she had discovered so far still rested at the surface of . . . of what exactly?

She has written of how it was her sensation of swimming through herself that led her to wanting to move beyond reading, to plunge into the experience of dissolution, of deconstruction at the core of psychoanalytic work. She asked a close friend, Iván Fónagy, for advice on the right analyst. Fónagy, a Hungarian linguist, had done an analysis with Ferenczi and had recently settled in Paris, working at the National Center for Scientific Research.[131] His work on the relationship between the Freudian drives and phonetics,[132] which she highlighted in the context of elaborating her concept of the semiotic in *Revolution*, was of great interest to Kristeva because it was getting at "the life" of language located in its enunciation. It was on the drives present in infantile language, more specifically on how the erogenous zones participate directly in creating phonemes (units of sound that help distinguish one word from another). A well-known example is "mmmmmm" at the mother's breast that then becomes *mama*.

Fónagy understood exactly what Kristeva was looking for because he shared a link with both her Eastern European past and her emergent interest in psychoanalysis. When she had asked him why he had immigrated to France and broken completely with the communists, he responded in a manner that solidified her trust in him. He said that his decision to leave communist Eastern Europe had crystallized during the Slánský Trial—a show trial in Prague in 1952—where the Party (supported by Soviet Stalinists) accused mostly Jewish, dissident communists of being "agents of imperialism" and had them either executed (as was the case with Slánský) or imprisoned. As Fónagy watched the carefully orchestrated forced confessions (given under terrible duress, usually torture), he realized that the accused, in a desperate effort to save their souls, were "confessing" only in the third person. He was so moved by their linguistic heroism, by the fact that such a small linguistic mark—a shift to third-person discourse— could change so much, that he dedicated himself to scholarship at the intersection of linguistics and psychoanalysis.

When Kristeva asked Fónagy to recommend an analyst for her, he told her that she needed to go see his German friend, Ilse Barande. Barande (maiden name: Rothschild) was born in Germany in 1928. Her family left Germany in 1935 amidst the rise of Nazism and antisemitism. In Paris, she pursued her education in medicine and psychology, even as her mother was captured in the Vel d'Hiv Roundup in Paris in the summer of 1942 and was never seen again. Barande became a neuropsychiatrist, but in 1953 she also undertook a training analysis with the Psychoanalytic Society of Paris and became a practicing psychoanalyst. In 1954, she married the writer Robert Barande, and they collaborated together on many book projects, including the well-known *History of Psychoanalysis in France*.[133] She was a renowned expert on Ferenczi, a translator of the complete works of Karl Abraham, and widely known for her work on the maternal. In short: Kristeva got lucky.

Kristeva's first appointment with Barande did not last long. Barande asked Kristeva why she wanted to do an analysis, and Kristeva responded in tune with her characteristic intellectual self: she did not have "a problem"; she simply wanted to traverse linguistics for epistemological reasons, to move beyond the purely linguistic approach to language. As she repeated a couple of times, she really did not have any "problems." Barande was not having it. She responded: "And besides that?" Kristeva recalls:

> It just so happened that that very day, my mother and I think maybe my father too were visiting from Sofia. They didn't come often, but I was still afraid at that time to go to Bulgaria to see them because of my fear that I wouldn't be allowed to return to France. Things went a little better later on once I had my French citizenship, became a mother, etc., and

David and I were able to fly to Sofia. [Sollers never went out of fear of being put in a labor camp as a dissident!] But that time, my mother was in Paris. I explained to Barande that my mother and I were very close, except that I had the impression that I had never really touched her except perhaps like a ball that touches the floor and then rebounds . . . and I would like to stay a bit on the floor . . . "Is that all?" she asked: "We can start whenever you're ready."

Kristeva did her analysis in French.[134] This was crucial since it allowed her to develop a different relationship to the language. Even though she had learned French quite young, she had not spoken it at home (her mother did not speak French). Her father did speak some French, but the young Kristeva quickly spoke better than him (at the same time as she was also supplanting him financially, making more than him as a paid journalist). Speaking French with Barande, while talking about her childhood, was a way for her to enter into what she calls "baby talk," into ordinary, everyday language, to give everyday language a dignity beyond the litany of "pipi-caca." It was also a way into sensations, such as the taste of food. Sometimes, when she entered into the twists and turns of a complicated dream in French, Barande asked her to say the same thing in Bulgarian. This led to various wordplays that served as keys to bits of her past locked up in her native language.

It also led to maternity. Kristeva had thought a bit about becoming a mother, but not seriously. In hindsight, she has realized that there had been for a long time a kind of "insufficiency" in her life that had to do with her relationship with her mother. She had always been daddy's little girl. This shows clearly in the photos from Kristeva's childhood: she is almost always pictured with her father, often at the market holding giant melons! In her childhood, her mother was in the background.

As we have learned, when she was a young woman, Kristeva often mused about the difference between her mother and Blaga Dimitrova (see Part I), the famous Bulgarian writer and politician, who was almost the same age as her mother. Dimitrova wrote poetry. One of her poems in particular was famous and was recited at concerts, readings, and even soccer games in Kristeva's youth. Kristeva had learned it by heart.

She even wrote a long study of Dimitrova's poetry and embraced her public image. However, Dimitrova was not only a celebrated writer, not only the vice president of Bulgaria after the fall of the Berlin wall, but she was also, fairly late in her life, a mother—the adoptive mother of a Vietnamese daughter she adored.

Initially, Kristeva had seen her mother and Dimitrova as mutually exclusive models for her own life. But when Dimitrova opted for motherhood, Kristeva realized that she did not need to choose between living a full life as a writer-intellectual and living it as a mother—that she could perhaps do both. Kristeva and Dimitrova eventually became good friends, and Kristeva realized that her mother was quoting Dimitrova to her when she said: "I don't want to smother you with my feathers; I want to give you wings to fly."

As Kristeva told these stories to Barande, she realized that motherhood was an indispensable experience for her, a way to understand what was missing in her life. She came to understand that the crazy sexual atmosphere of post-1968 France was not satisfying her, that in the final analysis she valued the Bulgarian mindset of monogamous fidelity, and that maternity could perhaps provide the connection she sought between the sexually blissful body and loyal attachment.

But what about her freedom? Did Kristeva worry about maternity as a loss of freedom? She did not. It is true that before her son's birth in 1975, she could not have imagined what it would be like to have a severely handicapped child about whom one had to be vigilant every waking moment. Even so, even today, she has never thought of maternity as a burden, as a negative thing—not in the least. This has set her apart from many second-wave feminists in both France and the United States. She has explicitly contrasted herself to Beauvoir, to what Beauvoir says about motherhood:

> In Beauvoir's writing, there are horrible images of maternity as a polyp that eats you . . . that makes you vomit. In my book dedicated to her,[135] I tried to pay her the homage she is due but also to illuminate the texts where she speaks of maternity in such a negative way. It's understandable: women at the time were enslaved, sent into the

kitchen, had no right or access to education, and so it was necessary to fight for the pill and abortion rights, etc.[136] I was of the generation that had more rights, for whom maternity didn't necessarily mean slavery. I didn't quite know how I was going to do it, but as usual, I didn't ask myself too many questions. I wanted to do it, so I did.

Kristeva has always spoken fondly of Ilse Barande and has never failed to acknowledge how incredibly formative her analysis with Barande was for her, not only privately, but also as a published intellectual. Even as Barande was the closest participant in Kristeva's emergent personal contemplation of motherhood, it was also on the couch that Kristeva found many of her best ideas, including—as we will see later—her famous concept of "abjection." In a 2017 interview, Kristeva speaks with some wistfulness of her analyst as underappreciated in the Parisian analytic scene:

> Ilse Barande is not well known enough by the Psychoanalytic Society of Paris. Her writings on primary greediness, perversion, "mother-version," and *Le Maternel singulier* [*Singular Maternity*] are completely ignored. Even I, at a conference on "the maternal," I had planned to quote her. I saw her sitting in the front row, but pressed for time, I did not once pronounce her name. I found her in the hallway later and apologized. But it was too late. I felt complicit with what seemed to me to be a forgetting, if not a censoring on the part of our Society. Ilse Barande died not long after that [in July 2012] and I never saw her again.[137]

Revolution in Poetic Language (1974)[138]

In the early days of her analysis with Barande, 1970–74, Kristeva pursued with great dedication and energy her analysis, moving ever closer to her decision to have a child, while at the same time forging new ideas, new formulations, and new articulations of the poetic in her constant writing—mostly for her *Revolution in Poetic Language* but also for many articles on fiction writers that were published in journals from the marginal *Tel Quel*, through the more established *Critique* and *Communications*, to the mainstream *Quinzaine Littéraire*.[139] While exploring baby talk on the couch, in the library she pursued with incredible focus her research and writing toward her doctorate, bringing psychoanalysis, semiotics, and her ruminations on foreignness, strangeness, and the uncanny into dialogue with each other. One could almost say that it was during those first four years of pursuing an analysis in French *in between* her intensive research into the poetic process in French literature that the Kristevian voice most familiar today to her followers began to emerge with confidence.

Her personal and theoretical focus on language during those four years was intimate and determinant—revolutionary. In the documentary—*Strange Foreigner*[140]—made about Kristeva's life as a foreigner in France, there are images of her as an adult returning to Bulgaria to attend the Festival of the Alphabet of her childhood, marching along with the crowd, singing the triumphant marching song in praise of the alphabet, remembering perfectly the words to the song in Bulgarian. Keeping rhythm with the crowd of celebrants, she sings at the top of her lungs, with strong emotion, and with a beaming smile, about the power of language, writing, and knowledge:

March on, people revived!
March on toward a serene future
Through the strength it gives you,
May writing renew your destiny!
March on toward knowledge all-powerful!
March on, take part in all the battles!
May immutable duty be your guide
And God will bless you.
May immutable duty be your guide
And God will bless you![141]

As Kristeva's relationship to French became more intimate on the couch in the early 1970s, her relationship to Bulgarian shifted and has remained more or less in place even decades later. In the 2005 documentary, as she walks among the church ruins along the Black

Sea where she played as a young girl, she ponders the evolution of her linguistic self:

> I find that I speak today a very stereotypical Bulgarian at this point in my life. I continue to dream in Bulgarian; I can rediscover my childhood and other important events of my young life in Bulgaria. But I can't think in Bulgarian. During these past forty years, I've done everything in French. The fact of having learned French at a young age, having done an analysis in French, raised a child in French, written novels in French—that has given me the possibility to live inside of French as a constant creation, a constant invention.

In the film, Kristeva talks about how she would swim in the Black Sea as a child, but then go sit in the shade and work obsessively on her French vocabulary. French was her "window of dreams," a way to be elsewhere without being exiled. She dreamed of France. But she did not need to go there—and never imagined she would—because she had her books in French. As she reminisces, she sees what she calls an albatross (probably a *Larus marinus*) land nearby. She wonders if perhaps it is the same one that visits the Île de Ré in France . . .

Kristeva's belief in the power of letters, of syllables, of words, of the sonorities of language to creatively shape all invention, to evoke mystery unrecoverable by logic or syntax, to profoundly change any status quo, runs deep—I would argue, all the way back to her childhood. There was the celebration of the Slavic alphabet, and her parents gave her access to a foreign tongue. But she has also insisted that her father's love of nature and her resultant love of walking in nature also provided her with an opening, an emptiness, a yogic practice, where she could enter into a space between waking and sleeping and "move with the sensations of the world." It is one of the reasons that she fell in love with the Île de Ré: "It is my space of un-rootedness, a place that has protected its wild spaces in a very elegant, careful way."[142] She has also pondered the extent to which her immersion as a young child in the atmospherics of Orthodox Christianity may have embedded in her a curiosity about mystery that has remained alive even through her repeatedly articulated atheism: "Christian orthodoxy permeated me, and not in a dogmatic or religious way, *stricto sensu*. Rather, it constituted for me a somewhat fleeting spiritual climate . . . I can still smell the incense, see the profusion of flowers on the altar."[143]

Kristeva's time on the couch in Paris in the 1970s confirmed what she already knew: at the heart of the linguistic process is something mysterious, something visible only perhaps to the artist—or to the analyst.[144] Even in the early 1970s, she was already trying to dig into the interior (unconscious) of banal, communicative language in order to find that which disturbs codified systems of all kinds. She had the sense that the poetic disruption of codified language (linguistic politics, small-p) could tell us a great deal about social arrangements, about Politics (Real Politics, capital P). She links her still at that point fleeting access to the "alchemy of the word," her sensitivity to the sensations and sonorities of literary language, to her foreignness. For Kristeva, there is no doubt that it was her life as a foreigner living within a foreign language that finally truly opened the door to the mysterious "inside" of otherwise superficial, banal, syntax-produced, communicative meaning, ultimately allowing a *resurrection* of meaning and self. And (her) psychoanalysis provided the key to that door.[145]

In the early years of her work, in order to excavate this "mystery in the letters" through which meaning is produced, she mostly turned to writers and artists working at the "limits" of comprehension, disturbing meaning at multiple levels, self-consciously pushing forward an avant-garde practice usually from within an intense political environment: Céline, Artaud, Lautréamont, and Mallarmé.[146] Decades later, Kristeva turned to more canonical writers such as Colette and Proust to find the mystery.[147]

In *Revolution in Poetic Language*, Kristeva put into theoretical language her conviction that literature and art are a vital laboratory for understanding how meaning is produced at a given time, in a given place. *Revolution* is a difficult book that engages with history, philosophy, semiotics, literary theory, and some almost incomprehensible poetry. But it is also in this book that Kristeva, in almost Sherlock Holmes fashion, searches for and retraces the struggle between meaning and the "mystery" that gives meaning its shape. In addition, it is also in this book that Kristeva's "political difference"—as I called it already in 1986—begins to take shape for the reading public.

In 1986, I proposed that part of what Kristeva wanted to show in *Revolution* (though perhaps not explicitly at that early point in her work) was that the two totalitarian extremes of the twentieth century— fascism and Stalinism and therefore inevitably antisemitism—besides being political phenomena rooted in concrete historical and economic contexts as well as in personalities, were also rooted in the psychic mechanisms of the human subject which are laid bare in the psychic traces of the radically poetic text.[148] In the 650-page *Revolution* (only half of which has been translated into English), the difficult texts of the late nineteenth-century poets Mallarmé and Lautréamont serve as perfect case studies for understanding psycho-symbolic micro-politics in relation to the macro-political events of their time. Kristeva uses their texts to illustrate that by taking literature as a laboratory for understanding the sociopolitical economy of a given time and place, we can look beyond the "message" of a text to its form, to its networks of fantasies, to the rhythm, articulation, and style of its sentences, *which are bound up in a conceptuality that we cannot hope to change only at the level of what is said.*

This, I think, is ultimately Kristeva's key message in the immediate post-1968 period: we cannot change the world without changing the way it is imagined and spoken. This is what the communist regimes of Eastern Europe failed to understand.[149]

In order to pursue her analysis in *Revolution*, Kristeva invents and/or highlights several key terms, and in particular two functions that will become probably her best-known theoretical legacy: the semiotic and the symbolic. The *semiotic* element is the bodily drive— rhythm, tone, and intonation—as it is discharged in signification. The *symbolic* element is associated with the grammar and structure of signification.[150] In the same way that thinking about movies, maybe especially mainstream movies, can help us understand the fantasies of a given society's "daydreams," *Revolution* invites us to think about texts as laboratories of the political. Furthermore, it shows that texts that contain so much disruption that the symbolic is cracked open wide enough to make the semiotic visible constitute especially fertile sites for this type of investigation. We are asked to consider literature and art (and, she will later argue, movies) as laboratories for grasping the forces shaping a given Political (capital P) reality, particularly at crucial moments in history. Kristeva suggests that through an analysis of the symbolic/semiotic dynamic, one would even be able to create a typology of "texts." For example, in the category of texts where the symbolic reigns with little or no semiotic disruption, one might place scientific treatises or training manuals—or the phone book. Where the semiotic holds sway without (or without much of) the organizing principle of the symbolic, one might in turn point to surrealist poetry or mystical chants—or babies' babble. Yet it is important to remember that this symbolic/semiotic dance does not exist in the abstract, does not take place in a void—or only within an individual—but rather is grounded in an intensely interdisciplinary set of historical and material constraints.[151]

The complexity of Kristeva's argument in *Revolution* is often lost when critics rush to focus on the symbolic and semiotic functions as gendered tools for feminist analysis, with the symbolic function carrying the burden of masculinity and the semiotic function that of femininity. Along with the Platonic concept of the *chora* as the pre-symbolic maternal space (as the pre-condition of the symbolic), the semiotic— due to its association with the maternal space—has been gendered as "feminine" by many critics (myself included). Kristeva has tried to complicate this received understanding. In the 2005 documentary, she acknowledges that her readers have identified the semiotic as being on the feminine side of things, but adds that she "was really thinking of it more as having to do with the very particular relationship between the infant-as-yet-without-language and its genitrix who holds and reassures it, and who permits the infant to survive through the other." For her, the semiotic is not about fusion with the feminine or the maternal but about a space of ab-jection: a "state between fusion and subjectivity" in which "I am undergoing fusion, and I don't want it." In this state, subject and object do not yet exist. Rather, the infant is in the process of becoming a subject: "My mouth vomits or cannot vomit . . . my anus rejects or masters." Kristeva is here getting at "the constitution of the body's architecture and limits" that takes place just before separation from the maternal body.

In this context, Kristeva evokes Klein and Winnicott to emphasize that "no one has a recipe for a good separation from the mother." She also notes that no matter how well this separation is lived, it is always tinged with sadness, which sometimes—as Klein already argued—results from an awareness of one's own violence: "She left me! Perhaps I killed her!" However, above all, separation is the pre-condition for verbalization: "It is at this moment that echolalia, the semiotic, starts to become the symbolic. We see how this sadness is the other side of language acquisition. One speaks because one is capable of enduring the depression."[152] In addition, the ways in which the semiotic intrudes into the symbolic in later life can tell us a lot not only about the psycho-physical architecture of a given writer or artist but also about how this architecture was socially, culturally, and politically constituted in a given time and place.

Kristeva defended her doctoral thesis in 1973 at the University of Paris-Vincennes under the direction of Jean-Claude Chevalier, the respected French linguist, with the other members of her dissertation committee being Roland Barthes, Jean Dubois, and Lucien Goldmann.[153] She has described the defense as a "truly initiatory experience before a 'university body' in the process of putting itself back together in the wake of 1968."[154] At the defense, Chevalier challenged Kristeva by claiming that with all her emphasis on human subjectivity, she had left the social out of her interpretation of poetic signification.[155] What saved the experience for Kristeva was Barthes proclaiming at the end of the exam what she took as a supreme compliment (although it did not please everyone in the room): "The novel today, it is this thesis."[156] This compliment coming from Barthes meant much more to her than all the praise—all the success—that followed the publication of *Revolution* in the *Tel Quel Collection* by Éditions du Seuil on March 1, 1974:

> You speak of "success"? I didn't really notice. The diffusion [of the book] took place at first in fairly restrained circles, but it must have benefited from the impact of *Tel Quel* on intellectual life. And the reactions were not all positive. I've been told that the literary *establishment*—the guardians of the classical and academic temples—didn't understand and were quite shocked. But others, creators and younger authors, appreciated the book. When today, "senior deciders" tell or write me that they were influenced by my first books, of course I am touched. But I can't help but wonder who they are talking about.[157]

By the time the first half of *Revolution* was published in English in 1986, it was hard for some American readers not to read Kristeva's theory as "anarchistic" or "anti-Marxist." Her efforts to fight against the closure of meaning, the suffocation of innovation, did not quite translate in those years right before the fall of the Berlin Wall and what seemed to many in the West like the beginnings of a new, freer world order. In retrospect, her main question seems clear: How might totalitarianism's return be averted?[158] In some ways, this is still her driving question today when the closure of meaning and the suffocation of innovation passes by way of what she describes as corporate-mediated fantasies of hyperconnectivity: the "automatization of the human species . . . a new form of totalitarianism."[159]

The Pedagogical Imperative

Once Kristeva had her *doctorat d'État* and *Revolution* was out in the bookstores, she was able to make her teaching situation more stable. This did not mean that she stopped writing: her articles were being published constantly and increasingly (and not only in French). However, as Kristeva continued her analysis and writing, she began in earnest her teaching career—one which has by now impacted almost three generations of students via a practice of transmission that she has consciously and even enthusiastically embraced.

While writing her dissertation and undertaking her analysis, Kristeva was a researcher at the National Center for Scientific Research and a teacher at the University of Paris 7-Jussieu.[160] But once she received her *doctorat d'État* in 1973, she was able to leave the National Center for Scientific Research and become a full professor—a *maître de conférence*—at what is called simply "Jussieu."[161] This may sound impressive, but Kristeva's position was impressive mostly in a symbolic way. Its material reality was staggering. I studied at both the University of Paris-Vincennes and Jussieu in 1973 and have vivid memories of the old Jussieu building. Not as derelict as the Vincennes campus, it was nonetheless a shock for the average American student: broken-down hallways and classrooms made out of rusted concrete and steel covered with frenzied and layered graffiti of all kinds. And the odor was unbearable. (The bathrooms didn't work.) There was no drinkable water to be found. Furthermore, in order to find a course or a classroom (there were no catalogues and this was pre-computer), one had to become a detective of the highest order, able to wade through hundreds of notes scotch-taped to the walls with handwritten details about what was happening on any given day. Once you had a time and a place, you had to ask directions multiple times since none of the doors were reliably labeled.

Sollers has evoked in many interviews his first impressions of Kristeva's small office: "A Jussieu office, central tower, second floor. Mediocrity of asbestos dust walls."[162] However, Kristeva was excited to be part of a small group of professors working across three disciplinary intersections: literature and linguistics, literature and psychoanalysis, and literature and history. When asked why she entered this new world, she responds quite honestly:

> It's simple: anguish, solitude . . . I didn't have that many possibilities for dialogue. The work at the CNRS was extremely individualized and offered very few opportunities for the confrontation [of ideas] . . . I love to share my research, my doubts, my discoveries with students;

to watch for their reactions, their responses. One doesn't completely escape solitude; but one has the impression at least of being heard, of being discussed—perhaps a false impression, but it does stimulate.[163]

Kristeva has written of her teaching as an adventure where she has been fortunate to be able to teach more or less whatever she wanted and has also been free to experiment: for example, in the 1970s, when she was presenting some of her most difficult interdisciplinary connections between semiotics, psychoanalysis, and avant-garde texts, she took her doctoral students to the nursery at the University of Paris 3 where they studied the babies' sounds and movements. It was life-changing to watch the infants uttering and acting in ways one had read about in Kristeva's seminar on Freud and semiotics.

Kristeva has made it clear that all of her books after 1973 emerged to some degree from her doctoral seminars and the list of her students who have gone on to produce their own important books, many of which started in her Jussieu seminar, never stops expanding.[164] While it may be easy to assume that teaching has been secondary for Kristeva, she has spoken a great deal about how much she believes in the transmission of knowledge across generations—new generations acting as "repetitive resurrections" for her. She does not mean "resurrections" in the sense of bodies coming back to life but rather in the sense of a series of re-beginnings. As she puts it, "I think across and through the idea of university transmission."[165]

The Desire for China

Nothing that Kristeva has done, said, or written over the past fifty years has brought her as much criticism as her trip to China with four of her *Tel Quel* compatriots in 1974—unless it is the publication of her book, *About Chinese Women*, upon her return.[166] Over the years, she has explained and re-explained how and why the trip happened and why it was definitely not a case of "naïve Maoism." In the 1970s, French and indeed Western politics were beginning a new epistemological, economic, and cultural

Figure 3.6. Kristeva with Roland Barthes in China, 1974. The Julia Kristeva Archive.

era. One could argue that in that era can be found the beginnings of the technocratic neoliberalism that has for decades characterized Western ideology and policy—at least until very recently. President Pompidou died two years before the end of his term and a young technocrat named Valéry Giscard d'Estaing won the election, defeating the socialist candidate, François Mitterrand. In 1974, *Tel Quel* was still (had for some time been) in a precarious but serious alignment with the French Communist Party (CP). But the young Telquelians were increasingly becoming disenchanted with old-school communist bureaucracy:

> The members of *Tel Quel*—and first of all I myself who came from a discredited and therefore rejected communism—had the impression that certain intellectuals of the CP were trying to do something different than what Stalinism had tried to impose on the East. And this something else seduced us. We held the conviction that a French communism that wouldn't repeat the errors and the horrors of the East could actually exist. But we soon became disenchanted, hence our rupture with [the French Communists]. [This led in part to our trip

to China.] There are two elements [to consider here]: First, we were very interested in what one might call the national foundations of a political movement. There is no such thing as a universal politics . . . If we became interested in China, it was because we had the impression that Chinese history, Confucianism, Taoism, the place of writing, the particularities of the Chinese language, the role of women in the culture, etc. might be able to influence the socialist ideology that was seen as global and lead it toward some interesting mutations, where the impasses would not be the same [as in the West].[167]

In addition to this fascination with the possibility of a different destiny for socialist or even communist ideology, there was also the question of the intellectual, whose very function—as I have noted—for Kristeva is to resist, to revolt, and to contest while being careful to avoid complicity, or worse, with reactionary movements of either the Right or the Left. For Kristeva, intellectuals by definition take upon themselves "the anguishes of the era in which they are living": "This possibility of contestation can lead to impasses, but it is the life itself of thinking. If intellectuals abandon it, they renounce their role quite simply, in order to become aesthetes or specialists. *Tel Quel*'s approach contained this contestatory spirit and that's why it seduced me. It is important never to lose that spirit."[168]

Tel Quel and Kristeva in particular have been much criticized for their break with the French Communist Party and their enthusiasm for the Maoist experiment in the early 1970s. In Kristeva's opinion, these critiques are too simple. In an at-times contentious conversation with her former doctoral thesis director, Jean-Claude Chevalier, and the linguist Pierre Encrevé in the 1980s,[169] she elucidated once again how her trip to China fit into her overall intellectual trajectory, including the ways in which it contributed to her eventual rejection of macro-politics in favor of studying ideology's micro-political underpinnings. Asked about *Tel Quel*'s difference from the French Communist Party, she responds:

It wasn't the same Marxism. The one we were calling for was not the Marxism of dialectical materialism; we took from Hegel the idea of a dialectical transformation of the subject in his relationship to language and the body—which was closer to Freud than to Marx. The communists were not fooled and they looked at us with an evil eye. The retrograde bourgeoisie and the revindications of the CP apparatchiks were both in the process of dissolving given the liberating push of May 1968. At the same time, we had abandoned the shackles of structuralism and the theoretical, formalist superego. The audacity of linguistic imagination was—and is—the unavoidable sign of the subject in revolt. For example, the attention given to form as meaning; or, even more so, in a novel, the importance given to dream narratives, word games, or the upheaval of narrative time.[170]

When Encrevé responds that Artaud and Céline were already doing this much earlier in a way that was perhaps even more modern than that of Barthes, Kristeva pushes back: "With the risk of psychosis (Artaud) or political abjection (Céline) . . . whereas our attention, focused on ideologies, philosophy, and Freudianism, allowed us to avoid those symptoms."[171] And when Encrevé insists that this "didn't stop the leaning—if briefly—toward Maoism," Kristeva responds with uncharacteristic annoyance: "That wasn't the same thing as an antisemitic pamphlet!"[172]

Kristeva shared with her friends an intense interest in new possibilities for communism and for intellectual (noncomplicitous) revolt, but it is clear that her primary interest in China was cultural. She had been deeply influenced by Joseph Needham's *Science and Civilization in China*.[173] In her 2005 documentary, she adds that while perhaps the "bourgeois boys" were fascinated by Russia and China, she was not. It was the whole of Chinese civilization that intrigued her.[174] She did not need to "cross through the Marxist screen." She was already "behind the screen." She was asking questions: What would China be like when it awoke? What are the differences between Confucianism and Taoism? She did not want to represent Marxism; she wanted to represent the opening of France toward other cultures. She wanted to invite young people to open themselves up to the world.

Sollers, too, was an avid reader of Needham and has spoken of his and Kristeva's attraction to China—to its poetry, painting, calligraphy, and thought—since the 1960s. He has also evoked the Jesuits as being somewhat at the root of his China fascination: "A Jesuit came [to my *lycée*] to give a talk on China, and my interest in China has never let up ever since."[175] He has argued that the clandestine Jesuits in China inspired in him hope for the future and that it was really China and the Jesuits that radicalized him from a very young age.

Kristeva tends, in retrospect, to evoke the more playful aspects of their 1974 encounter with China. She talks about how they had fun with Mao's slogans, and she has often repeated the two Mao sayings that most influenced her: "You can only count on your own strength" and "Two steps back, one step forward, until victory!"[176] She even tends to laugh at some of the stories surrounding the trip, for example, the story of why Lacan did not go.

The trip to China was set for April 11–May 4, 1974.[177] Lacan—along with his mistress (designated as his "secretary"), Thérèse Parisot—was supposed to accompany Kristeva, Sollers, Barthes, Marcelin Pleynet, and François Wahl on the trip.[178] The trip, and Lacan's participation in it, was taking place against the background of the Chinese Cultural Revolution that began in 1966. Lacan himself had always been interested in China, having learned Chinese at the School of Oriental Languages in Paris during the Occupation. He had also worked with the same sinologist as Kristeva, François Cheng, in order to delve into the subtleties of Chinese philosophy, in part so that he could better negotiate the tidal waves of Maoism swamping not only psychoanalytic circles but also the entirety of the French left.

The story of why Lacan ended up not going was never widely told for a long time, most likely in deference to the wishes of Lacan's family. But Kristeva tells it willingly now, with a smile. The evening before the departure, she and Sollers were to have dinner with Lacan and Thérèse Parisot in order to finalize their plans for the next day. They went to pick up Lacan at 5 rue de Lille. Lacan was upset because he could not reach Parisot by phone. They all then went across the street to Lacan's favorite restaurant, La Calèche (8 rue de Lille), where they were supposed to have dinner, but she was not there. They began to drink their habitual rosé champagne while waiting for Parisot, but Lacan was becoming increasingly worried, even edgy, because he was afraid of a patient ("the recorder man") who was haunting him. He tried again to reach Parisot by phone to no avail. Everyone was beginning to panic, so they drove to her apartment. There was no answer when he rang the bell, so Lacan decided to use his key, but the lock was blocked on the inside by a key sitting in the lock.

They went downstairs to talk to the concierge. When they turned the lights on in the courtyard, Kristeva saw the shadow of a man in Parisot's window and—completely naively—shouted "A man!" Lacan screamed "Assassin!" Sollers said to Kristeva, "I think we should leave." But instead, they went back upstairs and there was Thérèse Parisot with Moustapha Safouan, a well-known Lacanian analyst. They tried to make up a story about a train strike . . . Lacan and Safouan started to yell . . . so Kristeva and Sollers left. Lacan and Parisot did not leave with them for China the next day. And Kristeva never again attended Lacan's seminar.

Many of the details of the China trip are recounted in Kristeva's book on Chinese women. Several well-known photos show Kristeva surrounded by singing and dancing children, Barthes sitting by himself off to the side, and Sollers deciphering signs. There is also a silent black and white 16mm film that, like many home movies of that era, does not show much besides endless buildings and the occasional glimpse of Kristeva walking in a park. Occasionally, she was mistaken for a Chinese woman, but as soon as she opened her mouth, her basic Chinese gave her away.[179]

The *Tel Quel* comrades, as they were called, were particularly impressed by several of the women they spoke with, for instance a young archaeologist who showed them prehistoric pottery where, the historian insisted, it was clear from fingernail traces on the pottery that it was women who had been the artisans and artists of matriarchal times. There was also an illiterate woman artist whose paintings reminded Kristeva of Van Gogh even though the artist had never seen any paintings but her own. Kristeva has also told stories about how she had to watch over Barthes carefully to keep him from getting arrested.

One time she told one of their guides that Barthes, "the Eldest Master," needed always to be seated with them at the center of the row. This was so that he would not flirt with the young Chinese men at the ends of the rows of seats. Most disappointing to Kristeva was the fact that the group was not allowed to visit any psychiatric hospitals. They were told in no uncertain terms that there was no need for psychoanalysis in China because there were "no crazy people in China" because, according to Mao, "one is divided in two."

Immediately upon returning from China, Kristeva did three things: she wrote her book on Chinese women; she decided to become a practicing psychoanalyst; and she decided to get pregnant.

About Chinese Women (1974)

Regarding her book on Chinese women, Kristeva was asked by a friend, Sarah Georges-Picot, who was a member of the group Psychoanalysis and Politics (*Psych et Po*), if she would like to meet Antoinette Fouque, the leader of the group, and perhaps write a book on Chinese women in the context of the Cultural Revolution. Antoinette Fouque (1936–2014) was a writer, editor, and militant known in part for being the co-founder of the French women's movement—Mouvement de libération des femmes (MLF)—with Monique Wittig. She is even better known for her public and strongly worded break with Wittig, which was when she rejected feminism as an aberrant form of "female machoism" (she loathed Simone de Beauvoir; the feeling was mutual). She then founded and directed, with her lifelong companion, Marie-Claude Grumbach, the group *Psych et Po*.

Fouque and *Psych et Po*, including the important writer Hélène Cixous, rejected feminism utterly and completely, grounding their theory instead in what most American feminists would see as an essentialist view of the eternal feminine. Today, many feminist theorists would argue that the matter was in reality much more complicated than that given *Psych et Po*'s complex relationship to Lacanian theory.

Through François Wahl at the Éditions du Seuil, Fouque had become familiar with Lacan's work and did an analysis with Lacan at the same time as she pursued an analysis with the feminist philosopher Luce Irigaray. (One can only imagine the cacophony that this experience set up in her unconscious!)

Fouque, *Psych et Po*, and their publishing house, Éditions des Femmes,[180] were at the heart of a heated controversy within the MLF over many years, especially in battle (sometimes literally) with Wittig's feminist publishing house and journal, *Questions féministes*. The controversy came to a boil in 1979 when Fouque *legally* claimed the MLF insignia for herself. Doing this meant that all scholars, journalists, government representatives, lawyers, etc. with questions having to do with feminism in France had to work with her first before consulting anyone else. This act was roundly condemned by feminists, led by Beauvoir, in France.

When I asked Cixous why they claimed the insignia, she answered simply and unapologetically, "Well, someone had to take the lead." Fouque was followed without question by legions of young women. She had been confined to a wheelchair since adolescence with a neurodegenerative disease. Some have argued that this added to her aura and her ability to gather completely devoted young women from around the world to her cause, in a cult-like atmosphere where whatever she said reigned supreme. Ironically, just before her death in 2014, Fouque was planning to publish a series of dialogues with the staunchly second-wave feminist historian Michelle Perrot, who had just won Kristeva's Simone de Beauvoir Prize.[181]

As you might guess from my description, Kristeva's encounter and arrangements with Éditions des Femmes did not go well.[182] For one thing, Kristeva was astonished that she was unable to correct page proofs before the publication of the book, with the result that its first edition was full of typos and awkward expressions. However, the book was a wild success, known especially for the way it documents the matrilineal traces of ancient China: burial rites with the arrangement of the entire family around the grandmother, the importance of the mother in general, the beauty of the maternal divinity in Taoism, etc. She also documents the scars of Confucianism and the enormous but unsuccessful attempts to better the condition of women in Mao's China: "Dogmatism took everything back in hand, extinguishing any hope of liberty."[183] Kristeva was as disappointed in the way women in China were being re-oppressed as she was with Fouque's "central committee's" autocratic handling of her fragile attempts to paint a complex picture of what she had discovered on her Chinese adventure.

In the wake of her disappointments both in China and Paris, she decided to pursue feminism in her own way, "without belonging to a group, but with my French and especially my American, Canadian, and Chinese students."[184] But the publication of *About Chinese Women* and her tumultuous experience with *Psych et Po* were only the opening salvo in Kristeva's long struggle with Western feminisms and the received image of her by many Anglo-feminists as an *anti*-feminist—a charge that to her is patently ridiculous, at least at the level of the fight for women's rights.

I want to signal three primarily biographical determinants of this perceived ambiguity: 1) Kristeva's coming of age in a communist country where the equality of men and women, while frequently merely a matter of lip-service, and obviously uneven, was nevertheless an explicit and often achieved *given* as political goal; 2) Kristeva's, I think, almost involuntary resistance to any habit of thought that even hints of dogmatism, intellectual rigidity, or what to her reads as militarism; and 3) Kristeva's early fascination with and erudite pursuit of psychoanalytic logic as the strongest tool that we have in the West for understanding sociopolitical reality at the tense border of rationality and irrationality.

It is the philosopher Kelly Oliver who has perhaps best mapped for the English-speaking world Kristeva's complex and ambiguous relationship to Western feminism and its postwar history. Oliver summarizes well the three areas where Kristeva's often very abstract thinking about sexuality and gender gets lost in cultural translation. First, Kristeva is deeply resistant to "identity politics." She is against limiting sexual difference to two kinds of bodies (male and female).

For her, there is no easy "natural sexual difference," and she is just as against the classification of sexualities into just two kinds (hetero and homo). Because of this complexity, she bristles at what she has called "herd feminism" and insists upon the links between the psychic logics of sexuality and other logics of violence against "strangeness" of all kinds, often racial. Second, she sees the oppression of women in patriarchy as "misplaced abjection"—that is, as a result of a historically impossible, largely un-thought relationship to the mother. Kristeva has often stated that it is a symptom of this problem that it is difficult to talk about maternity in a feminist context without sounding (or being accused of being) reactionary. Third, Kristeva insists on a politics of "radical differentiation"—a politics based on the recognition of the fundamental decenteredness of subjectivity—which makes the applicability of Kristeva's thought to practical feminist politics extremely difficult. Oliver turns to another Kristeva scholar, Jacqueline Rose, who articulates this "doublebind" concisely as the question of "how to challenge the very form of available self-definition without losing the possibility of speech."[185]

Kristeva published her first text explicitly on the question of women the year she visited China, 1974: "Woman, It's Never That."[186] This text is an interview with the women of *Psych et Po* around the time of the publication of her book on Chinese women. It is there that the aforementioned "doublebind" first shows up, although it is not acknowledged. A few short sentences from her 1974 article illustrate the problem perfectly:

> Believing that "one is a woman" is almost as absurd and obscurantist as believing that "one is a man." I say almost because there are still things to obtain for women: freedom of abortion and contraception, childcare centers, recognition of work, etc. Therefore "we are women" is still to be maintained as an ad or slogan of revindication. But, profoundly, a woman, that cannot *be*: it's even the problem in *being*.[187]

In other words, yes, there is a sociological category that we recognize historically, empirically (and increasingly normatively) as a group designated in patriarchal, especially metaphysical, history as having certain characteristics (starting with a vagina). But philosophically "woman" has never been part of Western/patriarchal articulations of "being," has never had existential worth within the larger category of "Man," which, as Foucault has shown us, is finished anyway. Kristeva was insisting as early as 1974 that the empirical and (empirically) historical could not be thought outside of the history of the philosophical, including the history of religious philosophy. Yes, we can talk about and even fight for "women," but only temporarily and self-consciously, before moving onto other more urgent matters of subjectivity in history, onto how all identity models must be accounted for historically and then shifted in the name of revolt, when not revolution, both conscious and unconscious.[188]

The Intimate Acts of the Modern Personality

It is perhaps not surprising, then, that the second thing Kristeva decided to do after returning from China was to become an analyst. One of the first people she told about her idea was Benveniste: "Little one, they are all crazy and you're not—what are you going to do inside of all that?," he responded.[189] Others saw it as a logical move: the day of her induction to the Psychoanalytic Society of Paris—Société Psychanalytique de Paris (SPP)—an old man on the jury asked her, "Tell me, my dear, how is it possible to be Sollers's wife?" She responded, "It's not easy, but it's never boring." The jurist concluded, "I think you can be an analyst."[190]

The one thing Kristeva was entirely sure of when she returned from China was that she wanted to become a mother, which meant that she had to figure out how she was going to manage things practically. For example, she knew that she would need to go to the university as little as possible. Being an analyst, seeing patients privately at a home office, seemed more doable. She started to ask herself and others which psychoanalytic society she should align herself with and, within that society, who should be her sponsor. In those days, there were lots of different societies, each aligned differently—some closer to Freud, some closer to Lacan—with many offshoots and subgenres.[191] She was most drawn to the Psychoanalytic Society of Paris, which was the closest to Freud's teachings.

Because Kristeva had already completed four years of analysis with Ilse Barande, she qualified for a sponsor. Immediately upon returning from China, she went to see Lacan to ask him who he thought would be best for her. She told him: "So I've finished my analysis, I've joined the SPP, and so now, in order to be protected and become licensed, can you give me the name of someone who would be a good sponsor for me?" Lacan said: "Safouan." Kristeva was so completely flabbergasted that she left in a rush, forgetting her umbrella. She never saw Lacan again. Had he lost it? Or had he merely forgotten the embarrassing incident with Parisot and Safouan just before the trip to China? Or was there something more "sleazy" going on?

She went with the Freudians (the SPP) under the supervision of André Green and Serge Viderman. Egyptian-born Green has been characterized as one of the most important psychoanalytic thinkers of twentieth-century France. Most of all, he is known for his independence of mind: he was a resolute Freudian who also knew well and integrated into his thinking the work of thinkers as diverse as Lacan and Winnicott, although his rejection of most of Lacanian theory was well known. Romanian-born Viderman was also an independent, even rebellious thinker who worked to open up the SPP to interdisciplinary, and particularly philosophical, questions. Kristeva does not hesitate to acknowledge that it was Green who taught her psychoanalysis.[192]

Part of the bond between Green and Kristeva was that they shared a theoretical and literary corpus from Freud, Hegel, and Saussure to Proust, Conrad, and James. Like Kristeva, Green was fascinated by affect and the drives and, also like Kristeva, he was a serious reader of Klein and Winnicott: "Through his example as an impenitent clinician who innovated by teaching and by writing, Green taught us that psychoanalysis is a political art that requires as much an affinity with madness as with respect for the 'general interest.'"[193] Kristeva felt that she had found her calling. Her sadness and loneliness began to lift even though her parents had just been denied a visa to come visit her in Paris. Her youthful enthusiasm returned to her:

> [It returned to me] when I was able to fully assume this therapeutic position, the one which allows the deceptions and dramas of those who have placed their faith in us to reverse themselves into possible new beginnings. It's another relationship to time. For the analysand and myself. That whole period was sparsely punctuated by moments of discouragement, solitude, and disillusionment, but not really any depression. It was punctuated by rebirths that carried me through, supported by "a marriage considered as one of the fine arts." That's fundamental. [I was] recognized and encouraged by Sollers, Barthes, Green. And Émile Benveniste who I am not forgetting.[194]

Kristeva discovered ever new beginnings when, with the guidance of her formidable mentors, she went outside the boundaries of conventional practice in order to hear the "mystery in the letters" wherever it might be found—for example in the broken symbolic systems of psychosis at the La Borde Hospital or in the first echolalias of infants at the university nursery where, as I have mentioned, she took her students "just to listen" to these strange humans at the frontier between nature and culture.

Kristeva is at her most poetic when she describes why and how her work as an analyst with an analysand coincides with and intersects with her work as a critic with a literary text. She searches across practices—on the couch, in literature and art, in religious and especially mystical expression (she has often said that psychoanalysis could never have existed without the mystics)—for a freedom that is, above all else, creative as well as an encounter with otherness that breaks the chain of cause and effect, that revolts against adaptation to any pre-ordained plot. For her, the unconscious is where the social subject is decentered, much like meaning is decentered in a poetic text, and most acutely in modern literary texts. The unconscious and the poetic text are about the articulation of desire, love, and hate, but without ready-made words or conventional moral codes; they are about what is too much for words, a dive into the unnamable, into strangeness, at the borders of the communicable. Analysis, for Kristeva, is a form of poetic listening—she has a sculpture of a large human ear on her desk—with the analyst facilitating an interpretation that neither an analysand nor a poetic text can generate on their own. From the beginning, she has wanted each analytic session to operate like a poem—or a dream. After all, to analyze literature is to interpret a culture's dreams, as she learned directly from Freud's book hidden in her Sofia home.

Psychoanalysis quickly became for Kristeva not only an art but also an increasingly convincing approach to politics. She has said that her initial discovery of psychoanalysis felt revolutionary, like a fragile resistance against totalitarianism. More recently, she has argued that psychoanalysts today are uniquely situated to fight the automatization of the human spirit, to critique the ordinary, to "problematize the present, find an audible language, and occupy a freely determined position" in the context of a deep, increasingly global crisis.[195]

Kristeva believes that we in the West have for some time been living in a period of a wide mutation where, for example, our relationships to time and space are being rapidly transformed by technology; where there is also a rapid redistribution of sexual difference; and where the "need to believe" is making a dramatic comeback, often in distorted ways. She is not necessarily opposed to these mutations, but she is alarmed by some of their effects on a world culture badly prepared to incorporate them. Caught in the midst of these mutations without the necessary tools for understanding or integrating them, our psychic space is being crushed. According to the Kristeva who has been a practicing analyst for forty years, this is one of the greatest political dangers we face today.[196] While I do not think that she could have or would have diagnosed and described this political danger in the mid-1970s the way she does today, her excited and serious discovery of psychoanalysis back then already contained her sense that something needed to be rethought, and that psychoanalysts were up to the task. She decided to take the path of the unconscious and has never regretted it.[197] As a journalist in the British newspaper *The Guardian* recently put it:

> In today's cynical world of media manipulation, fragmentation, globalization and "banalization," Kristeva sees herself as "an energetic pessimist" who can still envisage something better, a world to be striven for in which each individual should be enabled "to question themselves and their backgrounds, and their own dead-ends, and to have the courage to speak up." She believes that "politics has to take into account the intimate acts of the modern personality," and why, for her, psychoanalysis has such moral value. It is not only a subject on which she has written theoretically—most famously in her book *Black Sun: Depression and Melancholia* (1987)—but a practice woven into the fabric of her life: the one-to-one intimacy of seeing patients is as important to her as writing books.[198]

David

The project of becoming a mother was soon on its way to being as important to Kristeva as her patients and her writing. Motherhood

Figure 3.7. David as a baby with Kristeva in NYC. The Julia Kristeva Archive.

was Kristeva's third life-altering initiative upon her return from China in 1974. She was pregnant by April 1975 and she greeted her pregnancy with joy, anxiety, and, of course, acute thought. The question of maternity and motherhood—as another limit site where mystery seeps into the letters of the law, where the psychic spaces of human subjectivity are shifted, questioned, and reshaped—will move to the forefront of some of Kristeva's most important thinking over the next several decades. But maternity will no longer be examined from the abstract intellectual space of theory, as it had been up until then through concepts such as the chora and the semiotic, but will turn visceral. Even decades later, her intense evocations of her physical, emotional, psychic, and intellectual transformation while pregnant cannot help but give goose bumps to anyone who can even remotely relate. Whether reading *The Samurai* or watching Kristeva's 2011 film, *Reliance*, one cannot escape the realization that for Kristeva, pregnancy was not just life-changing; it was the discovery of an entirely new world.[199]

Sollers was not as into the idea of a baby as Kristeva was. Although he finally agreed to her plan, fatherhood did not come to him easily. Kristeva has explained that, as was the case with their legal marriage, he was neither enthusiastic nor reticent. Kristeva knew that she could count on him emotionally and materially, but remained worried that she might not be able to count on him at all on the everyday practical level. Her parents would be unable to come from Sofia, even though they were very eager for a grandchild. And she was quite sure that Sollers's parents would not leave the Île de Ré for any length of time. Kristeva has admitted that she engaged in a bit of wishful thinking at that stage: perhaps her parents would somehow find a way to come to Paris . . . or perhaps she would go there. She knew that such plans were unrealistic, but she also knew that she could count on her parents from afar and, in the end, decided that she "would just have to figure it out."

As I just intimated, Sollers was initially quietly neutral: he did not in general want to participate in the ideals of society—family, children. He relied on an anarchistic vision of the life of an artist, which has in fact remained his official discourse. But he did come through at the material level, always finding a way to make sure that Kristeva had help, from the very beginning, with childcare, housework, etc. He was very honest with her about the fact that he could not take responsibility for these kinds of things. Kristeva generously concedes: "He's not wrong . . . A fiction writer is always, constantly functioning, writing . . . even when not at their desk. To take even three minutes to think about something else, this functioning disappears. It's all a very fragile matter. As Proust put it, it is a 'fresh and pink matter' that can fade and die."[200]

However, as soon as David was born—on December 16, 1975— Sollers became a loving and devoted father; he was inseparable from his son:

> Philippe had chosen without hesitation the first name David—which enchanted me! David Joyaux, the name of his paternal family, son of Philippe Joyaux alias Sollers and of Julia Kristeva wife Joyaux. Without forcing himself, totally spontaneously, the new papa showed himself to be attentive, holding, of an exceptional tenderness. I can still see him now, holding David against his heart, all swaddled, singing to him . . . obviously not *Au clair de la lune*, but Mozart, *Mon cœur soupire la nuit, le jour* . . . And Bach, *Gloria Patri et Filio*.[201]

Kristeva has compared what came next to the awful feeling that overtook her when she first arrived in France, as if a kind of symbolic death had installed itself inside of her. Something was terribly wrong with David. He was having psychomotor, neuro-muscular problems. He was having tremors soon after birth. And every time he suffered an attack, she felt like it was she who was going to die. There were comas where the infant was literally balanced between life and death. Each time he stabilized, she felt like they were reborn, getting another chance in life. The young parents' feelings ran the gamut—fear, pleasure, anguish, hope. The doctors ran all kinds of tests but could not figure out what was wrong. No test showed anything at all. It was not epilepsy. It was not anything they could name. They called it "an orphan disease"— and still do today.

An orphan disease is a pathology for which there is no known treatment. Most are rare and not particularly profitable for drug companies to research. Some orphan diseases, such as Alzheimer's, are not as rare, but they cannot be treated beyond the alleviation of some symptoms. There are actually about seven thousand such diseases affecting over 350 million people worldwide. Kristeva did not want to believe that her baby boy was one of them:

> During his first coma at the Salpêtrière Hospital, I was watching over him, sitting next to his bed, talking to him, having him listen to the music he seemed to like. And in the intervals, I read Hannah Arendt, who establishes the difference between *zoe,* physiological life, and *bios,* life as recounted, shared, life as biography, life with meaning. I felt, I knew, in these moments of co-presence, that David himself was regaining strength to lead both of them: *zoe* and *bios.* And that I could, on my side, bring to him the care necessary for him to get there in his own way. Never has "the miracle of life" seemed so simple and so obvious to me—stripped of all religiosity, and with a breath of Arendtian revolt against barbarism—as it did in this hospital room where I was watching carefully over my son's breathing.[202]

They were in and out of the hospital constantly. Sometimes the doctors would keep David for observation for ten days. And they often kicked Kristeva out of his room while they ran tests—which she fought against tooth and nail. She was with David every minute she was allowed to be, with music boxes and lots of singing and baby talk. After several of these episodes, and weeks spent in exhausting apprehension, Kristeva's mother-in-law—who had been wonderful from the beginning—said to her: "Listen, we are going to help you take care of him because it is absolutely essential that you not abandon your work. Your work must continue to be a priority."

This was unexpected, but also a relief. Kristeva compares how she was feeling at the time to a Picasso painting. She was out of joint, with her head cut off, suffering a kind of castration, feeling constantly under the threat of death: "It is a fatal blow for a mother to be confronted with the mortality of her child constantly, to think of nothing else but how to do everything possible so that he can live, and live his life in the best possible conditions . . . have a relationship to language, be socialized." Given Kristeva's intense relationship to language, one can only imagine the weightiness of the situation.

As for her mother-in-law, well, "people are complicated." This is a woman who did not push her daughters or granddaughters to get a good education but who had a completely different way of thinking when it came to Kristeva. She even went to see her local priest to get his blessing, to tell him that Kristeva needed her and that she wanted to help her in her "battle as a woman." She came to Paris to take care of David. She even accompanied Kristeva to New York to help with David in the fall of 1976 so that Kristeva could teach at Columbia.

Meanwhile, Kristeva and Sollers decided that they needed to consciously and for the foreseeable future live frugally and use every penny they made for taking care of David and for taking care of household chores so that they could do their work. Philippe helped; his parents helped both on the Île de Ré and in Paris. The only social institutions in France available to help with severely handicapped children were Catholic, and their resources were scarce. They did help, but not enough given the level of care needed by David, and so Kristeva began entrusting a series of helpers with the material details of their lives on a daily basis. This is still today how she copes with the complexity of her life. It is why, in part, she travels to give lectures and takes on new patients whenever she can: in order to afford for David to have the 24/7 care he needs but also so that she and Sollers can keep writing. As she explains, "I was lucky to have fallen into a certain type/ art of living with the Joyaux family, with a little bit of money—not a lot—but enough that we could distribute it to those who could help us."

Compartmentalizing

Kristeva has talked a lot about how strange it is to her that so many people see her as a diva, even as a rich diva, with an easy life: "You can't imagine how difficult it is even to stand up straight when one is a woman with an unusual husband, an unusual child, and an unusual job."[203] It is mostly Kristeva's characterological qualities that have helped her manage everything. There is first and foremost what I have emphasized since the beginning of my account: her energy and single-minded devotion to whatever she is doing, thinking, or writing about. Her insatiable curiosity is propelled by a combination of what she calls her "naïve ardor" and her mantra, "Whatever comes at you, just carry on!"[204]

Kristeva is also very disciplined. She follows a routine: she needs nine hours of sleep at night but rarely gets it because since her father's death in 1989, she routinely wakes up at around 2 a.m. each night and works for a bit, either answering emails, writing, or making notes for future books. She gets up for good at 8 a.m. and has tea, cereal, and fruit with Sollers and David. After taking a few minutes to delegate tasks to her helpers, she sits with David to plan his day with him. Then she takes a walk or does some exercise. By 10 a.m., she—depending on the day—is writing at her desk, seeing a patient, or teaching at the university. (When David was small, she worked at the university only two to three days a week.) Around noon, she often has lunch with students, colleagues, or editors and then works until 8 p.m., after which she has dinner and spends time with her family until bedtime.

I believe that Kristeva's capacity to juggle so many demands from others while writing so much is due to her ability to compartmentalize. Compartmentalization is usually thought of as something negative, but for Kristeva it is a matter of *intensity* more than anything else. She has explained that one cannot have intensity with everyone: it is necessary to choose. Once one does, it is possible to proceed with the kind of ethic of care—what she calls *une reliance* (a reliance)—that is not a projection. In such an ethic, there is a strong connection, but with room for the other's difference, strangeness. She *invests*.[205] What she describes is an ability to completely, intensively dedicate herself to whatever she is doing or whomever she is with, in all its or their difference, strangeness, and complexity. She describes herself as *multiple*, as having multiple intense relationships, each of which she can devote herself to for a given amount of time, short or long. When she is with David, she is a hundred percent with David, not worrying about what comes next or what she has not yet done. Then she is a hundred percent with a patient, a hundred percent with a student. She admits that this was hard in the beginning: she could hardly bring herself to leave David's side. And she acknowledges that it was a hard choice to spend all their money on helpers so that she could structure her life in this way.

Energy, compartmentalization, intensity, investment—Kristeva's seemingly boundless activity is legendary. She attributes a lot of this to David having conferred upon both of them the energy of "survivants"—of sur-vivors. Indeed, in my experience, David has always been very intense all by himself. He has a photographic memory, a piercing intelligence, a wicked sense of humor, and an uncanny wisdom. He also has a lot of self-knowledge. As Kristeva explains:

> David is very lucid about his situation, but never complains. Perhaps only once in a while when he has trouble finding words to name the experience of coma or other limits. He writes of his suffering in laconic, tightly wound poems. Gifted with perfect pitch, he adores the Mozart and Vivaldi his father gave him a taste for—it's their own little world, and I admire them for that. Very affectionate and demanding in friendship, those two consider themselves anarchists when it comes to politics. David keeps up with his parents through irony. Some of his formulations from his childhood are unforgettable. For example: "Papa is like God, he exists but one doesn't see him very often." David prefers "Madame Joyaux" to Julia Kristeva. And puts me on alert: "Be brief! You talk too much!"[206]

Some of my other favorite aphorisms from David include, "Men are fragile and women work," "Papa is at war with humanity," and "I dream, therefore I am."

Kristeva's "energetic pessimism" and "survivor's energy" take her a long way. In addition, she refuels daily by reading. She reads all the time, always has—books only, though, because she hates reading on the screen (she also hates the new high-tech National Library in

Paris). She also likes to take long walks, especially in what she refers to as "my France": the Luxembourg Gardens, but also Versailles and the Chateaux de la Loire, when she can. She has never moved away from the Luxembourg Gardens, having over time lived on various nearby streets—rue des Gobelins, boulevard de Port-Royal, rue Michelet, rue d'Assas—just so she can refuel close by.

However, what really gets Kristeva's energy moving is writing. She says that writing actively puts her energy "into movement." But not just any writing has this effect: it must be *writing* related to her *thinking* about what she is *living* at any given moment. When I ask her how she has managed to raise David, be married to Sollers, have a demanding full-time job as a professor and psychoanalyst, and write so many books, she always first evokes those who have helped her, starting with Sollers, but quickly moves onto her thinking, philosophizing, theorizing, and, of course, writing about what she is in the middle of living. When asked how she does it all, she responds that she has the capacity to compartmentalize because she has learned to be a "multiverse," adding that this is something that we all need to grapple with in today's world:

> I do not write about my universe; it is my multiverse. Cubism captured that. Picasso saw human beings within a compartmentalization that was not superficial. Today, I would say that the challenges are slightly different. We are all caught in a globalization, a radical form of multiculturalism that some are finding difficult to transform into a multiversalism . . . in part because we are all limited within the leveling logic of neoliberal flows of capital. But if we want to be up to the level of what science is telling us about the criss-crossings of global culture, we need to face up to it without making of it a fragmentation. There are people who suffer from this, who feel fragmented, unable to put themselves together, to feel whole. Where am I? How do I unify myself in the midst of all this? That is why we must constantly revisit this problem, find ways to think it, communicate it, speak it, write it . . . We mustn't stop thinking it . . . trying to find a new language for all of it.

Those who cannot find their multiverse are prone to depression, but also to violent militantism, desire for revenge, and a revindication of their primary identity. Kristeva's own living of and thinking about her multiversalisms, in addition to being a matter of practical concerns, quickly becomes a matter of ethical and political quandaries in her writing.

Reliance: An Ethic of Care

One of the situations that Kristeva has lived most acutely is David's disability. However, for a long time she kept David's situation private, not putting it into writing until 2003 when she published her *Open Letter to the President of the Republic on the Situation of Handicapped Citizens*.[207] Since this book, she has written and spoken widely on the question of disability as well as participated in considerable activism to change the really quite shocking negligence of the French government with regard to the rights of handicapped people. I would argue that Kristeva's living, thinking, and writing the situation of the handicapped subject has rendered her reflections on non-normative subjectivities and multiversalisms even more nuanced and diverse. It has made her more attentive to the suffering of others, helping her develop an ethic of care—an ethic revived from the project of the French Enlightenment and evoked in the name of furthering the creative singularity of the handicapped as an antidote to their current forced integration into the individualistic normativity of our society, which emphatically demands producer-consumers:

> Careful! *Le souci*—caring—should not make one worried, anxious, or somber; caring simply means maintaining intense contact with the strangeness in others as in oneself; caring is the dawn of proximity. It is so rare in the egocentric world of consumption and digital virtuality, that a kind of pedagogical urgency impresses itself upon us to introduce caring along with the capacity *to care for*, as a first line value, coming before any other secular teachings about morality.[208]

David's disability has brought Kristeva closer to understanding how new forms of fear of otherness, indeed of mortality itself, can perhaps be calmed, even rechanneled.[209] The proximity of the disabled subject to the poetic subject has crystallized for her.[210]

David's gift to his mother was the experience of reliance, an ethic of care, an understanding of the singular bond that we call love and that Spinoza called the intimate foundation of ethics. For Kristeva, reliance is the heart of motherhood, the enactment of care, and the creation of a true connection. Motherhood, in turn, is a source of optimism in an otherwise uncaring world. As I have mentioned, Kristeva believes that there are only two discourses available in the West to talk about maternity: science/medicine (which reduces the mother to nature) and religion (which makes the mother sacred). Indeed, her sense that the West is missing a theoretical discourse on maternity was already visible in her earliest work, including in her gendered discussions of abstract concepts such as the *chora* and the *semiotic* in *Revolution*. Her account of reliance is a more recent attempt to build some of the missing vocabulary.

In her 2011 film *Reliance*—as well as in an article related to the film[211]—Kristeva traces models of reliance from the Greeks through the heights of Christianity to its greatest crisis to date in the Western world, namely the Holocaust. She places a special emphasis on the grotesque paintings of Max Beckmann—especially his 1937 *Birth* and 1938 *Death*—and their terrifying hallucinations of a destroyed maternity and the resultant loss of caring, of reliance. Kristeva furthermore believes that reliance is in crisis again today. She believes that another possible discourse on maternity—a feminist one—has been weighed down by negative, even murderous, visions of motherhood. She hopes that this can change. More specifically, Kristeva hopes that besides working to make the lives of mothers more possible with adequate childcare, parental leaves, decent educational systems, and so on, feminist intellectuals will take the lead in rethinking maternity symbolically. This is important because she is convinced that there can be no freedom for women until there is a *maternal ethics*, a discourse and practice of reliance: "'The free woman is just being born,' wrote Simone de Beauvoir in the *Second Sex* (1949). There will not be a free woman as long as we lack an ethics of the maternal. But this ethics is just being born; it will be a herethics of reliance."[212]

Since David's birth, Kristeva's writing has never been the same. All of her writing is grounded in her personal experience, and motherhood is no exception. For example, in 1975, the year of David's birth, her "Maternity According to Bellini" highlighted the maternal luminescence of Bellini's vision, one that is in danger of being undone by the victory of patriarchal forms of rationality in the West.[213] More generally speaking, she explains: "My life as a mother, I live it with the gravity [it deserves], certainly as a result of psychoanalysis, it is integrated into [all of] my work. My readings, my writings, my patients themselves are clarified in new ways by what I live with David. He helped me understand worlds that were opaque or closed to me before his birth."[214]

Kristeva's most important articles from the early to mid-1970s do not all focus on women and maternity, but the question of the vulnerable, cognitively unusual subject is always there (and is also, at least sometimes, us). Some of Kristeva's most influential articles continue her research at the intersection of subjectivity, linguistics, and ethics. "The Predicative Function and the Speaking Subject," published in 1975 in honor of Benveniste, is a dense rumination on the ways in which such odd bedfellows as Benveniste and Faulkner contributed to a twentieth-century redefinition of subjectivity through an emphasis on the limits of subjectivity, on how examples of the "extinction of communication" challenge conventional linguistics.[215] Another example is "The Ethics of Linguistics," published in 1974 as a meditation on ethics in Chomsky, Jakobson, and Mayakovsky.[216] In this essay, Kristeva brings the insights of psychoanalysis into dialogue with signs of vulnerability that are intrinsic to subjectivity but that are ignored by conventional scientific disciplines, such as linguistics.

About the same time, Kristeva also began to widen her attention to what precedes and disrupts the symbolic in arts other than writing. Already in 1972, after a trip to Padua and Assisi, Italy, with her sister, Kristeva published "Giotto's Joy," where she focused on the plastic arts.

Specifically, she analyzed the beginnings of Western representational painting and the centrality of color, especially of blue—which was associated with the maternal—in Giotto's paintings.[217]

Kristeva's 1975 "Ellipsis on Dread and the Specular Seduction," in turn, takes the movie-viewing subject into account, emphasizing the ways in which psychoanalysis can help us understand the breakdown of the normative, armored subject that takes place through the disruption of images (the symbolic) by traces of what precedes representation (the semiotic). Kristeva's explanation of how we as cinematic spectators are undone and seduced—in the terminology of film theory, "sutured"—and then taken to new limits of fear, joy, sadness, or abandon while lost in a screen became one of the earliest texts of film theory to receive widespread critical attention.[218]

I would moreover argue that Kristeva's first explicit foray into reading politics psychoanalytically also appeared in 1975 and pre-figured what would become her first book published in the 1980s: *The Powers of Horror*. Her article, "From One Identity to an Other," marks the moment when Kristeva formalizes her emphasis on "fragile subjectivity"—the speaking subject's symbolic experience within a collective symbolic order as impacted by the body, by instinctual drives, by affect—through her invention of the term *sujet en procès*: subject-in-process-on-trial.[219] This subject is all of us, of course, but some of us do not completely repress our instinctual drives, do not hide behind the carapace of our social identity, but are compelled to engage in a practice where the battle between the symbolic and the semiotic is stylized, narrativized, and made visible for all who are not blind to it. Literature and art become laboratories—privileged spaces—where the battle between rationality and irrationality can be mapped in order to better understand the forces at work in the larger society in which the artist or writer is living. Kristeva purposefully chose a Nazi-sympathizing writer, Céline, in order to illustrate through textual analysis how the economy of his poetics corresponded to the economy of his politics, showing the underbelly of fascism as it were. She also claims that language cannot be tamed by anyone and that it is poets—especially troubled, mad, ecstatic, or just obsessed ones—who know best how to stretch language to its outer limits.

The Crossing of Signs (1975)

There also appeared in 1975 a collection of essays based on Kristeva's 1973–74 seminar at the University of Paris 7: *The Crossing of Signs*. This ambitious collection of eight articles by members of the seminar broadens Kristeva's emerging theories of signifying practices to include the signifying systems of poetic texts across several cultural symbolic systems. Kristeva describes the aim of the volume as follows:

> To open up, then, to the consideration of the student and researcher in French and more generally Western literature, the conceptions of "language" produced by the great civilizations that are increasingly interpolating our own: China, India, Islam, Judaism . . . To follow the path toward a new historical conception of signifying practices, paying attention to their form but also to their subjects and the time of their sociality, without enclosing them within the rigid base/superstructure dichotomy which, as a consequence, will itself be thrown into question.[220]

Kristeva's own article in the collection, "Signifying Practice and Mode of Production,"[221] continues her argument that signifying practices must be taken seriously because, by illuminating the relationship between the process (trial) of speaking subjects and the social structures within which these subjects are immersed, they can help diagnose how instinctual drives are—or are not—being socialized in a given time and place. It is in this article where Kristeva begins to take an explicit distance from vulgar Marxist theory, for the signifying practices that she is interested in take place in much the same way across many different cultures grounded in different, often heterogeneous modes of production. It is also in this article where she most explicitly begins to explore the place of religious belief and symbolics in shaping speaking subjects, their poetic practices, and their culture's available—or unavailable—imaginary constructs.

New York City

In 1972, Kristeva met my soon-to-be professor and dissertation director from the Department of French at Columbia University, Leon Roudiez. *Tel Quel* was hosting a conference that summer on Artaud and Bataille at the International Cultural Center of Cerisy-La-Salle in northwestern France, where Kristeva presented two talks, most notably her now famous piece, "The Subject in Signifying Practice" (which can also be translated as "The Subject-in-Process-on-Trial").[222] Her passionate defense of the centrality of art and poetry for understanding culture and society, via an in-depth consideration of Artaud, deeply and irrevocably impressed Professor Roudiez, a specialist in twentieth-century literature at its most experimental. He invited Kristeva to teach at Columbia and became an admirer, protector, and translator of her work, struggling until his last days on earth to bring her work to a broader public.[223] Kristeva became very fond of him as well, and has often mentioned to me how warm and welcoming he was to her and the little David, stepping up with his wife, Jacqueline, as temporary grandparents during Kristeva's stays in New York.[224] Roudiez was also instrumental in founding and organizing what was called the Troika: the appointment of three world-famous European intellectuals in 1976 as Permanent Visiting Professors, each to teach one semester at Columbia every three years: Umberto Eco, Tzvetan Todorov, and Julia Kristeva (the linguist and poet, Henri Meschonnic, also was part of the Troika at one point).

I arrived at Columbia in 1975, and as a graduate student in the French and Comparative Literature departments, I felt like I had fallen into a hall of mirrors at an intellectual circus—or perhaps into a strange, intellectually violent, though non-lethal, warzone: in one corner, there was Roudiez, an erudite liberal-left specialist of avant-garde fiction as well as of Marxist, psychoanalytic, and poststructuralist theory; in the other, there was Michael Riffaterre, an erudite conservative-right specialist of nineteenth-century poetry as well as of structuralist semiotics and stylistics. These two disliked each other intensely, rarely spoke, and fought about their influence over graduate students. Graduate students quickly learned that to work with one meant that the other would write you off both professionally and personally.

There was also Sylvère Lotringer, the rebellious founder and editor of *Semiotext(e)*, the journal through which most of so-called "high" French poststructuralism entered the United States.[225] In addition, there was the trio of brilliant young feminist theorists—Nancy K. Miller, Naomi Schor, and Susan Suleiman—who were revolutionizing the field of feminist literary studies.[226] Upstairs, in one corner of the embattled English Department was Carolyn Heilbrun, the godmother of American feminist literary criticism, and in the other, Edward Said, the godfather of postcolonial theory. This made for interesting elevator rides in Philosophy Hall. It also gave most of us students the certainty that we had arrived at the center of the universe. I could not quite keep track of who did and did not speak to whom, although I was aware that I had landed in a place where intellectual history was being made.

When Kristeva arrived for her Troika semester at Columbia in the fall 1976, I had only read one article by her, "The Subject in Signifying Practice." I do not think that I understood very much of it, but I was utterly fascinated by what I managed to grasp; I was sure that there was something to understand in it. I remember reading it over and over again—I must have read it fifty times—especially after I met Kristeva. I became Kristeva's busy research assistant and met the then ten-month-old David, Kristeva's mother-in-law, Marcelle, and their au pair, Jacqueline, spending some time with all of them at their apartment on 28th Street. Mostly, I was utterly mesmerized by how many books Kristeva could look at every day. At one point, I had to hire my friends to help me get her the library books she wanted because there just were not enough hours in the day.

In addition, Kristeva was very anxious to experience the "New York avant-garde." In November 1976, Philip Glass and Robert Wilson rented the Metropolitan Opera House to stage *Einstein on the Beach*. Kristeva and I went at her insistence. I could not for the life of me figure out what was happening on that stage, although I could not really look away—except that every once in a while, I glanced over at Kristeva to see if she was enjoying it. As far as I could tell, she was completely absent to herself, lost in the spectacular visuals and the repetitious, minimalist music. She talked about it non-stop for days afterward and, of course, eventually wrote about it as an important example not only of new forms of artistic practice in the United States but also of new forms of subjectivity. Invoking artists such as Michael Snow on the one hand, and Yvonne Rainer and Robert Wilson on the other, she did what she always does: she weaved together her own experience with a theory of new anti-authoritarian arts and subjectivities—this time to be found on American, or at least *new-yorkais*, shores.[227]

The Dissident

Kristeva and *Tel Quel*'s interest in the United States had already been evident for a while even as their critics ridiculed them for their spin-on-a-dime "intellectual tourism," first to communist China and then to capitalist New York City. They were accused of shifting from left-wing concerns for the masses via Sinophilia to right-wing concerns for the individual via a new Atlanticism.[228] It is true that as the 1970s proceeded, given what was happening in the Soviet bloc—and no doubt with a lot of input from the now enthusiastically Western European Kristeva—*Tel Quel* became publicly less and less enthusiastic about Marxism and more and more enamored of Louis Althusser's analysis of the workings of the "ideological state apparatus" as a modern form of social power.[229] The Telquelians appreciated the ways in which Althusser's account of power elucidates the unconscious, and at times even irrational, mechanisms of causality, which often leave no one in particular accountable for what happens no matter how awful. The Telquelians also increasingly aligned themselves with dissidents from Eastern Europe and the Soviet Union, such as Solzhenitsyn, as well as with the so-called "New Philosophers": a group of disparate thinkers in 1970s France who shared a deep distrust of Marxism and what they saw as its adoration of power. Here is how Danielle Marx-Scouras, one of the best interpreters of the Telquelian 1970s, puts it:

> Kristeva maintained that the role of the writer was no longer to deal out "globalizing doctrines," but instead to express "the impossibility of cohesion." For "social consensus—even when it advocates the well-being of the majority—represents in its *massiveness* a germ of *totality,* and ultimately a promise of *totalitarianism*" . . . *Tel Quel*'s crisis with Marxism in the mid-1970s stems precisely from a fear of the massification of culture and society and the subordination of the individual to the collective. This explains *Tel Quel*'s total abandonment of Marxism in favor of human rights during its last phase.[230]

I hope that my reader can see by now why Kristeva could not but have found this new perspective deeply appealing. Along with her *Tel Quel* comrades, she began to argue that the best rampart against totalitarian tendencies, whether of the fascist or Stalinist variety, is *artistic practice* because—in short—both of these authoritarian psycho-socio-political worldviews share a "hatred for the diversity of languages and for what such a diversity opens up, that is, a transgressive and critical position with respect to normative codes."[231] For her, the clichés and codes of the European left, solidified in response to the experience of fascism, echoed the worst intellectual and discursive habits of both the fascism and communism that she had run away from.

Although Kristeva worried about the impact that her pro-Western and at times pro-American intellectual positions might have on her parents and other family members in Bulgaria at such a tumultuous time, she did not hesitate to speak up publicly. In two important articles published almost simultaneously in 1977, she focused on the new understandings that she was gaining from her time spent in the United

States and from her conversations with philosophers like Bernard-Henri Lévy—the most visible member, and some would say founder, of the New Philosophers—in France. I would argue that these two articles, first, marked the end of a certain kind of "pedagogical impulse to convince" at the heart of her publications, and second, hinted at the ethical fervor, even alarm, with which Kristeva would later focus on the need for a deep understanding of the crises of the Western World—in order to save it—over the next decade.

The first of the articles in question was an introduction to *Tel Quel's* triple issue on the United States in 1977. This introduction, entitled "Why the United States?," consisted of a conversation among Kristeva, Sollers, and Pleynet.[232] Kristeva had already published an article, "From Ithaca to New York," on the United States in 1974, during a visit to Cornell and Columbia, but it had been largely a personal evocation of her status as a traveler, a foreigner, a woman intellectual at a time of immense challenge and change in a country caught in the throes of dramatic events. In this article, Kristeva marvels at the complexities of the Vietnam War, the Yom Kippur War, the Women's Movement, Watergate, the oil crisis; she almost affectionately critiques the American left and particularly Chomsky; and she praises with enthusiasm artists from the elite John Cage and Robert Wilson to the massively popular edges of rock and roll. Through her remarks runs a streak of naïve discovery and genuine wonderment. Was Europe or the United States the sign of the future?[233]

"Why the United States?" is less dreamy, more analytical, and posits the United States as a polyvalent set of breaks with history and culture, as opposed to China which—Kristeva is very clear on this point—is just a "re-run" of the Marxist-Stalinist model. At the heart of American polyvalence is an artistic practice that is "non-verbal"—that is all about sound, gesture, and color. However, this artistic practice is not a matter of the semiotic gone wild because of the ways in which it is marginalized by a mainstream culture based on Protestantism and on corporate discursive structures that worship only sex and money. This article arguably launched Kristeva into a new era in which her "adoption" by the United States combined with her loyalty to European culture opened up her theoretical and literary corpus in ways that had not been previously possible.

The second "threshold" article published in 1977, "A New Type of Intellectual: The Dissident," is almost a manifesto.[234] In it, Kristeva makes clear her break with the past and calls for a new type of intellectual who is capable of stepping up to the challenges of the century.

Polylogue (1977)

For Kristeva at the end of the 1970s, it was crucial for the progressive left intellectual to ignore the "machinery of politics," and instead focus on language, dreams, and jouissance. In "A New Type of Intellectual," she moreover described her vision of social change as follows: "Communal but particular, addressed to all and yet carried out by each individual: such is the culture of our age, that is, when it is not only an echo-chamber of the past. From this point on, another society, another community, another body start to emerge."[235] In spite of this optimistic—some would say utopian—vision, Kristeva was clearly already worried that this process of renewal would not be able to continue. Her worry proved to be enduring, for the warnings about the crisis of society that she issued in this article only grew louder in the 1980s and 1990s.

For the Kristeva of 1977, there were three kinds of dissidents: 1) the rebel who attacks political power (but who is destined to remain within the master-slave dialectic); 2) the psychoanalyst (who, in his battle with religion, ultimately remains loyal to rationality); and 3) the writer who experiments with the limits of identity (and reinvents the relationship between desire and the law). In Kristeva's view, the third genre of dissident is our best hope. In this context, Kristeva once again raises the question of women and mothers, claiming that "at the pivot of sociality—*she* is at once the guarantee and a threat to its stability."[236] There are of course also others in exile who are capable of dissidence: Jews; exiles from the gulags; writers such as Kafka, Joyce, and Beckett, whose language pulverizes meaning; and intellectuals-in-exile such as Kristeva herself. Kristeva thus concludes that "true dissidence today is perhaps simply what it has always been: *thought*." That is, she posits that now that the Prince has joined the Politbureau or the Corporation, and that reason has been absorbed by technology, there is perhaps only "thought in language" that can serve as the cutting edge of dissidence and save the West from itself.[237]

After 1977, *Tel Quel* continued ambitiously to publish articles about and by American writers and artists—Pound, E. E. Cummings, Rothko, Ashbery, Rauschenberg, etc.—but Kristeva's nod to the new spaces for the imagination that she had discovered in the United States showed up only in a few varied contexts, often quite obliquely, and mostly in relationship to her emerging defense of cosmopolitanism. An example of such scattered glimpses is her essay "Post-modernism?," which was initially given as a paper at the 1978 Modern Language Association convention in New York.[238] In the late 1970s, the word *postmodernism* did not have the same currency in France as it was beginning to have in the United States, and in fact it would only be employed intellectually at any length—and in a very different way from how it was used in the United States—by the philosopher Jean-François Lyotard in his 1979 *The Postmodern Condition: A Report on Knowledge.*[239] However, for Kristeva in 1978 the American concept of the postmodern text was in the same territory as her European "limit-text" insofar as it served as the kind of thought-in-language that increased the possibilities of what could be represented; it incisively approached the limits of thought-in-language in order to make visible what can only be called "truth."

From another short text of that period, a 1976 essay on Samuel Beckett, it is clear that Kristeva's immersion in what she began to elaborate as a very Protestant American avant-garde culture made a deep and lasting impression on her, albeit in an unexpected way, at the level of a new kind of focus on religious psycho-symbolic structures. The pain of a close friend at the death of his father moved Kristeva to work on Beckett's *First Love*,[240] which is a narrative of a man whose father's death causes him to meditate upon the absurdity of his sexual adventures with women. Kristeva's essay, eventually included in her major collection of essays published in 1977, *Polylogue*, is mostly a celebration of Beckett's limit-texts.[241] But through her emphasis on Beckett's bi-culturalism—on his Irish *Protestantism* and his French *Catholicism*—Kristeva makes larger points about representations of women, the maternal, and cultural innovation. For example, she observes that only Catholicism gives symbolic (sacred) space to women as mothers through the imagery of the Virgin Mary. Protestantism does not do this at all, authorizing a more abject image of the female body, usually in the form of the prostitute. From this contrast, Kristeva explores Beckett's ambiguous and ambivalent representations of both maternal and prostituted bodies, which are interspersed with the ironic seriousness with which he displays (for all to see) the death of the Father in Western culture and society.

Even as Kristeva and *Tel Quel* continued in public to celebrate cultural dissidence and the cosmopolitanism of exile, Kristeva became increasingly focused on the individual in her thinking and writing. She was especially interested in how the practice of psychoanalysis and the history of religion, *thought together*, could address the most difficult questions facing humanity, primarily through new understandings of the maternal and of its impact on representation.[242] This is understandable: she had just become the mother of a very fragile child. She was married to an artist who was a practicing Catholic. She was in the middle of her training as a psychoanalyst. She was herself an Other, in the process of leaving behind her old identity and giving birth to her new French self.

One of the first interviews of Kristeva we have on video was filmed in 1976 for the French television show *Free Tribune* (*Tribune Libre*). The episode was entitled "Julia Kristeva: The Infancy of Art." A young, strikingly beautiful, un-smiling Kristeva sits rigidly still in a chair, dressed in a black and white pin-striped raincoat, with her hair pulled back in a bun. She answers the reporter's somewhat impossible questions bluntly and seriously, in perfect if staccato Parisian French.

When asked how she situates herself within contemporary thought, she replies that she is someone who crosses frontiers and engages in internationalism. When asked what the role of the intellectual is today, she replies that it is to give voice to the impossible in a given culture. She insists that *Tel Quel* is all about language in the process of becoming. Her responses are in keeping with what one would expect and, perhaps because she is so young, it is the interviewer who initially must keep things going.

However, when Kristeva gets her bearings, she begins to open up and speak more easily, going straight to the heart of what interested her most at that time: the human subject at the intersections of maternity, childhood, religion, psychoanalysis, and language. For instance, she notes that the infant and child are (at) the frontier between nature and culture and at the limit of rationality, and that artists and writers are children inasmuch as they also inhabit frontiers and margins. She argues that psychoanalysis is uniquely devoted to the discovery and, ultimately, the health of the fragile child in each of us attempting to find ourselves in language. She picks up speed and begins to talk about how the larger society lives its most intense moral crises almost entirely through children—in relation to abortion, contraception, marriage, and pornography. She adds that Christians have represented their God as a child on earth, yet the Church has no idea how to deal with these crises in the modern world. She emphasizes that it is psychoanalysis and psychoanalysis alone that offers a lucidly rational exploration of this "living limit," which is the child both literally and figuratively. She claims with profound seriousness that only psychoanalysis and modern art, faced with this situation, manage to revolt, to contest institutions, while exploring the limits of rationality.

In an essay Kristeva published about that same time, "Place Names,"[243] she focuses again on the child as a challenge to reason, on infantile language as the space where the infrastructure of all meaning is constructed in relationship to the maternal body. She explains that naming, attaching words to people and things, is a spatial processing that is about finding replacements for the mother even as the mother remains intractable. In addition, in 1977 Kristeva published one of her most enigmatic and well-known texts, "Stabat Mater," which is both a personal evocation of her experience of childbirth and motherhood and a philosophical and psychoanalytic meditation on the damage being done to men and women in the wake of the demise of religion, especially the demise of the only religion that offers a philosophy of motherhood, as unreal—as hallucinatory—as that philosophy might be.[244]

Crazy Truth (1979)

I would argue that by 1979, when Kristeva was thirty-eight, the basic infrastructure of her thought familiar to English-language readers today was more or less in place. That year she also became a fully licensed psychoanalyst and, in parallel, became more forceful in her writing about claiming that psychoanalytic insight was an important, perhaps even the primary, firewall between humanity's best and worst qualities. Her 1979 article, "Language Has No Master," is a defense and illustration of the urgent necessity of psychoanalytic insight at the end of the twentieth century. She argues that it is the capacity of the analyst to listen for, hear, and transform the unsayable, the impossible, and the heterogeneous—to decipher the hieroglyphic inscriptions of what escapes logic in the discourse of those who are suffering on the couch, who are writing the unnamable, living the unthinkable—that might help save humanity from unthinkable crises. Her ruminations take her from the destructive struggle of women to find places in discourse other than those that have been assigned to them to the ramblings of Céline, who showed us the psychotic underbelly of the disaster that was the Second World War. In 1979, psychoanalysis was for Kristeva the "only discourse capable of addressing itself to this untenable place our species finds itself in, exposed to madness under an empty sky."[245]

In 1979, Kristeva also published "Women's Time" in a small journal run by her students.[246] This essay became one of her most famous articles in English. What is best known about it is its diagnosis of the twentieth-century women's movement. Kristeva maintains that there have been three generations of women in this movement: the first generation of egalitarian feminists demanded equal rights in "linear time"; the second generation emphasized women's difference from men and the need to maintain a relationship with "monumental time"; the third generation—which Kristeva hopes will materialize—would be able to reconcile maternal time (motherhood) with linear (political and historical) time. However, I think that what has been less noticed about the article is the way that Kristeva places the third generation of women—and some men not devoted to patriarchal time—at the cutting edge of the ethical leadership that humanity needs in order to move forward. This would require a movement away from what we today call the "identity politics" of historical forms of feminism in order for women to take a lead in what she sees as a much larger struggle with and through symbolic practice, especially aesthetic practice. Over the coming decades, Kristeva will often refer back to this article and the optimism that she more than hinted at in it regarding the possibility that there will, in fact, be new generations of women who will be able to lead the human species to a more tenable place.[247]

As Kristeva was embracing psychoanalytic practice in France as a way to hear the rumblings of that which had been banned (even foreclosed) historically from the rational "city of words"—banished as madness, mysticism, or poetry—theorists in the United States were beginning to incorporate the work coming out of France under the rubric of postmodernism. Some celebrated it; others hated it. However, everyone agreed that it was a moment of profound transformation.

First, postmodernism introduced new definitions and forms of subjectivity (for example, those who had been excluded from white Christian heteropatriarchy were demanding to be included). Second, it examined new forms of representation (for example, the fact that television was literally turning the world inside-out and outside-in). And, third, and most importantly, it insisted on the impossibility of determining truth (for example, by emphasizing the breakdown of authority figures such as the father and his institutions). Because

Kristeva focused on the dissolution of symbolic structures of meaning by semiotic energies—on the breakdown of language, including the discourse of psychosis—in the context of modernist and postmodernist art, she was in the vanguard of many of these conversations. Among other things, her invention of the term "the true-real" (*le vréel*) in 1979 rang true as a description of something increasingly sought after by entire populations in postmodern times.

Truth was in crisis, and it seemed as if everyone was looking for something else in its stead, something less rational. Kristeva's term for this "something" contains three words in French: *le réel* (the real), *le vrai* (the true), and *elle* (she/her and a trace of the feminine/maternal). What worried her, though, was how to include this new genre of sought-after truth in a new, more inclusive social contract: how could this *vréel* be made *vraisemblable*? That is, how could "the true-real" gain verisimilitude without psychosis—the inability to distinguish between what is real and what is not—becoming the norm. Now, some three decades into the era of banal virtuality and "post-truth," her 1979 worry seems more than prescient.

"Le vréel" became the title of Kristeva's article in a 1979 collection of essays, *Crazy Truth*, that came out of a seminar that she co-organized with the Jesuit philosopher and psychoanalyst, Michel de Certeau.[248] The seminar, "Psychosis and Truth," was held in Paris at the Hospital of the Cité Universitaire in 1977–78. This is when Kristeva became close friends with Certeau, absorbing his scholarship on the relationship between psychosis and religious faith with great admiration and much fascination. Kristeva felt like he was teaching her what genuine revolt could look like, and together they returned time and time again to Kristeva's concerns about what was historically afoot in the world.

When Certeau died in 1986, Kristeva was deeply saddened. The Jesuits in Paris held a huge mass at the Saint Ignatius Church on rue de Sèvres. The church was packed with luminaries from the Collège de France and the École des Hautes Études, along with some forty Jesuit priests from all over Europe. One person after another stood up to speak to some quality of Certeau. Many said that he was a true Jesuit, which turned more than a few heads since it was rumored that he was gay. When Kristeva was privately wondering what it meant to be "a true Jesuit," one of the speakers specified that Certeau was a true Jesuit "because he was the most in revolt of anyone" and "true Jesuits were always in revolt."

Kristeva was impressed that the respected scholar could also be remembered as such a strong rebel. Just then, Certeau's spiritual leader announced that as he had closed the dying Certeau's eyes, Certeau had whispered his last wish. Suddenly the voice of Edith Piaf singing "Non, je ne regrette rien" filled the church. Kristeva started to cry, which is still one of her rarest responses, at least in public. She found the whole thing quite scandalous, quite carnivalesque, but also impressive . . . very true . . . and very, very moving. After the mass, Kristeva went up to Father Vallat, the Superior of the Order, and asked him: "Do you have women Jesuits? Because if you do, I will become one of them." He responded, "No, we don't deal with women, no." Kristeva did not dare to even chuckle at the priest's response. She merely made a hasty retreat, with tears still in her eyes—the same way that she left the 1970s behind as she moved forward.

Part III

Becoming Julia Kristeva (1980–Today)

A Vertical Present

I agree with Kristeva when she says (more and more often) that she has been talking about the same things, in different ways, since her youth, in a kind of vertical present tense. But I would add that since the beginning of the 1980s, she has been doing so with an increasingly precise and insistent vocabulary and an ever-increasing sense of urgency arising from her diagnosis of an ever more dire crisis affecting the entire world.

Never has she been more succinct about this crisis than in a 2016 lecture and a 2017 interview, both published by the Psychoanalytic Society of Paris. In the 2016 lecture, "Psychic Life in Times of Distress," she emphasizes the responsibility and capacity of interdisciplinary approaches within the humanities—with psychoanalysis leading the way—to help stand up to some of the most complex and frightening challenges we humans find ourselves facing in the twenty-first century:

> The twentieth century blew a hole in historical time by this crime without precedent against humanity which is the Shoah, and [today] the duty to remember [that crime] is implacably bumping up against repression, against defense mechanisms, yes, even against denial. The rise of science and technology in the third millennium is prolonging the duration of human life and modifying the possibilities of its reproduction; spectacle, hyperconnectivity, and virtual reality are shaking up the family unit when not replacing it; ancient adjustments made between sense and sensibility, among speech, writing, and other "languages" no longer hold together; transhumanism carries out the theory of man-machine; and immortality is within reach for android

automats who "speak" among themselves in "languages" their creators cannot understand. Never has temporality been so open: from the vibrations of cosmic depths passing through prehistoric grottos, right up to simulations of cosmic expansion. But since at the same time, the inequalities regulating access to those temporalities have never been so drastic, frustrating and explosive, never have humans lived such heterogeneous temporalities, from one end of the globe to the other, from one community to the other, from one individual to the other— even as [these temporalities] are superimposing upon and confronting each other inside of each of us, in spite of and alongside the ongoing banalization of behaviors and values.

This context durably impacts the psychic apparatus . . . and accentuates hysterico-obsessional symptoms by fragilizing them, all the while rendering them permeable to psychotic fragmentation, somatic incorporations, and [eventually] the eroticization of the death drive.[1]

For Kristeva, cultural, social, and political events inscribe their temporalities within the most intimate spaces of the self, and the profound temporal mutations described above have, in her opinion, deeply affected the human psyche in the last few decades—and not for the better. Time is now at once hyper-accelerated and suspended: most of us are trapped in a bizarre mixture of fast and slow, presence and absence. We live in a time of "sacrifice" and/or "maniacal narcissism"—a time that is, ultimately, perfect for the "avid consumers we all are and must be."[2] Kristeva believes that this temporal chaos, which threatens to shut down psychic space (whether one calls it mind, spirit, or soul)—which threatens to render human subjects more robotic and subservient to spectacle—must be fiercely resisted. She has increasingly outlined strategies for keeping the psychic space of our species alive in the struggle against developments that ultimately lead to nihilism. She sees this struggle as a fight literally to the death in the name of liberty— which should not be confused with choice in the liberal sense of the term—and especially in the name of renewed human connection, of reliance in the sense that I described earlier.

In her 2017 interview, "A Psychic Life Is a Life Lived in Time," Kristeva specifies that the above mentioned shifts in temporality, aided and abetted by rapid technological changes, represent only one of three great anthropological mutations that accelerated during the late twentieth century.[3] She believes that the other two mutations—in the realms of sexuality and religion, respectively—are potentially, though not invariably, more hopeful. The mutation in human sexuality involves a positive, if at times difficult, redistribution of sexual difference, which renders bi/polysexuality more omnipresent and inventive— that is, increasingly creative. The third mutation, taking place across all the religious territories of the world, involves the global embrace of modern secularity. This is the part that Kristeva sees as hopeful. However, this mutation can also unevenly but surely result in nostalgic, often deeply reactionary religious belief systems that lean toward not only fundamentalism but also violent, paranoid, sadistic—and even murderous—destructiveness.

An understanding of this third mutation was difficult for the atheist Kristeva to achieve. It was only her psychoanalytic work on what she calls the universal "need to believe" experienced by all human children as the first step toward the "the desire to know" required for fully alive subjectivity that helped her make sense of twentieth- and twenty-first-century global shifts in religious claims. It is this third mutation that has been at the center of Kristeva's work since the late 2000s.

What has Kristeva been talking about since before she left Bulgaria? My list would have to include poetry, fiction, art, the sacred, the beauty and sensuality of the natural world, mothers and fathers, women and men, love, hate, justice, freedom (especially from political authoritarianism), the diversity/polyphony of human beings, all things philosophical in the French/European tradition—and, most centrally, the preciousness of what she today calls "psychic space." Her themes and vocabularies have changed, but it is the delicate interiority at the heart of each of us as singular beings that has always fascinated Kristeva. Indeed, her desire to protect this interiority from the noise and data-driven chaos and violence of our twenty-first-century world has led her to continue defending most loudly, above all else, the human imagination as it manifests in artistic and literary practice. It has moreover led her controversially to defend psychoanalysis as the discipline most able to hear, respond to, and protect the kinds of polyphonic, kaleidoscopic subjectivities that she believes can provide resistance—a counterweight—to the digitalized, market-driven world that has overtaken our hearts and souls.

How is this the case? According to Kristeva, it is only through the process of what psychoanalysis calls *perlaboration*—a working through, a reinvention, a *trans*figuration—of history and cultural memory that humanity can avoid a cataclysmic end.[4] For Kristeva, it is when society stops remembering, stops (re)thinking, stops working through its history, that authoritarianism and its deadly consequences come to reign. She essentially argues that we who are situated within Western traditions should reconsider throwing out the baby with the bathwater. For instance, she emphasizes that we should not assume that rejecting organized religion will eradicate humanity's "need to believe": in the absence of religion, human beings will simply choose something else to believe in and idealize. Along related lines, she argues that those who reject universalism should not be surprised to find themselves desperately calling for respect for universal human rights when suddenly some lives are deemed more disposable than others.

For Kristeva, it is the responsibility of intellectuals and artists to help sift through the cultural and intellectual history of our Western traditions, in dialogue with other epistemological traditions from around the world, in order to critique, but also to determine what can be salvaged, redefined, and reconceptualized—what is still meaningful in a fully globalized scenario. This can seem like "too little too late" given the current state of the world—hence Kristeva's admission that she is but an energetic pessimist. But I would add that she is also—as she has always been—a very determined, sometimes stubborn person. Every time someone says that nothing can be done about a given situation, she feels compelled to retort, "So, what shall we do?"

Over the last four decades, as the Cold War unraveled, as late capitalist neoliberalism took root in the 1990s, as nationalism, ethnocentricity, racism, and antisemitism surged in the first decade of the 2000s, and as the market-driven internet and hyperconnected media overtook our lives in the 2010s—that is, in the midst of rapid subjective, spiritual, temporal, technological, and sexual changes—Kristeva has shifted slowly from analysis to advocacy and an insistence on the urgency of dialogue among those who disagree. She has shifted from x-raying the individual human psyche and its artifacts to advocating for a strategy based in a renewed secular humanism, in increased respect and space for what she calls "universal singularities."

This notion of universal singularities may be utopian, but Kristeva insists that only when there are universal rights for all can each person's singularity be valued. Toward this end, she has continued to write without pause. But she has also invented new institutions, organized dialogues among those who can barely tolerate each other, and continued her advocacy for human rights and dignity for the most marginalized. While continuing to work in both abstract and concrete ways to improve the status of identity-based populations, especially women, she sees these struggles as but part of a more important battle, which is to vanquish the instrumental reason at the heart of robotic subjectivity caught in spectacle-driven, market-based consumerism and, most urgently in her view, to stop the inevitable slippage of this condition toward totalitarianism and what she sees as its always-accompanying death drive.

She has traveled all over the world sharing these ideas, leading a strangely solitary life in spite of all the public accolades and critiques, all of which propel her back at regular intervals to David, to Sollers, to her patients, to her writing table, to the Île de Ré . . . in order to regain her balance.

Yes, Yes, of Course, but What Shall We Do Now?

Over the past four decades, Kristeva has acknowledged in depth the crimes of Western, especially European, ideologies and their institutionalized actors, but—again, much as she has done since her youth—she has then insisted upon moving on quickly to "yes, yes, of course, but what shall we do now?" What she has decided to do is to call for a "new secular humanism." When she does so, she is obviously speaking in the wake of the profound critique of traditional humanism undertaken by the progressive left since French poststructuralism led the way in the second half of the twentieth century. Kristeva was an important voice in the postwar rejection of that old humanism, which protected the integrity of Man at its center by rigid boundaries of inclusion—which deemed only straight, white, Western men as worthy of admission—and exclusion, which marginalized women, people of color, the poor, the colonized and/or enslaved, the disabled, the LGBTQ community, and so on. Against this backdrop, Kristeva's call for a reinvention of secular humanism today has to be seen as a call for a deep reworking of humanism—one that would safeguard the polyphonic, polycentered, singular, and, above all, relational subjectivity of each and every one of us.

What I attempt to do in what follows is to accompany Kristeva living-thinking through these complex arguments over the past forty years, over the long and tortuous path of her "becoming Julia Kristeva"—both the "real" person and the international icon to whom she cannot seem to relate. But I also try to guide my reader through Kristeva's writing (her way of living) to communicate to my reader the *desire* to know Kristeva's thought in a way that will help us re-think while moving forward, not backward—that will help us refuse to stay stuck in place while history moves on.

Death, That Strange Voice . . .

For Kristeva, the 1980s were framed by two gut-wrenching deaths: that of Roland Barthes—whom she adored—in early 1980, and that of her father—whom she adored—at the end of 1989.

The facts surrounding Barthes's death are well known to those who admire him (even as these facts may have been muddied in the reader's mind by Laurent Binet's ferocious rewriting of them in 2015).[5] On February 25, 1980, Barthes was crossing the street at rue des Écoles, after having had lunch with François Mitterrand, and was hit by a laundry van. Kristeva was inconsolable. After a painful month on both a respirator and a dialysis machine, Barthes died from his injuries on March 26, 1980. Since then, Kristeva has written often and eloquently about her friend and mentor, most notably in her 1996 *The Sense and Non-Sense of Revolt*.[6] But nowhere has her deep affection for Barthes been more palpable than in her 1990 fictional version of her last encounter with him in his hospital bed:

> There's nothing more convincing than a refusal to go on living when it's conveyed without any hysteria: no asking for love, just a deliberate rejection, not even philosophical but animal and final, of existence. You feel like a moron for clinging, yourself, to the bustle called life that the other is relinquishing with such indifference.[7]

The deaths of Émile Benveniste, Michel de Certeau, and Roland Barthes would not be the last to shake Kristeva to her core. Her father's death in 1989, her mother's in 2002, and her editor Claude Durand's in 2015—with many others along the way (Jacques Lacan in 1981, Michel Foucault in 1984)—would always astonish her: like Colette, she finds death to be but a commonplace defeat.

1. The 1980s: Strangers to Ourselves and Others

By the early 1980s, there were rumblings of serious trouble in socialist France—and Kristeva heard and felt them. The voices of antisemitism and ethnonationalism were getting louder. In 1984, the proto-fascist National Front began to make electoral gains and increased its so-called "populist" visibility.[8] By 1986, the right wing had significant presence in the legislature. And by 1988, Jean-Marie Le Pen was a household name.

Kristeva was worried and, like always, it was these concrete events in her life that sparked her next several books. First and foremost, she decided that she wanted to try to understand not only the social and political but also the psychic history of fascism. She knew something about Stalinism and suspected that the two psychic disorders were similar. She wanted to understand what makes a fascist tick. Kristeva has been direct about the fact that the shift in her tone in the 1980s was intentional and ethical. She was sensitive to the rise of the extreme right and, in tune with her decisions since her trip to China in 1974, wanted to tackle the problem at the level of "internal psychic experience": she attempted a *perlaboration* of evil.

Ça continue: Work, Family, the Île de Ré

Privately, the 1980s were a time of consolidation and relaunch for Kristeva. She entered the decade fully committed to her writing, her psychoanalytic practice (especially now that her own analysis was done), her students, and her family. She and Sollers had been living for some time in a crowded apartment constructed from several sixth-floor *chambres de bonne* on the boulevard Port-Royal. The space was purchased for them by Sollers's parents, but once David was born, there simply was not enough room. Sollers kept the space as his office—and still works there—but in 1980 the family moved to a larger apartment on rue Michelet where they remained until 1989. The Port-Royal apartment-turned-writing-space for Sollers soon filled with books to the ceiling in every room, so that there was not much space for anyone but Sollers himself. The rue Michelet family apartment was comfortable, with plenty of space for Kristeva to have a consulting room where she could see her patients. And the three of them continued to go to the Île de Ré for two weeks every Easter vacation and for two months every summer.

Kristeva missed her family in Sofia enormously. Communicating with them was extremely difficult and her parents were not getting any younger. After many visa refusals, things finally came together with help from Sollers's parents and the French government via Jacques Chaban-Delmas, the mayor of Sollers's beloved Bordeaux and a great admirer of

Sollers's writing. Kristeva's parents and sister were given permission to visit Paris every three years. They did not make the trip often, but they did the best they could. They had visited Paris briefly in 1969 and again in 1976 after David's birth. The visit to Paris that Kristeva best remembers was in 1982 when David was seven years old. Kristeva's father and David were inseparable. Her father loved Notre-Dame and spent every minute he could there with David during that visit to Paris. These were also magical visits for Kristeva who, surrounded by those she loved, felt an unusual calmness. Her sister played the violin for Sollers, and they all spent time with Sollers's family on the Île de Ré and in Bordeaux. Kristeva's mother visited one other time by herself sometime between 1984 and 1989 (it has proven to be impossible to determine exactly when).

Kristeva and David also visited Sofia in the winter of 1983–84 for Christmas vacation. Her parents took Kristeva and David to play in the snowy mountains and even managed to take them on a "curative vacation" to the famous Sandanski thalasso and spa in the foothills of the Pirin Mountains, in the southwestern part of Bulgaria. David was ecstatic playing with his grandfather, sledding in the mountains, and splashing in the hot pools of Sandanski. This was Kristeva's last trip to Bulgaria until January 1989, when, as I have mentioned, she was part of the formal delegation accompanying President Mitterrand.

Kristeva spent the vast majority of her time in the 1980s reading and writing. She has often said that she spent more time than usual in the early 1980s reading voraciously: Proust and Colette as always, but also lots of Shakespeare. She devoted quite a lot of time to *The Tempest*, one of Shakespeare's plays that means the most to her. She has acknowledged that its themes of exile and the enchantment of language, as well as its emphasis on the father, speak to her own life. She also read all of Philip Roth's novels, having been impressed with him in New York, and liked *The Human Stain* the most. And she returned to one of her great loves from her teen years: Dostoevsky. She remembers that she reread *The Devils* intently around that time.

It is fairly clear that across the decade of the 1980s, Kristeva was relatively oblivious to how fast her reputation was growing. She was becoming an increasingly respected literary and psychoanalytic theorist, and her five well-known books published in the 1980s enhanced her reputation exponentially. By association, both privately and publicly, Kristeva's relationship with Sollers was crucial to her life and work, whether he was bending her ear over dinner with bleak—and prophetic—predictions about how small computers and screens would soon take over a world where books would disappear,[9] or whether he was on television talking about his 1983 novel, *Women*, where she was embarrassingly profiled. She was teaching ambitious seminars and lecture courses throughout the 1980s, trying out her new ideas for her books. Her courses at the University of Paris 7 had been growing for some time. Foreign students flocked to her lectures. She rose in the professorial ranks, and in 1988 she was recognized as Director of Research in Psychopathology and Semiotics at the University of Pierre and Marie Curie (University of Paris 6). She was also being slowly recognized formally in France: she received the prestigious Chevalier de l'Ordre des Arts et des Lettres in 1987 and the Prix Henri Hertz de la Chancellerie des universités de Paris in 1989. Her publications were piling up and the first two important volumes of her articles came out in English translation: *Desire in Language* in 1980 and Toril Moi's *Kristeva Reader* in 1986.

Whatever Happens to Me, That's What I Write About

But what was most exciting and utterly absorbing for Kristeva at that time was her daily practice as an analyst: that is what was most intensively happening to her and that is what she wrote about. And this has never really changed. By 1987, Kristeva's practice as an analyst was officially recognized. She was welcomed as an affiliated member by the Psychoanalytic Society of Paris and the International Association of Psychoanalysis. She was becoming a bit of a global phenomenon, traveling to China and the United States and taking on Russian-speaking patients. Most importantly, Kristeva's daily practice as an analyst formed the primary infrastructure for all of her books—on abjection, love, foreignness, and new forms of mental illness, especially depression—in the 1980s, and has been at the heart of most of her work since then: from her theories of female genius and of modern forms of revolt to her emphasis on the necessary transfiguration of religious belief systems and philosophical concepts like universalism; from her loss of respect for politics in the age of spectacle to her renewed attention to the details of literary texts through an emphasis on singularity (via Proust and Colette in particular).

Even Kristeva's recent work on the "radical evil" inherent to terrorist attacks and on why male adolescents are particularly vulnerable to its pull began "on the couch" in the 1980s. It was then that she began regular analytic sessions with adolescent patients through the Experimental School of Bonneuil, a therapeutic school for teenagers in trouble founded by Maud Mannoni in 1969. As Kristeva listened to young people at the school, she became fascinated by the specific psychic structure of adolescence, one that could persist into adulthood and lead to what she even then called "a disease of ideality"—a concept that she would go on to develop in the 2000s.

As her psychoanalytic practice deepened over the years, Kristeva became more aware of how what she hears on the couch enters into dialogue with the ideas she is trying to write about. Kristeva's experience during the 1980s with psychoanalytic listening and analytic temporality propelled her directly to the question of intersubjectivity. This focus was simultaneously supported by her experience as a mother. The question of intersubjectivity, of the "implicated subject," that rises in the context of psychoanalytic transference soon led her to the most archaic of intersubjective relationships, the mother and child. This archaic state of subjectivity became central to her writing as she focused on abjection or love or depression, never again leaving herself out of the equation.

Questions of Civilization Cannot
Be Managed by Politics

Kristeva has argued that her focus on the history and modalities of love, on the new kinds of depression that she was hearing about from her patients, on foreignness—whether in the context of foreigners, against foreigners, or the foreignness inside oneself—led her to believe even more fervently that her turn away from politics after her return from China in 1974 had been the right thing to do. She decided that it would henceforth be *ethical* topics that would hold the most political resonance for her:

> In my innermost self, I was more preoccupied by subjective questions than by the political effects of those questions. Ever since I had returned from China, I had felt that political discourse was increasingly foreclosed, that politics was becoming a question of management, of what Hannah Arendt called "engineering." Human rights, the rule of law to resolve human problems, had to be pursued and protected of course . . . but I decided that henceforth I wanted to pursue ethical questions rather than political ones.

Or as Kristeva puts it in *Traveling Through Myself*: "There is no politics of psychoanalysis. In this third millennium, we psychoanalysts are the security guards for psychic space, and our responsibility is to explore its logics, to favor its metamorphoses and to warn about—and care for—its catastrophes."[10]

Powers of Horror (1980)

The first catastrophe Kristeva tackled was fascism and the psychic mechanism she found at its core: *abjection*. The first part of her 1980 *Powers of Horror: An Essay on Abjection* is an anthropological and historical reflection on the question of the abject in Western religious and philosophical texts—a long journey which is then combined with a Freudian analysis of the mother-infant relationship.[11] Kristeva examines abjection as a state of being that characterizes both infancy and "borderline personality" (which is neither neurotic nor psychotic). In abjection, the boundary between subject and object is unstable, with the result that the subject (or emerging subject) is defensively drawn to clarity, purity, identity, and definition, which in turn means that it is obsessively fearful of what it experiences as unclear, impure, other, mixed, unclean, or foreign—and, at the same time, maternal.[12] In the adult, this state echoes and reproduces the pre-Oedipal stage of the structuring of the individual, before the self is stabilized. And it is against this state of structural uncertainty that religion has historically offered at least a partial respite. Kristeva traces both the desire and the rites invented for the purification of the impure and mixed through the history of Judeo-Christianity. Across the history of religions, there are many different kinds of rites of purification. Kristeva catalogues these with an emphasis on alimentary restrictions and teachings about cleanliness, particularly with regard to the "stains" of women.

The second part of the book relates the concept of abjection to the texts of Céline and, more generally, to the politics of fascism. As I have emphasized, Kristeva drew the link between Céline and fascism already in 1975. In *Powers of Horror*, she was particularly interested in the fact that so many Europeans had been fascinated by the "radical," "emotive," and "tribal" sides of fascism, by the violent, emotional tug of the fascist promise to "fix" what was "infiltrating," "soiling," and rendering "sick" the seemingly "worn out" and "soft" democracies of the time.

Kristeva was becoming fairly overwhelmed by what she was finding when the word *abjection* came to her in a dream, perhaps because of the anxiety pervading her situation with David. It was not until she saw her analyst Ilse Barande the next day that it hit her that the word was much more than personal. In *Traveling Through Myself* she recalls the moment as follows:

> When on Ilse Barande's couch, I spoke of the joys and miseries of maternity: Am I subject or object? Empathy or rejection? Dependent and/or autonomous? On my couch, one of my patients confided

that she had dreamed about a scene in Céline's *Le Pont de Londres*
[*London Bridge*]: violent pitching, horrible "seasickness" [*mal de mer*],
mother and son clinging to each other, vomiting. I awoke with this
word: *abjection*. "It is what you are living as well, in a way," my analyst
commented.[13]

She returns to the same moment in her 2017 interview:

I remember that my mother was in France, taking care of David who
was cutting teeth and not sleeping at night—nor was I of course.
I'm on Ilse Barande's couch: "I just don't know how I'm going to
manage all of it—the baby, my mother, and this Céline with his *Voyage
au bout de la nuit*—unbelievable! . . . nothing but massacres, horror,
abjection!" My analyst says, "That's the word."[14]

Kristeva began to think about Céline as a particular kind of fragile
subject, one who was psychically confronted by a maternal body that
was both fascinating and revolting. She returned in detail via Freud
and Klein to the fragility of the earliest mother-infant connection—
where there is no subject, no object, just attraction and rejection—and
postulated that the adult ramifications of this inter- and intra-subjective
dynamic are made palpable by Céline's use of language. This in-between
state that pulls us in through fascination but then makes us want to spit
it out can become frightening. In the adult subject, it can lead to the
kind of defensiveness that I described above: the desire to no longer
live "at the border" but to retreat within, to defend oneself (and those
like oneself), and to exile (when not eradicate) the scapegoat seen as
causing the invasion of impurity.

Kristeva finds this dynamic at the root of Céline's antisemitism:
Céline "loves" Jews but also "loathes" them, thereby illustrating an
instability between self and other that is found at the core of all racism.
This is an identity catastrophe that can lead to acting out in reality if
not dealt with. What Kristeva most worries about is that those who
see phenomena like racism, misogyny, antisemitism, xenophobia, and
so on as *purely* social phenomena might think that through "[legal]
repression, or censorship, or through a sort of Protestant veil just

thrown over these phenomena, or simply through a cry of moral revolt, one can get rid of these phenomena. That is not at all my point of view."[15]

By the 1980s, Kristeva's point of view was solidly psychoanalytic, and in September 1982, she published an article in the American journal, *Critical Inquiry*, "Psychoanalysis and the Polis," where she tried to make her case to an English-speaking audience.[16] The article was published exactly a year after Lacan's death, and in it, she concisely laid out her argument that it is psychoanalytic theory that can provide the most powerful political insights. She also expressed her fear that American academic discourse might not be up to the task insofar as it seems only "to absorb, digest, and neutralize all of the key, radical, or dramatic moments of thought, particularly, a fortiori, of contemporary thought"—especially psychoanalysis. She argued strongly that psychoanalytic thought is more effective than political thought when trying to understand history.

Tales of Love (1983)

The psychoanalytic imperative runs through Kristeva's next four books as she dwells on various states of subjective fragility—even subjective catastrophe—as well as on the historical attempts to put these extreme states into words. She began with love, making the large claim that all stories come down to talking about love in the end. She set out to trace the various meanings of love across time and space, through multiple kinds of discourses and institutions. Her *Tales of Love* did receive a lot of recognition.[17] Soon after its publication, she was invited for the first time to appear on the well-known television show, *Apostrophes*, by Bernard Pivot who—having also invited several more predictable male authors for a special episode called "Lovers of Love"—singled out her and her book for the kind of utmost respect and deference that was unusual for him.

In *Tales of Love*, Kristeva elaborates on what Freud says about love and on what psychoanalysis more generally says about topics such as

Eros, narcissism, transference, male and female sexuality, and so on with regard to love. However, the largest portion of the book is dedicated to a lengthy history of different kinds of love, which is in reality nothing less than a history of different models of subjectivity. In prose that wanders between clarity and opacity, Kristeva moves from Greek *eros*, Jewish *ahava*, and Christian *agape* through the various protagonists who emerge from them—Narcissus, the Virgin Mary, Don Juan, Romeo and Juliet—all the way to modern and postmodern versions of the imaginary state we call love in authors such as Baudelaire, Stendhal, and Bataille.

The loudest critique of the book, especially in the United States, revolved around Kristeva's emphasis on religion and its treatment of love through the ages. She found these critiques to be tone-deaf and ultimately of minor importance. As was the case with her work on abjection and fascism, Kristeva wanted to rethink the Western heritage on love because she fervently believed that students of society and culture would be unable to understand the stakes of what was happening to them and to society at large—let alone find solutions to their problems—if they did not have any understanding of history, and particularly of the history of religion.

In the Beginning Was Love (1985)

A lecture that Kristeva gave in 1984 at Sollers's Catholic secondary school Sainte-Geneviève, in Versailles, was the source of her small but powerful 1985 *In the Beginning Was Love: Psychoanalysis and Faith*.[18] In some ways, I would recommend this book first to readers new to Kristeva's thought because it is an accessible bridge between her early and later work. She reviews the psychoanalytic "scene" of analysis as a transferential, linguistic space that can only be described as a space of love. She argues that analysis is one of the few spaces—along with certain spaces of religious faith—where the positivist rationality of the other human sciences can be challenged and the illogical, irrational, even un-real can be entertained. She describes it as one of the few spaces that the modern social contract allows for suffering subjects to speak of what ails them: almost always the lack of the kind of love they need and want. It is a space where it is acceptable to fall apart and be put back together again.

Kristeva also begins to trace the ways in which the "illusions"— at times hallucinations—at the heart of religious experience are co-extensive with the analytic scene. Kristeva recounts one of her analysands' experience of faith in the analytic process and tells her own story of resistance to the Orthodox Christian narratives of faith in the Father, Son, and Mother Mary of her childhood. Almost as a preamble to her equally small, equally important 2007 *This Incredible Need to Believe*,[19] she takes the desire to believe in God as one example of the "need to believe," to put one's heart into something. Even as early as 1984, Kristeva, unlike Freud, did not claim that religion was merely an illusion. Instead, she was already trying to convince her reader that it was important not to frighten either the faithful or the atheists, but rather to show them that it was time to investigate how the history of Christianity has prepared the Western world for secular humanism. She proposed that the successful invention of new belief systems for the modern age—the kind of invention that would not provoke the reappearance of fundamentalist and/or totalitarian demands for a return to the past—depended on this investigation.

Kristeva told me a story about the day she gave her talk on love and faith at Sollers's Catholic secondary school. Given Sollers's deep Catholicism, and Kristeva's deeply ambivalent relationship to that religion, it was a big deal for her to accept to give such a potentially controversial talk. She finally accepted, but as they were driving to Versailles from Paris—a forty-five-minute trip that they had made many times—Sollers, who was driving, kept getting lost. Round and round they went, finally arriving at the school where the audience had been waiting patiently for over two hours. Kristeva nevertheless gave her talk and it was well received, so much so that afterward the head priest came up to her and offered his observation that she was not really an atheist: "What would you say if I told you that you are a mystic?" Knowing little about mysticism at the time, Kristeva was overwhelmed. She responded: "Monsieur, if you say so, I will accept it!" Sollers was proud. She was exhausted and could not get over the fact that her husband had done everything possible—unconsciously?—not to arrive at the school . . .

Why did she argue in the mid-1980s that it was time to rethink love? I would say that this had a lot to do with her experience as a mother, a suspicion reinforced by the fact that the chapter of *Tales of Love* that has had the most enduring influence was her 1977 essay "Stabat Mater." The title echoes the thirteenth-century Catholic hymn to Virgin Mary, and the essay was a startling text laid out on the page in two columns, one a theoretical text on the maternal as symbolized by the Virgin Mary, the other a poetic incantation of Kristeva's experience of giving birth to and loving David.

In later interviews and lectures about her early work on love, Kristeva invokes love as the ultimate crisis of the subject, as a kind of vertigo of identity, a vertigo of words, that is in danger of no longer having a language in the late postmodern West. She emphasizes that along with the welcome breakdown of old moral codes through hard-fought battles for human liberation (for women, for people of color, for LGBTQ folks, etc.), new ethical languages need to be invented sooner rather than later. Above all, she proposes that because secular humanism lacks a language with which to speak of maternal love, indeed lacks an ethics of maternal love, this is where we should start.

Black Sun (1987)

Kristeva's next book, *Black Sun: Depression and Melancholia*,[20] starts from the same premise as her books on love: there is a particular state of subjectivity that can be catastrophic and that is now, currently and urgently, part of a large social crisis that needs to be looked at carefully so as to avert its worst consequences. *Black Sun* analyzes depression and melancholia, especially as they are indicative of larger social issues. However, despite Kristeva's continued emphasis on fragile forms of subjectivity, the blueprint of *Black Sun* is different from that of *Tales of Love*: while Kristeva foregrounds historical manifestations of depression and melancholia, she discusses them as elaborated by particular writers and artists.

Psychoanalysis still provides *Black Sun*'s infrastructure, but it is less an etiological history of an idea than an archeology of depression as translated by the literary and artistic imagination. Psychoanalysis is still the primary lever of interpretation, but it is not the focal point. Instead, literature is the primary carrier of thoughts about depression. It is also celebrated as one of the ways in which depression can be socially and culturally sublimated. As Kristeva looks into the "abyss of sorrow," she finds Holbein and Nerval, Dostoevsky and Duras rather than Plato and Descartes or Kant.[21] Indeed, the literary example in the book that caused an uproar was Duras: at that point in time, Duras was the only woman writer that Kristeva had ever addressed, and some took issue with the fact that she did so only in order to emphasize the depression at the heart of Duras's work.

Strangers to Ourselves (1988)

Kristeva's 1988 *Strangers to Ourselves* incorporates almost all of her textual strategies from the 1980s.[22] The catastrophic state of subjectivity at the heart of this book is the state of being a foreigner, a stranger. This topic has always been more personal than theoretical for Kristeva. By the end of the 1980s, it was also deeply political. The personal as the political runs right through even her most abstract analyses of foreignness. Over the years, she has alternated between evoking, on the one hand, the terrible negativity one can experience from being "too much," from being a strange foreigner, from not being accepted and, on the other hand, what one can accomplish with the liberating creativity derived from existing in this state.

On the negative side, Kristeva has said in many different ways that it is the way in which the French look at her that makes her feel unaccepted.

Sometimes she gets the feeling that the French are not interested in what she has to say. She tends to shrug this off. But the visceral attacks always take her by surprise.[23] In *Traveling Through Myself*, Kristeva evoked with unusual candor the extent to which the French have delighted in attacking her as an immigrant from Bulgaria: "Why is it in France that xenophobia takes this form of a mocking hatred, a foolish egotism supposedly all innocent."[24] She marvels at the viciousness of the attacks against her as an intellectual. Yet she also recognizes the freedom that her foreign status has given her and acknowledges that it was in part Sollers who helped her see this positive side.[25]

Very early in her Parisian life with Sollers, Kristeva adopted the attitude that if one was to think, one could not belong—that to *really* think, one needed to exile oneself. And as late as June 22, 2015, in a speech she gave in the context of accepting the prestigious Mondi Migranti Prize in Italy, she continued to evoke the complexity and urgency of the problem: "Foreigner: a strangled rage deep in my throat, a black angel troubling transparency, opaque trace, unfathomable."[26] Standing before an auditorium filled with those dedicated to coming to the aid of migrants, immigrants, and refugees in our own xenophobic moment, she argued that foreignness is the hidden face of our own identity and that it is only when we can learn to recognize it in ourselves that can we stop scapegoating others.

Strangers to Ourselves is structured like *Tales of Love*: it is primarily a history of the idea of foreignness/strangeness. Kristeva begins with the Greeks—in particular with women, the Danaïdes—as the first foreigners in the West. From there she moves through wandering Jews and crusading Christians to the European Renaissance, the horrors of the beginnings of colonialism, and what she sees as the bright spots of the cosmopolitan European Enlightenment. It is with the solidification of the nation state at the end of the eighteenth century that she begins her more theoretical ruminations on foreignness, always keeping in mind the totalitarian dangers of the concept of "nation"—dangers that erupted during the twentieth century. She wrestles with the question of human rights and universalism, as well as with her sense that it is precisely the "nation" that must be rethought without falling into the cult of origins which, for her, is always about hatred. Kristeva notes that this hatred all too easily becomes defensive, initiates a desperate search for a scapegoat, and fuels anger at one's neighbors, perhaps even at those suffering from the same tyrants or economic situations.

These thoughts on foreignness and strangeness will deepen and expand over the next three decades, as Kristeva keeps elaborating ever more precisely on the basic insight of her 1988 book. In a nutshell, toward the end of the volume, she states:

> The foreigner is a "symptom" . . . psychologically he signifies the difficulty we have of living as an *other* and with others; politically, he underscores the limits of nation-states and of the national political conscience that characterizes them and that we have all deeply interiorized to the point of considering it normal that there are foreigners, that is, people who do not have the same rights as we do.[27]

In this context, Kristeva alighted upon the project of redefining and transfiguring universality. Taking into account Freud's discovery of the unconscious—the uncanny foreignness inside of all of us that psychoanalysis investigates—she puts the matter as follows:

> With Freud indeed, foreignness, an uncanny one, creeps into the tranquility of reason itself, and, without being restricted to madness, beauty, or faith any more than to ethnicity or race, irrigates our very speaking-being, estranged by other logics, including the heterogeneity of biology . . . Henceforth, we know that we are foreigners to ourselves, and it is with the help of that sole support that we can attempt to live with others.[28]

Essentially, Kristeva believes that the hatred of others ultimately always amounts to a hatred of oneself.

Kristeva wrote most of *Strangers to Ourselves* on the Île de Ré because that is where she feels most at home.[29] She switched publishing houses, publishing her book on foreignness at Éditions Fayard, where the editor, Claude Durand, had captured both her and Sollers's admiration in the early days of *Tel Quel* at Seuil as the editor in France who had the courage to publish Aleksandr Solzhenitsyn's *The Gulag Archipelago*, García Márquez's *One Hundred Years of Solitude*, and many other "foreign outsiders." In Kristeva's view, Durand was waging a battle to save the Book, to rescue the act of reading, in combat against what both Kristeva and Sollers had diagnosed for years as a new form of digitally based totalitarian culture intent on destroying the practices of reading and writing . . . and hence of thinking. Durand enthusiastically embraced Kristeva's book on foreigners in 1988, encouraged her fiction writing in the 1990s, and remained her loyal editor and defender until his death on May 7, 2015. With regard to his death, Kristeva states: "His brutal death really left me orphaned. I think of it as the third major loss that I have lived through, after the deaths of my parents . . . Today, without him, I don't feel capable of finding the strength to publish a new novel, or even a new book."[30]

She did of course find the strength . . .

And Yet, It's up to Women . . .

Even taking into account Kristeva's resistance to identity-based politics, I tend to agree with Kelly Oliver that in order to see the political efficacy of Kristeva's work, one must accept her emphasis on an ethics grounded not only in psychoanalysis, in the placement of strangeness at the heart of identity, but also on an ethics grounded in maternal practice. Oliver explains:

> Maternity provides a fundamental metaphor for an ethics through which we can love the other in/as ourselves. Psychoanalysis provides a fundamental metaphor through which we can accept the stranger in/as ourselves. Both of these metaphors serve the same function. The ethics of psychoanalysis is born out of "herethics," and neither this ethics nor the politics it implies is enforced by an exterior paternal Law.[31]

By 1993, Kristeva herself expresses this idea even more directly: it may be up to women to lead us out of the historical crisis we are in.[32]

The strongest compliment Kristeva can give anyone—especially a woman—is that they are a fighter—*une battante*. In part this is because she herself is a fighter. But it is also because of the new ethics she calls for, an ethical movement led by women. I think that the search for such an ethics was perhaps the beginning of a turning point for the philosopher who never wrote about women. I say this because the same year that Kristeva published *Strangers to Ourselves*, 1988, she also published a little-known introductory essay on the American painter, Georgia O'Keeffe, for the catalogue for the 1987 O'Keeffe exposition at the National Gallery of Art.[33] The essay is a celebration of O'Keeffe's vision, of her independence, of her insistence on building her own community, of not following the rules, and of her ability to maintain the energy of her artistic practice while coupled up with a demanding male artist (Alfred Stieglitz). In this essay, one can viscerally feel Kristeva's admiration of O'Keeffe and of her art. One can recognize in Kristeva's appreciation of O'Keeffe's sensuality, bisexuality, and courage the harbingers of the themes that were, a decade later, to become central when she began her trilogy on female genius. Reading the essay on O'Keeffe today, one almost feels like Kristeva could have skipped several of her books in the 1990s and gone straight to Hannah Arendt, Melanie Klein, and Colette.

But something awful happened.

If You Could Just Die . . .

Ever since she could remember, Kristeva's father had suffered from terrible ulcer pains, especially at night. He could not sleep and had to be very careful about what he ate. When Kristeva was in Sofia in January 1989 as part of President Mitterrand's delegation, she asked her father pointedly if the ulcer was still bothering him. He told her not to worry, that he was being treated, that he was fine. Later that year, in September, when his ulcer formed a scar that blocked his intestine, he wrote and told his daughter that he was going to have a simple, inexpensive operation. It was just a matter of re-opening the scar and sewing it closed again properly. Kristeva was terribly worried and asked him if he wanted to come to Paris for the surgery. He reassured her and said no, absolutely not. It would be too expensive and, besides, it was really a very simple procedure.

The reality was that the communist regime in Bulgaria at the time was in a fiscal mess and the medical system was one of the first public services to suffer. Resources to train physicians were uneven and the government began recruiting doctors trained in other contexts. As Kristeva has recounted it many times, Stoyan Kristev was assigned a surgeon who had been doing risky experiments on the elderly. Considered to be expendable because of his age, Kristeva's father became the victim of a horrifying, corrupt-to-the-bone medical system that condoned such things in the name of "the greater good." The surgeon decided to "experiment" by cutting out the part of the intestine that was affected by the scar and grafting there a piece of intestinal wall from elsewhere. Whether through medical error or intentional malice, the results were devastating.

By the time Kristeva received an alarming telegram from her mother, the situation was dire. A raging infection had set in. Stoyan Kristev was in isolation, unable to see anyone, not even his wife, "for fear of microbes." Kristeva kept sending telegrams saying she was working on getting him to France. She wondered if her parents even got them. (Sadly, we now know that they did not because all of her letters and telegrams were being intercepted by the Bulgarian Secret Service.) Kristeva became increasingly alarmed and called Mitterrand at the Élysée Palace. He remembered well meeting her distinguished father in January and said that they would try to get him to France. But Bulgaria had to give permission. After herculean efforts, the surgeon himself said no: "But madame! Socialist medicine is performing miracles!"

Stoyan Kristev died alone two days later.[34]

In November, the Berlin Wall fell.

Barely able to hold herself together, Kristeva began the process of trying to get to Bulgaria. Alongside her intolerable grief, she was genuinely terrified. Because she had stayed in France, she worried that she might be arrested upon returning to Bulgaria. As had happened to others, she might be detained until she had "paid back her education." She was a French citizen by marriage, but the Bulgarian embassy advised her to get a Bulgarian passport to "show that she still had esteem for her country of birth." She took both her French and Bulgarian passports with her and got on a plane, but the plane was re-routed because the airport in Sofia was closed. She landed at the last possible airport in Yugoslavia before crossing the Bulgarian border. Thankfully, Mitterrand had arranged for officers stationed at the French embassy in Yugoslavia to pick her up.

When Kristeva got to the hospital, all she could do was to comfort her mother and sister. But she soon had another battle to fight. As a devout Orthodox Christian, Stoyan Kristev had wished to be buried in a local cemetery with a Christian service. But he was not allowed to be buried in a grave, because graves—the distraught Kristeva was informed—were only available to members of the Communist Party in order to avoid religious processions. The official in charge of grave sites coldly stated: "If you could just die . . . since you are famous . . . we could bury your father with you." The bureaucrat added that, as a bonus, they might even be able to throw her husband in with her and her father.

For Kristeva, these words and the detached look on the face of the bureaucratic apparatchik uttering them have come to epitomize communism before the fall of the Berlin Wall. She tried everything she could think of to buy a grave. She offered to pay in (strong) dollars. She begged friends in Sofia for help. But while she was doing so, the bureaucrats simply went ahead and cremated her father—against the wishes of him and his family. This was a violent shock for Kristeva. She could not even cry in the moment. She was enraged and pierced through by sadness and, worst of all, by a sense of guilt that she had been unable to prevent what for her father was a sacrilege.

In Kristeva's mind, this was the ultimate crime. She has never recovered from her sense of helplessness and outrage in relation to the evil that she encountered in the midst of her grief. Despite the bureaucratic prohibition, she and her family and friends gathered at the cemetery for a religious ceremony, thereby putting themselves at risk for arrest. But the ceremony did not offer much comfort to Kristeva or her family, in part because the urn containing her father's ashes had been placed in a dirty, rundown crematorium situated by a stream that stank of chemical pollution. She and her family managed to install a small piece of marble with the urn. There they inscribed her father's name, a Christian cross, and a photo. Every year since, they have had to replace the marble because it is inevitably sold by the poor who live near the polluted stream. She might be able to replace it now, so many decades later, but the obstacles are still daunting.

As I have mentioned, even today, in her late seventies, Kristeva wakes up every night at 2 a.m.—the hour she associates with her father's murder—with a bit of insomnia.[35] In this way, Kristeva is daily reminded of the horrible days that preceded only by two months the fall of the Berlin Wall in November 1989. Just like her father's death, "no one foresaw either its rapidity or its consequences."[36] For Kristeva, the two events are forever linked: a before and an after that can never be separated.

2. The 1990s: Revolt, She Said

Kristeva has never stopped believing in the kind of strong thinking that is needed to trace the historical links between intellectual movements and political moments, especially when the two seem unrelated. For example, as I have emphasized, for her the popularity of semiotics in Eastern Europe and the Soviet Union from the 1960s through the 1980s was a sign of revolt against the mindset of Stalinist social realism, even if there was still no way to foresee the fall of the Berlin Wall.[37] She has written about how even during her visit to Sofia in January 1989, it was not yet entirely clear what was going to happen. But there were signs:

> No one imagined that the Wall was going to fall. We knew that the system was rotting, festering and crumbling, but it seemed like it would take years. Retrospectively, one can see that the situation was already "ripe." We certainly had to speak with dissidents only in the semi-clandestine cafés in the very early mornings. But we did manage to meet with them. I also remember a gathering organized at the University of Sofia. In the grand amphitheater, François Mitterrand and Todor Zhivkov were supposed to debate with students. Only communist students were invited, but many others got in. One young man asked Mitterrand what he thought of countries where dictators stayed in power against the will of the people. These were embarrassing questions for Mitterrand, given how obvious was the allusion to Zhivkov. He responded: "In certain circumstances, it is more important to ask a question than to get a response." And it's true that the audacity of this young man was a sign that a complete overthrow was being prepared.[38]

Nine months later, in September 1989, when Kristeva returned to Sofia in grief, she was stupefied by the change:

> Well, in contrast, in September 1989, I didn't recognize my country anymore. Awful lines wound around in front of the stores. I remember waiting two hours to buy cherries for my mother. In vain. But besides the economic crisis, I was struck by the violence [that had taken over] human relationships. I didn't recognize this new hard, brutal language full of insults that exasperated people were throwing in the faces of others . . . Like wolves, literally.[39]

This strange new world would consolidate during the 1990s. In short, Bulgaria found the transition to capitalism extremely painful. Anticommunist groups privatized everything fast, starting with agricultural land, and these efforts—combined with uneven modernization inherited from communist rule—fueled massive unemployment and dislocation. The dismantlement of the Communist

Party and its State Security Apparatus was a great relief to most Bulgarians, but the rapidity of its demise and the lack of any kind of organized police force or justice system contributed to a level of criminality never before seen in Bulgaria. Mass stealing of capital, machinery, materials, and even furniture led to the collapse of one industry after the other. Bulgaria was on the verge of becoming what we now call a mafia state.

Meanwhile, on the Western side of the crumbled Iron Curtain, a paradigm shift was also the order of the day even as a fragile but loud resistance thrived. For example, Kristeva has more than once posited that the popularity of postwar French thought in American and British universities from the 1960s through the 1980s was linked to a growing discontent among intellectuals and students with the increasingly dominant socioeconomic order we now call capitalist neoliberalism. For this reason, French poststructuralists—including their interlocutors working in Marxist, psychoanalytic, semiotic, feminist, queer, and race theory—were deemed by neoliberal intellectual foot soldiers to be devils in disguise.[40]

In this troubling context, Kristeva began thinking more deeply about "radical evil," which for her—as she became more and more shocked by new genocides and began reading Hannah Arendt—represented a condition that declares some humans expendable, thereby allowing what Freud called the "death drive" (*Thanatos*) to take over. Her mounting focus on the death drive was, unfortunately, increasingly prescient as the decade progressed.

Accolades and Accusations

It was during the 1990s that Kristeva became a public intellectual of international importance. She did not, however, experience herself that way. She was absorbed by her disciplined writing every day (the 1990s produced thirteen books). She was seeing patients most days.[41] She was also teaching full time. In 1992, she was named Director of the Doctoral Program in Language, Literature, and Image at the University of Paris 7. But she did not only teach in Paris. She was also a Permanent Visiting Professor of Comparative Literature at the University of Toronto, traveling back and forth through the entire decade. She also occasionally taught at several American campuses, including Georgetown. In addition, she was traveling at an ever-faster pace—among other places, to England, Germany, Italy, and Spain—to give lectures and receive prizes.

She was running her small household now on rue d'Assas—no simple task. Mostly she was busy with David who, on the one hand, was a fairly typical, demanding adolescent but, on the other, was also a severely handicapped young man who needed physical care around the clock and even more importantly, the loving guidance of his parents as he tried to build a social life for himself in an inhospitable world.[42] Sollers was writing full-time, rarely leaving his office. In part to keep the three of them together at the table for at least one meal a day, Kristeva was developing her love of cooking. She specifies that she did not cook "as well as Colette." Nevertheless she created delicious dishes that she still today cooks for her family and friends. She states, "I think of Colette and her language for eating . . . I love to cook, but I rarely have time: ginger salmon, pork with pineapple, veal stew, veal head, veal tongue . . . it takes time! Colette eats words . . . she 'cooks' with the taste of words . . . it's never as tasty as when she writes it. Me? Well . . ."

Kristeva also spent significant time and energy mourning and honoring many of her contemporaries who died of old age—or committed suicide—in the 1990s: in 1992, Félix Guattari died of a heart attack; in 1993, Yuri Lotman passed away of old age; in 1994, Guy Debord shot himself (some have said because he felt that our society of spectacle was out of control); in 1994, Sarah Kofman committed suicide on Nietzsche's birthday; in 1995, Gilles Deleuze jumped out of a window; and in 1998, Jean-François Lyotard succumbed to leukemia. The intellectual loss of these strong thinkers seemed to reinforce the feeling that a certain era of intellectual history was ending.

On the one hand, Kristeva's work was being increasingly engaged with and honored. In 1991, she was named Chevalier de l'Ordre National de Mérite; in 1997, Chevalier de la Légion d'Honneur; and in 1998, Member of the American Academy of Arts and Letters. She was awarded honorary doctorates from Western Ontario University (1995), Victoria University in the University of Toronto (1997), and Harvard (1999). Her essays were being collected and translated and entire books were beginning to be devoted to her work, especially in English.[43]

On the other hand, the first loud and brutal attacks against poststructuralist thought in general and Kristeva's work in particular were coming in loud and clear. The most notorious among them came to be known as the Sokal Affair. In 1997, two science professors, Alan Sokal of New York University and Jean Bricmont of the Catholic University of Louvain, as part of a larger tirade against postwar French thought, published *Fashionable Nonsense: Postmodern Intellectuals' Abuse of Science*, in which they accused a whole list of postwar French thinkers of intellectual fraud because of their "misuse of mathematics."[44] Their attack against Kristeva was particularly insulting and demeaning: she was genuinely shocked by the level of verbal violence they hurled at her. She responded in an even-tempered voice that did not reveal the depth of her distress. In an article in *Le Nouvel Observateur*, she explained with an annoyed patience that "the human sciences and especially the interpretation of literary texts, as well as psychoanalytic interpretation, do not obey only the logic of the exact sciences."[45]

New Directions: Fiction and Revolt

As the 1990s version of the postmodern era began to sink in, Kristeva's writing took two radically new turns: 1) toward writing fiction and 2) toward adjusting her psychoanalytic ear directly to political traumas in order to suggest a way out.

Deciding to write novels was risky. An argument that Kristeva used with herself to justify taking the risk was that she had been raised on the French novel, especially the eighteenth-century French novel: she had internalized a way to "think in novel form," much like Rousseau, Voltaire, and Diderot. Her decision to use psychoanalysis to think about political trauma, in turn, led her to a new way of thinking about revolt. In the years between her 1974 *Revolution in Poetic Language* and her 1996 *The Sense and Non-Sense of Revolt*, she had changed her primary tools of interpretation from those in linguistics to those in psychoanalytic theory. However, during those years, it was the political trauma of Bulgaria that irrevocably moved her: her whole world shifted. *The* wall had fallen; *the* revolution had failed. The word *revolution* itself had become trivialized: the focus of dark comedy or slapstick. Yet something else—something immensely significant—had also happened: the people of her country and of other countries in communist Europe had *revolted* in 1989; they had revolted against the revolution.[46]

I have divided Kristeva's books from the 1990s into four categories and will try to provide a few brief insights into each grouping: 1) her three novels and a long, dreamy, and novelistic treatise on Proust; 2) her four books diagnosing new maladies of the soul that require a new theory of revolt; 3) two short books and a museum catalogue consisting mostly of popular explanations of the new status of citizen-subjects (while revealing Kristeva's own new status as an emerging public intellectual); and 4) two books where she returns to questions of maternity, women, and woman—ultimately to *a singular woman genius* named Hannah Arendt.

Thinking Through the Novel

In retrospect, Kristeva has most often attributed her turn to writing fiction to the shock of her father's murder, even if this was only the most shattering of the reasons. Other reasons, both internal and external, include her analysis, the birth of David and the discovery of his disability, the intense intellectual questioning of the relationship between fiction and theory by such writers as Jacques Derrida, and the fall of the Berlin Wall. Kristeva's choice to write novels started out as an overwhelming desire and only began to make sense to her years later. Over the years, she has elaborated at great length on how she was drawn to the vertical time of fiction writing, including its similarities to the time of analysis as anamnesis; she appreciated fiction's ability to "touch time," even the vertical time of "the cosmos."

Kristeva has also always seen fiction as a space of revolt, as a way to "truthfully lie," and as a way to reconnect with the maternal in language. She has spoken of her love of dreamlike states where the self disappears and another way of thinking—a state of "anti-thinking"—comes to the fore. She has insisted that she was not drawn to writing straightforward autobiography or autofiction, but rather to the process of transposition required by the novel form. She has emphasized her status as a kaleidoscopic subject, and especially as someone divided between at least two cultures, two sensibilities: "I am made of this Orthodox sensibility, and if I discipline it in the daytime, I am submerged in it at night: my unconscious is an Orthodox land enveloped by a French atmosphere."[47]

Critics and reviewers were not kind to Kristeva in the early days of her fiction writing. As elaborated by Benigno Trigo in 2013, in the first serious collection of essays considering Kristeva's fiction, popular reviewers were the most brutal, while academic reviewers were more civil, even if their assessments were mixed.[48] The former found her writing "boring"; the latter found it either "fascinating" in relationship to her theory or "conservative" in relationship to her politics. Some argued that the hostility Kristeva encountered in the popular press was really directed against Sollers (Kristeva and Sollers decided that this meant that all was going well).[49] Kristeva's defenders argued that she had folded philosophy and serious thinking into her narratives, thereby making them as difficult to read as, say, the earlier "New Novel" (Trigo); yet others saw her fiction as an undoing of her formal thought (Nikolchina). Kristeva took in the nevertheless mostly negative critiques, suffered at their violence, and kept writing: "The 'literary world' disgusts me, and I hear the bluntness of that remark, but why retract it? I will never be part of that world, and it doesn't want me either."[50]

The Samurai (1990)

Kristeva's first novel, *The Samurai*, was a fictional rendering of her early years in Paris starting with her arrival in the city in 1965.[51] The novel links together the lives of three women—Olga Morena, Carole Benedetti, and Joelle Cabarus—from the "revolution" of 1968 to the end of the 1980s. Olga (a graduate student from the Eastern bloc, only lightly disguised) and Joelle (a psychoanalyst, also lightly disguised) live through turbulent times, intellectual revolutions, and lots of men. Olga and Hervé (a French novelist, lightly disguised) are the couple at the center of the novel as Olga finds love and eroticism, the pleasures of the seaside in a place very much like Île de Ré, the affections of an adopted family, and the intellectual excitement of post-1968 France.

The Samurai reintroduces 1968 smack dab into the middle of 1990, painting a social fresco of the inventive, radical intellectual world at that earlier moment in Paris in counterpart to the depressingly anti-intellectual worries of the early 1990s. Part of the fun of reading the novel for the first time is the challenge of deciphering who is who—lightly disguised. Brehal (Barthes), Strich-Meyer (Lévi-Strauss), Lauzun (Lacan), etc. populate the fresco in the style of a *roman à clef*, never leaving behind Olga and her almost picaresque adventures in Paris, Île de Ré, China, and New York.

The most interesting reading of the novel that I have seen is that of Trigo, who points out that most academic critics like this of Kristeva's novels the least because its symbolic matricide vis-à-vis Simone de Beauvoir is so obvious that it does not need interpreting by critics. That is, Trigo argues that *The Samurai* grabs the place of Beauvoir's 1954 *roman à clef, The Mandarins*, a novel about her and Sartre's generation in Paris after World War II.[52] Trigo puts forward the rather audacious hypothesis that Kristeva defends her authorial voice from inquiries into the unconscious of the text, thereby refusing to make of it a laboratory for critical reflection. He suggests that this may be because the matricide that the text enacts was necessary for Kristeva's ability to really begin writing. Be that as it may, matricide was, for Kristeva, at that point slowly becoming a key concept situated at the heart of patriarchy, and she places it even more overtly—albeit more complexly—at the heart of her novels to follow.

Whatever one thinks about Trigo's theory of *The Samurai*, it would be fascinating to look closer at the only character in the novel who remains completely unidentified, anonymous, and secret—Olga's secret lover in New York, Ed Dalloway—in comparison to Beauvoir's acknowledged lover in the United States, Nelson Algren. In my reading, the entirely disguised Dalloway conforms to a typical, almost stereotypical model of 1990s American masculinity. Kristeva renders him invisible, unnamed, and left behind.[53] Dalloway is a far cry from the down-and-out real poet and novelist, Nelson Algren, who remained central to Beauvoir's public fantasy life for the rest of her days.

The Old Man and the Wolves (1991)

After exploring the *roman à clef*, Kristeva's next two novels, written in the direct aftermath of her father's death, attempted to form a new genre: that of a "metaphysical murder mystery." I found the first one, her 1991 *The Old Man and the Wolves*, excruciating to read.[54] It is about her father's murder, and because I know Kristeva personally, perhaps the raw autobiographical voice in it was too loud for me. But I suspect that any reader who has ever experienced—or who is able to imagine—the murder of a loved one in a sociopolitical situation that seems beyond redemption would have the same reaction. It is a book of rage, of helpless indignation at the wanton cruelty and corruption of the world. Kristeva wrote it right after her father's absurd death as she struggled to grieve and continue her work once she was back in Paris. She has called the novel the record of her internal *coup d'état*.

The novel is divided into three parts: The Invasion, Detective Story, and Capriccio.⁵⁵ In short, an old man, a former classics professor, named Septicius Clarus (Kristeva's father, lightly disguised) lives in a country, Santa Varvara (Bulgaria, lightly disguised), that is being overtaken by wolves. The wolves are relentless, gruesomely devouring thousands of citizens while other citizens, to escape the wolves' violence, become wolves themselves. Everyone tries to ignore, deny, or "spin" the wolves' presence. The increasingly mimetic, monster-making violence spreads even into the deeply intimate recesses of a formerly loving couple, Vespasian and Alba, without them realizing it. Into this desperate situation arrives a French detective-reporter named Stephanie Delacour, the daughter of the French ambassador to this strange country. She begins to try to make sense of what is happening, what has happened, and what is going to happen in a whirlwind of philosophical questioning.

The old man, Septicius, ultimately dies. But before he does, he contemplates the end of civilization, evoking terrifying images borrowed from Ovid (who once wrote on the banks of the Black Sea now overrun by the Eastern mafia). Septicius rails against "the charlatanism of the scientists and intellectuals," "the venality of the lawyers," and "the vanity and frivolity of the ruling classes." He exclaims: "*These are the men who devour us. And what big teeth they've got!*"⁵⁶ Stephanie Delacour's father also dies, and her grief at her father's death intermingles with the brutal images of torture and death evoked by Septicius in a crescendo of ferocious rage. I was particularly struck by the rage expressed in the novel against "the ordinary," described as the lowest form of human arrangement that produces—or at least condones—oblivious savagery among the masses.⁵⁷

Alas, you cannot win against ordinariness:

Lousy old ordinariness. A permanent waste product of the everyday, of which people are ashamed though at the same time they secretly enjoy it. But is it as secretly as all that? The secrecy of the ordinary is a kind of psychological dirt: the psychological as unconscious excretion. Soil your neighbor as you soil yourself; don't fight; don't have aspirations;

don't breathe; shrink, be sly, be vengeful, wear a mask, be realistic—
you know what illusions lead to.

But is savagery really any more harmless when it's ordinary?
"There's no solution," thought the Old Man. But he went on pursuing
his visions. Septicius Clarus was no ordinary pessimist.[58]

This is indeed a metaphysical murder mystery: a philosophical
detective novel about evil, where Kristeva wants to inscribe the
traumas of a given time and place as both internal and external. It
connects the dots between religion, totalitarianism, and the loss of
freedom, conveying the impossibility within this nexus of forces of
finding justice, of finding the guilty parties, for they are disseminated
throughout society and devoid of any accountability. Kristeva wishes to
show the relationships between psychic and political traumas.

Critics were not all convinced, but even one of the harshest critics
of Kristeva's fiction, Michael Wood, admitted that Kristeva's prose
becomes incandescent when Stephanie Delacour's unbearable grief at
her father's death is connected to the deathly crisis of the strange Santa
Varvara that Stephanie no longer recognizes.[59]

Possessions (1996)

Stephanie Delacour returns in Kristeva's second and her (and my)
favorite metaphysical murder mystery, *Possessions*.[60] This novel,
published in the thick of right-wing consolidation in France, was in
part inspired by the National Front's call for, and the French public's
growing support of, the reinstatement of the death penalty in France,
which inevitably evoked symbolic echoes of the French guillotine.
Kristeva found this development deeply disturbing. Her distress was
mostly about what she sees as the social contagion of the death drive,
of the "killer instinct," especially when it comes to women. In the novel,
Stephanie Delacour's old friend, Gloria Harrison, is found brutally
decapitated in her Santa Varvara home and Stephanie reluctantly
returns to that city to try to find out who did it.

Stephanie is a detective in search of a void, for at the core of her pursuit of truth and accountability, there is a whirlwind of possibilities but no absolute certainty: there is a lacuna akin to the missing head of the now dead but formerly accomplished, independent, demanding, and beautiful Gloria. The reader accompanies Stephanie on an evocative journey among those who were most important to Gloria, especially Gloria's handicapped son. This journey eventually leads to the interrogation of multiple suspects. It appears that Gloria may have killed herself through an overdose, but she was probably also strangled by her lover, stabbed by a serial killer, and decapitated by another woman, Pauline Gaudeau, her son's speech therapist. Nothing is definitive in this search for truth except the ways in which some people possess other people, especially the way in which the speech therapist who works with Gloria's son is possessed by her love for him and by her resentment of his mother's insistence on having a life outside of motherhood, on not only reconciling her professional life with her love life but also both of these lives with her life as a mother. For Pauline, the embittered, traumatized, lonely speech therapist, this complexity is an impossibility that cannot be tolerated. The only truth in Stephanie's search for the truth is the realization that one can become possessed by love, by hatred, by resentment, or by anger. And there is of course the truth that if we are not careful in this circumstance, *Thanatos* will catch up with us.

Kristeva is the first to admit that in this second novel after her father's murder, she herself was still possessed by rage. She is also the first to admit that the decapitated woman, Gloria, and the detective-journalist, Stephanie, are different parts of her own psyche.[61] Kristeva felt "decapitated" by her father's murder, by the heartless and cruel social contract that she saw overtaking her beloved Bulgaria. She admits that as an intellectual woman, and as the daughter of an intellectual father, she felt decapitated and that her encounter with this manner of "putting to death" forced her ever more insistently to keep her head when serving as a witness to—and a detective examining—the murderous world she was living in.

Time and Sense (1994)

Kristeva's book on Proust, *Time and Sense: Proust and the Experience of Literature*, appeared between her two metaphysical murder mysteries.[62] It is obviously not a novel, but it is a bit of a literary experience both in terms of its subject matter (the nitty-gritty literary details of Proust's *In Search of Lost Time*) and its style (it is a long, flowing, and at times dreamy rumination that mirrors Proust's way of writing). Proust has been one of Kristeva's most important inspirations for her entire adult life. When Kristeva was twenty, Proust was her "go to" writer, the one always on her bedside table. This began a love and an interest that has continued to this day.[63] Here I will merely emphasize briefly what I think are the three most important aspects of this 1994 book for the English-speaking reader of Kristeva.

First, I agree with Miglena Nikolchina that this is Kristeva's *last* long rumination on the sexuality of artistic men. Though it is a summary of sorts, it is also definitely a turning point. For anyone who wants to understand Kristeva's overall theory of artistic masculinity in relationship to the mother, this is the book.[64]

Second, this book is Kristeva's *only* book-length rumination on trans-, inter-, bi-, and polysexuality. She approaches her topic from a theoretical perspective that may be unfamiliar to many Anglo-American readers, except perhaps ones who are well versed in poststructuralist, postcolonial, feminist, and queer theoretical critiques of identity politics (and the deconstruction of identity that tends to accompany such critiques). Although Kristeva acknowledges and supports homosexual identities—lesbians and gay men, for example—she does not see these identities as viable sites of revolt in the long term. Like much of contemporary queer theory—which frequently finds itself at odds with the ways in which mainstream LGBTQ activism rallies around nonnormative *identities*[65]—she values polymorphism over identity, disruption over acceptance, and subversion over settled law.[66] She stages an aesthetically driven political challenge against heterosexual hegemony which, instead of valorizing non-heterocentric identities, valorizes what disrupts psychic unity in order to reinvent identity.[67]

Kristeva has been clear over time that while she abhors the "macrocosmic" sociopolitical enforcements of homophobia, she is most interested in its psychic—"microcosmic"—causes. Although she explicitly supports LGBTQ issues politically, what she celebrates intellectually is polysexuality. The situation is comparable to her relationship to feminism: she supports women's rights yet simultaneously critiques the intellectual assumptions of mainstream feminism. *Yes, of course, but . . .*

Third, Kristeva's book on Proust is her *first* long rumination on time. She values Proust for his fight against the speed of the twentieth century.[68] Proust's writing (like psychoanalysis) is a way of restoring time to language, a way to journey away from the conscious mind toward our "inner wealth" and slowly give a language to the sensory. Kristeva sees Proust's writing—which represents an exemplary playing out of a polymorphous imaginary—as a form of resistance against no less than the speedy "eruptions of banality" overtaking us all.[69] For Kristeva, Proust's writing was a form of visionary resistance to the emerging society of technological efficiency and spectacle—an appeal to the imagination as an alternative to the political disasters about to descend on Europe and elsewhere. Perhaps it was even a form of resistance against death.[70] Hers is a *political* Proust also grappling with the *metaphysical* in a way that can be understood today: "A 'political' Proust in the complex sense of the word, torn apart by his Jewish, Christian, homosexual, 'committed' (in the Dreyfus Affair) identities, and whose worries resonate with the interrogations of identity happening today."[71]

The last four pages of Kristeva's book on her beloved Proust are entitled "Time for a Long Time." They enact a personal, melancholic embrace of prolonging childhood and sensation by delaying death and meaning—as Proust also did. This book perhaps needed to be written before Kristeva could move from her mourning toward a new witnessing of the world through strong thinking.

Revolt After the Revolution

The second group of books Kristeva published in the 1990s focuses on what she had diagnosed as the most urgent problem of the late twentieth century—the death of psychic space—and, more importantly, on the solution to this problem: revolt. For Kristeva, the novel has clearly always been a space of revolt, but by the mid-1990s she felt compelled to address more explicitly the broader question of what could possibly propel change "after the revolution" in a society of spectacle and psychic death—a society, in her view, on the precipice of returning to totalitarianism. If the Velvet Revolutions—the revolts against the communist revolution in Eastern Europe—were the spark of this new direction in Kristeva's thinking, her rising concern about our globalized techno-future in the West became its flame. The revolution had killed revolt, had destroyed the spirit of questioning, critique, and invention. Kristeva preferred the search for universality through audacious, singular experiences. She became intent on finding new means of unveiling, overturning, displacing, reconstructing, and reinventing the past so as not to allow the human psyche and the spirit of revolt to be crushed.

It is in an interview published in a French communist newspaper in July 2001 (that is, just before 9/11) where Kristeva best summarizes for a non-specialist audience why the question of revolt came to occupy the center of her thinking in the 1990s.[72] She outlines the history of the word *revolution*, emphasizing that its most common meaning of "overthrowing a political system" emerged at the end of the eighteenth and throughout the nineteenth centuries. She sees this definition as too restrictive for the twenty-first century. What is more, she claims that the ideal of revolution has had its chance but that it has repeatedly failed by falling into totalitarianism when not terror. She wants to take the word out of the realm of the political and move it closer to the more intimate domain of subjective or psychological "turning."

Kristeva explains why she believes that this new form of revolt is important in our time: our planetary era of new technologies, including the rapid expansion and globalization of the media, is bringing about a radical—and highly problematic—change in forms of social cohesion and modifying the definition of the human. Omnipresent and uniform representations shrink human psychic space. This situation, in turn, leads to the inability of human beings to represent for themselves their own life conflicts. Instead, they turn to images, including "reality shows," to avoid reality. As the screen becomes a substitute for "inner experience," the image replaces the psyche: everyone tries to escape both personal and social conflicts by turning to (social) media or, worse, alcohol and drugs. This leads to illness, depression, violence and, eventually, the angry search for a scapegoat who is deemed to be the cause of all that is dissatisfying or painful. Against this backdrop, Kristeva clearly states that she does not believe that revolution is the answer to our emerging planetary situation.

New Maladies of the Soul (1993)

New Maladies of the Soul set the scene for Kristeva's subsequent books on revolt.[73] It is a collection of essays that dig deeply into new forms of psychic, social, and physical pain that Kristeva was hearing about from her patients:

> Do new [kinds of] patients exist? New pathologies? What one finds is an upsurge and diversification of kinds of serious depressive disorders, psychosomatic diseases, vandalism, drug addiction, and, most recently, what I have called extreme "diseases of ideality" which lead to radicalization and gangsterism . . . My psychoanalytic practice encourages me to speak of these "new patients" who fall outside the usual categories of psychopathology.[74]

In her book, Kristeva includes clinical vignettes from her patients, drawing out patterns and repetitions in psychic destruction. Years later, she will add that the internet and the expansion of the round-the-clock media have made things worse: there has been a homogenization of the psyche and the soul as images have become ever more toxic and as language has been reduced to codes, to sound bites, that are used to advertise, sell, buy, or produce PR for the "self."

Kristeva herself has resisted the internet, only using email to communicate and even that as little as possible. She worries that the internet has become a huge space of mimeticism, that communication has become a goal in and of itself no matter what one communicates. Can this growing space be used creatively? Kristeva hopes so and hastens to add that we do not really know yet. For now, she still writes her books in pencil, with an eraser at hand. She believes that this keeps her texts alive:

> What will happen to Western society if . . . psychic space finds neither the time nor the space to grow? Perhaps we are approaching the ideal of a superman who would be satisfied with a pill and a television screen . . . For now, at any rate, those who try to live without a psychic space are quickly exposed to exhaustion, relationship difficulties, and extreme frustration.[75]

Kristeva offers many practices and activities that can help keep our psychic space alive even as we are bombarded by ready-made, repetitive, toxic languages and images. For example, she advocates artistic endeavors, reading and writing, spiritual practices, and physical activities such as dance or sports. However, she almost always comes back to psychoanalytic practice—both literally (on the couch) and figuratively (perlaboration)—as a privileged space where the subject's unconscious psychic space can be made known and modified through interpretation within a transferential relationship. Like love, analysis is a state of being open to the other. And if you have a psychic space, you are alive. This in turn means that you can revolt.

The Sense and Non-Sense of Revolt (1996)

Kristeva's *Sense and Non-Sense of Revolt* was based on her 1994–95 seminar at the University of Paris 7. The first half of the book addresses at length many of the questions I have already evoked: Is revolt even possible today? What is the history of the word and concept? Why do we need to reinvent it for our current situation? She argues that those who have been excluded from society—the unemployed or underemployed, the alienated youth of the suburbs, the homeless, foreigners, and so on—cannot achieve happiness without revolt. Indeed, we all need revolt to save ourselves from robotization. She goes so far as to say that, going forward, revolt may be the only thing that can save humanity. The second half of the book studies three important twentieth-century figures of revolt: Louis Aragon and his adventures with surrealism; Jean-Paul Sartre and his insistence on the imaginary as revolt; and Roland Barthes and his semiological revolt against both Marxist doxa and bourgeois moralism.[76]

Intimate Revolt (1997)

Kristeva's *Intimate Revolt* revisits many of the themes regarding revolt already mentioned, but goes further and is in some ways more explicitly political.[77] Kristeva stays close to psychoanalytic theory, but only in order to reiterate her warning about the dangers of searching for scapegoats and especially of the political desire for purification (especially from women and mothers). She praises Sartre for his explorations of negativity and nothingness at the edges of the human psyche and Aragon for his understanding of the equivalencies between fascism and communism.

The Future of Revolt (1998)

Kristeva's third book on revolt, *The Future of Revolt*, is more personal, evoking language as the hinge, the seam between the (social) body and the (personal) psyche through which she has explored her own suffering most successfully.[78] Simply put, she revolts as a constructor of language. At the crossroads of languages and durations, Kristeva designates herself as a *monster* when alluding to the writing of her first three novels.

Over the decades, the theme of revolt as a precondition of psychic aliveness has remained a consistent one in Kristeva's work. For instance, in 2014 she published a text in English entitled "New Forms of Revolt." I have heard her give a version of this text as a lecture several times in several different places, and I have always been amazed by the consistency of the line that connects Kristeva's mid-1990s books on the definitions of, antecedents to, and needs for revolt to her later books about returning to religion for historical models of understanding revolt (for example, in books such as her 2007 *This Incredible Need to Believe*). In "New Forms of Revolt," Kristeva brings up to date her conviction that only through revolt can any kind of psychic space—inner experience—be saved. She also renews her commitment to the new kinds of rebels that she sees and hears around her, especially on her psychoanalytic couch.[79]

Nations Without Nationalism (1990)

It was in the 1990s that Kristeva also began to focus consciously on the question of how to reach a larger audience as a public intellectual. For example, she began working in earnest with UNESCO, giving talks on human rights.[80] She campaigned hard to have Freud included in UNESCO's "Memory of the World," a program launched in 1992 to document and preserve some of the world's most significant legacies. Along with Émile Malet, the director of the journal *Passages*, and the psychoanalyst Charles Melman, she helped organize a series of colloquia in Paris, New York, Israel, and Tunisia that were dedicated to this cause. She accepted invitations to write for art exhibition catalogues. She began to accept invitations from journalists to speak about her most recent work. And two small books of hers—one published at the beginning of the decade, in 1990, and the other toward its end, in 1998—provide a more journalistic window into themes that we have already looked at in the context of her more specialized work since the fall of the Berlin Wall.

Kristeva's 1990 *Nations Without Nationalism* offers some of Kristeva's main arguments in a straightforward form.[81] It advances the idea that people should not be reduced to their groups of origin. And it posits that debates about nationality—which raise questions such as "What is Frenchness?" or "How can we rethink the legacies of cosmopolitanism?"—should be opened up so as to keep humiliations and resentments from festering. I think that one of her most important points is summarized in a sentence in the opening essay that is unfortunately left out of the English translation: "I fear . . . that judgement [both judgement and rational thought] is not the best method for destroying racist and nationalist perversion and that, on the contrary, simply to underline evil is to authenticate it and fix it in place."[82]

Revolt, She Said (1998)

Kristeva's *Revolt, She Said* is a series of interviews that continue to bring her thoughts on the 1990s culture of exploding antisemitism, anti-immigration, and extreme right-wing social agendas to a larger audience.[83] Along related lines, when a journalist from the magazine *Marianne* asked her to write a piece on depression, she chose to write on national rather than personal depression, depicting it as a barrier to the spirit of revolt. She goes back to 1968 as an incisive moment of revolt. Moreover, she worries that it is the general depression of the 1990s—characterized by a constriction of psychic space, an inability to cope, and a lost confidence in a common cause—that is carving out space for Le Pen and stifling the demand for revolt and social justice.

In particular, Kristeva focuses on the challenges that women are facing as "superwomen."[84] Kristeva furthermore makes it clear that the woman she is thinking the most about in 1998 is Hannah Arendt and her efforts in her own time to "rehabilitate anxious/worried thinking (*la pensée inquiète*) against calculated thinking that is just 'computerizing.'"[85] Kristeva underlines the fact that Arendt pointed out that there were two hugely damaging abolitions in the twentieth century:

> The Nazis abolished the injunction against murder (given in the commandment "Thou shalt not kill") and the Stalinists did away with the prohibition against slandering ("Thou shalt not bear false testimony against your neighbor"). Stalinism, in its incitement of slanderous accusations, repudiated the principle of respect for the other.

> We should ask if today, in our democracies, we are not in danger of sliding into a "soft" type of totalitarianism in which moral prohibitions . . . are being eroded along with the capacity to represent. Without restraint, without the internalization of a superego or an ideal ego, there can be no values, no meaning, no representation; everything is allowed, including suicide, somatization, acting-out, vandalism, and even murder. We live in a time in which civilization is on the brink of collapse. Fortunately I am referring only to extreme cases, but there are certain fringes of society where this danger is imminent.[86]

The Severed Head (1998)

Well before ritualized, televised beheadings began to terrorize the world in 2002, Kristeva was thinking about the loss of the head—through a violent beheading—as an inaugural and enduringly central fantasy throughout the history of Western, Judeo-Christian art. Kristeva has emphasized that her interest in the topic has been longstanding and theoretical, and should therefore not be confused with the spectacles of political barbarism staged by extremist groups. As we have seen, in 1996 she had published a novel that had a beheaded character at its center. Consequently, even though she was a bit intimidated when Françoise Viatte of the Louvre asked her to organize an exhibition for the Napoleon Hall in 1998 on a topic of her choice, Kristeva immediately proposed the theme of decapitation in Western art. The exhibition covered ground from about 6000 BC through the well-known images of Medusa, David and Goliath, Saint John the Baptist, and Judith and Holophernes all the way to twentieth-century paintings by such artists as Max Ernst and Picasso. The catalogue for the exhibition, *The Severed Head*, was published in 1998.[87]

There is a great deal to say about this volume beyond its central thesis, namely that severed heads are part of a fantasy central to the very possibility of representation. However, instead of explicating Kristeva's theoretical journey vis-à-vis this hypothesis through the centuries, I would like to propose that this large book on a long segment of the history of Western art serves as a point of transition between the books that Kristeva had published earlier in the 1990s and the topic she returns to at the end of the decade and during the 2000s: woman and women.

In *The Severed Head*, Kristeva proposes that the representation of decapitation, of severed heads, serves as a sublimation of our fear of death and, most importantly, of what is akin to the fear of death for the infant in each of us: the fear of separation from the mother or, even worse, her exertion of overwhelming power over us. In examining this sublimation of fear through artistic representation, Kristeva postulates (not for the first time) that the representation of violence can prevent violence in reality. That is, by refusing to erase what makes us fearful and violent, by finding a way to articulate and represent it, we avoid acting it out in real life. In this sense, representation functions in the same way as analysis does. By avoiding repression and embracing sublimation, representation can compensate for our loss of the loving maternal face and even accumulate joy through creativity. In the end, with any luck, the creative representation can circulate in the world as a singular act of revolt—sometimes for centuries.

Transcend Yourself!

By the end of the 1990s, many of Kristeva's colleagues, readers, and students—especially in the United States—were practically begging her to write a book on feminism. She replied that she was not interested in defining feminism, summarizing it, or recommending what "it" should do. She stated publicly and privately that she was more of a "Scotist" than a feminist. By this she meant that she felt more compelled by the medieval philosopher Duns Scotus's theory of "haecceity"—of the discrete qualities, properties, or characteristics of a thing or living being that make it a particular thing or being—than by any homogenizing mass movement, even feminism.

Kristeva nevertheless made a special plea for the feminist movement, for she believes that it still has the chance of being one of the few -isms to claim a vibrant leadership position during the twenty-first century without backsliding into rigidity. However, she argued that this will only happen if feminism invites each woman to embrace her singular creativity, her own specific genius, which can then be shared with others through new forms of social connection and revolt. She said that she did not want to participate in telling women what they should or should not do or say or be. Rather, she wanted to provide examples of women who, against incredible odds, resisted, carried on, fought back, became *sur-vivantes*, not survivors but aliver than alive: *les battantes*. She said that she was most interested in examining deeply the writings of women who had the strength to reconstruct, to "rebirth," themselves.

While feminist thought was still very much alive in the 1990s in the United States,[88] in France Kristeva was often busy supporting individual women artists and writers without being attached to any feminist movement per se.[89] In any case, there were none to attach to. Consequently, what Kristeva decided to do in the late 1990s was to choose three strong, highly singular women in domains she knew a lot about in the European context: philosophy, psychoanalysis, and literature. She especially wanted to choose women who, when faced with situations where everyone felt that there was nothing to be done, figured out what to do—women who resisted, who did not get crushed by history.

For example, although Kristeva was fascinated by Simone Weil, an excellent philosopher, she was not interested in presenting to the world—as an example of female singularity—a woman who was both ill and struggling for "personal salvation." Kristeva was more interested in Simone de Beauvoir and Hannah Arendt. As for fiction writers, she thought about Virginia Woolf, Sylvia Plath, and even the Russian writer Marina Tsvetaeva because all three were of great interest to her. But, again, Kristeva wanted to put forward examples of strong women who did not get beaten up by history, who were able to transcend themselves and their situation—women who did not commit suicide but were *battantes*. She ended up choosing the indomitable Colette, who, according to Kristeva, positively "spit fire."

The Feminine and the Sacred (1998)

Kristeva's 1999–2002 trilogy on three strong women—on *life* (Arendt), *madness* (Klein), and *words* (Colette)—were joined together by the word *genius*. But in 1998, just before publishing the first volume of the trilogy on Arendt, she published a book of correspondence between herself and her old friend, the French philosopher and novelist Catherine Clément, a book whose key word was *sacred*: *The Feminine and the Sacred*.[90] This book is a compilation of letters the two women exchanged over one year, between November 1996 and November 1997. They begin with one question: Is there anything sacred that can at the same time be considered as strictly feminine? They are referring primarily to "women" but also to all the symbolic functions ascribed to women over the centuries and across cultures, especially within the domain of world religions.

The one definition of the sacred that Kristeva and Clément can agree on is that it seems to be a symbolic economy that helps human beings make sense of their existence. Beyond this vague definition, it would be difficult to summarize the exchange between Kristeva, the "Christian Atheist" whose references are primarily European Christian/Catholic, and Clément, the "Jewish Atheist" whose references are primarily Eastern (e.g. Hinduism and Buddhism) and African (Animism).

They argue, sometimes with quite an edge, about African, Indian, and European women, about demons and witches, but also about the Catholic Virgin Mother (Clément is very hard on Kristeva on this front), about maternity (including their own loves and fears as mothers), about Eva Perón and Princess Diana, but also about Voltaire, Proust, Edward Said, and Jacques Lacan. They rarely get personal, but Clément does so when she describes the various cultural practices that she observed while living in The Gambia and Delhi, and Kristeva does so when she evokes David's surgery in March 1997.

Kristeva also conjures up occasional memories of her childhood: for example, her childhood bed, placed under a portrait of Saint Juliana, her father having wanted her to pray to the saint. She explains that it was her inability to do so that led her to the understanding that the only thing she valued in the face of death was *thinking*. She also stresses that when she was working at a communist youth camp on the Black Sea, she realized that given that there is nothing to be done about death, the important thing is just to do one's absolute best in the face of it.

Kristeva and Clément's book was reissued in 2015 with a new and moving preface written by Kristeva.[91] Although taking account of this 2015 preface here involves jumping ahead in time, I think that its language provides a retrospective bridge between Kristeva and Clément's 1998 epistolary book and the other book Kristeva was finishing at the time: her 1999 intellectual biography of Hannah Arendt. In the new preface, Kristeva announces that she has three urgent preoccupations that relate to their 1998 book: the attack on *Charlie Hebdo*; the sacrifice of young girls in the name of "sacred tradition"; and the interior experience of facing God.

Kristeva wrote the preface in the wake of the January 7, 2015, deadly terrorist attack at the Parisian headquarters of the French satirical weekly magazine, *Charlie Hebdo* (as well as the attack at the Hypercacher, a Porte de Vincennes kosher supermarket two days later). One of the twelve people murdered at the *Charlie Hebdo* offices was Elsa Cayat, a French psychiatrist, psychoanalyst, writer, and columnist at the magazine. Kristeva dedicates the new edition of her book with Clément to Cayat's memory and to Delphine Horvilleur, France's third female rabbi, who paid homage to Cayat at her funeral. Kristeva praises Cayat's love of books, of serious thought, and her struggle to live freely—her spirit of revolt. She admires Horvilleur's understanding that "('sacred?') texts are there to be interpreted, to be digested, sometimes far from their literal meaning. Without that, they alienate us, close us into suffering, soak us in their abuse. They condemn us."[92] Kristeva wants to "dedicate to these two women, Elsa Cayat and Delphine Horvilleur, this new edition of our exchanges. In order to salute their courage, their sense of revolt through interpretation, their innovation of tradition."[93]

Regarding her second urgent preoccupation—crimes against women—Kristeva states: "Today, more than 700 million adult women currently alive were forcibly married as children. Every year, 15 million girls fall victim to these practices."[94] Kristeva then enumerates other injustices committed in the name of the "sacred" before turning to her third urgent concern: the inability of intellectuals to imagine new ways of thinking about "internal experience" without religion. She chides Clément for accusing her of becoming "religiously possessed" when she writes about Teresa of Ávila or talks to Pope Benedict XVI—as she did in 2011—about her suggested principles for a new twenty-first-century secular humanism: "You know this, I ask myself: what are we proposing, we the descendants of the Enlightenment, faced with identitarian tensions, dogmatisms, fundamentalisms, fanaticisms, jihadisms . . . ? Not very much. Nothing but a large question mark after the most serious concepts: identity, man, woman, God himself, the sacred of course, the feminine too."[95]

Hannah Arendt (1999)

Kristeva's mixture of optimism about the power of interpretation and her pessimism about the situation of the world at the end of the twentieth century comes through loudly and clearly in her last book of the 1990s, *Hannah Arendt*.[96] Published in 1999, this is the first volume in her trilogy on women and the question of genius, a trilogy focused on the lives and works of three remarkable women who, I would argue, echo and highlight Kristeva's most cherished value: a vibrant psychic space where thought and life are one.[97]

Kristeva dedicates her three volumes to Simone de Beauvoir, thereby underlining her main reason for choosing Arendt, Klein, and Colette to think through the question of women and genius, namely that they had the privilege of being able to act and did not waste it. They did not wait for Beauvoir's successful liberation of women to be a *fait accompli* in order to exercise their freedom to think, to create, and to be continually reborn: "Is not genius precisely the breakthrough that consists in going beyond the situation?"[98]

Kristeva outlines the three general characteristics of women's genius as it manifests in each of her three examples.

First, all three writers are invested in the originality of each individual, but only as manifested within a web of human relationships: "In these affirmations of a *self that cannot be separated from its various attachments*—political, psychic, sensory, amorous, or literary—I would be tempted to distinguish a constant of feminine psychosexuality."[99] Arendt is distinguished by her position as the only philosopher of the twentieth century to bring about a philosophy of a connected life.[100]

Second, all three women identify thought with life. Arendt undertook a political struggle against the destruction of life by totalitarianism through her engagement in a philosophical struggle to defend thought:

> By diagnosing a radical evil in totalitarianism, which dared to announce "the superfluidity of human life," Arendt set herself up as the champion of life if (and only if) *this life has a meaning*: life not as *zoe* but as *bios*, giving rise to a biography that becomes part of the memory of the city-state. Through an investigation of the meandering paths of the acts of *willing*, *thinking*, and *judging*, she attempts to understand the meaning of an existence such as this, in which life is coextensive with thought and which the two versions of totalitarianism of the twentieth century started to destroy in order to annihilate, with thought, life itself.[101]

Third, all three women have a relationship to temporality that allows them to imagine "beginning once again." Arendt in particular was a loud champion of freedom defined as the possibility of new beginnings:

> Without having experienced maternity herself, Arendt attributed a nodal function to the temporality of birth in her ideas about freedom: it is because men *are born* "strangers" and "ephemeral" that freedom— which is the very possibility of starting anew—can be given its ontological foundation. "This freedom . . . is identical with the fact that men *are* because they are born, that each of them is a new beginning, begins, in a way, a new world." In contrast, Terror eliminates "the very source of freedom which man receives from the fact of his birth and which resides in the fact of his capacity of being a new beginning."[102]

Kristeva cautions that these three characteristics shared by her three geniuses—a capacity for attachment, life as thought, and an emphasis on the temporality of birth and rebirth—are undoubtedly not the only attributes of feminine psychosexuality. She also argues that they might be found in the work of male writers as well, given the psychic bisexuality of both sexes. Indeed, she insists that it is important to go beyond the dichotomy of the sexes and to examine creativity in its uniqueness. This uniqueness is nevertheless something that can be shared with the rest of the world. As Kristeva states with regard to her three examples:

> At the heart of the precarious solitude of their pioneering work, which was the price they paid for their unique creativity, Arendt, Klein, and Colette managed to create the conditions that give rise to a necessarily public opinion and, why not, a school and, at best, create an effect of seduction that solicits a communion of readings and a community of readers.[103]

I would argue that Kristeva has also managed to create a community of readers through her careful enactment of singularities within commonly shared codes. I would also propose that of the three geniuses Kristeva engages, it is Arendt with whom she shares the closest political affinity. Both Kristeva and Arendt refuse to freeze themselves into any identity whatsoever, afraid as they both are that truth will become massified, convinced as they both are that the banality of evil is the destruction of the capacity to think.

I Cannot See Any Light . . .

In 1999, Kristeva was interviewed by the British historian and philosopher, Jonathan Rée, for a British Channel 4 television series called *Talking Liberties*. During the interview, Kristeva revisited her work from the 1970s up until that moment with friendly, accessible idiom and with impressive grace even when the questions became tedious. Toward the end of the interview, Rée asked Kristeva if she still felt the optimism of her youthful writings or if she thought that there was a new sense of crisis at the end of the century, the end of the millennium. Kristeva's tone and presence shifted noticeably. Her voice took on a deep, rather ominous seriousness. I remember that when I heard the interview in early 2000, I got goosebumps. I was not sure at the time whether I was reacting to what seemed to me to be a new kind of conservatism about Europe on her part or whether I was uneasy because she was again sounding prescient of . . . I did not know what. Here, in part, is what she said that evoked my confused response:

> I think [the crisis] has gotten worse . . . [In *The Old Man and the Wolves*], I portray the world—East and West mixed together—as comparable to the crisis experienced by the Roman Empire which has no more values, is filled with hatred, and doesn't know where it is going . . . [It] knows perhaps what it doesn't want: We don't want any Stalins, we don't want any Hitlers—although there may still be some nostalgia for them—but we don't have any positive values, or when we do have some positive values, they are archaic values, derived from some religion or another, values that are incompatible with the demands of sexual independence and sooner or later people collide with these phenomena . . . Religious values are seen as necessary but are difficult to bear. So I have painted an even bleaker picture, for I think, alas, that we are in a period of transition and I cannot see any light, I cannot see any

positive outcome . . . It's very clear in France at the moment. Political parties are aware of it. They talk of the public's sense of gloom. People are disappointed. They don't see any way out. I think politicians are wrong to say, "Oh, come on now, it will all sort itself out." It's a grave miscalculation because we are living a depression. Our civilization is experiencing something like a personal depression. And the last thing you should say to a depressed person is, "Pull yourself together, you'll be fine." You have to find the roots of the problem and delve into the cause of the malaise. I think that's where we are now. And as intellectuals, we should seek out the causes of this discontent before sorting out the future . . . But I would certainly not give an optimistic prognosis . . . We must face up to our problems and see them for what they are. And for the moment, it wouldn't be honest to go beyond that. So for now, I remain rather pessimistic. And as I said at the beginning of our interview, the pressure on the geographical [and symbolic] borders of Europe from the East [including the Middle East]—in a state of economic and moral misery—and the pressure from the South, from Africa for example, with its high levels of suffering, of starvation, are such that if we don't face up to these difficulties, and adding to that the unhappiness of Western populations, who have lost their values, who believe in nothing . . . or if they do, their religious values enter into conflict with the new sexual freedoms, it's a pretty negative diagnosis . . . Perhaps I am more worried by these phenomena because I come from a part of the world where people are more damaged than here . . . It seems to me that [Western] Europe is still a bit of a protected zone, but it is time for us to attend to the problems that surround us . . . Otherwise, I fear we are in great danger.[104]

And then, suddenly, it was 9/11/2001.

3. The 2000s: An Intellectual Who Works on the Invisible

Even as the globe was shifting consciousness, often violently, over the course of the first decade of the 2000s, Kristeva continued to write without pause, with an explicit emphasis on what is not obvious, on the opposite of the evident: on the unconscious and its often illogical effects increasingly being felt in Western Europe and the United States.[105] Between 2000 and 2010, Kristeva published thirteen books (including two novels), consolidated her presence on the world stage, and continued to defend psychoanalysis from increasingly direct attacks from both the right and the left. She also continued her work on the question of female genius while expanding her interest in how the sacred and its relationship to the unconscious needs to be rethought for the twenty-first century if humanity is going—literally—to survive.

Kristeva worried about the slippage of some into cynicism, reductionism, or reactionary identity politics after the 9/11 attacks: for her, it is crucial to resist saying to oneself, "Well, it's all so bad, what's the point of thinking? I'll just protect my own." Her defense of psychoanalysis frequently took the form of an emphasis on alternative logics of care, reliance, and rebirth, always with the insistence on the fact that what escapes Western definitions of rationality need not be limited to madness or evil. She continued her analysis of the importance of re-evaluating cultural and aesthetic memory, especially in the public sphere, in the *res publica*, in the *polis*. She repeatedly wrote about reinvention and transvaluation, more and more often with reference to the project of the secular humanities taking over from monotheistic religion through a grappling with what she began to call "the universal need to believe." And she elaborated in more depth her concept of singularity and her view of its critical importance for new forms of political thought.[106]

In order for "universal singularity"—a universalism based on the recognition of the irreducible singularity of each and every one of us—to have a shot at existing in the world, Kristeva knew that some deeply controversial debates would need to take place. She began to pursue some new intellectual directions, step-by-step, over the decade. First, she argued that the European Enlightenment had completely underestimated the capacity of human beings to indulge in radical evil, which she defined, after Hannah Arendt, as a situation in which one group of humans determines that another group of humans is no longer necessary and must be eliminated. According to her, this means that both Enlightenment thinking and radical evil need to be rethought for the twenty-first century. Second, she argued that the forms through which radical evil currently spreads must be re-examined: she posited again that hyperconnectivity is not providing humanity with more freedom, but on the contrary, is in the process of banalizing and globalizing barbarity, and ultimately, the death drive. Finally, she argued that in the face of death, of nihilism, there still remains the possibility of repairing genuine social connection, starting with those who are most immediately and acutely impacted by that nihilism: those caught in the throes of an inevitably fragile adolescence in the midst of overwhelming social, economic, and political injustice. And she decided to start there: with the crisis of the European subject filled with both unfettered rage and terrible gloom.

Against Cynicism

Over the 2000s, the use of antidepressants in the United States doubled. France was not far behind. In fact, as Kristeva planned her year of radio shows, *Chronicles of a Sensitive Time*, on France Culture, from September 5, 2001 to July 24, 2002, she decided that her first broadcast—"The Festive Exclusion"—would be about the staggering increase not only in prescriptions for depression but also in addictions to hard drugs like oxycodone and heroin in France and around the world. She describes this worldwide phenomenon as being due to a profound malaise induced by a new world order which creates new forms of exclusion. She maintains that the banalization of the business and use of hard drugs has led to a new division in global culture, the utility of which the "old capitalism of exclusion" could not even have envisioned: a division between those who are lucid deciders and those who are anesthetized, dead-alive consumers whose oceanic state deprives them of desire and agency.

Kristeva's next broadcast, "The Film Was Silent," which took place a week after the 9/11 attacks, announced that a complete "recomposition of economic, political, ideological givens is taking shape." Kristeva evoked the cognitive dissonance of the attacks as a traumatic silent film drowning in the inflationary chatting of commentators. She argued that deepening the Western understanding of the economic, political, and cultural causes of terrorism should not preclude an investigation of the unconscious roots of such behavior in the death drive, nor should it impede an examination of its wide-open circuits of global contagion.

In what remains for me the most striking of her broadcasts on the topic of 9/11, "The Newly Disengaged," on November 21, 2001, Kristeva vividly chided French intellectuals such as Jean Baudrillard for being so fascinated by the ultimate "silent film" of global spectacle (the collapse of the twin towers), for being so engaged in intellectual narcissism that they were denying the reality of the event itself as well as the reality of the totalitarianism represented by new forms of global terror. Kristeva had no patience for the dismissal of the "real" in favor of the "hyper-real." She also took umbrage at the French media's "cynical" judgement that both globalization and terrorism were beyond good and evil (i.e., the argument that because the United States was the primary architect of globalization, it was its fault that it was attacked). Moreover, she began to place 9/11 and the reactions to it within the context of a much larger crisis, one of truly traumatic, global proportions only beginning to become more visible to the average citizen.[107]

And crisis there was: terrorist attacks,[108] the growth of the "big brother" security state, and the 2008 financial crisis.[109] Kristeva's diagnosis of widespread social depression became literalized on a global scale.

I Can Only Rely on My Own Strengths

In May 2002, Kristeva was invited to Sofia to accept an honorary doctorate—one of many such doctorates that she received in the

2000s—from her own University of St. Kliment Ohridski in Sofia. Pope John Paul II was also there for the Festival of the Alphabet, as well as to celebrate both the unique Bulgarian co-habitation of Jews, Muslims, and Christians and the Bulgarian refusal to deport its Jewish citizens during World War II. Kristeva was honored to find herself in the presence of this Pope who had worked so hard to bring about one of Kristeva's fondest dreams: the full reconciliation of the Western Catholic Church with the Eastern Orthodox Church, which she sees as a crucial step toward a united Europe.

However, while Kristeva was in Sofia, she received an urgent call: her mother had suddenly fallen ill and within hours had been declared to be in mortal danger from acute bacterial meningitis. Kristina, in fact, died. Kristeva was in shock. She does not talk or write often about her mother's unexpected death, but when she does, she contrasts it with that of her father. When he died, she could not cry: she was too enraged. But when her mother died, she could not stop crying for ten days. It was if she were enveloped by silence, unable to speak. She has written about how her mother was always the silent one, the "background" to her life, but also the very fabric of it in a kind of "curious transubstantiation in which we form a unity, even as each of us preserves our own place."[110]

In *Murder in Byzantium*, written while mourning her mother's death and published in 2004, one finds a description of at least a certain part of what Kristeva felt at the loss of this "source," this "foundation," or even this "condition" of her very being that was her mother. In a letter entitled "Silence, My Mother Is Dead" written by the novel's protagonist Stephanie Delacour and addressed to the protagonist's lover—the handsome Chief Inspector Rilsky—she recalls that "this woman let us believe that she was content to open a path for us, that she didn't suffer or scratch and gave nothing but a caress. 'I didn't tie you down, I gave you wings.'"[111] Ten years later, Kristeva stresses that her mother embodied "the 'mystery' of the maternal passion that I later called a *reliance*. To allow the newcomer, ephemeral stranger, to acquire his own originality. Which makes me cry: 'You cry from joy' says David."[112]

Once Kristeva was back in Paris, she returned, if with deep sadness, to what she always does: writing daily, seeing patients, teaching, and caring for her son: "What I *invest* in: I become 'one' with . . . mine, Philippe and David. My patients. My books."[113] Among other things, Kristeva pursued her life with Sollers, a life of travel, conversation, and writing. She often responded in public to the steady stream of his novels and dealt with an increasing number of interviews that touched on their life together.[114] However, mostly Kristeva continued to work on her own. She undertook two major institutional initiatives that continue to mean a great deal to her today even though she retired from the university in 2010. First, in 2000 she established the Roland Barthes Center with Dominique Lecourt, Pierre Fédida, and François Julien at the University of Paris 7.[115] Second, in 2008 she founded the annually awarded Simone de Beauvoir Prize for Women's Freedom. The Beauvoir Prize was founded on the 100th anniversary of Beauvoir's birth with the help of Beauvoir's adopted daughter, Sylvie Le Bon de Beauvoir, Claude Lanzmann, Élisabeth Badinter, the militants of the League for the International Rights of Women,[116] and a jury of around thirty distinguished scholars of Beauvoir's work. Kristeva chaired the committee from 2008 to 2011 and has remained very proud of its record.[117]

Throughout the first decade of the twenty-first century, Kristeva continued to receive numerous awards and honors. This frequently required her to do international traveling, which she came to find less and less enjoyable as the practicalities of air travel became more onerous after 9/11. Most of the time Kristeva has seemed almost oblivious to the large number of her honors. Yet it is also clear that they have come to mean a lot to her as she has struggled to gain respect—especially in France. Among other things, she received honorary doctorates from the Free University of Belgium (2000), the University of Bayreuth (2000), the University of Toronto (2000), the University of Sofia (2002), the New School (2003), and the University of Cyprus (2007). In 2002, she was named a member of the British Academy and of the Académie Universelle des Cultures. In 2006, she received an

Award of Merit from Bucknell University. Some of these awards were related to her popular presence on campuses: for example, besides the permanent visiting professorship at the University of Toronto that I have already mentioned, she received a comparable visiting professorship at the New School for Social Research in New York City. She has valued this relationship a great deal because of her admiration for the university's Philosophy Department as well as because of her access to the Hannah Arendt Center, which was founded in 2000 in honor of Arendt, who taught at the New School from 1967 until her death in 1975.

I am tempted to argue that it was the awards and honors that Kristeva received in France that were most meaningful to her, for they were hard-won. The list is long but includes several that are important at least to mention: in 2000, she was named a member of the Institut Universitaire de France; in 2004, she was elected Officier de l'Ordre National du Mérite; in 2003, she was extended the honor of membership on the Conseil économique et social, in the Section des relations extérieures for a period of five years; and in 2009 she was named a member of the Délégation aux droits des femmes et à l'égalité des chances entre femmes et hommes. She was also awarded in 2005 the Grande Médaille de Vermeil de la Ville de Paris and in 2007 the Trophée Créateurs Sans Frontières, "Essai" Quai d'Orsay Cultures France.

In 2008, Kristeva reached the heights of French honor when she became an Officer of l'Ordre National de la Légion d'Honneur. On the occasion of this award ceremony on May 28, 2008, she gave what I think is one of her most concise and moving public addresses. In this acceptance speech, Kristeva describes herself as a European citizen of Bulgarian origin who considers herself a cosmopolitan intellectual, specifying that the word *cosmopolitan* alone would have sufficed for one to be persecuted in the Bulgaria of her childhood. She evokes her mother and her father and the gift that they gave her of the French language and its culture, in particular its insistence on skepticism, on questioning, on interpretation, and on debate as antidotes to "national depression as well as its maniacal form: nationalism." She emphasizes the contributions of the French human sciences to world culture in the postwar period through their insistence on analyzing how meaning is produced and how subjectivity is constructed. She credits this for having led her to a contemplation of "foreignness and strangeness" in the context of modern literature and psychoanalysis, always in pursuit of her dream: a new Europe constructed not as an association of identities, but as a federation of mutually respected "foreignnesses," a federation based on a "solidarity of differences" and open to the diversity of the world.

In a lightly coded description of her own experience in France, Kristeva acknowledges that this will not be easy for foreign women. Kristeva evokes Madame de Staël as the first French woman intellectual who wrote about how women intellectuals tend to provoke jealousy when not wholesale pity on the part of the public, how they are often attacked "violently, and the first blow reaches the heart."[118] Kristeva acknowledges her own struggles for respect and honor in France, while also conceding that inevitably "every honor is won on the battlefield, that the battle is never finished, and that for men as well as women, there is no greater guarantee of honor than . . . vulnerability."[119]

Kristeva's awards were of course not limited to France: in 2005, she received the Gonfalone d'Argento Award of the Region of Tuscany and the Regional Council of Florence; in 2006, she was awarded the Hannah Arendt Prize for Political Thought by an international jury; in 2008, she was deeply touched to be granted the Václav Havel Vision of European Culture Prize in honor of the "president-philosopher" whose vision of Europe had in part inspired the Velvet Revolutions; and in 2009, she was honored by the Oslo Høgskole with a week-long conference on her work, in her honor.

However, nothing compares to what most would consider to be the apogee of a career such as Kristeva's: on December 3, 2004, in Norway, she was awarded the first Holberg Prize, the equivalent of the Nobel Prize for the Human Sciences.[120] Kristeva's acceptance speech for this honor reflects the seriousness with which she took it. Entitled "Thinking About Liberty in Dark Times," Kristeva's talk is a moving account of where her thought was taking her in the early 2000s.[121] After evoking her parents, her love of French literature and culture, her work on women geniuses, her reputation as a so-called French theorist, and her love of North American hospitality, she turns to the world and its need for a new, positive definition of humanity, for a new ethics, for new ways to think about the sacred and—at the very heart of her message—the need to think and rethink "freedom." She contrasts two kinds of freedom: on the one hand, the kind of freedom that she fears is dominant—and that involves the capacity to adapt to instrumental, calculated causes outside of oneself within the logic of capitalism, science, and technology— and on the other, the kind she values, namely freedom as an eternal questioning, as a way of being in the world prior to any cause or calculus.

In short, in the 2000s, Kristeva developed at greater length her idea of "singular humanism"—or "humanism in the singular"—in response to deepening divisions between two (differently limited) politico-intellectual factions: "identity politics" based on rigid binaries and "anti-capitalist struggles" that were so narrowly focused on economics that they were oblivious to the emerging poly-identities of the transmodern world. She began to promote a universally applicable analysis of socioeconomic injustice that would allow for an emphasis on singularity rather than on identity. Although she makes it clear that she supports identity-based struggles that are undertaken strategically, she also argues that intellectuals must embark on a broader and more complex critique of socioeconomic injustice, one based on an analysis of how capital-induced injustice *combines* with psychosocial fears of difference (which cause racism, xenophobia, etc.)—an analysis without which, in her view, nothing can be done. And she concludes that for such a complex undertaking to succeed, we need psychoanalytic insight.

Psychoanalysis Is a Humanism

In the twenty-first century, there has been perhaps no intellectual or political task more complicated for Kristeva than to find ways to translate—for her peers, students, readers, and increasingly a global (especially American) public—her firm belief that psychoanalytic theory and practice are essential for understanding and building the future of humanity if, indeed, it is to have a future. Almost none of her defenses of psychoanalysis in the 2000s are new, but they are articulated in new ways and in a new direction that converges with her primary new interest in the 2000s and 2010s: the history and philosophy of religion.

For example, in a 2006 interview she brings up to date her worries already expressed in her 1993 *New Maladies of the Soul,* stating emphatically that it was the combination of her intellectual explorations of literary and artistic modernity with her personal experiences of a totalitarian regime—one that punished creativity within a "paranoid-schizoid political and cultural framework"—that convinced her of the necessity to open up her psychoanalytic ear to the new psychic configurations emerging within the crisis of what Nietzsche called "monotonotheism." She decided to do this publicly in spite of (and in response to) the emergence in the 2000s of new mixtures of terroristic and nihilistic attitudes spawned by globalization. Otherwise, she argued, through our silence in the *polis,* we all risk being complicit in spreading "the plague of complacency (more or less occultist), with regression, fragmentation, madness."[122]

Kristeva became more explicit about her longtime sense that psychoanalytic listening is a form of resistance against totalitarian tendencies in all of us, and that in late capitalism, it offers a bulwark against the banalization of the ordinary and the commodification of everything. Throughout her publications, interviews, and public lectures in the 2000s, she talked about the necessity for political theory to include an analysis of the intimate facets of the modern personality, which can be revealed and explored through theoretical and clinical acts of psychoanalytically inspired perlaboration. She chided psychoanalysts for being afraid to go public, for being unwilling to take into the public sphere their discoveries of the often-disturbing new psychic structures that they were discovering in the private therapeutic spaces they inhabited daily.[123]

Kristeva was perhaps a bit unprepared for the virulent attacks aimed at her as she tried to make her more psychoanalytically precise ideas public in the media. The best known of these attacks came from the Nietzschean philosopher, Michel Onfray, whose 2010 book criticizing Freud, and by extension, psychoanalysis, *The Twilight of an Idol: The Freudian Confabulation*, kicked up a media storm.[124] It was a nasty and challenging attack. Kristeva decided to take on Onfray publicly. For her, it was no less than a matter of life and death, a matter that must be understood at the intersection of psychoanalysis and religion in order to rethink universality urgently in a diverse, globalized world. She began explaining publicly the link between psychoanalysis *and* religion (not psychoanalysis *as* a religion):

> Humanism came after religion, but it did not get rid of the need to believe . . . and Freud founded his whole system on it. Will it continue? Or will we move towards a nihilism where there is no language, where no one believes in anything, where there is no proximity . . . this would be another [kind of] humanity.[125]

Singular Universalism and Human Rights

The thirteen books Kristeva published during the first decade of the twenty-first century can roughly be divided into four groups: 1) Kristeva's forays into the world of governance and the media as a public intellectual; 2) two works of fiction; 3) her continued examination of women, motherhood, and "female genius"; and 4) new explorations of secular humanism in terms of its debt to the histories and philosophies of organized religion.

Kristeva is very hard on herself now when she looks back at her efforts in the early 2000s to reach a larger public via the media, going so far as to suggest that it was just her "five minutes of fame." When asked in 2016 whether she had retained her distrust of official journalism from her youth in communist Bulgaria, she replied bluntly:

> I do realize that the empire of the media, today invaded by information and communication technologies, has replaced totalitarianism, for better and for worse, and that its powers are of a different but still formidable efficiency. Nothing can defeat it. In every manager of opinion, I smell a cop, in the broadest sense of the word, ready to manipulate information and everything attached to it, at the service of the highest bidder, and of course in terms of power. This is not the "fault" of this or that person; it's the unconscious in certain cases and inevitable because there is no more *one* power, but only networks of power, and if you want to be "part of things" you have to be at least a double agent. So I invent and I stay away. Well, not completely.[126]

"Not completely" is right. In the early 2000s especially, Kristeva sounded the alarm in the media widely as well as bluntly and passionately. She argued that we are threatened by both nihilism and radical evil and that we are globalizing barbarism—the death drive in Freudian terms—through an unconscious embrace of hyperconnectivity. She asked whether it might be possible to weld back together our broken social links and to reformat the tools that we have inherited from the European Enlightenment in order to question, interpret, and rethink the historical division between "us" and "them." She tried to bring the force of her ideas directly to situations on the ground, to often-controversial political and social problems. She especially did so vis-à-vis her vision of new kinds of citizen-subjects who would embrace inter- and pluriculturality and promote universal human rights grounded in the respect of radically different singularities. She advanced a "singular universalism"—a universalism that would esteem each person's singularity—that was utopian yet, in her view, worth aspiring to.

For example, on the question of whether the West should accept President Hamid Karzai's project of allowing Taliban leaders to join the government in exchange for peace, Kristeva was of the opinion that every other effort—no matter how seemingly *impossible*—should be made before agreeing to sacrifice human rights, especially women's rights.[127] And she did not limit herself to just writing about the issue. She pursued her concerns actively via the Delegation on the Rights of Women to the Comparative Education Society in Europe. She moreover donated her Hannah Arendt Prize to medical and educative organizations in Afghanistan that were trying to stop young women from setting themselves on fire in protest against their treatment by fundamentalist men. She promoted a fight for freedom for all people in overtly Sartrean terms, a fight not stymied by a so-called respect for "diversity," exclaiming, "Why not [respect] Chinese foot-binding?!"[128]

In Geneva, Kristeva called unabashedly for a "transvaluation" of patriarchal law and a "transmutation" of religious memory. In Jerusalem, she called for new educational initiatives for Jews, Christians, and Muslims in the teaching of the history of world religions via psychoanalytic theory. At the end of the decade, she waded into journalistic controversies surrounding the Arab Spring, vocally supporting the revolts in the name of human rights.[129] She spoke out about the new, emerging field of Francophone Studies, urging scholarship and policy to address the need for France (and Europe) to take accountability for its "errors and horrors" as well as to simultaneously take responsibility for inventing new intercultural connections and more flexible global structures:

> Colonialism, the Inquisition, the European man's machismo, the Shoah, many well-known phenomena. Particularly the left, which I belong to, has been made extremely uncomfortable by such historical weight and has failed to see the progress and achievements of European culture, which could help us think and overcome these errors and these horrors and also to invent new relations.[130]

Crisis of the ~~European~~ Subject (2000)

What was especially new at the time was Kristeva's attempt to connect her public statements with actions on the political level through her leadership in governmental committees and her writing of formal policy reports.[131] What was also new was Kristeva's increasing transparency about her personal life and history in print. For example, during the first week of 2000, she wrote a week's worth of short texts—"Diversity in the Tempest"—for the French newspaper, *Libération*, where she anchored her otherwise familiar remarks on diversity in France and Europe and on Colette and Arendt with remarks about David and her home on the Île de Ré.[132] That same year, Columbia University Press published a collection of her essays where English readers began to catch a glimpse of the woman behind the prose. This collection, *Crisis of the European Subject*, contains articles on Colette and Arendt, and on Europe and equality, but it also includes her very moving meditation—"Bulgaria, My Suffering"—on the loss of her maternal tongue, as well as on the social and political nightmare emerging in Bulgaria as the mafia state was taking hold.[133]

At the Risk of Thought (2001)

In 2001, Kristeva published *At the Risk of Thought*, the title of which—as I mentioned in the introduction—served as the inspiration for the title I chose for this biography.[134] *At the Risk of Thought* contains a collection of interviews that were originally conducted by the journalist Marie-Christine Navarro and broadcast on France Culture in 1998. In this collection, Kristeva evokes in detail the Valley of Roses and the Slavic alphabet of her native Bulgaria, her beloved father and his cruel death, her early exposure by French nuns to French language and culture, and her personal experience with totalitarianism that in part at least explains her persistent calls for intellectuals to engage in revolt.

Such revelations of autobiographical material stand out because Kristeva is such an abstract thinker. Kristeva's rejection of girls' toys in a totalitarian state in the 1950s, her empty pockets and wet shoes when arriving in Paris in 1965, her ecstasies and terrors upon becoming a mother in 1975, her rage about her father's murder in 1989, and so on, provide the concrete anchors readers need to find their way through the density of her theoretical texts.

Micropolitics (2001)

From September 6, 2000, to July 25, 2001, every Wednesday morning at 8:25 a.m., Kristeva spoke on France Culture about current events or reviewed books. The broadcasts were collected in her 2001 volume entitled *Micropolitics*.[135] Among Kristeva's books, this is one of my favorites. It is a dizzying array of her unfiltered thoughts on politics, movies, art, and writers such as—listed here in the order of their appearance—Djebar, Woolf, Barthes, Aragon, Dostoevsky, Celan, Foucault, Bacon, Lacan, Céline, Colette, and Philip Roth.

Kristeva even talked about sexual politics, for instance about the debate in France over giving a child the mother's last name. Kristeva found it ridiculous that conservatives were using psychoanalysis to defend their rejection of this idea when, she argued, psychoanalysis would be the first to approve it because it recognizes the bi-poly-sexuality of everyone. I would argue that the importance of these broadcasts was due less to her revelations of details about her private life than to the fact that she touched her listeners because of the ambiance of the broadcasts: her listeners felt like they were in a private conversation with her over breakfast every Wednesday morning.

Chronicles of a Sensitive Time (2003)

I have already mentioned the continuation of Kristeva's broadcasts on France Culture (a bit earlier, at 7:55 a.m. on Wednesdays) from September 5, 2001, to July 24, 2002. These broadcasts were collected as *Chronicles of a Sensitive Time* in 2003 and were, overall, in the wake of 9/11, more political than the year before.[136] For instance, besides what I have already delineated, Kristeva emphasized the need to understand the unconscious depths of terrorist inspiration; she cautioned against underestimating "the psychic microcosm" as we organize our "macroscopic treatment" of violence and injustice; she worried about "biometrics," the security state, and privacy; she posited globalization as one of the causes of the unleashing of the death drive worldwide; and she once again praised artistic practice as a way to face up to the horrors propagated upon so many peoples of the world.

Kristeva did not hesitate to jump headfirst into controversy. For example, she talked about a deeply controversial letter published in the world media and sponsored post-9/11 by the conservative Institute for American Values. It was signed by academics across a wide political spectrum, but basically upheld the "clash of civilizations" school of thought put forward by the Institute's conservative Christian members. She recounted in her radio address how at a conference at Georgetown University, she had publicly agreed with the letter insofar as she agreed that terrorism must always be fought as an attack on universal values. However, because she recognized that the letter was one-sided, she had also used the occasion to praise—and to defend from righteous conservative indignation—contemporary artists and writers who were reflecting back to us the complex horrors of the world in their work. She argued that art is not only, or always only, about beauty. Rather, she argued that art must sometimes be ugly, that we must value the aesthetic process in some part because it can help protect civilizations from horror breaking out. Additionally, she reminded everyone that it was only in a democracy where such a conference could be held on such a contentious topic without fear of censorship or some kind of more violent retribution, even death.

Open Letter to the President (2003)

Kristeva's investment in helping David build an independent life has been immense over the years; from the outside, it has seemed herculean. She has stated publicly that, thanks to David and Sollers,

and thanks to her analysis as well as to her practice as an analyst—
and thanks to her daily writing practice—she has escaped the worst
suffering faced by mothers of handicapped children.[137] She has, of
course, also described dramatically harrowing moments, such as the
many times when David has inexplicably descended into a coma and
she has watched over him desperately at the hospital, herself feeling
as if she were hovering between life and death (she wrote most of
her book on Hannah Arendt while lying on a mattress at the foot
of David's hospital bed during one of his episodes). But most of her
caring for David, especially since he has been an adult, has been of the
quiet, everyday kind. Additionally, she has determinedly pursued the
conditions necessary for his independence.

As David became an adolescent and then a grown man, Kristeva ran
all over Paris, indeed all over Europe, in an attempt to find resources
to support her son as an intelligent and curious adult. She and Sollers
had managed for years to puzzle together both public and private
educational frameworks where David, with his parents' constant
support, managed to thrive intellectually and creatively. Kristeva
rearranged their apartment on rue d'Assas to accommodate his physical
disabilities. Furthermore, even though they had around-the-clock help
providing for David's well-being, Kristeva and Sollers carved out as
much time and space as possible to personally accompany him as he
explored music, painting, writing, and cultural events in Paris.

One of Kristeva's most disappointing efforts in the 2000s was to find
suitable housing—an arrangement along the lines of "assisted living"—
for David. Only a handful of organizations, such as the Catholic Simon
de Cyrène Association, offers such housing in Paris, and none of them
worked out long-term. This is how Kristeva and Sollers came into close
contact with people dealing with all kinds of disabilities as well as with
people who were trying to help them. As a result, Kristeva became
acutely aware of how little France recognizes disability as an issue. She
did not take well to hitting one wall after another in her quest to find help
for David. She became angry and frustrated, but because she is never
one to give up, she began to ask herself what could be done. It was in

the early 2000s that her private life (which had always been the basis for her thought, writing, and engagement), her role as a public intellectual in the media, and her activist yearnings to make things happen through creating new organizations came together powerfully around the issue of disability. She began to ask herself how she might help bring about an urgently needed social, economic, political, and ethical transformation in the treatment of disabled subjects in France. She even folded this question into the mix of her work on subjectivity and the need for a new humanism, thereby opening up new avenues of research.[138]

Little could Kristeva have imagined that her new research and institutional initiatives would take place with the help of a president and a priest. She started her efforts by wrangling an appointment with the President of France himself, Jacques Chirac, who had a handicapped daughter and who had built housing communities for the handicapped in the French region of Corrèze.[139] He asked her to write a report, which was published in 2003 as a book entitled, after Diderot, *Open Letter to the President of the Republic on Citizens with Disabilities, for the Use of Those Who Are Disabled and Those Who Are Not.*[140] She put together the National Council for the Handicapped and got busy reforming outdated laws from 1975.[141]

Kristeva and her colleagues worked tirelessly on multiple fronts from 2002 to 2005, engaging well-known celebrities to help shift public discourse, publishing articles and reports, producing public service announcements on television and radio, and organizing a Tour de France in support of disability. In 2003, in the wake of a deadly heatwave that killed many vulnerable citizens in France (indeed, all of Europe), Kristeva published an article in *Le Monde* with her colleague Charles Gardou, imploring the public to get involved in fighting against the "ignorance, indifference, even arrogance and barbarism with a compassionate face" in France.[142] She invited all French citizens to remember the systematic sterilization and murder of the vulnerable, including the disabled, under Hitler in 1933–45. She and Gardou— and this is the initiative of which she is most proud—also organized a special meeting of the General Assembly of UNESCO on May 20,

2005. To this meeting, entitled "Disability: Time for Engagement," they invited Jewish, Muslim, and Catholic intellectuals, including Jean Vanier, the founder and director of the Catholic Community of L'Arche.

Their Look Pierces Our Shadows (2011)

Most of Kristeva's work on the question of disability was a mixture of pragmatic initiatives and abstract thought, asking her readers to rethink "difference," modify the calculating and individualistic ideologies of secular society that keep us from thinking about our fear of death and hence push us to reject the ill, the poor, the elderly, and the disabled instead of considering them in terms of their uniqueness and singular, creative capacities. She reminded her readers that Jesus was a disabled God, carrying Christians' mortality for them, carrying their fear of their mortality. And she evoked her decades of psychoanalytic practice as well as her experience as the mother of a handicapped child.[143]

However, as time went on, Kristeva gradually became discouraged: public opinion was glacially slow to change, schools were stuck in their bureaucratic ways, and businesses were resistant to hiring the disabled. But Kristeva did not stop her efforts entirely. For example, she helped create the International Disability Movement: Solidarity, Equality.

With the help of the French national train system—the SNCF—she organized a cross-country tour so that the abled and the disabled could meet in cities across France to raise money. She continued to work with other countries, such as Norway, where more progress had been made than in France. But there was never enough money.

Meanwhile, Kristeva continued to search for opportunities for David without much luck. She got back in touch with Jean Vanier, the founder of L'Arche, which is a federation of one hundred and forty-six communities in thirty-five countries that welcomes the disabled to participate in workshops, social activities, cultural events, and in some

cases, to live in an Arche community permanently. L'Arche is inspired
by the Catholic faith of its theologian founder but is open to all. When,
in 2009, Kristeva became furious because the city of Paris abruptly
canceled a project for the handicapped that she and David had been
working on and also counting on for him, she went to see Vanier: "I
visited L'Arche de Compiègne where he lives, and I was overwhelmed
by the generous solidarity of the 'friends' (as they call themselves) who
live there."[144] Although David did not end up living there, Kristeva and
Vanier began talking about the plight of the disabled and they decided
to publish the letters they exchanged between June 2009 and August
2010 in *Their Look Pierces Our Shadows*.[145] The book's title is a haunting
line that evokes the 1894 play by Ibsen, *Little Eyolf*, where the memory
of the eyes of a drowned handicapped boy never leaves his mother in
peace.

Kristeva and Vanier's epistolary volume cannot possibly leave its
readers in peace either. Although Kristeva and Vanier are at their
best when they disagree over terms, philosophical assumptions, and
functions of the psyche, they come together in perfect agreement when
it comes to the need in modern culture for more care, for making more
time and space for love. I think that the book is Kristeva's most moving
publication, one where the strange mixture of a secular psychoanalyst's
call and a Catholic philosopher's response (and sometimes vice versa)
is guaranteed to haunt the reader for some time after closing the book.
When asked in 2016 how she would sum up her efforts to change
French society with regard to its most vulnerable, she said this:

> I think with gratitude about the medical, psychological, sociological,
> musical, and so many other teams that surround David and that I
> have met through him and his friends. It's true, I have a tendency to
> forget the fears, the tears, the errors, the unease . . . There only remains
> David's smile which gathers in everything he loves, all those with
> whom he shares his contagious vitality, wherever he wants, whenever
> he can, on the Île de Ré or in Paris, with his "I dream, therefore I am":
> that's life (*c'est la vie*). I just try to live up to this state of urgency that
> is life.[146]

Murder in Byzantium (2004)

I have suggested all along that, for Kristeva, life is writing and writing is life. And sometimes this life-as-writing/writing-as-life brings surprises. When I closed Kristeva's third "metaphysical detective novel," the 2004 *Murder in Byzantium*, I wrote to a friend and said, "Wow, I've been reading Julia Kristeva for three decades and I've never ... There's a wild woman in there somewhere!"[147]

Kristeva never tries consciously—intentionally—to translate her theoretical work into her novels, writing her theory primarily by day and her fiction by night. But all the grave theoretical and political matters that Kristeva was writing about in the 2000s are present in this novel: the question of how to get individuals and societies to interrogate their deepest truths; how to get Catholic Europe to engage culturally with Orthodox Europe; how to find ways for the formerly religious subject to experience bliss without resorting to drugs or television in a culture where the only event resisting the remote control is one's death; how to save the human psyche from robotic depression as we global subjects become unequally but inevitably immersed in the dizzying globalization of the death/suicidal drive through hyperconnectivity; how to reinvent social connections as the old symbolic order and its authority—its institutions writ large—implodes throughout the global village inebriated by spectacle and under the boot of mafia-infused governmental control; and how to sidestep the temptation of the "radical evil" that she herself once viscerally experienced as Stalinism and that seems to be re-emerging in the twenty-first century. All of this can be found in *Murder in Byzantium* as smoke, fog, echo, and an intricate web of background noise to what is ultimately a light-hearted, carnivalesque, kaleidoscopic—in her words, a polylogical/polyphonic—novel. But mainly it is an amazingly wild romp through time and space, love and loss, truth and its impossibilities, the need to believe and the desire to know.

Without aspiring to sum up this novel—which would be a ridiculous task—I will try to trace briefly its main pathways. Stephanie Delacour, the intrepid journalist detective, is once again sent to Santa Varvara—the corrupt place that might be Bulgaria or Eastern Europe but is mostly the global village—to report on a series of murders by the Purifier (Xiao Chang) who is killing off members of a drugs-mafia-religion cult called the New Pantheon. Stephanie becomes lovers with the police chief, Northrop Rilsky. Hence we have the first murderer (Xiao Chang) and the first love story (Stephanie and Rilsky). Meanwhile, Professor Sebastian Chrest-Jones (note *Kristev* meaning "of the cross" plus the letter *J* evoking Julia), a professor of human migration, is secretly writing a novel about the first woman historian—indeed the first woman intellectual in Western history—the Byzantine princess, Anna Comnena. Sebastian goes off to find out more about (and in fact even hallucinates becoming) Anna's great lost love, Ebrard, who is probably the professor's ancestor and who roamed across Europe all the way to Byzantium during the First Crusade. Hence we have a second murder (Sebastian kills along the way his pregnant Chinese lover, Fa, sister of the Purifier) and a second love story (Sebastian is "in love" with Anna). And so it goes.

The climactic scene of the novel takes place in the Cathedral Notre-Dame du Puy, the famous World Heritage Site in southern France, ending Sebastian's footsteps in the shadow of the First Crusade as well as his and the Purifier's lives in a blaze of gunfire. Stephanie returns to Paris, slowly absorbs the death of her mother, but almost as soon as she does, and just as her boss is demanding that she finish her article on what happened in Santa Varvara, the entire Louvre explodes, going up in flames from a terrorist attack. This turns out to be just a nightmare. But Stephanie decides that she cannot stay in Paris with this nightmare in the back of her mind, so she goes back to Santa Varvara, where there is already a new Purifier at work. She needs to investigate.

Who is the real heroine or hero of the novel? Stephanie is, at least on the surface. Some have argued that it is really Anna Comnena. Or maybe it is Sebastian. What is clear is that the authorial voice is deeply fractured among Stephanie, Sebastian, and Anna, the journalist and the professor and the historian, all sensual, all searching for answers. And where is Byzantium? It is not really to be found; it is not on the map. There is the historical empire of course, one which we come to know through Sebastian's (a.k.a. Ebrard's) travels and Anna's biography. But the Byzantium that Kristeva sketches does not exist yet, or only does so as a dream, as an imaginary place of the future where the dark times of the novel as well as the dark times of Kristeva's time of writing the novel are long past. Kristeva started the novel in 1995 and published it three years after 9/11 and one year after the invasion of Iraq. She has called these years the time of demons, of killer instincts: Dark Times. In 2013, Kristeva argued that Byzantium is the Europe that is in the process— that could/should be in the process—of being built.[148]

Over the years, Kristeva has been increasingly explicit about some of the things that she was trying to accomplish in the novel, many of which are familiar by now. She wanted to talk about Bulgaria and the Orthodox faith and the difficulty that Europe as a whole has in overcoming the historical schism between Rome and Byzantium. She wanted to explore the depression of Orthodox Europe and why it was there that communism was able to gain such an ironclad hold. She wanted to write a novel of the subject, not of the ego, exploring the limits of identity (where there is no more self) and the optimism of asking questions (of oneself especially), of believing that it is possible to know an answer to an enigma with enough investigation. She wanted to explore time, the diversity of time frames we all live in all the time at the same time, with murder as the ultimate "catastrophe of time."

Murder in Byzantium was her best-received novel to date, at least according to the French newspaper *Le Monde*. The media overall expressed surprised but solid praise. *The New York Times* called it a "total novel" *à la* European eighteenth century. And in May 2005, Kristeva was invited to Sofia and Sliven to celebrate the publication of the novel. In Sofia, she told a journalist that "there are also characters in the novel, who are Bulgarian foreigners—like me. They have left this country many years ago, but always come back"—just like Stephanie Delacour who went back to Santa Varvara in the end.[149] Likewise, in an important interview about the novel, one that concludes her 2006 collection of essays, *Hatred and Forgiveness*, Kristeva makes explicit many of the connections between her own life and what happens in the novel. However, despite the media's relatively positive reception, Kristeva did not feel that the novel was genuinely appreciated. Most telling to me is what she says in the interview about feeling not heard, about being once again rejected as foreign, as strange, and what she postulates as being the consequences of that deafness:

> While writing this novel, as well as after publishing it and listening to you now, I kept asking myself: "Who is ready to hear this?" . . . And yet I threw myself into this saga of immigrants that *Murder in Byzantium* is with a sort of enthusiasm, the kind you have when, surrounded by walls, you knock [on them], thinking in spite of everything, it might be heard one day.[150]

Hatred and Forgiveness (2005)

Almost a companion to *Murder in Byzantium*, *Hatred and Forgiveness* is a collection of some forty articles, lectures, and interviews, all but one written between 1998 and 2005, most of them between 2001 and 2005.[151] A map of Kristeva's thinking over the period in which she was writing her novel, the essays in *Hatred and Forgiveness* address cultural politics (China, Europe, secularism, disability, linguistic diversity, etc.); sexual politics (parity, maternity, beauty, etc.); psychoanalytic practice (cases, concepts, etc.); religions and their concepts; literary and artistic figures from Beauvoir and Duras to Proust, Aragon, and Celan; and less familiar figures to English-speaking audiences, such as the philosopher Sylvie Courtine-Denamy and the French artist Annette Messager.

Most of the articles that comprise the French 700-page edition were translated for the American edition, and several of them are well known, such as her Holberg address, her thoughts on vulnerability, on Barthes, and on Georgia O'Keeffe. She has described the volume as a record of her life during those seven years: a record of her thought in action, a kind of "current events of her intelligence." All the essays address her primary effort of the first decade of the 2000s: her insistence that intellectuals rethink our Western heritage through a transposition of its values. But there are a few things that struck me as being "new" in *Hatred and Forgiveness*, especially for those who follow Kristeva's intellectual journey at a distance: her thoughts about her work's reception in China (originally written for the Chinese edition of her much-criticized *About Chinese Women*); her comments about the publication of her 1980 *Powers of Horror* in Chinese; and her fervent plea for new forms of secularism, articulated in her 2003 talk before the French Senate, "Secularism: 'Values' at the Limits of Life."[152]

Of the many ways in which Kristeva was thinking her living-while-writing in *Hatred and Forgiveness*, let me mention just one additional formulation. In a chapter entitled "Desire for Law," she discusses the horrors at the Abu Ghraib Prison in 2003–4 as the new normal for the Santa Varvara which is our global village.[153] Her intellectual, ethical, and moral outrage is palpable. She proposes that in our global village, on the one hand, we are dealing—in part through our increasingly instrumental educational system—with an adherence to professional rigor and law and, on the other—in part through the internet and its social media—with a complete disinhibition of drives:

> Never before has the high level of technical perfectionism required from such a large number of people such an effort of coded apprenticeship, of conformity with the law, but a law reduced to *regulations* organizing the efficiency of a system and its underlings, a law calling for surveillance, concentration, and self-control: in short, ferocious repression turning the functionaries of the "new world order" that we are into robots. The desire for Law has become a desire subjected to a supposedly winning set of regulations. In counterpoint to this coded Puritanism and these regulations, the rush toward uninhibited satisfaction explodes. Never before has the influence of the image over the body laid our sadomasochistic drives bare so lightly: the rule is for robots to have a blast, film themselves, and communicate through discharge in all innocence! The desire for the other is deviated into a manic jouissance that is sustained by the sexual victimization of others.[154]

Kristeva ends by stating categorically that "we lack the words, instruction, and discussion that would allow us to reflect on the urgent measures that should be taken to try to remedy this psychosis, this split, this abyss that today separates *desire for Law* from *desire for the other*. Unless it is too late."[155]

Kristeva's interest in hyperconnectivity persists beyond *Hatred and Forgiveness*. In a 2006 article entitled "Truth and Art," Kristeva reads Claude Lanzmann's film *Shoah* along with the work of the American psychoanalytic critic Shoshana Felman in order to offer a striking hypothesis about how, during the Shoah, it was the refusal to see what was happening that allowed for its horror.[156] She goes on to claim that today we see this old problem in reverse: everything is "seen." We can "see" everything via the internet. Everything is visible via satellite technology:

> Have we taken the measure of the historical catastrophe that the Shoah has inflicted upon us? We have reacted by counter-investment in the visible: the look is everywhere at once; there is not a single event that escapes the register of the visible. But this inflation of vision is deprived of *intelligence*. Is this privation the most insidious endurance of the *catastrophe*, of the Shoah? This train in motion, without end.[157]

Alone, a Woman (2007)

Against this grim backdrop, I once again want to emphasize Kristeva's insistence that no less than the future of humankind may be up to women—at least to those women who, along with their allies, struggle in their lives and work to surpass the historical, social, political, and psychic situation in which they find themselves. Between 2000 and 2005, Kristeva published four books on two women who did just that. That is, she published four books on the two women who, besides Hannah Arendt, make up her trilogy on female genius: her 2000 *Melanie Klein* and her 2002 *Colette*, as well as two companion volumes to her book on Colette, namely her edited volume on Colette, the 2004 *Our Colette*, and her pithy 2005 essay on sublimation and/in Colette, *Self-Love and Its Avatars*.[158] The entire decade (in fact since the late 1990s) she was also, in tandem, writing her novel on Saint Teresa of Ávila: *Teresa, My Love*, published in 2008. Kristeva also published a collection of journalistic articles, talks, and interviews on women: her 2007 *Alone, a Woman*.[159]

Alone, a Woman consists of three parts: first, there are articles that Kristeva wrote in the late 1980s mostly for the popular women's publication, *Femme*, on topics ranging from "superwomen" to "seduction." The second section contains articles on singularly accomplished women from the seventeenth and eighteenth centuries (Madame de Staël, Olympe de Gouges, etc.). The third section collects articles from the 1970s to the 2000s on a range of topics having to do with her thoughts on women and femininity, most of which I have already touched upon.

Most interesting to me in this volume is Kristeva's introductory interview with Navarro—the journalist who had interviewed her for *At the Risk of Thought*—where she repeatedly comes back to the question of freedom for women, to how important it is for women not to confuse "choice" with freedom, to how essential it is for each woman to make herself "strange" to herself. Most importantly, Kristeva repeatedly encourages women to push beyond their situation toward their unique capacity for thinking, however "singularly" this might manifest itself in the world.[160]

As I have emphasized, Kristeva's focus on the singular contributions of three exemplary women's thoughts on life (Arendt), madness (Klein), and words (Colette) was organized around the need for women's genius in the future. Recall that her assessment of female genius is that it can be found where there is 1) an emphasis on singularity/originality but only within a web of human relationship, linkage, and care; 2) an identification of thought with life, where to live is to think-sublimate-create; and 3) an insistence on the temporality of starting anew, of re-birth, of continual flowering—of getting up and continuing to run even after falling down.

Melanie Klein (2000)

Kristeva admires enormously the sometimes controversial Austrian-British psychoanalyst Melanie Klein for her innovation in all three of these domains (especially the first), and in many ways, identifies with her intellectual efforts as much as she does with those of Arendt:

> Both [Arendt and Klein] were interested in the object and the social bond, were drawn to the destruction of thought ("evil" for Arendt and "psychosis" for Klein), and resisted linear modes of reasoning. To those similarities were added some existential parallels: the two intellectuals, both of whom emerged from secular Jewish worlds, appropriated Christian philosophy, Enlightenment humanism, and contemporary science in a uniquely critical and highly personal way.[161]

Kristeva sees Klein as the most original innovator of the "psychoanalytic century." She sees Klein as having gone further than Freud, not by breaking with his teaching, but by filling in his blind spots, and especially by moving the psychoanalytic lens from the father to the mother through a focus on the infant's bond with the mother. Kristeva emphasizes that through her analysis of that bond, Klein articulates matricide as an essential piece of psychic development, indeed as the primary mechanism required for creativity, for the journey from fantasy to thought. That is, Klein illustrates that the child's transition to psychic life requires a traumatic separation from the mother, a separation that, in the best of circumstances, induces the child to seek to repair the damage that it—phantasmatically, due to this very separation, to this very matricide—has inflicted on the mother. In other words, what Klein famously called the paranoid-schizoid position, under ideal conditions, generates the desire for restorative reparation, which in turn functions as the foundation of creativity. However, because the impulse to repair only arises from matricide, matricide resides at the core of Klein's theory of psychic development. Through this line of reasoning, Klein single-handedly raises the mother to the position of being the source of thought itself.

For Kristeva, Klein's psychoanalytic innovation was "to listen to—and to solicit—*a desire that thinks*," as well as to recognize that it is matricide that resides "at the origin of our capacity to think."[162] Furthermore, Kristeva believes that the Kleinian understanding of our capacity to think can help to save the world.[163] In Kristeva's view, the preservation of the mind and the spirit of humanity can only be accomplished through a new ethic of care, an ethic that is grounded in the mother-infant bond and that turns us outward toward others. As we have seen, Kristeva calls this ethic *reliance*. Kristeva developed this concept primarily through Klein. And she struggles to bring it into existence concretely through, for instance, her actions to protect and support the vulnerable, especially the handicapped, in France. She is quick to point out that the realization of this admittedly utopian vision would require a complete transformation of civilization; it would require us to begin to value those who care for others in our society.

Colette (2002)

If Kristeva's book on Arendt is a political love letter, and if her book on Klein is an analytic one, her book on Colette is an ode to sensual delight. Kristeva admires and respects Arendt and is full of curiosity regarding Klein, but when it comes to Colette, she is mostly enchanted and overcome with the pleasure of reading. Although the three women of Kristeva's "female genius" trilogy are linked—and in some ways represent different facets of Kristeva herself—with Colette she moves onto the terrain of "an alphabet written as part of the world's flesh."[164]

For Kristeva, Colette invents new alphabets, providing Kristeva with "jubilant memories" of the annual Festival of the Alphabet of her youth. When she was learning French in Bulgaria, Kristeva was given short excerpts—some of which were about flowers—to read from Colette. Kristeva has always loved flowers. She has talked in French magazine interviews about her love of gardening at the Île de Ré, all in precise descriptive detail. And when, as a little girl, she climbed to the treetops to read, she read Colette out loud, learning passages by heart. She is drawn to Colette's rapturous textual absorption of the scents of food and perfumes, and of the hushed sounds of lovers' voices. She is also drawn to the melancholic sobs of Colette's disappointments in love. She has argued that, like most artists, Colette had a healthy—even extravagant—dose of self-love which was thankfully sublimated into an aesthetic practice that often helps her, Kristeva, to understand her own feelings, disappointments, and attitudes: Yes, death is but a commonplace defeat, and yes, after love is over, life can be gay again.

Kristeva also tries to address the ambiguous—some would say willfully blind—attitude that Colette adopted toward politics during the French Occupation. While detailing Colette's naïve dismissal of politics, Kristeva also emphasizes Colette's resistant cult of happiness, her will to survive, to write, to describe the world with compassion— her affirmative genius. While never excusing Colette, Kristeva attempts to understand why Colette in her last years was so lost in the imaginary she could not see what was happening before her very eyes. Kristeva has also always been fascinated by the strange mother-daughter relationships in Colette, by the textualities of motherhood in Colette, and by the omnipresence of the mother in many of Colette's novels. In addition, she is intrigued by Colette's representation of sexuality. When asked whether the university has been so slow to accept Colette because Colette's writing is seen as fiction for girls in bordellos rather than for university professors, Kristeva jokes: "My university experience, for two decades, persuades me that university professors do not necessarily have the finesse of certain bordello girls."[165]

In my opinion, some of Kristeva's best readings of Colette are about "illicit" sex, about the "hypersensitive intimacies" and "erotic excitations" of Colette's enthusiastic Dionysian relations with everyone and everything—men, women, plants, beasts, and monsters—and about "their constant metamorphosis into writing."[166] Expressing her relief that "psychoanalysis is currently abandoning the normativity that taints its fundamental notions"—that it is finally moving beyond the dichotomy of the sexes and its binaristic vision of sexuality—Kristeva dives into an exploration of Colette's psychic and bodily sexualities, her bisexuality, her polysexuality.[167] For Kristeva, Colette's polymorphous sexualities and her incestuous experiments (with her stepson, Bertrand) were an important laboratory where her self-love was transmuted into an almost mystical song of desire where "it is my body that thinks" and "my whole skin has a soul."[168] Bisexuality. Mysticism. The Body. To the extent that Kristeva believes that "the passion for unconscious truth is the indelible mark of both the man and woman of genius," we are not far at all from a saint like Teresa.[169] We have, in fact, never left her behind.

Teresa, My Love (2008)

Kristeva has been fascinated by—and philosophically interested in—the mysteries of spirituality for a long time. In some sense, this has been true since, as a child, she accompanied her father and sister to Orthodox services at dawn. But it has certainly been true at an intellectual level since at least the 1970s when she and Michel de Certeau began looking at religion from a psychoanalytic point of view in their seminar on "Psychosis and Truth." A series of intellectual interests and historical forces then brought religion, especially Judeo-Christian philosophy, to the very forefront of Kristeva's attention in the 2000s. She had been focusing for a while on how to rethink—to transvalue—the Western tradition, including its dominant religious infrastructure of Judeo-Christianity, and on how, as the ultimate goal, to re-found, to re-formulate secular humanism. Her 2005 *Hatred and Forgiveness*—on atheism, on the question of peace, on Catholicism, on Israel, and so on—clearly signaled her increasing focus on religious history, culture, and politics. On a different track, through her work on Melanie Klein she had begun to focus psychoanalytically on adolescence as a time of deep identity crisis—a time that frequently includes strong mystical yearnings—and sometimes as a time of disconnection when not disappointment, depression when not abjection. Simultaneously, she was becoming deeply concerned about the rising violence in the 1990s and 2000s perpetrated mostly by adolescent men at the heart of Western democracies: the cascade of fundamentalist terrorist attacks in the name of Islam after 9/11, the explosion of riots in the Parisian suburbs in 2005, and the extreme rantings of anti-immigrant and Islamophobic white nationalists across Europe. It was, however, a surprisingly pragmatic moment that laid the foundation for the transformation of these intersecting interests—spirituality and religion, the psychic structures of adolescence, and political and social violence—into a more focused and sustained inquiry.

In the late 1990s, Kristeva's former student, Frédéric Boyer—who had written a dissertation under her direction on spiritual experience in the works of Proust, Dostoevsky, and Marguerite Duras—called her. Since finishing his studies, he had become a successful novelist, a translator of the Bible, and also the Director of Bayard Press, one of the oldest publishing houses in France associated with the Catholic Church. Boyer told Kristeva that he was publishing a small collection of books on Western spiritual leaders and asked whether she would be interested in writing one of them from a psychoanalytic perspective.

Kristeva was in the middle of writing *Murder in Byzantium*, so she was not sure. She also stated bluntly that she just did not "know much about all that." She did, however, suggest that perhaps a volume could be devoted to Anna Comnena, the deeply impressive and prolific eleventh-century writer and historian of the crusades (and also a character at the heart of Kristeva's novel) who had converted to Christianity. Boyer said no: no one had ever heard of Anna Comnena. But he wondered about "the mystic, Saint Teresa of Ávila." Kristeva replied that she did not know anything about her. Broyer suggested that she read some of the mystic's work and give him a call back.

Kristeva did not stop reading for several years. She read everything she could get her hands on by or about Teresa and, as always, she started writing. Slowly but surely, the pages mounted . . . hundreds and hundreds of them . . . so much so that she eventually told Boyer that she was not capable of writing a short book on Teresa of Ávila. She told him that she had become transfixed by this amazing woman writer, historian, founder of convents, mystic, and rebel who inspired the age of the Baroque, who was in some ways the missing link between the Renaissance and the Enlightenment. Kristeva could not bear the thought of applying three or four psychoanalytic concepts in a short text to such a prolific, brilliant, and important woman—another woman genius. As a result, Boyer and she canceled the book contract, and she turned to her editor at Fayard, Claude Durand, asking him to help her figure out how to cut the pages down, how to tame the manuscript. He said that he did not want her to tame it. He wanted to publish it as it stood. Thus came about Kristeva's 700-page *Teresa, My Love*, published in 2008.[170] This story, essay, or novel—what I can only call a *cri du cœur* (or in English, less accurately, a "cry from the heart") caught fire with the European—especially Italian—reading public.

This Incredible Need to Believe (2007)

At about the same time, because Kristeva felt badly about having broken her contract with Bayard, she submitted to them a long interview on "the need to believe" that she had originally published in Italian, combining it with several short texts addressing Christianity and the question of Europe. Bayard published this collection in 2007 as *This Incredible Need to Believe*.[171] Like her enormous book on Saint Teresa, this little book on "the need to believe" as the foundation of "the desire to know" attracted a great deal of attention, with the consequence that Kristeva spent a lot of time on the radio and television talking about both books, together and apart.

Kristeva spent a lot of time, especially in the beginning, answering the question of how an atheist, a Freudian psychoanalyst, and a "liberated woman" to boot, could become so deeply invested in understanding religious thought, its different forms, its histories and political implications—especially for human subjectivity. She tended to defend her interest in religion by discussing the ways in which philosophy and theology had divorced in the twentieth century, arguing that the human sciences cutting ties with religion, with theology, had been a disastrous mistake because of the ways in which the human psyche works.[172] She argued that humanity is at a turning point and that religion, along with time and sexuality, is an important "mutation" that we are undergoing in the West. She proposed that it has become vital to understand "the need to believe" as a universal, pre-religious, and pre-political need for human investment, for an investment in oneself, others, and especially language.

Kristeva's reasoning relied on a psychoanalytic interpretation of how infants become invested in things, including themselves, but she did not hesitate to extrapolate from this interpretation to a much larger argument about belief and its vicissitudes. She explained that the problems facing civilization today cannot be solved politically, that while remaining a firm atheist, she could perceive that the widening gap in Western democracies between secular politics on the one hand and religious belief on the other has caused the *ethical* dimension of politics to recede from view, making it impossible for "the need to believe" to transform into "the desire to know."[173]

Kristeva agreed that we all have an obligation to continue the critique, the deconstruction of world religions, and of Christianity in particular, in order to understand better all the ways in which they have been destructive. Christianity, for example, has an ugly history from the Inquisition and witch hunts of earlier times to the denial, control, and even abuse of the body and its sexuality today (which has been especially detrimental to women). At the same time, she insisted that Freud's examination of religion (as not only an illusion) is crying out to be continued today because only psychoanalytic work on the psychic mechanisms of belief—work interrupted by the horrors of World War II—can resist the rising destruction of psychic space which is also a spiritual space. She stated in different ways that she wanted to mobilize her insight and knowledge as an atheist, a psychoanalyst, and a woman to explore these problems. She had to constantly insist that her interest in religion did not mean that she was getting "religious." She pointed out that the Catholics were much more accepting of her as an avowed atheist than the mainstream press.[174]

I would argue that Kristeva's interest in spirituality over the course of the 2000s resulted principally from two by then deeply entrenched experiential components of her life. First, there was her experience as an analyst.[175] But the second, and perhaps deeper port of entry into the question of faith was the one that she had entered as a child via her father's deep religiosity. She draws a link between these two influences as follows: "During my childhood, my father's faith not only seemed incomprehensible to me, but also irredeemably archaic—no point in knowing about it or in questioning it. It was only my discovery of Freud later on that was going to clarify things for me as to the interdependence of faith and reason."[176]

Reinventing Secular Humanism

Kristeva set out to lead an interdisciplinary conversation about how to reformulate secular humanism through an understanding of the logics of the religions that no longer hold us together socially:

> It's a mission, I accept the word, and it's a long-term and delicate mission. And it is important at each step along the way to refine the means used to carry it out. It is not a question of being "Counselor to the Prince" nor of becoming satisfied in the role of "Media Intellectual." Even less is it a question of playing a political "role." Quite simply, it is a question of trying to *think deeply* about [today's] symptoms, about anguishes and the ways they get expressed and to communicate that [thinking] to others. [This is] a form of engagement that is without political affiliation, transversal to political parties, but one which shares neither the nihilism of an "end to history" nor the abstentionism of an "end of the political." Yes, the re-foundation of humanism is a political act, a bet placed on [the possibility of] a different kind of politics.[177]

Kristeva's published work and public appearances on the topic of religion led to a stream of invitations which in turn led to new initiatives on her part to bring her work to different kinds of publics. For example, in 2006 she accepted an invitation to participate in the Lenten Lecture Series held every March at the Cathedral Notre-Dame de Paris. On March 16, the topic was "Suffering," and Kristeva was shocked to be invited to speak: "What can Catholics expect to hear from me in the fabulous space of Notre-Dame de Paris?" It must have been strange for her to find herself an honored guest in the very cathedral that she had ducked into during her first couple of days in Paris in 1965 in order to gain some solace from her loneliness as well as to stay warm and dry and where, to her not yet recalibrated communist eyes, the Parisians and tourists inside the cathedral had seemed like brightly wrapped Christmas gifts. Her 2006 talk on Christian models of suffering and its sublimation into words and images, beginning with Christ, was deeply psychoanalytic and focused on how humanism might remodel Christian empathy and compassion in the age of globalization and the internet. Her talk was published in *This Incredible Need to Believe* along with an interview about the experience. What she emphasizes most is the necessity of more such crossings of boundaries, more interdisciplinary, intersymbolic conversations.[178]

Kristeva went on to help invent such a conversation in Jerusalem. In November 2008, she was invited to participate in a conversation among psychoanalysts, theologians, art historians, social historians, scientists, doctors, and others at the inaugural meeting of "The Standing Interdisciplinary Forum: Psychoanalysis, Belief, and Religious Conflicts." She came prepared to think big, and in her talk, "Jerusalem," she did exactly that.[179] This talk would be a great place to start for those who are new to this aspect of Kristeva's thinking. From Freud through Lévi-Strauss to Lacan, from women and mothers to modern forms of subjectivity, Kristeva skims the interface between psychoanalysis and religion while outlining her theory of the "need to believe"; love and hatred for the father in Freud, Christianity, and Islam; the invitation by modern secularism to see so-called "transgressions of the symbolic order" not as faults but as opportunities to invent new forms of kinship, new kinds of families, and new legalities.

A few years later, Kristeva launched another interdisciplinary initiative, the Montesquieu Project, in Paris at the Collège des Bernardins in the 5th arrondissement. This initiative is still going strong today, most recently focusing on the rise in antisemitism in Europe. Kristeva has spoken there several times on the rights of the handicapped and on female genius, but mostly it is a space where the unlikeliest of interlocutors come together to take up her challenge to work through their antagonisms in order to invent new forms of secular humanism.[180]

The "French Death of God Theologian"

Kristeva's personal atheism and her politico-intellectual emphasis on secular humanism throughout all of these initiatives have not stopped some in the media from calling her "a mystical atheist" or a "psychoanalytic theologian." In fact, some distinguished philosophers and theologians have praised her as one of the world's *most important* theologians. For example, Thomas Altizer, the famous radical theologian who has joked about being the "American Death of God Theologian," has said that Kristeva (sometimes called the "French Death of God Theologian") is a *great* theologian second only to Karl Barth, the Swiss Reformer reputed to have been the greatest Protestant theologian of the twentieth century.[181]

Kristeva finds these accolades a bit overwhelming and strange. But she has noticed that it is often the theologians of the world who hear her argument best even though they also insist that if she is saying many of the same things as they are saying, this must be because God is inside of her. Kristeva usually smiles patiently and nods sympathetically at these remarks. She sometimes retorts that it was precisely Saint Teresa's sense that Jesus was inside of her that invited others to call her mad and indeed brought on the danger of being burned at the stake for heresy by the inquisitors. Kristeva then usually goes on to talk about how her psychoanalytic exploration of the "interior château"—of psychic space— no doubt echoes their spiritual exploration, but that it nevertheless is different. For her, it is an exploration of language-with-the-unconscious where no absolute values, no laws (or institutions) can be found, where the singular genius of each human can (hopefully) be gathered into a multitude of singularities within an ethical project of humanistic—rather than religious—understanding, learning, and expression.

With the publication of *This Incredible Need to Believe* in 2007, Kristeva was in some ways continuing her work on revolt from the 1990s, but she was doing so by focusing on the adolescent as an archetype of rebellion. She was also continuing her practice of following Nietzsche's advice to put a giant question mark after all big ideas, this time after "God." And she was staying faithful to her practice as a psychoanalyst, pursuing a "diagnosis" of what she sees as a pre-religious "need to believe" as an inner experience common to all of us. Further, she was doing so because she believes that an "emotional, experiential, and sharable knowledge of the inner experience is possible" because it is *discursive*.[182]

Kristeva always begins her discussion of faith with the Sanskrit word *credo*: "to give one's heart, one's vital force, in the expectation of a reward," an "act of confidence" (which will eventually extend to the idea of "credit"). The investment of *credo* on the part of the infant is psychoanalytically complex, but what it leads to is a sense of holding onto, a sense of "I hold this to be utterly true," a sense of safety and belonging. It is a truth that falls upon you, that you stumble across: it is vital, solid, absolute, and indisputable (not unlike the belief that an analyst must feel for the stories told by an analysand in order for transference and countertransference to work). It is on the basis of this believing that the child can look away from the caring parents, especially the mother, toward the world and develop a desire to know: exploding with questions, language arrives.

The Crisis of Ideality

This strong foundation of belief trembles at the advent of adolescence when a new kind of subject, "the teenager"—still a true believer—rejects the parents and searches for an erotic object, an *ideal erotic object*, in order to find a paradise in which to invest *à la* Romeo and Juliet. Structured by idealization, by a desire for absolute satisfaction, the fragile adolescent is almost always in some kind of crisis because nothing can quite measure up to the ideal. That is, the adolescent is a subject in a state of what Kristeva calls an "ideality disorder": "Remember that adolescence breaks out of childhood at the very moment the subject is convinced that *there is another ideal for him*—partner, husband, wife, professional-political-ideological-religious ideal—and that this ideality is already present in the unconscious; the adolescent unconscious is structured like this ideality."[183]

When the psychic identity of an adolescent, even a fragile one, is satisfied, sublimation takes over and the death wish is integrated into an identity and an ideal, usually through a form of love. This prevents destruction. But if things do not go well—if there is severe disappointment, if ideals are deceptive or unavailable or impossible, and especially if this happens repeatedly—one falls into pieces. There is a void-hallucination-obscurity that sets in, the ego explodes in release, the subject feels intense suffering, and the result can be the punishment of oneself (drugs, depression, eating disorders, suicide) or of others (the parents, the disappointing object). That is, the adolescent acts out, which, in extreme cases, can take the form of delinquency, and ultimately, nihilism, violence, or murder:

> Endemic to and connected to every adolescence, the *ideality disorder* risks becoming a form of profound psychic disorganization, if a sociohistorical, personal, traumatic context pushes it in that direction. In that case, the avidity of absolute satisfaction resolves in the destruction of everything that is not this satisfaction, abolishing the border between myself and the other, the inside and the outside, between good and evil. *No link* to any "object" exists for these "subjects" who are no longer subjects but are prey to what André Green calls disconnection, with its two versions of desubjectivation and deobjectivation. [This is] where all that triumphs is the death drive, the malignancy of evil.[184]

Kristeva frequently spoke about the riots and fires in the Parisian suburbs and in Marseille—led mostly by disenfranchised, often immigrant young men—at the time she was writing about adolescence. However, for her these disturbances were not a matter of any kind of interreligious, interethnic, or civilizational identity or clash; rather, they were about the cruelties of denying the idealized aspirations of adolescents. They were about brutal discrimination. What were burning in the suburbs were idealized, envied, and denied objects—cars, stores—or symbols of adult authority figures who had disappointed or excluded or mistreated the enraged young people running through the streets: schools, police stations, churches.[185]

The crisis of ideality does not of course necessarily always end in violence, at least not right away. Kristeva also wrote about how dreams of "paradise" could be manipulated by bourgeois culture into idealized domesticity and soap operas that would, however, one day disappoint. And from a psychoanalytic perspective, violence that is deferred will always ultimately return.

Kristeva was adamant that organized religion could not fix the problem of the nonintegrated, desocialized adolescents who were traumatized by merciless globalization and succumbing to violent crises of ideality. She rejected both the handwringing of politicians and the moralizing of religious readers. For instance, she explicitly argued against Jürgen Habermas and Joseph Ratzinger's calls for "normative presuppositions," "conservative conscience," and a "correlation between reason and faith."[186] Instead she made a plea for "ideals adapted to modern times and to the multicultural soul": "On the political level, this need of ideals, of recognition and respect crystallizes into a single battle, and it is a huge one, considering the suffering it reveals and the extent of the changes needed: the battle against discrimination."[187]

Kristeva argued that she was part of a generation that might be able to help through an attempt to redefine the ideals of humanism—away from "soft humanism, this fuzzy 'idea of man,' devoid of substance, bonded to a utopian fraternity, which harked back to the Enlightenment and the postrevolutionary contract."[188] For her, humanism is instead a state of perpetual questioning, a permanent interrogation. It is an interrogation neither *for* nor *against* religion but only *of* it to the extent that it can help us understand the need to believe and how to transvalue this need for modern times. She insisted that religion must not be rejected as an illusion under new extreme forms of secularism (such as the communism she grew up with) but must remain an important part of the conversation.

When Kristeva moved her seminar, "The Need to Believe," from the University of Paris 7 to the Maison de Solenn—a multicultural clinic of ethnopsychiatry for adolescents at the Cochin Hospital—she invited philosophers, psychologists, sociologists, and practicing psychoanalysts to participate in building "a new anthropology." But she especially invited religious leaders of all persuasions. "We must not be afraid," she stated, "to pursue this work of reevaluation of traditions with which secularization has cut ties ... Certain analysts respond to it, for example, Fethi Benslama with Islam, Daniel Sibony with Judaism. I questioned, for my part, Catholic mysticism, beginning with the texts of Teresa of Ávila.[189]

Teresa, Our Contemporary

Kristeva dedicated her 2008 "novel-essay" on Saint Teresa to her father. In the French edition of the book, the dedication is placed immediately before (and in the English edition, immediately after) a photo of the famous Bernini statue of the saint in a state of ecstasy or—in Lacan's words—*jouissance*. It is a striking if unintentional juxtaposition.[190] What follows is a wildly ecstatic, pleasure-filled text whose basic theme is, quite simply, real, deep, and infinite love—and not exclusively erotic love. In the text, Sylvia Leclercq, a psychoanalyst who shares many qualities with Kristeva, is the unstable but dominant narrator who discovers the writings of Teresa of Ávila, the sixteenth-century Spanish writer, mystic, and founder of seventeen Carmelite monasteries in twenty years. The two together—at times they are indistinguishable—

set out on a voyage of discovery while Sylvia also sees patients, engages in romance, travels to Ávila, and raises her son Paul, who shares many qualities and more than a few favorite sayings—"I dream, therefore I am"—with David.

However, the real story consists of Sylvia and Teresa's loving travels together to the edges of subjectivity, where they together skim the boundaries of meaning through ecstasy, even rapture. Beyond the ego is the id—this Freudian insight is updated by Kristeva when she describes her text: "The outside-of-time nature of the unconscious dilates the ecstasies of *Teresa, My Love*."[191] This ecstasy runs through a hybrid mix of biography, history, fiction, psychoanalytic theory, case studies, a three-act play, and ends with a letter to Diderot. But mostly it is a dialogue between Teresa—a kind of linguistic precursor to James Joyce who joyfully transforms her (semiotic) visions into writing—and Sylvia, the twenty-first-century psychoanalyst who confesses to Teresa (and to the reader): "I receive your illuminations."[192] Sylvia moreover admits to Teresa that "in this cavalier adventure you are, investigative Teresa, my unwitting accomplice in lunacy."[193] However, this lunacy is sometimes interrupted by present time, for example, when Sylvia has long talks with her American writer lover, Andrew—who complains that Sylvia is a workaholic—about the 2005 London bombings or when Sylvia rants about the world caught between new fundamentalisms and nihilistic consumerism. But mostly Sylvia remains captured like a fly in a spider's web in Teresa's semiotic-beyond-symbolic language or perhaps within the sense of "liquid immersion" that one gets when reading this book.[194]

Yet there is a method to the madness, a method that is boldly political both symbolically and practically.[195] One thing that Kristeva emphasizes in her public comments about Saint Teresa is her modernity and the ways in which she is our contemporary: "I see her as a contemporary, as a modern woman, energetic, ecstatic, but in reality, very pragmatic."[196] The second claim Kristeva advances is that without Teresa's kind of mystical practice, there would be no psychoanalysis. Exaggerating only slightly in saying this, Kristeva refers to Teresa's deeply passionate experience of reading scripture, which was often jubilatory or even trance-like, at times even bringing Teresa to the point of fainting. However, Teresa was able to put into words these destabilizing states, first through confession and then through constant writing. In this sense, the experience became therapeutic and, through becoming a writer, Teresa was more or less able to cure herself of her trance-like states bordering on madness.[197] This is the most important reason for Kristeva's admiration of Saint Teresa: "This extravagant, suffering and sensual mystic, perfectly spiritual and [also] a business woman as she defines herself—is a great writer."[198]

Representing the Atheists of the World

As I have noted, *Teresa, My Love* got a lot of attention across Europe: parts of it were performed in 2014 by the actress Isabelle Huppert at the Odéon Theater in Paris, and it drew crowds at the National Croatian Theater of Zagreb that same year as well as in Genoa in 2015. Kristeva

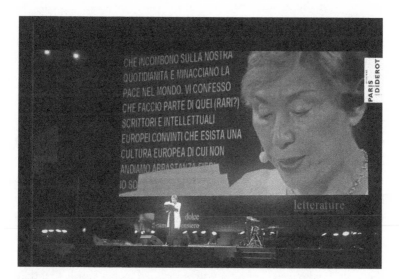

Figure 4.1. International Literature Festival at the Roman Forum, June 22, 2010. Photo from *Julia Kristeva—Une étrangère, citoyenne du monde*, dir. Alain Monclin.

traveled to Ávila for the 500th anniversary of Teresa's birth where she was greeted with open arms and was able to speak with Carmelite nuns from all over the world. She argued there and elsewhere that the most important thing that Teresa and her form of mysticism can offer in support of her twenty-first-century dream of a new kind of secular humanism is an intimate knowledge about love.

Media and academic critics heard this message. Carol Mastrangelo Bové wrote, "Mysticism enables an empathy with the at times painful desires of other people."[199] Carlene Bauer wrote, "Through reconsidering the life of this saint, she is calling those of us 'trapped between secularism and fundamentalism' to reconsider what we think we know about love."[200] And Maria Margaroni wrote, "Hence her turn to Thérèse's mysticism which, she believes, opens a third pathway that promises to lead us beyond the deadly dilemmas we are currently facing."[201]

Finally, on a warm night in Rome, Italy, on June 22, 2010, Kristeva found herself standing in front of a large audience nestled among the ruins of the Roman Forum. She had been invited to speak at the International Literature Festival held annually at the site of the Basilica di Massenzio where a frescoed and coffered vault offers a dramatic background for gatherings among the strikingly lit ruins in the Forum.

Standing there in the evening heat, at sixty-nine years old, with the words and images not only of herself but also of all of her women geniuses (Arendt, Klein, Colette, and Teresa) projected onto a giant screen behind her, Kristeva made an impassioned plea for new understandings of love in secular Europe, understandings that could be accessed through the writings of mystics like Teresa of Ávila.[202] She worked hard to make her ten years of labor on love accessible to those who had braved the heat to hear her words. What she did not know was that in the audience were several high-ranking religious leaders from the Vatican who were so profoundly impressed by her words that they approached her with an invitation that she could not refuse: Would she do them the honor of representing the atheists of the world at an inter-religious conference convened by Pope Benedict XVI to be held in Assisi, Italy on October 27, 2011? She did not hesitate. She responded with a surprised but enthusiastic *Yes!*

4. The 2010s: Traveling Through Myself

One of the men who was deeply impressed by Kristeva's presentation in Rome was Cardinal Gianfranco Ravasi, the "Minister of Culture" of the Pontifical Council for Culture in Rome, and someone very close to Pope Benedict XVI. Cardinal Ravasi is, by anyone's standards, a fascinating character for someone so thoroughly inside Vatican circles. For example, in 2008 he confirmed the compatibility of the Darwinian theory of evolution with the Bible and the teachings of the Catholic Church; in 2017 he created the historically unprecedented group "Feminine Consultation" within the Pontifical Council. He reads literature across cultures and languages and has always been an avid fan of David Bowie and Lou Reed.

Ravasi clearly saw something in Kristeva and asked her to be part of the Courtyard of the Gentiles, an initiative that he was undertaking at the Pope's request to foster conversation and debate between "noble atheists" (i.e., not polemicists) and "believers" (i.e., not fundamentalists). The initiative's name makes reference to the Court of the Gentiles and Pagans at the ancient Temple of Jerusalem, in Latin the *atrium gentium*, which was a space where Jews and anyone—mostly Greeks and non-Jews and others regardless of culture, language, or religious affiliation—could meet and discuss all issues of interest. Kristeva pointed out to Ravasi that this was perhaps not the best name for an initiative designed to bring the humanists and atheists of today into conversation with Catholics, pointing out that European humanism emerged *after* those times and that, well, the Catholics are themselves the non-Jews. Ravasi replied that because it was the Pope who had come up with the name, it could not be changed. Kristeva accepted the invitation mostly because she thought that the project could potentially provide an infrastructure for what she had been calling for: a conversation between believers and nonbelievers about the most urgent issues of the day. In addition, it was—and remains—an ambitious project with meetings already held or planned in cities and countries all over the world, including Eastern Europe.

The first meeting—on the theme of "Enlightenments, Religions, Common Reason"—was held in Paris in March 2011, with sessions at UNESCO, the French Academy, and the Sorbonne.[203] Kristeva's talk, "To Dare Humanism," lays out Kristeva's vision for the new form of humanism she advocates, one that critiques and leaves behind the attitudes and practices of the old, inherited "soft humanism" with its racism and imperialism disguised as enlightened care, and turns to what she regards as the potential new actors of a new humanism: the elderly, the handicapped, women, people of color, LGBTQ citizens, and so on. She had assumed that her message—especially when she said outright that her form of humanism is a feminism and that its leaders would no doubt be women—would not be taken well by the Catholics in the audience. But she was mistaken.

No One Owns the Truth

In June 2011, Kristeva received the formal letter from the Pope requesting that she lead a delegation of atheists to the "Inter-Religious Gathering for Peace" to be held in Assisi in October 2011. She was quite honored. Pope John Paul II had started this inter-religious event in 1986, and there had been two more in 1993 and 2002. But after John Paul II died in 2005, Pope Benedict XVI had decided not to continue them. However, in part because of world events post-9/11, he changed his mind and proclaimed that there would be a gathering again at Assisi on the twenty-fifth anniversary of the first meeting. The gathering was billed as being organized for "Pilgrims of Truth, Pilgrims of Peace" in an effort to promote "a commitment to peace in justice" around the world. What was dramatically different about the 2011 meeting was that it was the first time that atheists were invited. And it was the first time that

Figure 4.2. Kristeva as the only atheist with the Pope and representatives of multiple religions at Assisi, Italy, 2011. Julia Kristeva Archive.

a woman was going to speak on the same stage as the Pope. Kristeva stepped up to the plate and took charge of a delegation made up of three other distinguished scholars: the Italian philosopher Remo Bodei, the Mexican philosopher and activist Guillermo Hurtado, and the German economist and former National Chairman of the Communist Party of Austria, Walter Baier.

Kristeva was moved to find herself once again in Assisi. She had traveled there with her sister in 1966, right after her arrival in France, and had been deeply affected by the glorious Giotto frescoes at the Church of Saint Francis. As I have mentioned, she wrote quite lovingly about Giotto in one of her most famous essays, "Giotto's Joy." She also placed a Giotto detail of multiplying angels on the cover of *Polylogue*, in devotion to the artist as well as in praise of all that is polylogical. That she was returning to Assisi, to Giotto, at seventy years old, as the first woman and the first atheist to speak in the Pope's presence at such an event, was almost beyond belief.

Thousands and thousands of pilgrims of every imaginable religion descended upon Assisi on October 26 and 27. On the evening of the

26th, Kristeva presented a paper at the University of Rome: "Ten Principles for Twenty-First-Century Humanism."[204] Cardinal Ravasi was present and in dialogue with her. That was a fairly ordinary occurrence for Kristeva: academic and organized. But the next day was different.

There were nine representatives of multiple religions—plus one atheist—in a row, with the Pope in the middle, standing in front of a huge audience of an endless sea of mostly male faces. They stood for some time at attention in front of the Basilica of Saint Mary of the Angels.[205] Enormous television screens outside the Basilica brought the event to thousands more pilgrims eager to see and hear as well as to millions of viewers in Italy and around the world. The ten dignitaries spoke for ten minutes each and Kristeva was last.[206] She began by quoting John Paul II: "Don't be afraid!" Then she presented a condensed version of her Ten Principles. In short, they state that:

— The humanism of the twenty-first century is not a "theomorphism." It has no "superior value" or "goal" and it is where Man (with a capital M) does not exist. It is where each of us must put our personal, historical, and social situation into question in order to work toward "a system of global governance of universal and ethical solidarity";

— Twenty-first-century humanism is a process of continual refoundation that progresses through rupture as innovation, for "the moment has come to take up again the moral codes built throughout history, without weakening them, in order to problematize them, to renew them in the face of new singularities";

— Twenty-first-century humanism "is a feminism. The liberation of desires could only lead to the emancipation of women. The battle for economic, legal, and political parity necessitates a new kind of reflection on the choice and responsibility of motherhood";

— Twenty-first-century humanism "teaches us that the loving care for each other, the care of the earth, the young, the sick, the disabled, the elderly dependents, constitute inner experiences that create new proximities and surprising solidarities";

— "We do not make history, we are history. For the first time, *homo sapiens* is capable of destroying the earth and himself in the name of his beliefs, religions, or ideologies . . . The diversity of our meeting here, at Assisi, shows that this hypothesis of destruction is not the only one possible";

— "The age of suspicion is no longer enough. Faced with increasingly grave crises and threats, we have arrived at the age of the wager. We must dare to bet on the continuous renewal of the capacity of men and women to believe and to know together so that in the multiverse surrounded by a void, mankind can continue to pursue its creative destiny for a long time to come."

I urge my reader to watch the videos (available on Kristeva's website) of the amazing minutes while she is speaking. The cameras hover over the crowd, capturing the stone-cold, entirely expressionless faces of the hundreds of people (mostly men) seated in the church, from many nations and faiths, as they read along with her in their own languages. Given the scene, I have to say that this is one of Kristeva's most courageous public moments. When Kristeva sat down, there was total silence as the Pope walked to the microphone:

> Benedict XVI . . . spoke after me as I was the last speaker. After celebrating this first participation by non-believers in such prestigious events, the Pope began to deplore the fact that we must be in a state of "great suffering" not having met the true God . . . [but only briefly] just before he turned to point out that, for [the non-believers], the truth is nevertheless an interior struggle, a search, a path. And [he wanted] to proclaim, addressing himself this time to the believers, that "no one owns the truth."[207]

The Pope went on to imply that it was the nonbelievers who understand this better than the believers, that it is always those who think that they are "the landlords of the truth" who bring violence, suffering, and eventually war to humankind. This was a surprising rhetorical turn, especially from a Pope!

Kristeva sat at lunch afterward with the only other woman she could find in the whole place: Betty Ehrenberg, Executive Director for the World Jewish Congress of the United States and North America. After eating, they caught one of the buses carrying the dignitaries up the hill toward the Church of Saint Francis and Giotto's frescoes. When they got out of the bus, they were surrounded by thousands of pilgrims caught up in a festival-like atmosphere of demonstrations for peace and justice. Kristeva continued to climb, following the long trail of men, headed by the Pope, up the hill and listening as the huge crowd began yelling "Benito! Benito!" Then, suddenly, with no warning, the crowd was yelling: "Benito! Julia! Benito! Julia! Benito! Julia!" for several minutes. She was overcome with emotion. It turns out that as Italian and especially French pilgrims realized that she was the only woman there, and after they heard what she had said in her remarks, they cried her name in honor. Some of those who started the chanting of her name were friends of Jean Vanier back in Paris, but the crowds quickly picked up the chant. She sent a text to Philippe: "You won't believe what just happened to me."

When Kristeva returned to Paris, the French press welcomed her back with the usual amused wink. For example, the magazine *Le Point* ran the headline "Benedict XVI's Favorite Atheist." However, for Kristeva the event had not been amusing at all, but rather deeply heartening and a source of optimism that has carried her quite a distance.[208]

The Why Rather than the How

France, led by the socialist François Hollande 2012–17, became a microcosm of what will most likely be judged by history to be two of the major forces giving shape to the Western world in the first two decades after 9/11. First, the 2010s saw the explicit and rapid rise of the extreme right wing in the form of the National Front, which won its first seats ever in the French Senate. White supremacy and Euro-skepticism (culminating in Brexit) have in many places formed some very strange alliances to protect white Christianity.[209] Second, fundamentalist terrorist attacks in the name of Islam hit France without mercy: the *Charlie Hebdo* and Hypercacher murders in January 2015 and the Bataclan and nearby restaurant murders in November 2015 shook France to its core. And of course there are the July 14, 2016, attack in Nice, the April and June 2017 attacks on the Champs-Élysées, and on and on.

These developments have affected Kristeva deeply: she has become increasingly vocal about the problems at hand. I think that it is possible to argue that Kristeva's early experiences under communism provided her with the political and cultural antennae necessary to detect the ways in which the cruel market logics of neoliberalism, rising ethnocentric paranoia, and the violence of fundamentalist terrorism are combining in the West to produce a totalitarianism that may be different from what she experienced growing up but is just as virulent. This new totalitarianism all too easily leads to the wholesale instrumentalization of the subject and therefore guarantees its subservience to what Arendt characterized as absolute evil: the callous belief in the disposability of certain human beings. In this context, Kristeva has wanted to insist on the "why" rather than the "how." She does not think that the historical confluence of forces that is creating twenty-first-century totalitarianism can be stopped by describing how it works. Rather, she has come to insist more and more on understanding why fascism has not disappeared from the interior of so-called democracies or from the psyches of their inhabitants.

Kristeva has continued to call throughout the 2010s for a problematization of all "clenched-up" identities and truths through an intense interrogation—a revisiting, a perlaboration—of cultural history. Faithful to many of the main insights of her earlier work, she has rejected what is rigid, solidified, certified, reified, or dogmatic, and has wanted instead to draw out what is polyphonic, kaleidoscopic, multiversal, flexible, and multidisciplinary. She has repeatedly made the case for the need in Europe to put thought into action through a reformation of the educational system. She has insisted on the need to teach with more relevance, to excite young people about their histories, especially their religious histories, in order for them to acquire the tools of interpretation provided by their complex cultures, and in order for them to be able to create new bridges among today's diversities. In particular, she has insisted on the need to teach the history of the three great monotheistic religions as laboratories for the future. This education would include reading Greek mythology, the Christian Bible, the Torah, and the Koran. She has gone so far as to say that the future of humanity itself may depend on the transposition of the values of the great world religions for today's world. She additionally believes that instead of raising identities and traditions into cults, they need to be treated as questions, experiences, and pathways that can help Europe create a genuinely pluralistic society. This alone would allow Europe to function as "a rampart against the chaos of antisemitism, nationalism, and fanaticism."[210]

For Kristeva, today's forms of radical evil, such as the violent extremism of alt-right Christianity or fundamentalist terrorism in the name of Islam, are frequently merely nihilism with religious pretensions. She believes that "if we want to escape the popularity of the extreme right that takes hold of identities but does not think them, does not problematize them, and does not look for bridges," we must revalue the best parts of secular humanism, with diversity at its heart, and do so without delay.[211]

As part of this effort, Kristeva has embraced her role as a public intellectual with a seemingly boundless energy, speaking at hundreds of events and writing countless articles for magazines and newspapers, addressing a European culture caught between the two forms of radical evil she focuses on: violently extreme right-wing ideologies and fundamentalist terrorism in the name of Islam. In so doing, she has emphasized both humanism and psychoanalysis. She believes that psychoanalysis provides an essential bridge between religious teachings and secular humanist ethics. Most of all, she revisits the Freudian formulation of the death drive and its seeming prevalence in today's world.[212] Regarding humanism, Kristeva continues to make the case for putting into question its inherited forms and for encouraging its transformation into new forms of collective, sharable singularities. For this reason, she is a strong advocate for the humanities, which she does not see as a set of disciplines but as a site where modern conceptions of the human are processed.[213]

In addition, there is the question of Europe. Kristeva has been a vocal and consistent defender of the European Union for many years.[214] In numerous talks, articles, and interviews over the past decade, she has asked in many different ways whether there is such a thing as European culture. Is there a European identity? She has laid out in detail what she sees as the "specificities of Europe." She has put "Europe on the couch," worrying about the nationalism and xenophobia at the heart of Brexit: "Europe is dead, long live Europe."[215]

Kristeva's position on Europe is complicated. On the one hand, she argues that it is important to recognize the terrible sins of hegemonic European culture and also to not idealize Europe or think about the world in a Eurocentric way. On the other hand, she believes that the complex intellectual history of Europe along with its cultural multiplicity and its polyphonic citizenry provide a powerful toolbox for putting identity into question, for questioning every absolute, and for celebrating and developing freedom as a genuine encounter with human diversity rather than freedom as an adaptation to market capitalism through an illusion of choice. She insists on the need to interrogate the complex density of European cultural memory in order to start again, much like an analysand on the psychoanalytic couch might want to understand what is wrong with the way he is thinking so as to be able to build a new psychic space, a new life.[216]

Kristeva's wish that Europe's uniqueness be appreciated can be difficult for American readers to peel off from garden-variety European ethnocentrisms. When confronted with this problem, I myself tend to hear echoes of Kristeva's first mentor in France, Lucien Goldmann: take them from the inside![217] What is clear is that in the 2010s, Kristeva has been acutely focused on undoing received ideas about Europe, on enumerating the challenges it faces, and on attempting to analyze its broken infrastructure, which politicians seem unable to repair.

No One Pays Attention to the Political Until
It Feels Spiritual

Across the 2010s, Kristeva's role as a public intellectual solidified and her relationship with the media warmed. Some of the media focused on projects with which she had been associated for several years, such as the Simone de Beauvoir Prize. Kristeva was always involved when the media announced that the prize had been awarded to some well-known, inspiring, and political "women warriors" in the 2010s, for example, the courageous Malala in 2013 and Giusi Nicolini—the mayor of Lampedusa who worked tirelessly to protect and lend dignity to migrants landing on Italian shores—in 2016. (Nicolini was brutally defeated by her anti-immigrant opponent in 2017.) Kristeva did short radio appearances on various themes,[218] almost always bringing the topic around to a political controversy.

What was new in the 2010s was Kristeva's willingness to take strong positions on deeply contentious political controversies *in public*. This is not to say that she had not done this previously: witness her wicked analysis of Sarah Palin during the 2008 presidential election in the United States.[219] But in the 2010s, Kristeva spoke out on issues that were often ferociously dividing the French public. For instance, in 2012 she came out passionately against the death penalty. And in 2017, she spoke out on the #metoo movement, voicing her deep support for every woman's right to justice while also issuing a stark warning: "Will the virtual streaming of 'me too' suffice to liberate us from these outrages, and to go beyond them? I doubt it."[220] She also got into anguished debates on the biopolitics of the medical humanities and took strong stands in defense of psychoanalysts under duress in authoritarian states.[221]

Kristeva has stated explicitly that she tries not to wade too deeply into other cultures whose history and language she does not know well. But she rarely hesitates to intervene when totalitarianism of any kind is a danger to intellectual work of any kind. In the context of the Middle East, Kristeva has increasingly come around to writing some of her most explicitly political and moving texts. Some of these efforts were brief but powerful, such as, for example, her endorsement of Gohar Homayounpour's *Doing Psychoanalysis in Tehran*[222]:

> Was Scheherazade a precursor to Freud? Psychoanalysis is a laboratory made of narratives. It offers the possibility to connect the stories of all those who suffer—whatever their anxiety, their traumas, their desires—and to give birth to individual freedoms—despite the religious, social, and economic obstacles presented by various political regimes. The roads to freedom found on Gohar Homayounpour's analytic couch are unexpected, secret, and ultimately irresistible.[223]

Rafah Nached, the first psychoanalyst to work in Syria for a generation, had studied at the University of Paris 7. Upon returning to her besieged and traumatized Syria, she decided to act. In revolt against the forced hospitalization of handicapped children with dying elders, Nached opened a clinic in Damascus to treat patients who were suffering from . . . fear. She came to the attention of psychoanalysts in France and around the world because, on September 10, 2011, as she was trying to visit her new granddaughter in Paris, she was detained by the Syrian police and thrown into prison. The French psychoanalyst Jacques-Alain Miller as well as noted intellectuals around the world (including Slavoj Žižek and Noam Chomsky) began to work for her release.

Nached was sixty-six and in poor health. The situation was dire. Why had she not been allowed to leave Syria? Most agree that it was because of her research, seminars, and analytic practice focusing on fear—fear of everything, from the fear of one's husband to the fear of death, from the fear of flying to . . . the fear of the government. She had been supported in her work by French and Dutch Jesuit priests in Damascus who had also helped her publish her new translations of Freud into Arabic. This is what got Kristeva's attention: earlier Arabic translations of Freud had only talked about sexuality in terms of death, never in terms of pleasure. But Nached had read Arab mystics who gave her a language of love, of living with God in erotic terms. As a result, with the help of analysts in Tunisia and Morocco, she retranslated Freud in order to bring new analytic tools to her culture without them being rejected as "corrupt imports from the West." At a huge gathering in support of Nached at the Palais des Congrès on October 9, 2011, Kristeva weaved together her multiple pathways at the intersection of psychoanalysis, women's rights and genius, and her life-long resistance to totalitarian tendencies as well as realities:

> Thus it was that faced with the outdatedness of psychiatry in Syria, faced with the difficulties Rafah encountered introducing psychoanalysis into a milieu dominated by behaviorism and behavior therapy, faced with the fear of saying "I" or "no" in a country where tradition does not encourage singular speech, and on top of that, under a regime of increasing violence and repression . . . and very precisely in the prayer spaces of Jesuits in Damascus—Rafah Nached ended up undertaking the work of group therapy founded in psychodrama . . .
>
> What does this act say, an act in its origins strictly clinical? It says: "Don't be afraid!"
>
> You heard me right, I am sketching out a comparison between the analytic work of Rafah Nached and . . . the words of John Paul II who unleashed the Solidarity Movement in Poland . . . before leading directly to, in the midst of and following a series of economic, political, and social causes, the fall of the communist bloc itself.[224]

Rafah Nached was freed from prison on November 16, 2011.

Kristeva also continued to write about artists and writers, some well known in the United States (Louise Bourgeois, Jackson Pollock), some less well known (Adel Abdessemed, Anish Kapoor), and some deeply controversial (such as Jonathan Littell).[225] The American-born, French-educated Littell's 2013 novel *The Kindly Ones*[226]—described as an intimate memoir of an ex-Nazi mass murderer and containing a psychopathic Nazi narrator—terrified readers in France, angered readers in Germany, and led American reviewers to write mixed when not disgusted reviews. Kristeva did not hesitate to praise his accomplishment, which was "to show how a virus can contaminate you, taking you hostage."[227]

However, by far the majority of Kristeva's interventions in the media after the 2015 terrorist attacks in Paris that shook all of France had to do with her work on adolescence—on the "need to believe" and the "desire to know"—and on how young men and women were being recruited daily via the internet by cynical recruiters posing as believers in the Muslim faith. She continued to intervene as a psychoanalyst who wanted to understand the "why" rather than the "how." She rejected the rhetoric of "the clash of civilizations" and "the clash of religions," focusing on what she knew best: clinical practice. Most of her public remarks were based on her continuing clinical work with adolescents at the Home for Adolescents in the Cochin Hospital in Paris. While she did not hesitate to extrapolate from what she was hearing in that venue from young people tempted by radicalization, by gangster-inspired extremism, she mostly left to others the analysis of why "Islam" was so frequently the rhetorical vector for recruitment. Instead, she continued to focus on "radical evil" in the current historical context; on what we can say about it based on our previous run-ins with it, especially in the twentieth century; and on what we can do to prevent its spread in the future.[228]

Perpetual Motion

Kristeva turned seventy in June 2011 but she has not slowed down for one minute over the last decade. Seemingly blessed with boundless energy, a minor need for sleep, and unlimited capacity for focus—not to mention what seems to be her unflappable patience with all kinds of interlocutors—she has continued through the 2010s to travel, give lectures, collect honors, deflect critiques and hurtful events, and attend to her family and friends, in a blur of motion that is hard to keep up with.

Kristeva continued to be recognized worldwide throughout the decade. In 2011 alone, she was awarded honorary doctorates from the University of Aristotle in Greece, the University of Buenos Aires in Argentina, and Queen Mary University in England. That same year, she was made Commandeur de L'Ordre National du Mérite in France. More honorary doctorates came soon thereafter: Haifa University in

2014 and the Hebrew University of Jerusalem in 2017. In 2014, she was named Commandeur de la Légion d'Honneur and "knighted" personally by President Hollande in 2015.

In addition, prizes for her books were legion: for example, the Prix Mondi Migranti in Genoa in 2015 for *Strangers to Ourselves* and the Prix Saint-Simon in 2017 for *Traveling Through Myself* (as well as her entire corpus). She was named President of the Prix du Livre Politique in 2015. That same year she was also declared as "one of the most daring interdisciplinary thinkers in the world" by Gianluigi Ricuperati in his *100 Global Minds*.[229] Other less noticed celebrations were just as, if not more, important to Kristeva: for instance, the small but fun and moving celebration of her retirement at the University of Paris in 2011 and the launching of an international research group—"The Kristeva Circle"—by Kelly Oliver in 2012.[230] An extraordinary film directed by Iskra Angelova, *Who's Afraid of Julia Kristeva?*, premiered in London in February 2018 much to Kristeva's delight.

Kristeva continued her travels around the world: for example, to China in 2009 and 2012; to Chile and Argentina in 2012; to the United States in 2013; to Sofia in 2014. She has written with great emotion about friends made and honors embraced during these travels. Her friendships with intellectuals in Beijing, Shanghai, and Nanjing grew as she lectured there, wrote for prominent journals and newspapers, and interacted with women's groups.[231] There was also a significant moment in Buenos Aires when the Rector of the university guided her into the Grand Theater where a famous tenor was singing Don Giovanni in her honor.[232]

Kristeva's return to Sofia in September 2014—her first since 2005 and my first visit to that part of the world—was astonishing. Everywhere we went, we were followed by national media. I had to learn to walk backward while being filmed as well as to sit quietly, pretending that I understood Bulgarian conversation, whether on national television or sitting in a café at the Rila Monastery drinking strong liqueur because we were freezing due to a power outage. But the most memorable moment for Kristeva had to be when she walked into the huge, packed amphitheater at the St. Kliment Ohridski University in Sofia to give her talk, "New Forms of Revolt." The whole place went wild with standing ovations and enthusiastic applause that just would not stop. Kristeva raised her arm in salute. As always, her shock at the adulation was apparent on her face.[233]

Despite these accolades, at the center of her life—always—remain her family and friends,[234] especially David and Philippe. David has mostly thrived over the last decade, painting, listening to music, boxing, and especially writing a lot of poetry while becoming more and more independent. There was one difficult period in 2013 when he fell into an extended coma and was hospitalized for quite some time. Kristeva was frantic, especially because his care in the hospital was subpar: at one point, his attendants dropped him on the floor, which led to a broken hip. When they went to do a hip replacement, he received a serious burn on the operating table, which led to infections.

Kristeva's heart-stopping experiences with these horrors are vividly captured in a line in her 2015 novel *The Enchanted Clock*. In the midst of hallucinations and meditations upon death—not to mention upon the less than admirable practices of the Salpêtrière Hospital in Paris—Nivi, the character taking on Kristeva's voice, notices that her best friend, a new mother, does not cry in front of her baby in an effort to protect it from distress. Nivi notes, "She learns to cry from the inside; she learns to be a mom."[235] David did finally recover and he and his parents have worked hard to put this particularly traumatic medical episode behind them. They have more or less succeeded, always beginning again.

In the 2010s alone, Sollers has published (to date) eight novels and as many new collections of essays, interviews, and letters.[236] The most important of the latter was no doubt his 2013 *Portraits of Women*, where his portrayal of both Kristeva and Dominique Rolin filled several news cycles in France. His evocation of Kristeva is loving and full of admiration. His evocation of Rolin, as "Cleopatra," is mostly sad. She had died in 2012. As I have noted, Kristeva harbors no ill feeling against Rolin. But it is said that Rolin was deeply hurt by Sollers's marriage to Kristeva. And it is hard to say how Kristeva lived the experience of watching the first two of four volumes of love letters (1958–80) between Sollers and Rolin be published in Paris in 2017–18 with all the to-be-expected media attention.[237] But I think it safe to say that she did not pay much attention. She was writing non-stop.

Kristeva's last six books, as of this writing, published between 2011 and 2016, find her "traveling through herself" more than usual. All of them differently but steadily move through a process of rememoration, almost of auto-analysis, even as they continue to analyze our present moment and to narrativize the past in order to thwart identities and complicate certitudes. I have already discussed three of these books, so I will not dwell on them here: the 2011 *Their Look Pierces Our Shadows* travels through Kristeva's experience and analysis of disability; the 2015 *Marriage as a Fine Art* travels through Kristeva and Sollers's philosophy of couples and marriage; and the 2016 *Traveling Through Myself*, which I have cited throughout this book, is Kristeva's long autobiographical interview with Samuel Dock.

Beauvoir Presents/In the Present (2016)

Even Kristeva's collection of articles on Simone de Beauvoir, *Beauvoir Presents/In the Present* should be familiar to my readers at this point even though I have not discussed it directly. In this little book, Kristeva celebrates Beauvoir's courage, her energy, her singular genius, her unending quest for freedom, and also her insistence on putting writing at the center of her life: As Beauvoir once put it, "Writing has remained the grand affair of my life."[238]

Kristeva discovered Beauvoir in 1958 when one of her friends from the other side of the Iron Curtain snuck *The Second Sex* to Sofia. Kristeva's explicit admiration for this *battante* for women's rights should put to rest any doubts in the Anglophone world about Kristeva's support of freedom and justice for all women.[239] Kristeva revisits, throughout her essays, many of her most important ideas, the ones closest to her heart: universalism, motherhood, bisexuality, resistance to coupledom, historical accuracy, the novel, freedom, the transcendence of self, Freud, polylogic and polyphony. She admires vividly Beauvoir's explorations of the United States and China, enthusiastically agreeing with Beauvoir that when faced with complex situations, it is necessary above all *to think.*[240]

Passions of Our Time (2013)

Kristeva's collection of essays, *Passions of Our Time*—much like her 2005 *Hatred and Forgiveness*—is a record of articles on her theoretical and political concerns while she was writing other books from 1999 to 2012. Forty-eight essays are collected in an almost 800-page volume, with most of the contributions dating from 2010 to 2012. Kristeva's topics are already mostly familiar to my readers: singular liberties, psychoanalysis, women, religions, humanism, France, Europe, and China.

In this volume, Kristeva revisits and refines her diagnosis of and recommendations for the twenty-first century, especially with regard to the responsibility of intellectuals to think . . . and re-think . . . the European legacies of humanism and religion. In *Traveling Through Myself*, Dock captures the energetic ambition of Kristeva's passion-in-time/our time as it is inscribed in *Passions*: "Rarely have the problematics of hypermodernity been described so accurately; rarely has the touchstone of our times been excavated, deciphered, with such acuity."[241]

The Enchanted Clock (2015)

But it is in Kristeva's novel *The Enchanted Clock* where her mind and her heart weave together across and through (out-of-joint) time. It is a lightly apocalyptic but loving tale for our times at the same time as she undertakes a true voyage through herself. In the novel, the character closest to Kristeva's own voice, Nivi ("my language" in Hebrew) Delisle (*de l'île*, of the island), is a psychoanalyst and magazine editor who is rescued from drowning off the Île de Ré by a mysterious astrophysicist named Theo Passemant (also called Astro). Theo becomes Nivi's mostly absent but adored lover. Nivi is the doting mother of Stan, who suffers from inexplicable comas, and it is with and through her poetically visionary son that Nivi discovers and becomes obsessed with a clock at Versailles created by an eighteenth-century engineer/astronomer/clockmaker for King Louis XV in the years leading up to the French Revolution.

The clock has two faces (one conventional one and another showing the positions of the planets in the solar system), no arms, four widely spread and sturdy legs, and a very suggestive swinging pendulum down below. It is set to run until the year 9999. This strange mechanical creature is at the center of the novel but only as a cipher for a much more complicated story than that of linear time. The novel spins the time of the clock in the eye of a hurricane of events, objects, and personas (alive and dead), telling many stories at once."[242] The enchanted clock, both apocalyptic and vital—still ticking as I write this—beckons the reader toward experiencing a new kind of time continuum between fiction and reality with characters from different eras who have in common only their dialogue with passing time. Whether Nivi is hallucinating conversations with Passemant or admiring the first woman to have a paper published by the French Academy of Sciences, Émilie du Châtelet; whether she is engaging with the crimes and misdemeanors of the twentieth century, wondering where her dear Theo is and what he is up to; or whether she is pondering the future of virility in Paris, time is a philosophical object. Is man a machine? Has the clock replaced God? Whatever the answers to these questions might be, Nivi becomes a neobody in a neoreality, exploring an eternity that is not divine but rather cosmic and scientific.

Through the multiple ripples in time that make up this novel, the reader can get glimpses of the life of Julia Kristeva as explored in this book. Nivi's son, Stan, with his terrifying comas, stands out, as he awakes from his involuntary sleep and asks his mother about the clock: "He lives in time, Stan, and brings me back into it."[243] And there is Theo and the story of Nivi's linguistics professor inscribing the word *THEO* as he lay dying. There are also familiar places, such as the Luxembourg Gardens and the Île de Ré with the swan outside Nivi's window. There are the rose laurels of Nivi's childhood and the denied dreams of being part of the Sputnik revolution as a young woman. But mostly there are the glimpses of Kristeva's travelings through herself as affect: her sensation of living in a beehive of words, her lack of capacity for hatred or jealousy, her questions about her Frenchness, and her son's sense of her as being very much like a Picasso painting. And both via Nivi in the novel and Kristeva in real life, there is an insistence on the playful. In 2018, when the radio station *France Inter* asked Kristeva how to fight off melancholia, she listed writers like Proust, singers like Ella Fitzgerald, filmmakers like Hitchcock, islands near the sea like the Île de Ré, and of course "the fabulous astronomical clock of Claude-Siméon Passemant."[244]

And there's of course Dostoevsky: Kristeva's "first great literary shock."[245] She was working hard on her brand-new book on Dostoevsky's demons, criminals, and idiots in March 2018 . . . when her phone rang. It was history calling, time spinning in reverse into a tightly coiled spring and then releasing in a whirl—and a wham! Kristeva was about to get one of the most painful shocks of her life.

It's a True Nightmare or a Pitiful Farce, I'm Not Sure Which . . .

Kristeva explains:

> That day I was working on Dostoevsky. I was starting a book about him for "Les Auteurs de ma vie," [a Buchet-Chastel series], and I was thinking of his life: a revolutionary, a convict, loving his Holy Russia, enraged against nihilism, but especially a novelist of the general carnival, capable of probing the death of God and absurd crime including Stavrogin's pedophilia in *The Possessed*. I was wondering how to restore its bewildering resonance with contemporary times and what it brought me day after day. From time to time, a message alert lit up my cellphone. A friend advised me "not to worry" without

specifying why. Another proposed to "discuss all of this" as soon as possible, without specifying what. Not enough to distract me from Dostoevsky's sinuous sentences, which meander through the true and the false.

In early evening, I can see that the same stranger has called me several times before sending me this text by mistake: "Kristeva unreachable, let's drop it." Intrigued by this error, I dial the number. He is a journalist from the weekly, *Le Nouvel Observateur*. He is speaking quickly: "Do you know what's going on? It's very serious." I don't understand. He shares his scoop: in the 1970s, when I was already living with Philippe in Paris, I'd worked as a secret agent for Bulgaria. "Me? That's a hoax." But he's sure of what he's telling me: the authorities in Sofia have just unearthed my recruitment record, he says, it's very clear. Now he would like my reaction. As I remember it, I sweep it away ironically: "Someone probably wants to make me feel good."[246]

I was one of the people trying to reach Kristeva. I had received an email late on the evening of March 27, 2018, with an article from the *Balkan Insight* attached: "Bulgaria Alleges Julia Kristeva Was State Security Agent." I, too, thought that it was a hoax. The article stated flatly, in bureaucratic prose, that Kristeva was recruited on June 19, 1971 by Senior Lieutenant Ivan Bozhikov of the Communist State Security's Foreign Intelligence Department. This was being reported by the Committee for Disclosing Documents and Announcing the Affiliation of Bulgarian Citizens to the State Security and Intelligence Services of the Bulgarian National Army. *What?*

Variations of this headline and basic information were repeated between the evening of March 27 and March 30 in, among other outlets, *The Sofia Globe*, *The Sofia News Agency*, (strangely) the *Irish Times*, and (even more strangely) *ArtForum*, *Reuters*, *The Guardian*, *Le Monde*, *Le Nouvel Observateur*, *France 24*, and *Le Point*. I was flabbergasted, confused, angry, and worried all at once. Kristeva quickly issued a denial:

> I have never belonged to any secret service—not Bulgarian, not French, Russian or American! These archives are a perfect illustration of the

methods used by police in the service of a totalitarianism that I have in fact helped to denounce by explaining in many of my publications how its mechanisms work. Furthermore, I have not offered my support to a regime that I fled, and I have never written reports for it. The fact seems to remain that the still too little understood methods of totalitarian regimes—naming and amassing secret files on people without their knowledge—remain formidably efficient today if we are to judge by the credence given to these files, without there being any questioning about who wrote these counterfeited documents or why. Ultimately, this episode would be comical, and might even seem a bit romantic, were it not for the fact that it is all so false and that its uncritical repetition in the media is so frightening.[247]

When I was contacted by *The New York Times* on March 29, I knew exactly what I was going to say: that I believed Kristeva. Why? There were—are—many reasons: her adamant opposition to totalitarianism and totalitarian tendencies from since before she left Bulgaria (and especially after the murder of her father and friends); her loud and articulate defense of Europe and of Western thought since her twenties; the myriad ways in which her integrity shines through whatever she writes even when one might not agree with what she is saying. But, in the end, the reason for my sureness that I found myself repeating over and over was simple: if she had been forced to do such a thing, if she had had no choice but to comply to protect her family and friends, let alone herself, she would have written about it the minute the Berlin wall came down in 1989. She would not have been able to resist. I told *The New York Times* that "no one who knows anything about her or her work believes this." At least the old Gray Lady had a double headline in a vague gesture toward balance, different from all the others up until that point: "Bulgaria Says French Thinker Was a Secret Agent. She Calls It a 'Barefaced Lie.'"[248]

There are many strange, bizarre, and creepy things to say about this episode. But none are as uncanny to me as the fact that Kristeva was writing about Dostoevsky when the DS crashed back into her life and that Kristeva's former Bulgarian boyfriend, Tzvetan Stoyanov, was writing his much-praised book on . . . Dostoevsky,[249] when he was probably killed by the DS. (His book was published posthumously.) As I discuss in Part II, Stoyanov met with Georgi Markov in London in January 1971 in an attempt to convince Markov to return to Bulgaria. It did not work. Markov stayed in London and was murdered by the Bulgarian Secret Services in September 1978. Stoyanov was last seen by friends in Sofia mid-June 1971. He was sick by July 1 and dead by July 3, 1971. When the headlines hit the global press in March 2018 about Kristeva, giving the date of her recruitment as "June 19, 1971," several friends in Europe responded quickly: "Kristeva must have chosen to live." Others, including myself, have speculated—with only circumstantial evidence—that the communist bureaucrats were so upset about their failure with Markov (and so worried about what their superiors might think) that they doubled down in "mid-June 1971" on their other two most visible and celebrated intellectuals of the time: Stoyanov ended up dead; Kristeva became "Sabina" and an object of surveillance.[250]

It is clear to me that the article that hurt Kristeva the most was the one—actually two—published by *Le Nouvel Observateur*, a left-leaning weekly in Paris that has always been a great friend to intellectuals and artists, both French and foreign. *Le Nouvel Obs* published one article on March 28, 2018, at 7:04 p.m., that declared that "Julia Kristeva was recruited by the Bulgarian Communist Secret Services."[251] It basically repeated what had already been reported in the press, but with a mean-spirited twist: it brought up the 2015 novel by Laurent Binet, *The Seventh Function of Language*, where a character named Kristeva is portrayed as a communist agent responsible for the death of her friend and mentor, Roland Barthes. At 8:13 p.m., *Le Nouvel Obs* triumphantly proclaimed that they had procured the infamous "archive" from Sofia, writing in a definitive tone: "However, the dossier of the Darzhavna Sigurnost, obtained exclusively by the *Nouvel Observateur* from the Official Commission of the Archives of the DS in Sofia, does report a recruitment in 1971 by the Espionage Services, and not a surveillance."[252] (They kept repeating "obtained exclusively.")

Kristeva wrote a scathing "Right to Respond" piece a few days later, decrying their "naïve" and "complacent" reporting: "These 'archives' are ideological fossils that have been disavowed and fought by democracies: why give them such blind faith today? How can one not step back as such methods once again demand, and learn from them for the present and the future? We must always ask ourselves the question: who benefits from this?"[253]

The so-called Dossier Committee in Bulgaria, established in 2006, is similar to committees set up in most of the post-communist satellite

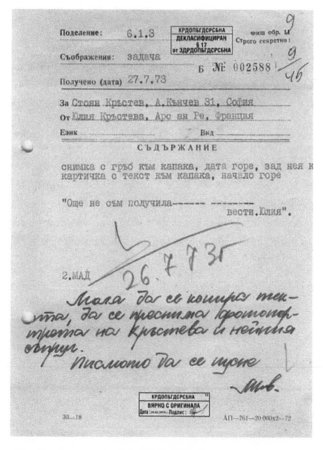

Figure 4.3. Document #10 of the "Sabina" Dossier, March 2018.

countries in order to "reconcile" with a violent past. Bulgaria was one of the Soviet Union's closest satellites, and as the Soviet Union disintegrated, Party loyalists—the Bulgarian equivalents to the KGB—grabbed all the records they could and burned them in an old factory near Sofia. But they were not able to destroy everything and what was left was gathered by the Dossier Committee and organized into some 15,000 files on so-called collaborators during the forty-five years of Sovietized rule. They are supposed to flag the dossier of anyone running for public office or who works in journalism, education, and so on. Kristeva had been on the masthead of a literary magazine in Sofia, *Literaturen Vestnik*, since 1995. She was suddenly flagged in 2018. The file is marked "Sabina."

In the file are about 400 pages of materials, including reports, letters, and postcards between Kristeva and her family and a few other documents, which were all immediately published on the web by the Dossier Committee when they realized how famous Kristeva is. The document pictured above is labeled simply "Document #10."[254] It is a standard, communist-era, dull yellow bureaucratic file in the voice of the investigative agent describing in detail a postcard mailed by Kristeva from the Île de Ré to her father in Sofia on July 27, 1973. It is quite "uncanny" and "creepy," according to my friends who read Cyrillic. The one-page document describes the postcard, reproducing Kristeva's message that she was not receiving any mail from her parents:

> Picture with its back to the envelope flap, date on top, behind it a postcard with the text facing the envelope flap, text begins on top

> "I still haven't received ----------------
> news. Julia."

The sentence, "I still haven't received . . . news. Julia," reflects the fact that, as I have emphasized, the majority of correspondence between Kristeva's mother and father in Sofia and Kristeva in France was being confiscated by the Secret Services.[255]

The agent then gives instructions on how to handle the postcard: "Please copy the text and take a picture of the photograph of Kristeva and her husband. Release the letter." The instructions are clear: only release the letter for delivery to Kristeva's father after it has been copied and photographed. Most Orwellian to me is the black stamp at the bottom of the document that authenticates the original date of the postcard (July 27, 1973) and is itself dated March 30, 2018—the date the Sabina Dossier was released to the public. As a matter of fact, the latter date on the stamp embodies what Kristeva has said repeatedly: the most painful thing about this episode for her has been how no one seems to care that not only were she, Sollers, and David followed and spied upon in Paris for years, but her private correspondence from her younger self to her deceased mother and father has now been published on the web for all to see.

The ascription of the code name "Sabina" to Kristeva is only one of the weirdly hallucinatory details about this episode. The name Sabina immediately brings to mind Sabina Spielrein, one of the first women psychoanalysts in the world and the patient, student, colleague—and probable lover—of Carl Jung. She was also a friend of Freud, and one of her most famous patients was Jean Piaget. She is best known for her work on schizophrenia and the death drive. A Jew, she was shot, along with her two daughters and 27,000 others, in July 1942 by a German SS death squad and, even more uncannily, most of her family was later killed during Stalin's purges.

Moreover, if that were not enough strangeness for one proper name to carry, one cannot help but think also about Sabina, the free-spirited artist character in Milan Kundera's *The Unbearable Lightness of Being* who escapes totalitarianism in this novel set in 1968, during the Prague Spring. The novel was not published until 1984, which was mostly too late for the bureaucrats assembling the dossier on Kristeva. But Kundera's own life story—his slow but steady rejection of Soviet communism, his involvement as a dissident in the Prague Spring, his subsequent ejection from the Party, his eventual loss of Czech citizenship, the loss of his teaching job, the banning of his books in 1979, and the still controversial 2008 secret police file accusing him of having been an informant for the communists—adds more than a twist of *unheimlich* to the plot of why "Sabina."

The uncanny details mount as one reads through the Sabina Dossier. It is almost like an exercise, a test case, in working with Tzvetan Todorov's semiotic strategy of verisimilitude, a strategy that he uncovered as it was used in realist fiction to produce "reality effects": detail, detail, detail, and lots of proper names were, he argued, what was needed to produce the illusion of the real.[256] In the dossier, there are names of agents, handlers, and officers: for example, the station chief at the Bulgarian embassy in Paris—her supposed "handler"—whose "real name" is Luka Draganov and whose "code name" is Lyubomirov and with whom Kristeva allegedly spoke each time she went to the embassy to mail a letter to her parents or take care of other issues. There is Vladimir Kostov, whom Kristeva does not deny having known. You will remember that he sent books to Sofia for her and helped her many times with her work (see Part II). It seems that she met with him for coffee at Chez Francis near the Pont de l'Alma in October 1975 and that they talked and talked. What she did not realize was that he wrote it all down. He defected in 1977 and the Secret Services tried—unsuccessfully—to kill him in the Paris metro in 1978, right before Markov was killed in London. Kristeva swears that she had no idea that Kostov was a secret agent.

Who's Afraid of Julia Kristeva?

On March 21, 2018, Iskra Angelova's documentary *Who's Afraid of Julia Kristeva?* had its French debut at the University of London Institute in Paris. It was a huge success and, as it turned out, the calm before the storm. Within a week or two of the release of the Sabina Dossier on the web, articles by well-known critics and philosophers began to appear in a broad array of publications. There were a handful of articles— mostly by men—that were disgruntled, bewilderingly mean, and often uninformed. There were the usual right-wingers and haters of "French Theory." But there were also a couple of surprisingly sure-of-themselves pieces by young voices who have little understanding of what living under Stalinist-type communism was like.[257]

The storm raged on, on both sides of the ocean, especially across social media. In Bulgaria, the attacks on Kristeva via social media came swiftly and viciously: people hated the Eiffel Tower, Kristeva's face, or, more likely, Sollers. However, slowly a few strong voices—mostly women— emerged from the fracas. They began to make the case that today's Western media is naïve, too eager for "clicks," and consequently buying into manufactured reports from the same model of shady sources as the American public had given credence to during the 2016 elections— except that this time, they were giving credibility to sources deep within disinformation campaigns *actually*, *literally*, and *historically* designed and activated by the KGB and its surrogates *during* the Cold War.

Kristeva, in her multiple published rebuttals of the reports from the Bulgarian Secret Services, almost always comes back to this problem of the circulation of information with no analysis, no question marks, and no deep thinking. She denies the accusations, pointing in some detail to her published work over decades. She takes stabs at refuting odd entries in the dossier: yes, she had to go to the Bulgarian embassy in Paris to mail letters to her parents, to see about visas, and yes, of course she smiled, she chatted, but she never lingered. She circles back to what she cannot get over: the Bulgarian Secret Services target her, fabricating a dossier about which she had no knowledge; the often-critiqued Dossier Commission publishes it as "the Truth"; and the Western media then repeats and repeats it, "participating in a chain of post-totalitarian abjection."[258] This is dangerous stuff circulating from a dark and ugly past into the dark and ugly time of today, into our own time when it is becoming increasingly clear that an old cold-war strategy of disinformation remains at the heart of a Moscow-inspired effort to destroy Western democracies from within. It is the Western media's seeming blindness to her surveillance that finally gets to Kristeva. I quote her at length:

> For an alleged spy, I was especially very much spied on. The file reveals that no fewer than 16 officers worked on my case. I remember a former high school classmate who came to my door one day and said that he was bringing me a package from my parents—a jar of jam and some baklava. I welcomed him in; we had tea; he showed me a Bulgarian poem

that I found badly dashed off; and then I thanked him because I had work to do. Translated into the language of secret agents, this yielded a note that depicts me as "haughty" and "disdainful of [Bulgaria's] national poetry." And this other embassy employee, whom I took to be oafish and a bit too persistent, also went on in his report. One day when he insisted on seeing me, I sent him a postcard from Brussels to ask him to lighten up a bit, signing off with a ridiculous slogan: "Long live the people's power." Believe it or not, this missive is now submitted as overwhelming proof of my guilt.

I'm arriving at the last part of this affair, the most intimate, the most chilling: the reading of my mail by the police for years. I discover with horror that my letters addressed to my parents were systematically opened: from our most innocuous exchanges about their arrival dates in France, to the evolution of my father's health, the birth of my son, and my mother's worries. Nothing escaped police control, not even a reassuring letter from Philippe to my mother and father; or a word from my sister-in-law following a weekend by the sea. I must admit: this espionage and the online publication of these letters flooded me with disgust, revolt, and retrospective terror. To what pressures were my parents subjected? Were they harassed by the police? Did they not tell me to protect me? In a report about me, one hand noted: "Sabina is obviously very eager to bring her parents to France. But she is behaving as usual: she requests a lot without offering anything in exchange." I will never forget my father's last days in this sordid Sofia hospital, cut off from the world, no visiting allowed. In spite of all my efforts, I did not manage to get him out, and the regime ignominiously refused to bury him: burials were strictly for communists, to avoid the religious gatherings. My father would be cremated, contrary to his wishes. "If you had died before him," I was told, "as you have a certain notoriety, why not? We could have added him to your grave; but, in this case, you understand . . ." What was this payback for? My mourning took the form of a metaphysical detective novel, [*The Old Man and the Wolves*].[259]

I invite my readers to read through a series of smart, thoughtful, and informed articles published during the past year, mostly by women, in both Europe and the United States. There are recurrent arguments: the ultimate proof of complicity according to experts on the Bulgarian

Secret Services would be if there was something in the dossier written or signed by Kristeva, but there is not (even Kristeva's "registration card" is not signed by her); everything in the dossier is in second- or third-hand indirect discourse; there is nothing in it to prove that Kristeva knew that she was "Agent Sabina"; and the "information" in it is trivial, readily available in public accounts and the press, for example that Louis Aragon was upset when Elsa Triolet died, that the left was changing in Europe, and that the Israeli-Palestinian conflict seemed intractable. Those who question the dossier's veracity, especially those in Bulgaria, are incredulous that the Western media grants credibility to the sinister secret police—then or now—rather than to its targets and victims.

Sonia Combe, a respected French historian, writing in *Le Monde* on April 5, 2018, makes a plea for caution when it comes to reading the language of the secret police; Maria Dimitrova, a well-known writer in London, writing in the *London Review of Books*, ridicules the credence given to the files by the Western media; Sarah Pines, a journalist based in Berlin, writing in *Welt*, goes through the process by which totalitarian regimes in the cold-war period manufactured what we today call "post-factuality" and "fake news."[260] In one of the most passionate critiques I have seen in print of what has happened to Kristeva, Koprinka Tchervenkova, Editor-in-Chief of *Kultura* in Bulgaria, decries the Dossier Commission, along with the laws upholding it and the "small town militiam[e]n" showing off on the world stage, as a farce.[261] Nina Ivanova, another voice from *Kultura*, takes apart the claims of the Dossier Commission, arguing that many others "have already shown in their books how much the power of [the] security State is treacherous, ignorant and stupid, and at the same time devastating."[262]

A Violence that Reaches the Heart

As I have during the past year been pulled into the strange post-Soviet world that produced the Dossier Committee and its "procedures" and "truths," I have been as if possessed by the uncanny similarity between what is happening in post-communist Eastern Europe and in Trump's

United States: both seem to be caught in a web of post-fact, post-truth, and conspiracy-driven narratives, with no way to figure out what is truth and what is fiction. It is difficult to trace how much the disinformation campaigns that originated in post-Soviet Russia, but which are modeled on communist-era propaganda strategies, are to blame for the increase of disinformation on American social media under Trump—and this is not a topic for me to develop here.[263]

As for trying to understand post-communist Bulgaria, I tend to turn to literature in order to find the words to describe the dystopian aura I find there. I use words like *Orwellian* or *Kafkaesque* (I wonder if perhaps Kristeva felt like Gregor Samsa last year, waking up as a bug?). I am told that the Law is the Law and that the Dossier Commission is just following the Law. Sometimes I drift off into images of the *Handmaid's Tale*, Ionesco's rhinoceroses, or Alice's upside-down experiences on the other side of the looking glass. But then I am reminded: this is not fiction. And as many have said, it would all be comic if it were not so brutal.

So in this post-cold-war atmosphere, why Kristeva? Why now? Who benefits? Is this just old-fashioned misogyny? Jealousy? Is it garden-variety hostility toward intellectuals . . . or in the United States, against anyone associated with postwar French theory? Some see the attacks on Kristeva as "part of a wider project by right-wing, anti-democratic, and populist forces to discredit European institutions and pro-European intellectuals, politicians, and prominent ex-pats."[264] Others see the attack as specific to her. But what is clear is that this is not *only* happening to her. For example, over four thousand names of those accused of collaborating with the KGB have been published in Latvia recently, much to the traumatic surprise of many of those named.[265]

A Bulgarian journalist, Alexenia Dimitrova, who has worked diligently since 1989 to access Bulgarian intelligence documents (her father spent two terms in labor camps under the communist regime) was shocked recently to find her own name there:

> I was shocked to see my name in the list. I spent a month to research
> my own case. I traced and met two ex-officers responsible for that unit

and asked them how my name appeared there if I have never signed [a] contract to collaborate with the secret services and I have never written reports for them? I asked them how I was assigned a secret code name without knowing about it? These two ex-officers confessed that it happened that some lower personnel, trying to make quick career [progress], lied [about having attracted] agents just in order to fulfil [their quota for] recruited agents.[266]

Even an American woman named Katherine Verdery discovered herself inexplicably drawn into the spy web. The description for her recent *My Life as a Spy: Investigations in a Secret Police File* reads as follows:

As Katherine Verdery observes, "There's nothing like reading your secret police file to make you wonder who you really are." In 1973 Verdery began her doctoral fieldwork in the Transylvanian region of Romania, ruled at the time by communist dictator Nicolae Ceausescu. She returned several times over the next twenty-five years, during which time the secret police—the Securitate—compiled a massive surveillance file on her. Reading through its 2,781 pages, she learned that she was "actually" a spy, a CIA agent, a Hungarian agitator, and a friend of dissidents: in short, an enemy of Romania. In *My Life as a Spy* she analyzes her file alongside her original field notes and conversations with Securitate officers. Verdery also talks with some of the informers who were close friends, learning the complex circumstances that led them to report on her, and considers how fieldwork and spying can be easily confused. Part memoir, part detective story, part anthropological analysis, *My Life as a Spy* offers a personal account of how government surveillance worked during the Cold War and how Verdery experienced living under it.[267]

The best work on trying to understand the bizarre, paranoid-schizoid post-Soviet phantasy world at work in Bulgaria is of course being done either in Bulgaria or in Slavic studies elsewhere. Philosophers in Sofia like Miglena Nikolchina are analyzing in depth the dizzying impossibility of proving what the Secret Services were up to during the Soviet era. She has uncovered strategies that they used, such as "working in the dark," where the targets they were surveilling had no idea that this was happening to them—this may be the strategy that was employed with Kristeva—and how, in the present time, the victims of these strategies have no power to stop the "predictable avalanche of slander, abjection, and hate":

> And while the battle around the truth of Kristeva goes on, a more terrible and totally ignored truth emerges: the kudos of the communist secret services in Bulgaria seems to have never wavered. Few of us dare doubt *them, their* truth, *their* power to provide the truth. Well, why should we? The secret services were busy molesting and destroying intellectuals in the past; they seem to be able to go on doing this *decades after their presumed demise.* Look at what they can do to Kristeva *today.* She tried to escape them, she even got to Paris and New York, to world renown. Yet here they are, *they got her.*[268]

The Slavic studies scholar Vladislav Todorov has theorized what might be called the political unconscious of Soviet communism, coining the term "Political Dada Theory" to account for the superficial-conspiracy-simulation that was the web holding together the "Conspiratorial State" that is now the "Post-Conspiratorial Condition"—i.e. the "Crime State."[269] A graduate student in Prague, Martin Tharp, is also trying to understand what has happened to Kristeva in the larger context of the current post-Soviet condition as "evil postmodernism":

> All across post-communist Europe, it is possible to discern not merely the dismantling of the 1990s open society, but even more worryingly, the emergence of a "red-brown" coalition between old communists, Generation X rightists, and Pepe-meme-addicted millennials—all around the flag of nationalism and national purity. In Bulgaria, the foul regime of Todor Zhivkov is increasingly praised for the vicious anti-Turkish measures implemented at the end of the 1980s, rightly regarded by some Balkan observers as a dress rehearsal for Bosnia less than a decade later. An attack on a Western intellectual, and a leading defender of social openness at that, could definitely be interpreted as a disturbing attempt to split up the pro-Western forces as Bulgaria's xenophobia only swells in strength.[270]

It's Just Not My Life . . .

But none of this is Julia Kristeva's *life*. She was definitely side-swiped by history in 2018–19 (and not for the first time). And she will no doubt be haunted and harassed for some time to come. But I predict that the tumult will not last long, for none of it is really her life. What is her life? I hope to have convinced you that her life is writing, that writing is her life. Besides her family and friends, her colleagues, students, and patients, it is writing that is at the center of her life. To be more precise, Kristeva will always return to language, to the poetic at the heart of her intelligence, at the heart of her politics, at the heart of her process of living . . . at the heart of her writing. In a 2016 talk she gave at the Théâtre National de la Colline, in answer to Friedrich Hölderlin's question, "Of What Use Are Poets in Times of Distress?," she said, "If you find the meaning of the world in the fullness of language, the totalitarian hold cannot threaten you anymore." She continued:

> For me, the poet is above all a musician of language, he upsets the maternal and/or national language because he takes hold of its nerve—the voice and meaning accorded, and he excels in what the first Stoics called the "inner touch": the *oikeiois*, that impalpable sensation that connects each of us to the most intimate parts of our self and of the other, thus constituting the first sketch of what will be called a "conciliation," an "*amor nostri*" and later the "human race" and "fraternity." The poet is at the root of this "inner touch," he is the carrier wave of incarnated universality. Why the poet? Because by readjusting sense and sensibility, by testing unspeakable passions, the poet crosses through identities, borders and foundations, and he makes co-presence sharable. I am telling you that the alchemy of the poetic verb is an inseparable lining of the *fraternity* that has inspired our meeting tonight. It was inevitable, therefore, indispensable, that we should seek the poet when humanity collapses, and that we ask of him, and of him in the first instance, not *to be or not to be*, but quite simply just to begin again. For without him, there will be no more "inner touch" to be shared, there will be no more humanity.

A few minutes later, Kristeva evokes the poet again, this time in the persona of her son, David:

> Examples of these poetic multiverses, multiverses of life-giving power?
>
> There are some examples, on the part of those who are fragile: my son David Joyaux proves it; he publishes some of his poems in the newspaper, *Le Papotin*, open to people with disabilities. This is how he confides and confirms his sur-vival (with a dash) after a long coma at the hospital:
>
> *Writing*
>
> *From the white point to the point / black where is written / without / the day, without the night, the attraction / of words for the withdrawal / of the seas . . . The hidden objects / are sentences / Where I'm hiding so as / not to forget love. / The envelope, / it's silence. To perform / your writing / listen to the silence of the books. Writing allows / thinking. It is the / memory of life. / It allows the forgetting / of suffering, it allows / to love, it allows / to be together / surrounded /, in the / solitude. / Writing allows travel / When one wants / or does not want / . . . / Writing . . .*[271]

À suivre . . . as Colette once wrote. To be continued . . .

Figure 4.4. Julia Kristeva in her garden on the Île de Ré, Summer 2012. Photo by Anna Jardine.

Appendix 1: Document #10 of the "Sabina" File

Section: 6.1.3   top secret!
Consideration: assignment
Received (date): 27.7.73   [black ink stamp saying it was declassified]

To: Stoyan Kristev, A. Kanchev 31, Sofia
From: Julia Kristeva, Ars an Re, France
Language: Type:

CONTENTS

Picture with its back to the envelope flap, date on top, behind it a postcard with the text facing the envelope flap, text begins on top

"I still haven't received ----------------
                                    news. Julia".

2. MAD
[handwritten in pencil] 26.7.73

[handwritten in ink]
Please copy the text and take a picture of the photograph of Kristeva and her husband.

Release the letter.

[signature]

[black ink stamp: true to the original date: 30.03.2018 signature: [signature]]

Appendix 2: A Chronological List of Kristeva's Books in French

For the convenience of specialist readers, I have here listed the French titles of Kristeva's books in chronological order. Given that publication details are provided in the endnotes, only the titles and years of publication are listed below.

1. *Sēmeiōtikē: Recherches pour une sémanalyse* (1969)
2. *Le Langage, cet inconnu: Une Initiation à la linguistique* (1969)
3. *Le Texte du roman: Approche sémiologique d'une structure discursive transformationnelle* (1970)
4. *La Révolution du langage poétique: L'Avant-garde à la fin du XIXe siècle: Lautréamont et Mallarmé* (1974)
5. *Des Chinoises* (1974)
6. *La Traversée des signes* (1975) (ed.)
7. *Polylogue* (1977)
8. *Folle vérité: Vérité et vraisemblance du texte psychotique* (1979)— with Jean-Michel Ribettes
9. *Pouvoirs de l'horreur* (1980)
10. *Histoires d'amour* (1983)
11. *Au commencement était l'amour: Psychanalyse et foi* (1985)
12. *Soleil noir: Dépression et mélancolie* (1987)
13. *Étrangers à nous-mêmes* (1988)
14. *Lettre ouverte à Harlem Désir* (1990)
15. *Les Samouraïs* (1990)
16. *Le Vieil homme et les loups* (1991)
17. *Les Nouvelles maladies de l'âme* (1993)
18. *Le Temps sensible: Proust et l'expérience littéraire* (1994)
19. *Possessions* (1996)
20. *Sens et non-sens de la révolte: Limites de la psychanalyse I* (1996)

21. *La Révolte intime: Limites de la psychanalyse II* (1997)
22. *Le Féminin et le sacré* (1998)—with Catherine Clément
23. *Contre la dépression nationale* (1998)
24. *Visions capitales* (1998)
25. *L'Avenir d'une révolte* (1998)
26. *Le Génie féminin I: Hannah Arendt* (1999)
27. *Le Génie féminin II: Melanie Klein* (2000)
28. *Au risque de la pensée* (2001)
29. *Micropolitique* (2001)
30. *Le Génie féminin III: Colette* (2002)
31. *Lettre au président de la République sur les citoyens en situation de handicap* (2003)
32. *Chroniques du temps sensible* (2003)
33. *Notre Colette* (2004) (ed.)
34. *Meurtre à Byzance* (2004)
35. *L'Amour de soi et ses avatars* (2005)
36. *La Haine et le pardon* (2005)
37. *Seule, une femme* (2007)
38. *Cet incroyable besoin de croire* (2007)
39. *Thérèse, mon amour* (2008)
40. *Leur regard perce nos ombres* (2011)—with Jean Vanier
41. *Pulsions du temps* (2013)
42. *L'Horloge enchantée* (2015)
43. *Du mariage considéré comme un des beaux-arts* (2015)—with Philippe Sollers
44. *Beauvoir présente* (2016)
45. *Je me voyage: Mémoires* (2016)—interviews with Samuel Dock

Notes

Introduction

1 See Susan Rubin Suleiman, *Risking Who One Is: Encounters with Contemporary Art and Literature* (Cambridge, MA: Harvard University Press, 1994).

2 This angle is not lost on Kristeva herself: see her *Beauvoir présente* (Paris: Fayard/Pluriel, 2016).

3 Kristeva herself has over the last couple of decades focused on women intellectuals (Arendt, Klein, Colette, Teresa of Ávila), wanting to "tell their stories," "quote some of their best writing," and "make them contemporary," but also to give her "personal point of view" on them. I could not state my own goals here more succinctly. I feel that these goals are particularly important in light of the recent attacks on Kristeva and her work, attacks originating in Eastern Europe and then picked up and amplified in Western Europe and the United States. These attacks contain more than a shadow of misogyny. (See my discussion of these attacks at the end of Part III.)

4 Julia Kristeva, *Au risque de la pensée* (Paris: Éditions de l'Aube, 2001).

5 See my discussion of Kristeva on the topic of Europe in Part III. For an example of her optimism about European culture, see Gaby Levin, "Julia Kristeva: Humanities Can Help Thwart the Destructive Depression That Feeds Fanaticism," *Haaretz*, June 15, 2017. Kristeva's relationship to her native Bulgaria is sometimes examined in relation to her perceived Eurocentrism. For a particularly virulent analysis of how Kristeva's "abjection" regarding her Bulgarian roots distorts her general theory of human subjectivity, see Dušan I. Bjelić, "Julia Kristeva: Exile and Geopolitics of the Balkans," *Slavic Review* 67, no. 2 (2008): 364–83. For a positive reading of Kristeva's relationship to Bulgaria, see Miglena Nikolchina, "Julia Kristeva and the History of Bulgarian Women's Literature: Narratives of Transposition," in *Women's Voices in Post-Communist Eastern Europe. Vol. 1: Rewriting Histories*, ed. M. S. Draga-Alexandru, M. Nicolaescu, and H. Smith (Bucharest: Editura Universității din București, 2005), 19–35. For a detailed discussion of

Kristeva's relationship to nationalism, see Ewa Ziarek, "The Uncanny
Style of Kristeva's Critique of Nationalism," in *The Kristeva Critical
Reader*, ed. John Lechte and Mary Zournazi (Edinburgh: Edinburgh
University Press, 2003), 139–57. Kristeva's embrace of cosmopolitanism
must be considered in the context of her Eastern European education:
cosmopolitans (most often a code word for Jews) were demonized under
both fascism and communism.

6 For an important and now classic critique of Kristeva's use of
psychoanalysis to theorize social change, see Nancy Fraser, "The Uses and
Abuses of French Discourse Theories for Feminist Politics," *boundary 2*
17, no. 2 (1990): 82–101. For an equally important and classic example
of a critique of what is perceived as Kristeva's psychoanalytically based
heteronormativity, see Judith Butler, "The Body Politics of Julia Kristeva,"
in *Gender Trouble: Feminism and the Subversion of Identity* (New York:
Routledge, 1990), 79–93.

7 See, for example, Julia Kristeva, "New Forms of Revolt," *Journal of French
and Francophone Philosophy* XXII, no. 2 (2014): 1–19, 1.

8 Sollers made these remarks while sitting with Kristeva outside their home
on the Île de Ré. Quoted from the documentary *Histoires d'amour et de
passerelles* (2011), written and directed by Teri Wehn-Damisch.

9 Simone de Beauvoir, *The Prime of Life* (New York: Harper Books,
1976), 10.

10 Julia Kristeva, "Un Institut des Humanités à Paris-Diderot." Available on
Kristeva's website.

11 Julia Kristeva, "Nouvelles formes de la révolte," a lecture delivered at the
University of Sofia, St. Kliment Ohridski, Bulgaria, on September 26,
2014. The published English reference is given in note 7 above. I have
slightly modified the translation here.

12 For an excellent introduction to Kristeva's recent work on biopolitics
in our era, see Sarah K. Hansen, "Julia Kristeva and the Politics of Life,"
Journal of French and Francophone Philosophy XXI, no. 1 (2013): 27–42.

13 This struck me vividly as I got to know her better personally while
co-translating her *Desire in Language*, ed. Leon S. Roudiez, trans.
Thomas Gora, Alice Jardine, and Leon S. Roudiez (New York: Columbia
University Press, 1980).

14 *Histoires d'amour et de passerelles.*

15 Ibid.

16 Colette, *La Naissance du jour* (Paris: Flammarion, 1928), 133. The original French reads, "renaître, ça n'a jamais été au-dessus de mes forces."

17 Julia Kristeva, *Je me voyage: Mémoires*, interview with Samuel Dock (Paris: Fayard, 2016), 9; Irene Ivantcheva-Merjanska et Michèle Vialet, "Entretien avec Julia Kristeva: Penser en nomade et dans l'autre langue le monde, la vie psychique et la littérature," *The Cincinnati Romance Review* 35 (2013): 158–89, 158–9.

18 See, for example, Michel de Certeau, *The Writing of History* (New York: Columbia University Press, 1988).

Part I: Bulgaria, My Suffering (1941–1965)

1 Julia Kristeva, *Au risque de la pensée* (Paris: Éditions de l'Aube, 2001), 24.

2 Kristeva makes these remarks while looking at photos of herself as a child. Quoted from the documentary *Histoires d'amour et de passerelles* (2011), written and directed by Teri Wehn-Damisch.

3 Kristeva, *Au risque de la pensée*, 10–11. When she was older, Kristeva also spent summers by the Black Sea as a monitor of so-called "international pioneers" at a summer camp for children from France, Belgium, Italy, China, Vietnam, North Korea, and Africa. Kristeva worked and played with the children in French, producing shows of La Fontaine's *Fables*, among other literary events.

4 This is a tricky subject. Bulgaria did pass anti-Jewish laws and deportations almost happened several times. As Milena Savova-Mahon Borden notes, "A major clarification has to be made about the very definition of who actually were the Bulgarian Jews in the communist version of history. The communist theory about the saving of the Bulgarian Jews was based on the definition of the Bulgarian Jews as the Jews living in Bulgaria proper. The Jews living in the territories occupied by Bulgaria in Macedonia and Thrace were excluded from this definition. The Jews from these so-called 'occupied territories' were sent to concentration camps" (in "The Politics of Nationalism Under Communism in Bulgaria," PhD dissertation, University College London, 2001, 356–7). See also Michael Bar-Zohar, *Beyond Hitler's Grasp:*

The Heroic Rescue of Bulgaria's Jews (Holbrook, MA: Adam's Media Corporation, 1998) and Marshall Roth, "The Rescue of Bulgarian Jewry," *AISH.com*, October 23, 2011. The Bulgarian King Boris III died suddenly in 1943 after a visit to Germany. It was rumored that even though he was pro-German, the fact that he helped prohibit the deportation of Jews led to his being poisoned. Years later it was determined that he in reality died of a coronary occlusion. His six-year-old son, Simeon, took over the crown with the guidance of a Council of Regents. After Simeon's exile by the communists, he returned to Bulgaria after 1989, reunited with the intellectuals there, and became Prime Minister.

5   This short presentation of Bulgaria's history during the Second World War is constructed from multiple sources to give context for Kristeva's earliest childhood memories and the war stories that gave shape to these memories. Because many of the "facts" about the time are buried under multiple layers of propaganda, the material reality of what happened is sometimes unclear.

6   Julia Kristeva, "Nouvelles formes de la révolte," a lecture delivered at the University of Sofia, St. Kliment Ohridski, Bulgaria, on September 26, 2014. The lecture was transformed into an article, translated and published as "New Forms of Revolt," *Journal of French and Francophone Philosophy*, XXII, no. 2 (2014): 1–19.

7   Kristeva makes these remarks as images from her childhood and from historical Sofia scroll in the background. Quoted from *Histoires d'amour et de passerelles.*

8   She remains an avid swimmer today.

9   The Saint Nedelya Church stands at the center of Sofia. It is most famous for its choir and has also preserved many important and valuable icons.

10 Music has remained at the center of Ivanka's life. In 1966, she went to study music formally at the Conservatory of Music in Moscow. Later she studied in Basel and Paris on prestigious scholarships. In France, she became a renowned musicologist, a practitioner and theorist of music, eventually teaching music and music theory at the University of Paris 8 and working with many important twentieth-century musicians, including Pierre Boulez at IRCAM, Paris. She is the author of hundreds of articles and of numerous ground-breaking books, including *Entre détermination et aventure: Essais sur la musique de la deuxième moitié du*

Notes

vingtième siècle (Paris: L'Harmattan, 2004). Living up to Stoyan Kristev's dream for his daughters, she speaks seven languages. When she moved to Paris in the early 1970s, she changed her family name from Kristeva to Stoyanova, after her father. Ivanka Stoyanova and Julia Kristeva offer an interesting window into the abodes of sibling rivalry.

11 Kristeva has commented that the result of mixing religion and medicine is psychoanalysis: "I am therefore the pure product of this paternal heritage!" (*Au risque de la pensée*, 16).

12 One of his most important essays was on Vasil Levski, a revolutionary and a member of "Priests Against the Turks." Levski participated in the struggle for the liberation of Bulgaria from Ottoman rule, was tortured, and eventually executed. Young Kristeva played soccer in school and her team was named after Levski, a patriotic hero.

13 John Sutherland, "The Ideas Interview: Julia Kristeva," *The Guardian*, March 14, 2006, https://www.theguardian.com/education/2006/mar/14/highereducation.research1.

14 First published in *L'infini* 51 (1995): 42–52. Collected in *Crisis of the European Subject* (New York: Other Press, 2000), 163–83.

15 Kristeva, *Au risque de la pensée*, 15.

16 David Halperin, *Sabbatai Zevi: Testimonies to a Fallen Messiah* (Oxford: Littman Library of Jewish Civilization, 2007).

17 Julia Kristeva, "Du dessin, ou la vitesse de la pensée," in *Visions capitales* (Paris: Fayard/Éditions de La Martinière, 2013), 9–13, 9–10. Translated as *The Severed Head: Capital Visions*, trans. Jody Gladding (New York: Columbia University Press, 2011). The translation here is mine.

18 The image of the decapitated woman is sometimes mentioned by Kristeva with regard to her mother. One cannot help but think here of the famous text by Hélène Cixous, "Castration or Decapitation?" *Signs: Journal of Women in Culture and Society* 7, no. 1 (1981): 41–55.

19 In her interview with Samuel Dock, Kristeva tells this story slightly differently. There she remembers having herself been offered the spoonfuls of water [*Je me voyage: Mémoires* (Paris: Fayard, 2016), 22].

20 It is important to note that Kristeva has learned recently that the women who taught her might not have been Dominicans but rather members of the Oblates of the Assumption, a non-consecrated cult of women founded in Nîmes, France, in 1865 and dedicated to missionary work and inter-

religious dialogue. Bulgaria was their first destination as part of what has come to be known as "The Near Eastern Mission." It is also important to note that after the war there was a lot of confusion about grade levels, especially in the context of coordinating between Bulgarian public and foreign private schools. Kristeva was placed in the beginning classes at the maternal school but progressed up the class levels quickly.

21 In particular, Kristeva remembers learning by heart Victor Hugo's "Sur une barricade" and La Fontaine's "L'Abeille et le Papillon," as well as Colettian phrases dedicated to cats and geraniums amidst general theatrical festivities and brightly costumed children.

22 Hristo Botev (1848–76) is among Bulgaria's most famous poets. He is considered to be a national hero because he died in the struggle by the Bulgarian people against Ottoman domination. The anniversary of his death, June 2, is celebrated every year.

23 Kristeva, *Au risque de la pensée*, 11–12. Other Eastern European countries that use the Cyrillic alphabet have also occasionally adopted this holiday.

24 Julia Kristeva, "Mon alphabet, ou comment je suis une lettre," in *Pulsions du temps* (Paris: Fayard, 2013), 15–23. As I finalize this biography, a translation of *Pulsions du temps*, *Passions of Our Time*, is forthcoming from Columbia University Press.

25 Ibid., 23.

26 See Iskra Angelova, "Julia Kristeva, Interview," *Nochtni Ptitsi* ("Birds of the Night"), Bulgarian National Television, October 19, 2014. Available on *YouTube*: https://www.youtube.com/watch?v=fsQvQmZlOLY.

27 *Who's Afraid of Julia Kristeva?* dir. Iskra Angelova (Sofia: National Palace of Culture and Wonderland Productions, 2017). A trailer is available on *YouTube*: https://www.youtube.com/watch?v=ww7oqHDEZTcsp freload=1. The short version of the film debuted on Bulgarian National Television and the complete version was shown in Sofia on April 20, 2017. It debuted in London on February 9, 2018, via the Bulgarian Cultural Institute. The film made its French debut at the University of London Institute in Paris on March 21, 2018.

28 Blaga Dimitrova (1922–2003) is best known for her work published in the 1970s, where she critiqued the communist government. She received serious reprimands for doing so. In her early seventies, after the fall of the Berlin Wall, she served as the vice president of Bulgaria (1992–93). Some of her poetry has been translated into English, for example, *Because the*

Sea Is Black: Poems of Blaga Dimitrova, trans. Niko Boris and Heather McHugh (Middletown, CT: Wesleyan University Press, 1989). Recently, a text by Dimitrova in praise of Kristeva, "Crossroads, Encounters with Julia Kristeva," has been posted on Kristeva's website. Next to it, Kristeva has posted her "1963, 2016: deux regards sur Blaga Dimitrova," *La Revue de belles lettres* 2 (2016): 241–7, which includes both her admiring 1963 article on Dimitrova [originally published in *Septemvri* 7 (1963): 216–24] and a new 2016 essay in praise of Dimitrova.

29 John Updike, *Bech: A Book* (New York: Knopf, 1965). The story also appeared in *The New Yorker*, March 13, 1965.

30 Ibid., 63.

31 Julia Kristeva, "Zapadna Evropa prez pogleda na zhurnalista" ["Western Europe Through the Eyes of a Journalist"], *Septemvri* 8 (1962): 178–80. The review is translated into English here for the first time by Margarita Teneva, who has recently graduated with an MA from the English and American Studies Department, University of Sofia. The quotations that follow are from this review.

32 This kind of palimpsestic style was also used by Kristeva's Bulgarian sweetheart, Tzvetan Stoyanov, although in the end it did not save him.

33 This article appeared originally as an editorial in *Tel Quel*, no. 74 (1977): 3–8. It was translated in *The Kristeva Reader*, ed. Toril Moi (New York: Columbia University Press, 1986), 292–300.

34 The French New Novel came of age in the 1950s. Overall, the novels often grouped under this rubric share a certain depersonalization and resistance to character, plot, and especially psychological depth. Writers most often included in the category include Michel Butor, Claude Ollier, Jean Ricardou, Alain Robbe-Grillet, Nathalie Sarraute, and Claude Simon.

35 Kristeva did not meet Mireille Bourdeur in person until years later when Mireille showed up at one of Kristeva's book signings.

36 Until 1972, *Les Lettres françaises* was financially supported by the French Communist Party. But as it became critical of Stalin during the 1960s, it went out of business because it lost communist support. Under Aragon's leadership, it loudly supported the liberalization of communist regimes, sympathized with the Prague Spring, and criticized the Soviet invasion of Czechoslovakia. The Soviet government and the French Communist Party were not happy and the journal slowly died.

37 Always intrigued by social and intellectual connections, Kristeva began to hear in the new essays coming out of France—which insisted that it is only by radically changing style and language that subjective liberation and democracy can emerge—echoes of Russian formalism, the historical avant-gardes, and writers like Mayakovsky and Khlebnikov.

38 Vercors, *Le Silence de la mer* (Paris: Minuit, 1942). Translated as *The Silence of the Sea*, trans. Cyril Connolly (New York: Macmillan, 1944). By 1948, it had sold more than a million copies in twenty-seven languages. It was also made into at least two films.

39 I have no doubt that it is because of her own experience of learning French as a young woman that one of Kristeva's most focused efforts over the past few years has been the promotion of Francophone culture to international governmental agencies and educational initiatives around the world. By "Francophone culture," she is referring to all history, literature, and philosophy written in French, wherever that may be.

40 Julia Kristeva, *Harakterni Tendencii V Zapadnata Literatura Ot XX Vek* [*Characteristic Trends in 20th-Century Western Literature*] (Sofia: DKMS, 1964).

41 Miglena Nikolchina, "Byzantium, or Fiction as Inverted Theory," in *Kristeva's Fiction*, ed. Benigno Trigo (New York: SUNY Press, 2013), 143–54, 145–6.

42 Julia Kristeva, *Nations Without Nationalism*, trans. Leon S. Roudiez (New York: Columbia University Press, 1993), 15.

43 Julia Kristeva, *Strangers to Ourselves* (New York: Columbia University Press, 1991), 191.

44 Irene Ivantcheva-Merjanska and Michèle Vialet, "Entretien avec Julia Kristeva: Penser en nomade et dans l'autre langue le monde, la vie psychique et la littérature," *The Cincinnati Romance Review* 35 (2013): 158–89, 160.

45 Young Bulgarians were encouraged to emulate the cosmonauts: Senior Lieutenant Yuri Gagarin of the Soviet Air Force and Valentina Tereshkova, the first woman in outer space.

46 Recent attacks on Kristeva by sections of the Bulgarian government have implied that Kristeva was only able to leave the country in 1965 because she agreed to spy for the communist regime while in France. That is patently ridiculous given everything that she studied, published, risked before leaving—about which more in Part III.

Part II: The Crazy Truth of It (1965–1979)

1   Julia Kristeva, *Je me voyage: Mémoires*, interview with Samuel Dock (Paris: Fayard, 2016), 54–5.

2   One of the first places where Kristeva wrote about her arrival in Paris was in her text, "Mémoire," *L'Infini* 1 (1983): 39–54. *L'Infini* became the new title of Sollers's journal, *Tel Quel*, in 1982. This short but important account was translated by Athena Viscusi in the *New York Literary Forum* in 1984 as "My Memory's Hyperbole." It was reprinted twice, in *The Female Autograph*, ed. Domna Stanton (Chicago: University of Chicago Press, 1991), 261–76 and in *The Portable Kristeva*, ed. Kelly Oliver (New York: Columbia University Press, 2002), 3–22. In it, Kristeva mentions that she also carried books by Maurice Blanchot and Louis-Ferdinand Céline in her suitcase.

3   Kristeva has often noted that her Bulgarian education was of the "Germanic" variety (except that Freud, who was considered to be a decadent by the communists, was excluded), and one cannot overstate the influence that Hegel had on the young Kristeva, especially on her *doctorat d'État*, her state doctoral thesis, later published as *La Révolution du langage poétique* (Paris: Seuil, 1974). Translated as *Revolution in Poetic Language*, trans. Margaret Waller (New York: Columbia University Press, 1984).

4   Kristeva has not wanted to reveal the name of the person who was supposed to meet her at the airport out of fear of embarrassing him (he is named Boris in *The Samurai* and we know that he was a friend of Vladimir Kostov). But as we shall see, it was this missed connection that led to a whole set of successful meetings that helped her find her way as a young intellectual in Paris. Kristeva has wanted to thank him for a long time.

5   Julia Kristeva, "My Memory's Hyperbole," in *The Portable Kristeva*, 6.

6   Irene Ivantcheva-Merjanska and Michèle Vialet, "Entretien avec Julia Kristeva: Penser en nomade et dans l'autre langue le monde, la vie psychique et la littérature," *The Cincinnati Romance Review* 35 (2013): 158–89, 169.

7   A handful of women along the way offered her material aid, but none of these women had access to any kind of power or influence.

8   Miglena Nikolchina, "Addendum: The Discretions of Inverted Theory," in *Lost Unicorns of the Velvet Revolutions: Heterotopias of the Seminar* (New York: Fordham University Press, 2013), 112–13. I am indebted to Nikolchina's writings in what follows.

9 Julia Kristeva, *Intimate Revolt: The Powers and Limits of Psychoanalysis*, vol. 2 (New York: Columbia University Press, 2002), 244.

10 Ivantcheva-Merjanska and Vialet, "Entretien avec Julia Kristeva," 169. See also Kristeva, "Pour une sémiologie des paragrammes," *Tel Quel*, no. 29 (1967): 53–75. This article was translated as "Towards a Semiology of Paragrams," in *The Tel Quel Reader*, ed. Patrick French and Roland-François Lack (London: Routledge, 1998), 25–49.

11 Nikolchina, "Addendum," 113.

12 Ibid.

13 Ibid., 115.

14 Perhaps also linked to these earliest writing efforts is Kristeva's much critiqued habit of dismissing the "obvious" or "ordinary" politics of any given problem in order to dive into the mess. A well-known example in feminist politics is her tendency to say something like, "Of course, it is clear that women must have equal rights, but let's talk instead about the messy complexities of maternity."

15 Kristeva, *Je me voyage*, 56–7.

16 Posted on Sollers's website on March 7, 2014: http://www.pileface.com/s ollers/spip.php?article1478#section8.

17 Nikolchina focuses on these concepts in her Introduction to *Lost Unicorns* (see especially p. 4) and in her conclusion to that book, "Addendum," 115.

18 Julia Kristeva, "On Yury Lotman," *PMLA* 109, no. 3 (1994): 375–6, 375. More than one commentator in Bulgaria has hinted that the recent attacks on Kristeva by government officialdom may in part be in retaliation for her role in the 1960s excavation of the communist foundation in Eastern Europe.

19 *Balkan Departures: Travel Writing from Southeastern Europe*, ed. Wendy Bracewell and Alex Drace-Francis (New York: Berghahn Books, 2009), 123. Western pop music would later inspire the marches of 1989–90. See pages 123–4 for a description of the essays Tzvetan Stoyanov wrote on the 1960s signs of Western youth rebellion, flaunting references from medieval mysticism to Beatlemania. All of his essays were censored.

20 According to *The New York Times*, Kostov was still alive at seventy-seven years old in 2008, but it is hard to find any reliable information about him after that. See Matthew Brunwasser, "Fresh intrigue surrounds a Cold War murder," *The New York Times*, September 10, 2008. There are many

emerging accounts with James Bond–worthy plots of the Cold War Secret
Services in Bulgaria, but few are translated into English. For a reputable
journalistic account, see Kelly Hignett, "The Curious Case of the Poisoned
Umbrella: The Murder of Georgi Markov," in *The View East: Central
and Eastern Europe, Past and Present* at https://thevieweast.wordpress.
com/tag/vladimir-kostov/. See also Zygmunt Dzieciolowski, "Alexander
Litvinenko: the poison of power," in *openDemocracy* (http://www.ope
ndemocracy.net/globalization-institutions_government/poison_power
_4111.jsp) and Alexenia Dimitrova, "Bulgaria's 'murder bureau' targetted
emigre dissidents" (https://euobserver.com/news/30560). A recent and
reputable update on the case is Christopher Nehring, "Umbrella or pen?
The murder of Georgi Markov. New facts and old questions," *Journal of
Intelligence History* 16, no. 1 (2017): 47–58. The Markov case has now
been officially closed by the Bulgarian government, given the end of
the thirty-five-year statute of limitations. The prime suspect known as
"Agent Piccadilly"—Francesco Gullino—was successfully tracked to an
obscure Austrian town. Amateur sleuths abound. Moreover, these types
of murders have not stopped: there is the famous case of Alexander
Litvinenko, a former KGB agent, who was found dead in London
from radioactive poisoning in 2006; the Russian journalist and human
rights activist, Anna Politkovskaya, was murdered in Moscow in 2006;
Alexander Perepilichny dropped dead while jogging in London in 2012;
and Vladimir Kara-Murza has been poisoned twice (most recently in
2017). Many have joked that America has its guns and Russia has its
poisons. What is not funny is how painful the recent spy accusations
against Kristeva have been for someone like her who watched so many
dissident intellectuals die at the hands of the Bulgarian Secret Services.

21 Stoyanov married as soon as he realized that Kristeva was not returning
to Sofia at the end of her year in Paris, on November 13, 1966.

22 Dospat is a town in the Rhodope/Rodopi mountains, and the Rodopi is
where Orpheus lived.

23 For example, there is an annual national contest for best student essays
on Stoyanov's work. In 2010, the theme was "Tzvetan Stoyanov: Prophet."
The university student who won the contest wrote an essay about how
Stoyanov had an early vision of the internet when he warned about the
alienation in society that would result from the desire to create an image

of oneself. Cf. "De jeunes auteurs bulgares sur les prophéties de Tzvetan Stoyanov," Radio Bulgaria: http://bnr.bg/fr/post/100108075/de-jeunes-aut eurs-bulgares-sur-les-prophties-de-tzvetan-stoyanov.

24 Marie Vrinat, "Le Livre inachevé d'une 'vie inachevée,'" postface to Tzvetan Stoyanov, *Le Génie et son maître: Fiodor Dostoïevski et Konstantin Pobedonostsev*, trans. Marie Vrinat (Paris: L'Esprit des Péninsules, 2000), 215–20, 219. Nikolchina has written about Stoyanov and Kristeva's generation's belief in keeping alive "the utopia of the grand dialogue of humanity," which is not a bad definition of culture. See Miglena Nikolchina, "Reading the Communist Legacy through Non-Coinciding Coincidences: Tzvetan Stoyanov with Julia Kristeva and Georgi Markov," unpublished paper, 6.

25 Julia Kristeva, *The Samurai* (New York: Columbia University Press, 1992), 41.

26 See, for example, Kristeva, *Je me voyage*, 58–9.

27 Nikolchina, "Reading the Communist Legacy," 6. She is quoting and translating Tzevetan Stoyanov, *Izklyuchitelnata biografiya na Budi Budev* (Varna: Durzhavno izdatelstvo, 1969), 6.

28 Kristeva, *The Samurai*, 43.

29 Nikolchina, "Reading the Communist Legacy," 6.

30 Kristeva, *The Samurai*, 44–5.

31 See Nikolchina's "Reading the Communist Legacy" for an extended explanation of the strategy of non-coinciding coincidences.

32 I have read the French translation of Stoyanov's book on Dostoevsky (see note 24) with great admiration and with the hope that it will soon be translated into English. Given that Kristeva is currently writing a book on Dostoevsky which will undoubtedly be translated into English quickly, it would be fascinating to read the two volumes in tandem. There is a moving accolade on the back cover of Stoyanov's book written by Tzvetan Todorov, even if he does get the date of Stoyanov's death wrong (Stoyanov died in 1971, not 1977).

33 Nikolchina, "Reading the Communist Legacy," 10.

34 Ibid., 8, 11.

35 Yordan Vassilev, "Tsvetan Stoyanov—A Ray of Light (Marking 80 Years Since His Birth)." My sincere thanks to Nikolchina for sending me this very moving, unpublished paper by one of Stoyanov's closest friends. My thanks as well to my talented Bulgarian translator, Margarita Teneva.

36 Nikolchina, "Reading the Communist Legacy," 11.

37 I would argue that Pierre Daix was a more important figure for young intellectuals like Kristeva than he has been given credit for. His unique experience as editor and publisher during those heady times in Paris deserves its own chronicling.

38 See Kristeva on Aragon in *The Sense and Non-Sense of Revolt: The Powers and Limits of Psychoanalysis*, trans. Jeanine Herman (New York: Columbia University Press, 2000).

39 Kristeva returned to Rabelais many times via her interest in Bakhtin's readings of Rabelais and the carnivalesque. It is interesting that she is today returning to Bakhtin's other great textual obsession, Dostoevsky.

40 Julia Kristeva, *Le Texte du roman: Approche sémiologique d'une structure discursive* (Paris: Mouton, 1970). There are two levels of doctoral study in France even today: first there is the *doctorat de 3ème cycle* (equivalent to the American PhD) and then the *doctorat d'État* (for which there is no equivalent in the United States).

41 Tzvetan Todorov and Kristeva were never close friends, although they were of the same generation, shared many of the same interests, were both mentored by Roland Barthes, and were both completely integrated into French intellectual circles and, eventually, into French life as full citizens. Among Todorov's many institutional affiliations there was his appointment as Director of Research at the French Centre Nationale de la Recherche Scientifique (the National Center for Scientific Research) in 1968. In 1970, he helped found the journal *Poétique*, of which he remained one of the editors until 1979. He was a visiting professor at several universities in the United States, including Harvard, Yale, Columbia, and Berkeley. Todorov published a total of thirty-nine books. Many consider one of his best books to be *Introduction à la littérature fantastique* (Paris: Seuil, 1970). Translated as *The Fantastic: A Structural Approach to a Literary Genre*, trans. Richard Howard (Ithaca, NY: Cornell University Press, 1973).

42 It has been argued that Kristeva, in her early work, was trying to combine structuralism and Marxism. It has also been suggested that when she added psychoanalysis to the mix, she became a precursor of poststructuralism.

43 Lucien Goldmann was born in Romania in 1913, and spent much of his youth on the run from the Nazis, eventually ending up in Paris. In 1946,

he was appointed to the École Pratique des Hautes Études. His "Marxist
Humanism" is revered by many of my generation in the United States
as having brought clarity and respectability to the study of literature
and culture from a Marxist perspective. But there are just as many
who criticize him for having made Marxism "palatable" to the postwar
Western liberal academy. He eventually became very resistant to the
new forms of critical writing emerging in Paris in the 1960s, especially
psychoanalysis. His *Pour une sociologie du roman* will probably remain
one of his most influential works in the English-speaking world (Paris:
Gallimard, 1964). Translated as *Towards a Sociology of the Novel*, trans.
Alan Sheridan (New York: Tavistock Publications, 1975). Goldmann died
in 1970 at the very young age of fifty-seven.

44 Semiotics, the study of signs and the production of meaning, is at the
foundations of almost all of the critical theory that came out of France
in the postwar period. If one does not know what a "sign" is, the rest of
"postwar French thought" remains more or less incomprehensible.

45 Russian Formalism was a school of literary theory in Russia from the
1910s to the 1930s. It includes the work of a number of highly influential
scholars such as Viktor Shklovsky, Vladimir Propp, and Roman
Jakobson, and exerted a major influence on thinkers such as Mikhail
Bakhtin and Yuri Lotman.

46 Mikhail Bakhtin was a Russian philosopher, literary critic, and
semiotician who was very active in the Soviet Union of the 1920s. But he
was not famous until his work was rediscovered by Russian and Bulgarian
scholars in the 1960s. It was Kristeva who brought his work to the
attention of the rest of the world.

47 In postwar French thought, the term *speaking subject* refers to the
speaking human being, not only to the human person but to the person
who *speaks*, who symbolizes, who communicates. Human beings
experience each other as subjects and communicate with each other as
speaking subjects.

48 I remember vividly a day in Kristeva's 1976 seminar at Columbia when
she made this point about Marxism as well—mainly for the benefit of
the contentious Marxist student in the room. She drew on the board a
long flat line to represent the traditional Marxist notion of the base (the
economic arrangement of a society at any given time and place). She then

drew a long flat line above it and parallel to it to represent the Marxist notion of the superstructure (cultural products like literature) as an exact mirror of the base. In a series of almost frenzied gestures, she drew slashing lines vertically, cutting across the first two lines, and labeled them "subjects" and "histories" (by which she meant both histories and stories). She then warned us in a solemn voice to never leave human subjects and their stories, let alone history, out of the picture. She then dismissed us. As a graduate student, I was deeply marked by this class.

49 The talk was first published as "Bakhtine, le mot, le dialogue, et le roman," *Critique* XXIII, no. 239 (1967): 438–65. This article was translated as "Word, Dialogue, and Novel," in Julia Kristeva, *Desire in Language*, ed. Leon S. Roudiez, trans. Thomas Gora, Alice Jardine, and Leon S. Roudiez (New York: Columbia University Press, 1980), 64–91.

50 Roland Barthes, "L'Étrangère," *La Quinzaine littéraire*, no. 94 (1970): 19–20.

51 Julia Kristeva, "Roland Barthes, the Stranger" (presentation, *Inside Barthes* Conference, New York University, October 15, 2015). It is because of Barthes and Kristeva's deep affection for each other that the publication of the whodunit by Laurent Binet, *La Septième fonction du langage* (Paris: Grasset, 2015), was so hurtful to her. Binet's book was translated as *The Seventh Function of Language*, trans. Sam Taylor (New York: McMillan, 2017). I am convinced that Kristeva was chosen as the villain of the novel because she is Bulgarian by birth and because Binet calculated that the satirical humiliation of one of the best-known, still living French theorists of the postwar period would catch the populist wave of anti-intellectualism sweeping Europe.

52 Kristeva was visibly moved as she told me this story. Afterward, we talked about how her experience with Goldmann was so different from that of many intellectual women caught in these kinds of situations. When the male mentor has so much power, it is usually the female student reduced to tears.

53 Kristeva's tone is nonchalant, almost dismissive in 2014 when she talks about the necessity to change the form (rather than just the content) of any given practice if one wants true change. Yet I remember vividly Kristeva saying exactly this with great conviction in her course on poetics at Columbia in the 1970s. She insisted that literary discourse is necessarily, by definition, a form of contestatory logic, a form of revolt.

54 Julia Kristeva and Philippe Sollers, *Du mariage considéré comme un des beaux-arts* (Paris: Fayard, 2015). Translated as *Marriage as a Fine Art*, trans. Lorna Scott Fox (New York: Columbia University Press, 2016).

55 *Libération*, July 25–26, 2015.

56 Philippe Sollers, *Un vrai roman: Mémoires* (Paris: Plon, 2007), 162. The name Dominique refers to Dominique Rolin, Sollers's lover of over half a century. *Paradis* is a reference to his novel by the same name (Paris: Seuil, 1981). The full Nietzsche quotation is from a famous collection of Nietzsche's poems published in 1888, *Dionysos Dithrambs*: "Upon wide, slow stairs climbs your luck to me: come, come beloved truth!" [see Friedrich Nietzsche, *The Peacock and the Buffalo: The Poetry of Nietzsche*, trans. James Luchte (New York: Bloomsbury, 2010), 309.]

57 Created in 1881, L'École des Hautes Études Commerciales (HEC) is one of the most elite of the elite system of Grandes Écoles in France. A degree there would be roughly equivalent to an MBA from Harvard.

58 Philippe Sollers, *A Strange Solitude* (New York: Grove Press, 1959).

59 Philippe Sollers, *The Park* (New York: Red Dust, 1969); Philippe Sollers, *Event* (New York: Red Dust, 1986); Philippe Sollers, *Numbers* (not translated). Most readers of Sollers in English tend to know only a few of his texts and often do not have a sense of the overall shape of his work, which ranges from the experimental and even avant-garde texts of his youth—through the more conventional narrative of books like his *Women*, trans. Barbara Bray (New York: Columbia University Press, 1990) [*Femmes* (Paris: Gallimard, 1983)]—to his more political volumes of the 2000s seemingly caught up in a war against nihilism and cynicism. American commentators tend to limit themselves to calling him "the bad boy of French letters," "the chain-smoking Casanova," or "the anti-philosopher." A serious critical volume devoted to Sollers's overall writing career is long overdue.

60 As far as I can tell, treatments of various kinds and stages of viral hepatitis with cortisone are still today very much debated as to outcome. It appears to me that Kristeva was very lucky.

61 One of the best books in English on the history of *Tel Quel* is still Danielle Marx-Scouras's *The Cultural Politics of Tel Quel: Literature and the Left in the Wake of Engagement* (University Park: The Pennsylvania State University Press, 1996).

62 "L'Avenir est à eux!: Des membres du groupe *Tel Quel* s'expriment," Radiodiffusion-Télévision Française, April 6, 1963. Posted by the online French film archive Institut National de l'Audiovisuel: http://www.ina.fr/video/I11010118/des-membres-du-groupe-tel-quel-s-expriment-video.html.

63 Philippe Sollers, *L'Intermédiaire* (Paris: Seuil, 1963).

64 See Jean-Claude Chevalier with Pierre Encrevé, *Combats pour la linguistique, de Martinet à Kristeva* (Paris: ENS Editions, 2006), 276.

65 *Tel Quel* was largely Marxist 1968–75, but after that moved increasingly toward an ethics grounded in writing itself, leaving Marxist ambitions behind by the end of the 1970s.

66 See Chevalier and Encrevé, *Combats pour la linguistique*, 282, 290–1.

67 Ibid., 291–2.

68 *Julia Kristeva—Une étrangère, citoyenne du monde*, dir. Alain Monclin (University of Paris-Diderot, 2012).

69 Julia Kristeva, *Au risque de la pensée* (Paris: Éditions de l'Aube, 2001), 36.

70 In *Je me voyage*, Kristeva shares detailed stories about some of these "great men."

71 Kristeva has often talked about the psycho-sexual politics of the group, about how her and Risset's female masculinity played well with the young men of *Tel Quel*.

72 Julia Kristeva and Jean Vanier, *Leur regard perce nos ombres* (Paris: Editions Fayard, 2011).

73 She would, years later, be attracted to the writings and practices of Saint Teresa of Ávila precisely because the saint's faith provided her with an exile from herself.

74 See Kristeva's chapter on Aragon in *Intimate Revolt: The Powers and Limits of Psychoanalysis II*, trans. Jeanine Herman (New York: Columbia University Press, 2002), 181–219.

75 I had the pleasure of meeting Marcelle Joyaux when she accompanied Kristeva to New York City in 1976–77 for Kristeva's year of teaching at Columbia.

76 Centre national de la recherche scientifique.

77 This characterization of France as the best and the worst place for foreigners to settle opens Kristeva's *Strangers to Ourselves*, trans. Leon S. Roudiez (New York: Columbia University Press, 1991).

78 Kristeva, *Je me voyage*, 126.

79 Philippe Sollers, *Lettres à Dominique Rolin* (Paris: Gallimard, 2017); Dominique Rolin, *Lettres à Philippe Sollers* (Paris: Gallimard, 2018).

80 Josyane Savigneau, "Un amour clandestin de Dominique Rolin," *Le Nouvel Observateur*, May 27, 2012, on the occasion of Rolin's death at the age of ninety-nine. Savigneau emphasizes in the article that when Rolin was alive, no one dared to write or say her and Sollers's names together in public. It should be noted that Savigneau is a well-known Parisian journalist, a former editor at *Le Monde des Livres*, who has over the years written many articles and reviews in support of Sollers's publications. Some even thought that they were lovers at one time, although that was untrue. She praised him so consistently that she was demoted at *Le Monde* and accused of using her position to promote Sollers.

81 See the page of Sollers's website, *Pileface*, devoted to the March 24, 2000 edition of Bernard Pivot's television show, *Bouillon de culture* (*The Broth of Culture*). The quoted description of what transpired was written by Albert Gauvin for Sollers's site in a section entitled, "Presentation of the Broadcast." Posted by Philippe Sollers: http://www.pileface.com/sollers/article.php3?id_article=39.

82 As of this writing, the published letters are receiving a great deal of attention in Paris even as Kristeva has been defending herself against the accusations emanating from Bulgaria (see Part III). Given the aggressive behavior of the French media on the latter topic, it is hard to imagine the additional stress put on Kristeva by the media's curiosity about the former one.

83 Sollers, *Un vrai roman*, 240–1.

84 Ibid., 333.

85 Philippe Sollers, "Dominique Rolin, toujours," interview, *Études* 12 (2017): 87–96, 87.

86 Kristeva talks about the dangers and challenges for women who are publicly sexual in a joint interview with Sollers published as "Complicités, rires, blessures" in *Le Nouvel Observateur* in 1996 and collected in *Du mariage*, 31–3.

87 Philippe Lançon, "La vie à deux: Julia Kristeva Philippe Sollers—Tête à tête," *Libération*, August 5, 1996.

88 Kristeva, *Je me voyage*, 137. For an example of how hard the French media has been on Kristeva about Rolin, constantly wanting to stir up

rumors of a *ménage à trois*, see the interview with her—as opposed to the more gentle one with Rolin—in *Paris Match*, March 30, 2000. The two interviews were reframed in 2014 as "a triumph of literature and thought over vaudeville," as "Kristeva, Sollers, Rolin: l'art d'écrire, l'art d'aimer," on Sollers's website: http://www.pileface.com/sollers/spip.php?article1481# sommaire. For an example of how the media often treats Kristeva in person when she refuses to succumb to taunts about her intellectual explanations of love and marriage, see the May 16, 2015, interview with Kristeva and Sollers on the French television program, *Bibliothèque Médicis*: https://www.youtube.com/watch?v=yhNORgb-q5k. Rarely have I ever seen Kristeva that annoyed in public.

89 See "Julia Kristeva: 'Je suis une chercheuse d'humanité,'" *Le Soir*, December 22, 2016.

90 François Mitterrand, while completely dedicated to his legal wife, Danielle, had a second family that has become more visible since his death. For a public account of Mitterrand's "multiverse," see Philip Short, *Mitterrand: A Study in Ambiguity* (London: Bodley Head, 2013). Sollers has been very clear about his resistance to being "coupled" with anyone: "Above all, no apology for the couple please. [Any idea of] the couple is immediately tacky. Official intellectual, official couple: horror! Aragon-Elsa, Eluard-Nush [sic], the clichés arrive and it gets tacky . . . What would be interesting would be to have done something completely out of the usual. A creation. In our case, I think that's what it is. She is lucid and I am a joker" (Lançon, "La vie à deux").

91 Kristeva has said that Sollers exhibits the feminine side of his mother and she the masculine side of her father, so much so that "in the end, we form a kind of couple of four" (*Je me voyage*, 119).

92 Ibid., 139–41.

93 Julia Kristeva and Philippe Sollers, "Le vrai personnage du couple, c'est le temps," *Libération*, July 26, 2015.

94 Lançon, "La vie à deux."

95 Ibid.

96 On Kristeva and Sollers's views on the benefits of secrecy (or at least of discretion), see their *Du mariage*, 34–5.

97 Kristeva, *Je me voyage*, 134.

98 Kristeva, *Au risque de la pensée*, 87.

99 Julia Kristeva and Philippe Sollers, "Enfance et jeunesse d'un écrivain français," in *Pulsions du temps* (Paris: Fayard, 2013), 31–8. Also posted by Philippe Sollers on November 7, 2010: https://www.youtube.com/watch?v=k-j97w-ep6g. Sollers's further remarks are of great interest as he elaborates his theory that each of us has multiple births: biological, symbolic, sexual, political, geographical, etc. and that the sum of these births is biography.

100 Kristeva, *Je me voyage*, 128.

101 Kristeva's favorite story about her time at the National Center for Scientific Research is about a letter she received from Claude Lévi-Strauss reprimanding her for working too late because it cost too much to keep the lights on so late (see, for example, *Je me voyage*, 68).

102 The association and its journal were officially founded in 1969 with Émile Benveniste as its first president. Other members have included A. J. Greimas, Roman Jakobson, André Martinet, Roland Barthes, Umberto Eco, Thomas Sebeok, and Yuri Lotman.

103 Kristeva, *The Samurai*, 87–8.

104 This famous slogan of the 1968 protests was later associated with the Situationists. See, for example, *Beneath the Paving Stones: Situationists and the Beach, May 1968* (Chico, CA: AK Press, 2008).

105 See "Cultures of Protest," Department of Romance Languages and Literatures, Harvard University, 2018: http://culturesofprotest.io. Kristeva has recently published a retrospective consideration of 1968 for its fiftieth anniversary, "Le Corps français" in *Femmes et filles: Mai 1968* (Paris: Éditions de l'Herne, 2018), 104–11.

106 Kristeva's *Sēmeiōtikē: Recherches pour une sémanalyse* was first published under the *Tel Quel* imprint by Seuil in 1969. Two essays from the volume were included in *Desire in Language*. Several essays from *Sēmeiōtikē* remain untranslated.

107 A 1968 special issue of the journal *Communications*, dedicated to the concept of verisimilitude, launched the theoretical obsession in the 1970s with the process of "making to appear real" and the crisis of this process in the postmodern era leading to an inability to tell what is real and true.

108 As for Foucault, I am referring to *Les Mots et le choses* (Paris: Gallimard, 1966). Translated as *The Order of Things* (New York: Random House, 1970).

109 Kristeva, "Pour une sémiologie des paragrammes."

110 Julia Kristeva, "L'Engendrement de la formule," in *Sēmeiōtikē: Recherches pour une sémanalyse* (Paris: Seuil, 1969), 217–310.

111 Kristeva was always very careful to distinguish her genotext/phenotext dyad from Chomsky's concepts of surface and deep structure.

112 There is also already a fascination in these early essays with several other kinds of signifying systems that remain other than (or even resist) Western ratio-linguistic communication: gesture, dance, hieroglyphs, and non-phonetic languages like Chinese.

113 Kristeva, *Je me voyage*, 179.

114 Ibid., 179–80.

115 Kristeva's second 1969 book, *Le Langage, cet inconnu: Une initiation à la linguistique* was published under Julia Joyaux in the collection "Le point de la question" at SGPP Press, Paris. It was translated into English by Anne Menke as *Language, the Unknown: An Initiation into Linguistics* (New York: Columbia University Press, 1989). Kristeva's parents were disappointed that the only one of her books that they could understand was not signed with their name, Kristev, but with her married name Joyaux—an odd and complicated truth.

116 Chevalier and Encrevé, *Combats pour la linguistique*, 285. A few years later, in her *Revolution*, Kristeva describes linguistics as a discipline that listens to a sleeping body.

117 Chevalier and Encrevé, *Combats pour la linguistique*, 290.

118 Kristeva, *Je me voyage*, 95.

119 On Kristeva's discussion of Benveniste's intellect and heart, see Julia Kristeva, "Préface," in Émile Benveniste, *Dernières Leçons, Collège de France 1968–1969* (Paris: EHESS Gallimard-Seuil, 2012), 13–40. Kristeva's preface was collected as "Émile Benveniste, un linguiste qui ne dit ni ne cache, mais signifie," in *Pulsions du temps*, 97–132.

120 Kristeva, "Préface," 13.

121 Kristeva, *Je me voyage*, 99.

122 Kristeva, "Préface," 14.

123 Antonin Artaud, *Œuvres complètes, tome XI: Lettres de Rodez 1945–1946* (Paris: Gallimard, 1974).

124 Kristeva, "Préface," 15.

125 Ibid.

126 *Langue, discours, société: Pour Émile Benveniste*, ed. Julia Kristeva et al. (Paris: Seuil, 1975).

127 Kristeva, "Préface," 17.

128 Kristeva, *Le Texte du roman*.

129 Derrida's interview, "Sémiologie et grammatologie: Entretien avec Julia Kristeva," was first published in *Information sur les sciences sociales* VII, no. 3 (1968): 133–48 and then collected in Jacques Derrida, *Positions* (Paris: Minuit, 1972), 25–50. *Positions* was translated into English by Alan Bass as *Positions* (Chicago: University of Chicago Press, 1981).

130 Julia Kristeva, "The System and the Speaking Subject," *Times Literary Supplement*, October 12, 1973: 1249–52. The essay was collected in *The Kristeva Reader*, ed. Toril Moi (New York: Columbia University Press, 1986), 24–34.

131 Fónagy is perhaps best known for his book, *La Vive-voix: essais de psycho-phonétique* (Paris: Payot, 1991).

132 Iván Fónagy, "Bases pulsionelles de la phonation," *Revue française de la psychanalyse* 34 (1970): 101–36 and 35 (1971): 543–91.

133 Ilse Barande and Robert Barande, *Histoire de la psychanalyse en France* (Toulouse: Privat, 1975).

134 I also did an analysis in French and can therefore empathize deeply with Kristeva's decision here.

135 Julia Kristeva, *Beauvoir présente* (Paris: Fayard, 2016).

136 Kristeva had at least one abortion (in *Je me voyage*, she mentions two) before the Loi Veil was enacted. The Loi Veil was a hard-won law of 1975 that decriminalized abortion in France. It was written and orchestrated by Simone Veil, Minister of Health, under President Valéry Giscard d'Estaing. The law was made permanent in 1979.

137 Françoise Coblence and Marcela Montes de Oca, "Une vie psychique est une vie dans le temps: Entretien avec Julia Kristeva," *Revue française de psychanalyse* 81, no. 2 (2017): 351–67, 366.

138 Although already referenced, we repeat the reference for the convenience of the reader: *La Révolution du langage poétique* (Paris: Seuil, 1974). Translated as *Revolution in Poetic Language*, trans. Margaret Waller (New York: Columbia University Press, 1984).

139 Most of Kristeva's articles published between 1970 and 1976 were collected in her *Polylogue* (Paris: Seuil, 1977).

140 *Julia Kristeva, étrange étrangère*, dir. François Caillat (Paris: Institut National de l'Audiovisuel, 2005). Even though the film came out in 2005, at least parts of it were filmed during Kristeva's 2002 visit to Sofia.

141 Ibid.

142 Ibid.

143 Ivantcheva-Merjanska and Vialet, "Entretien avec Julia Kristeva," 175.

144 It will not be until a few years later that Kristeva begins to explore the access to this mysterious process as it was historically provided by religious belief, particularly through Catholic mysticism. Some early signs of her interest in this lost access through religion can be glimpsed in early articles on artists like Giotto and Bellini.

145 See *Julia Kristeva, étrange étrangère*.

146 See Kristeva, *Je me voyage*, 181–2.

147 See, for example, Julia Kristeva, *Time and Sense: Proust and the Experience of Literature* (New York: Columbia University Press, 1996). Originally published as *Le Temps sensible: Proust et l'expérience littéraire* (Paris: Gallimard, 1994).

148 See my "Opaque Texts and Transparent Contexts: The Political Difference of Julia Kristeva," in *The Poetics of Gender*, ed. Nancy K. Miller (New York: Columbia University Press, 1986), 96–116.

149 See Miglena Nikolchina, "Revolution and Time in Kristeva's Writing," *Diacritics* 45, no. 3 (2017): 77–99, 80.

150 For an excellent, concise definition of these two functions, see Kelly Oliver's 1998 "Kristeva and Feminism": https://www.cddc.vt.edu/feminism/Kristeva.html.

151 See Kristeva, *Je me voyage*, 67.

152 See *Julia Kristeva, étrange étrangère*.

153 The dissertation received the grade of "très bien avec félicitations."

154 Kristeva, *Je me voyage*, 67.

155 See Kristeva refute Chevalier in Chevalier and Encrevé, *Combats pour la linguistique*, 279–80. Recall that this text is a conversation between Kristeva, Chevalier, and Encrevé.

156 Kristeva, *Je me voyage*, 67.

157 Ibid., 182–3.

158 See my "Opaque Texts and Transparent Contexts."

159 Ivantcheva-Merjanska and Vialet, "Entretien avec Julia Kristeva," 160.

160 The most visible result of 1968 in many ways was the reorganization of the University of Paris into thirteen autonomous universities in 1970. In the early 1970s, the two campuses most devoted to the radical and exciting developments of postwar thought were Jussieu (Paris 7) and Vincennes (Paris 8). The latter was bulldozed by the French government in 1980.

161 Kristeva's position was in a new department known as UFR-STD. This acronym has become legendary: it stands for *Unité de Formation et de Recherche* ("Unit of Formation and Research") within a department called *Science des Textes et Documents* (Science of Texts and Documents). STD was later renamed LAC: Letters, Arts, Cinema. It became over the years an even more stimulating place, as transgressive as it was prestigious. The department diversified its audience. For example, it accepted as auditors residents from the La Borde Anti-Psychiatry Clinic and in later years worked with the Roland Barthes Center and the Institute for Contemporary Thought (both founded by Kristeva) to widen the experience of doctoral students.

162 Lançon, "La vie à deux."

163 Chevalier and Encrevé, *Combats pour la linguistique*, 281.

164 See Kristeva, *Je me voyage*, 206–7, for a partial list of her students over the years.

165 See *Julia Kristeva, étrange étrangère*.

166 Julia Kristeva, *Des Chinoises*, was first published by Éditions des Femmes in 1974 and re-edited by Pauvert in 2001 and 2005. Translated as *About Chinese Women*, trans. Anita Barrows (New York: Urizen Publishers, 1977). Later English editions have been published by the Marion Boyars Press, London, in 1993, 2000, and 2004.

167 Kristeva, *Au risque de la pensée*, 37–9.

168 Ibid., 41.

169 Chevalier with Encrevé, *Combats pour la linguistique*.

170 Ibid., 292.

171 Ibid.

172 Ibid.

173 Joseph Needham, *Science and Civilization in China* (Cambridge: Cambridge University Press, 1956).

174 Kristeva studied Chinese for four years but did not finish her degree.

175 Sollers, "Dominique Rolin, toujours," 91.

176 Lançon, "La vie à deux."

177 See Elisabeth Roudinesco, *Jacques Lacan* (New York: Columbia University Press, 1997), 353–4. This was the first trip by Western intellectuals to China since it was admitted to the United Nations in 1971.

178 Pleynet is a poet, critic, essayist, and long-time managing editor of *Tel Quel* and *L'Infini*. Wahl, a long-time member of *Tel Quel*, was also an editor at Seuil, where he published Derrida and Lacan among others.

179 See Kristeva, *Je me voyage*, 77–8.

180 Éditions des Femmes was funded by Sylvina Boissonnas, inheritor of the Schlumberger fortune, and is still open today at 33–5 rue Jacob, Paris.

181 For background, see Claire Duchen, *Feminism in France: May 68 to Mitterrand* (New York: Routledge, 1986).

182 Kristeva, *Je me voyage*, 90–1.

183 Kristeva, *Au risque de la pensée*, 45.

184 Kristeva, *Je me voyage*, 92–4.

185 Kelly Oliver, "Julia Kristeva's Feminist Revolutions," *Hypatia* 8, no. 3 (1993): 94–114, 107.

186 Julia Kristeva, "La Femme, ce n'est jamais ça," *Tel Quel*, nos. 57–8 (1974): 19–26. Interview with the women of *Psychanalyse et politique* for the magazine *Le Torchon brûle*.

187 Ibid., 20–1.

188 For a more recent example of Kristeva's complex manner of addressing feminist issues, see her response to the #metoo (#balancetonporc) movement: "Julia Kristeva et #balancetonporc: La parole libre est encore à venir," Lesinrocks.com, December 29, 2017. In short, echoing Simone de Beauvoir, but with more emphasis on the power of creativity, Kristeva argues that women must fight for and assume their full liberty (of expression, sexuality, and subjectivity), but that at the same time it is important also to look at the big picture of how desire, bodies, and identities are being controlled and manipulated in our current world of "mandated transparency" and "hyperconnectivity."

189 Kristeva, *Je me voyage*, 103.

190 Lançon, "La vie à deux."

191 For a detailed and fascinating history of psychoanalysis in France, see Elisabeth Roudinesco, *Jacques Lacan & Co: A History of Psychoanalysis*

in France, 1925–1985, trans. Jeffrey Mehlman (Chicago: University of Chicago Press, 1990).

192 Kristeva, *Je me voyage*, 86–7.

193 Ibid., 88.

194 Ibid.

195 Coblence and Montes de Oca, "Une vie psychique est une vie dans le temps: Entretien avec Julia Kristeva," 351–67, 355.

196 Kristeva completed her training in 1979.

197 Coblence and Montes de Oca, "Une vie psychique," 354–5.

198 Lucasta Miller, "Mother Complex," *The Guardian*, April 7, 2017.

199 Kristeva's film, *Reliance*, written by Kristeva and directed by G. K. Galabov was presented to the Congress of French Speaking Analysts in Paris on June 5, 2011. The film and its text are available on Kristeva's website. While Kristeva was pregnant, one person who was surprisingly attentive was Lacan: he would call her in the middle of the night to ask her how she was doing and whether they had decided on a name yet. David was a real presence to him, especially in 1977 when he invited Kristeva to give a talk in his seminar: Kristeva had to cancel her appearance because David was cutting teeth and Kristeva had not slept all night.

200 The reference is to the language of Marcel Proust, *Le Temps retrouvé*, in *À la recherche du temps perdu*, ed. P. Clarac and A. Ferre, vol. 3 (Paris: Gallimard, 1961), 871.

201 Kristeva, *Je me voyage*, 150.

202 Ibid., 154–5.

203 Ibid., 147.

204 Kristeva does not hesitate to attribute at least some of this "naïve ardor," the desire ingrained in her from her youngest age to forge ahead in the face of adversity, to the rousing political songs she learned as a young child in communist Bulgaria.

205 Kristeva discusses "investment" as part of her psychoanalytic training and with regard to her practice as an intellectual in *Je me voyage*, 194.

206 Ibid., 155–6.

207 Julia Kristeva, *Lettre au président de la République sur les citoyens en situation de handicap* (Paris: Fayard, 2003).

208 Kristeva, *Je me voyage*, 157.

209 Ibid., 165.

210 Julia Kristeva, "Liberty, Equality, Fraternity, and . . . Vulnerability,"
     Women's Studies Quarterly 38, nos. 1–2 (2010): 251–68.

211 See Kristeva's film *Reliance*. The text of the film was published as
     "Reliance: Qu'est-ce qu'aimer pour une mère?" in *Pulsions du temps*,
     25–9. Also see her "L'érotisme maternel" in *Pulsions du temps*, 197–214.
     The English version is "Reliance, or Maternal Eroticism," *Journal of
     the American Psychoanalytic Association* 62, no. 1 (2014): 69–85. In a
     talk, "Histoires d'amour, hier et aujourd'hui" (delivered at the Groupe
     Lyonnais de Psychanalyse Rhône-Alpes of the Société Psychanalytique de
     Paris, Lyon, January 17, 2015), and in an interview that same year with
     Radio RCJ, Kristeva begins to lay out a new ethics of love as *reliance*, as a
     link of confidence and as an idealization that should be transposed into
     the social contract today—as a gift toward the other.

212 This statement is from Kristeva's film *Reliance*. It can also be found in
     English in Kristeva, "Reliance, or Maternal Eroticism," 82.

213 Julia Kristeva, "La Maternité selon Giovanni Bellini," in *Polylogue*, 409–
     35. Translated as "Maternity According to Bellini," in *Desire in Language*,
     237–70.

214 Kristeva, *Je me voyage*, 154.

215 Julia Kristeva, "La fonction prédicative et le sujet parlant," in *Polylogue*,
     323–56.

216 Julia Kristeva, "L'éthique de la linguistique," *Critique* XXX, no. 322
     (1974): 206–16. The essay also appeared in *Polylogue*, 357–69. It was
     translated in *Desire in Language*, 23–35.

217 Julia Kristeva, "La joie de Giotto," *Peinture*, nos. 2–3 (1972): 35–51. The
     essay also appeared in *Polylogue*, 383–408. It was translated in *Desire in
     Language*, 210–36.

218 Julia Kristeva, "Ellipse sur la frayeur et la séduction spéculaire,"
     Communications, no. 23 (1975): 73–8. The essay also appeared in
     Polylogue, 373–82. The English translation appeared as "Ellipsis on Dread
     and the Specular Seduction," *Wide Angle* 3, no. 3 (1979): 42–7.

219 Julia Kristeva, "From One Identity to an Other," in *Desire in Language*,
     145. The essay was first published as "D'une identité l'autre," *Tel Quel*,
     no. 62 (1975): 10–27. It also appeared in *Polylogue*, 149–72.

220 Julia Kristeva, *La Traversée des signes* (Paris: Seuil, 1975), 7.

221 Julia Kristeva, "Pratique signifiante et mode de production," *Tel Quel*, no. 60 (1974): 21–33.

222 Julia Kristeva, "Le Sujet en procès," *Tel Quel*, no. 52/53 (1972/1973): 12–30, 2–38. The essay also appeared in *Polylogue*, 51–106. It was translated as "The Subject in Signifying Practice," *Semiotext(e)* 1, no. 3 (1975): 19–26.

223 Among Kristeva's texts translated by Roudiez for Columbia University Press are *Powers of Horror* (1982), *Tales of Love* (1987), *Black Sun* (1989), *Strangers to Ourselves* (1991), and *Nations Without Nationalism* (1993).

224 See Kristeva, *Je me voyage*, 230–43, for an account of her several stays in the United States and of the many friends she made there.

225 The journal *Semiotext(e)* was founded by Sylvère Lotringer in 1974 and brought together French, German, Italian, and American thinkers, writers, and artists in new and provocative ways. The journal and its spin-offs provided the primary gateway for radical European thought to enter the American university for more than a quarter of a century.

226 I could never have imagined in 1975 that all three would become close friends of mine.

227 Julia Kristeva, "Le Théâtre moderne n'a pas lieu," *34/44: Cahiers de recherche de STD*, Université Paris 7, no. 3 (1977–78): 13–16. The essay was translated by Thomas Gora and Alice Jardine, "Modern Theater Does Not Take (a) Place," *SubStance* 6/7, nos. 18/19 (1977), 131–4. We also went to see films and dance performances. One evening Kristeva begged me to take her to the precursor of the Mudd Club. I remember her asking me, but I do not remember if we went.

228 For this discussion of Telquelian politics in the 1970s, I am deeply indebted to Marx-Scouras's *The Cultural Politics of Tel Quel*.

229 Louis Althusser was a Marxist philosopher and professor at the École normale supérieure in Paris best known for (besides the murder of his wife) his concept of the "ideological state apparatus." I recommend his classic essay "Ideology and Ideological State Apparatuses (Notes Towards an Investigation)," in *Lenin and Philosophy and Other Essays* (New York: Monthly Review Press, 1971), 85–126.

230 Marx-Scouras, *The Cultural Politics of Tel Quel*, 180.

231 Marcelin Pleynet, *Transculture* (Paris: Union Générale d'Éditions, 1979), 232. Quoted by Marx-Scouras, *The Cultural Politics of Tel Quel*, 185–6.

232 Julia Kristeva, "Pourquoi les États-Unis?" *Tel Quel*, nos. 71–3 (1977): 3–20. The article was first translated as "The US Now: A Conversation," *October* 6 (1978): 3–11. It was reprinted as "Why the United States?" in *The Kristeva Reader*, 272–91. The important feminist philosopher Toril Moi, who edited the reader, pointed out in her introduction to the article that many criticized *Tel Quel* and Kristeva for positioning China and the United States as "voids" to be filled with high French theory in the 1970s.

233 Julia Kristeva, "D'Ithaca à New York," *Promesse*, nos. 36–7 (1974): 123–40. The essay was collected in *Polylogue*, 495–515.

234 Julia Kristeva, "Un Nouveau type d'intellectuel: le dissident," *Tel Quel*, no. 74 (Winter 1977): 3–8. As Marx-Scouras mentions, the article was based on her May 1977 lecture at the Pompidou Center. It was translated as "A New Type of Intellectual: The Dissident" in Moi's *The Kristeva Reader*, 292–300.

235 Ibid., 294.

236 Ibid., 297.

237 Ibid., 299–300.

238 Julia Kristeva, "Postmodernism?" translated from the French by Thomas Gora and Alice Jardine, *Bucknell Review* 25, no. 11 (1980): 136–41. This essay was never published in French.

239 Jean-François Lyotard, *La Condition postmoderne: Rapport sur le savoir* (Paris: Minuit, 1979).

240 Samuel Beckett, *First Love and Other Shorts* (New York: Grove Press, 1974).

241 Julia Kristeva, "Le Père, l'amour, l'exile," in *Polylogue*, 137–47. The essay was first published in a special issue of *Cahiers de l'Herne* on Beckett in 1976. It was one of the essays in *Polylogue* to be included in *Desire in Language*. Of the twenty articles collected in *Polylogue*, I have discussed all but seven, and these seven tend to be either very early (1971–73), heavily indebted to linguistics, or never published in English. The only article translated into English that I have not discussed here is "How Does One Speak to Literature?" (in *Desire in Language*, 92–123) in part because many of the ideas central to that piece have already been discussed in other contexts.

242 In 1978, Kristeva, Sollers, Pleynet, other Telquelians, and writers from both the political left and right, publicly joined CIEL: the Committee

of Intellectuals for a Europe of Liberties. CIEL saw as its purpose the celebration of culture over politics. It saw culture as the most important realm for intellectual work done in the spirit of resistance against totalitarianism of all kinds.

243 Julia Kristeva, "Noms de lieu," *Tel Quel*, no. 68 (1976): 40–57. The essay was also published in *Polylogue*, 467–91. It was published as "Place Names" in *October* 6 (1978): 93–111. "Place Names" was also included in *Desire in Language*, 271–94.

244 The article was first published as "Hérétique de l'amour" in *Tel Quel*, no. 74 (1977): 30–49. It was reprinted as "Stabat Mater" in *Histoires d'amour* (Paris: Denoël, 1983), 225–47. An edited translation was published in *Poetics Today* 6, nos. 1–2 (1985): 133–52. A later translation appeared in Moi's *The Kristeva Reader*, 160–86. The article is also a chapter in Kristeva, *Tales of Love*, trans. Leon S. Roudiez (New York: Columbia University Press, 1987), 234–64.

245 Julia Kristeva, "Il n'y a pas de maître à langage," *Nouvelle Revue de la Psychanalyse* 20 (1979): 119–40, 140.

246 Julia Kristeva, "Le Temps des femmes," *34/44: Cahiers de recherche de STD*, no. 5 (1979): 5–19. I co-translated the essay with Harry Blake in *Signs* 7, no. 1 (1981): 13–35. It is also included in Moi's *The Kristeva Reader*.

247 See Julia Kristeva, "Women's Time," in *The Kristeva Reader*, 211.

248 Julia Kristeva, *Folle vérité: Vérité et vraisemblance du texte psychotique* (Paris: Seuil, 1979).

Part III: Becoming Julia Kristeva (1980–Today)

1 Julia Kristeva, "La vie psychique en temps de détresse," remarks at the ninetieth anniversary of the Psychoanalytic Society of Paris, November 19, 2016.

2 Ibid.

3 Françoise Coblence and Marcela Montes de Oca, "Une vie psychique est une vie dans le temps: Entretien avec Julia Kristeva," interview, *Revue Française de Psychanalyse* 81, no. 2 (2017): 351–67.

4 The word *perlaboration* is a neologism created in 1967 by Jean
 Laplanche and Jean-Bertrand Pontalis to translate the German term
 Durcharbeitung which signifies "to elaborate or work through with care."
 It is at the foundation of analytic treatment, targeting the suppression of
 neurotic symptoms.

5 See Part II.

6 Julia Kristeva, *Sens et non-sens de la révolte* (Paris: Fayard, 1996),
 especially 283–325. Translated as *The Sense and Non-Sense of Revolt*,
 trans. Jeanine Herman (New York: Columbia University Press, 2000).
 Also see Julia Kristeva, "La voix de Barthes," *Communications* 36 (1982):
 119–23.

7 Julia Kristeva, *The Samurai,* trans. Barbara Bray (New York: Columbia
 University Press, 1992), 302–3.

8 For a concise history of the *Front National*, see Chapter 2 of Daniel
 Stockemer, *The Front National in France* (Cham: Switzerland, Springer
 International Publishing, 2017).

9 Philippe Sollers, "Le GSI (Organe central de la Gestion des Surfaces
 Imprimées)," *Tel Quel*, no. 86 (1980): 10–17. I remember vividly the first
 time I heard Sollers predict the end of paper books and the ubiquitous
 presence of something called "the internet" in our lives. I thought it was
 crazy. It was around 1977.

10 Julia Kristeva, *Je me voyage: Mémoires*, interview with Samuel Dock
 (Paris: Fayard, 2016), 200.

11 Julia Kristeva, *Pouvoirs de l'horreur* (Paris: Seuil, 1980). Translated as
 Powers of Horror: An Essay on Abjection, trans. Leon S. Roudiez (New
 York: Columbia University Press, 1982).

12 Julia Kristeva, "Fetishizing the Abject," interview with Sylvère Lotringer,
 trans. Jeanine Herman, in *More & Less*, ed. Sylvère Lotringer (Pasadena,
 CA: McNaughton & Gunn, 1999), 15–35, 18.

13 Kristeva, *Je me voyage*, 186.

14 Coblence and Montes de Oca, "Une vie psychique est une vie dans le
 temps," 365. Kristeva's parents visited Paris three times between 1965
 (her arrival in Paris) and 1989 (her father's death): 1969, 1976, and 1982.
 Her mother may have visited one more time, probably in 1984/85. This
 moment of discovery was no doubt during the 1976 visit of Kristeva's
 mother to Paris.

15 Kristeva, "Fetishizing the Abject," 22.

16 Julia Kristeva, "Psychoanalysis and the Polis," trans. Margaret Waller, *Critical Inquiry* 9, no. 1 (1982): 77–92.

17 Julia Kristeva, *Histoires d'amour* (Paris: Denoel, 1983). Translated as *Tales of Love,* trans. Leon S. Roudiez (New York: Columbia University Press, 1987).

18 Julia Kristeva, *Au commencement était l'amour: psychanalyse et foi* (Paris: Hachette, 1985). Translated as *In The Beginning Was Love,* trans. Arthur Goldhammer (New York: Columbia University Press, 1987).

19 Julia Kristeva, *Cet incroyable besoin de croire* (Paris: Bayard, 2007). Translated from Italian as *This Incredible Need to Believe,* trans. Beverley Bie Brahic (New York: Columbia University Press, 2009).

20 Julia Kristeva, *Soleil noir: Dépression et mélancolie* (Paris: Gallimard, 1987). Translated as *Black Sun: Depression and Melancholia,* trans. Leon S. Roudiez (New York: Columbia University Press, 1992).

21 Ibid., 24–5.

22 Julia Kristeva, *Étrangers à nous-mêmes* (Paris: Fayard, 1988). Translated as *Strangers to Ourselves,* trans. Leon S. Roudiez (New York: Columbia University Press, 1991).

23 Julia Kristeva, "En être ou pas," *Libération,* July 20, 2000. In this piece, Kristeva evokes her shock at the vulgar attacks against her Bulgarian origins.

24 Julia Kristeva, *Je me voyage,* 106. It is clear that in this 2016 book, she lets out some of her anger at the Bulgarian stereotypes in Binet's 2015 novel: "Between Bulgarian yogurt, the sodomite morals of the Bogomiles (ancestors of the Cathars, for the information of our readers), and the Bulgarian umbrellas of the secret police—toxic and phallic symbol if there ever was one—I had the right to be the object of any and all fantasies" (Ibid.)

25 Ibid., 117.

26 See on Kristeva's website her address given in Genoa on June 22, 2015 at the ceremony of the presentation of the Mondi Migranti Prize.

27 Kristeva, *Strangers to Ourselves,* 103.

28 Ibid., 170.

29 Kristeva, *Je me voyage,* 190.

30 Ibid., 108. See also Kristeva's very moving homage to Durand, "Le sacré du livre," on her website.

31 Kelly Oliver, "Review: Kristeva's Imaginary Father and the Crisis in the Paternal Function," *Diacritics* 21, no. 2/3 (1991): 43–63, 62.

32 Julia Kristeva, "Étrangeté, étrangèreté," in *Penser la rencontre de deux mondes* (Paris: PUF, 1993), 107–28, 121.

33 Julia Kristeva, "Georgia O'Keeffe: la forme inévitable." The essay was originally included in *Georgia O'Keeffe* (Paris: Adam Biro, 1989), 7–16. It was later collected in Kristeva's *La Haine et le pardon* (Paris: Fayard, 2005), 481–500. It was translated as "The Inevitable Form," in *Hatred and Forgiveness*, trans. Jeanine Herman (New York: Columbia University Press, 2010), 231–44.

34 Kristeva has told the story of her father's death many times. The first time was in an article entitled "Comme un polar métaphysique" available on her website.

35 Julia Kristeva, "Ma vie en dormant," in *Pulsions du temps* (Paris: Fayard, 2013), 133–7, 133. Written for the exposition "Promenades insomniaques" at the Gallery Passage de Retz in Paris, July 2008.

36 Julia Kristeva, "On Yury Lotman," *Publications of the Modern Language Association* 109, no. 3 (1994): 375–6.

37 The other major event capturing Kristeva's attention in 1989 was the Tiananmen Square protests in June. She commented extensively on post-1989 Chinese culture and politics in various interviews and radio and television broadcasts in the 2000s.

38 Julia Kristeva, "Comme un polar métaphysique." Zhivkov was the leader of communist Bulgaria until November 10, 1989.

39 Ibid. Kristeva's experience of her father's murder in September 1989—and of what she saw as the emerging mafia-society in Bulgaria—are at the heart of her novels in the 1990s.

40 I myself was attacked several times in the 1990s by such foot soldiers of neoliberalism. Two of these attacks stand out: one by Dinesh D'Souza when he was at the American Enterprise Institute, which forced me to engage in a year-long media battle with him, and the second, most notoriously, an attack in France via the conservative magazine, *Le Figaro*. For a detailed account of the latter event, see Susan R. Suleiman, "Big Bad Wolf: A Short Chapter in the Long Story of Franco-American Relations," *Sites* 4, no. 1 (2000): 145–51.

41 Kristeva became a signatory member of the Psychoanalytic Society of Paris and of the International Psychoanalytic Association in 1992 and a full member in 1997.

42 Given his overall medical situation, David remained in remarkably good health over the decade except for one trying bout with surgery in 1997.

43 There were a number of strong readings of Kristeva in the 1990s. See, for example, the work of Ross Guberman, John Lechte, and Kelly Oliver.

44 Alan Sokal and Jean Bricmont, *Impostures intellectuelles* (Paris: Odile Jacob, 1997). Translated as *Fashionable Nonsense: Postmodern Intellectuals' Abuse of Science* (New York: Picador, 1999).

45 Julia Kristeva, "Une désinformation," *Le Nouvel Observateur* 1716 (1997), 122.

46 See Part II.

47 Julia Kristeva, *Hatred and Forgiveness*, 301.

48 Benigno Trigo, ed., *Kristeva's Fiction* (Albany: SUNY Press, 2013).

49 Kristeva says, "The literary world takes revenge on Sollers through me. All of his enemies are my enemies . . . But [Sollers] tells me, 'We're being attacked so everything is fine'" (in Philippe Lançon, "La vie à deux: Julia Kristeva Philippe Sollers—Tête à tête," *Libération*, August 5, 1996).

50 Kristeva, *Hatred and Forgiveness*, 283.

51 *Les Samouraïs* (Paris: Fayard, 1990). Translated as *The Samurai*, trans. Barbara Bray (New York: Columbia University Press, 1992). I think that the meanest review of the novel I saw was by Wendy Steiner, "The Bulldozer of Desire," *The New York Times*, November 15, 1992.

52 Simone de Beauvoir, *Les Mandarins* (Paris: Gallimard, 1954). Kristeva has expressed her frustration with always being compared with Beauvoir, but it is a comparison difficult to resist.

53 See Kristeva's description of Ed Dalloway as a model of masculinity based in the desire for power and image in *Je me voyage*, 132–3.

54 Julia Kristeva, *Le Vieil homme et les loups* (Paris: Fayard, 1991). Translated as *The Old Man and the Wolves,* trans. Barbara Bray (New York: Columbia University Press, 1994).

55 A *capriccio* is a piece of music that is usually fast, intense, and fairly free in form. This just about describes the third section of this novel.

56 Julia Kristeva, *The Old Man and the Wolves*, 115.

57 Ibid., 45–6.

58 Ibid., 48.

59 See Michael Wood, "Time of the Assassin," *London Review of Books* 17, no. 2 (1995), 17–18.

60 Julia Kristeva, *Possessions* (Paris: Fayard, 1996). Translated as *Possessions,* trans. Barbara Bray (New York: Columbia University Press, 1998).

61 Irene Ivantcheva-Merjanska and Michèle E. Vialet, "Entretien avec Julia Kristeva: Penser en nomade et dans l'autre langue le monde, la vie psychique, et la littérature," *The Cincinnati Romance Review* 35 (2013): 158–89, 163.

62 Julia Kristeva, *Le Temps sensible: Proust et l'expérience littéraire* (Paris: Gallimard, 1994). Translated as *Time and Sense: Proust and the Experience of Literature*, trans. Ross Guberman (New York: Columbia University Press, 1996).

63 For example, as early as 1992, Kristeva presented a lot of the material for the book as lectures in English: the Eliot Lectures in Canterbury, England. In 2011, she gave a series of radio and television interviews on Proust. And in 2013, she gave a doctoral seminar at the University of Paris 7 as well as a series of interviews on France Culture with Proust as the primary focus.

64 See Miglena Nikolchina, *Matricide in Language* (New York: The Other Press, 2004).

65 For an account of this tension, see Mari Ruti, *The Ethics of Opting Out: Queer Theory's Defiant Subjects* (New York: Columbia University Press, 2017).

66 See Kristeva, *Time and Sense*, 85–6.

67 This has invited accusations of homophobia. The best refutation of this charge I know of is Sylvie Gambaudo, "Julia Kristeva, 'woman's primary homosexuality' and homophobia," *European Journal of Women's Studies* 20, no. 1 (2013): 8–20. I agree with Gambaudo's argument and I am also convinced that Kristeva is not personally homophobic.

68 Kristeva, *Time and Sense*, 310.

69 Ibid., 325.

70 Ibid., 173.

71 Ibid., 205.

72 Julia Kristeva, "L'avenir d'une défaite," interview by Arnaud Spire, *l'Humanité*, July 2, 2001.

73 Julia Kristeva, *Les Nouvelles maladies de l'âme* (Paris: Fayard, 1993). Translated as *New Maladies of the Soul*, trans. Ross Guberman (New York: Columbia University Press, 1995). This has been one of Kristeva's best received books in the English-speaking world.

74 Kristeva, *Je me voyage*, 190–1. Kristeva has recently included in her list of "new maladies" religious fundamentalism, nihilism, melancholic schizophrenia, and new kinds of maniacal extremes for "getting off" on death.

75 *Julia Kristeva: Interviews*, ed. Ross Guberman (New York: Columbia University Press, 1996), 86.

76 The essay on Sartre is especially important for understanding Kristeva's sense of "revolt."

77 Julia Kristeva, *La Révolte intime: Pouvoirs et limites de la psychanalyse II* (Paris: Fayard, 1997). Translated as *Intimate Revolt: The Powers and Limits of Psychoanalysis II*, trans. Jeanine Herman (New York: Columbia University Press, 2002).

78 Julia Kristeva, *L'Avenir d'une révolte* (Paris: Calmann-Lévy, 1998). This book is included in the English translation of *Intimate Revolt*.

79 Julia Kristeva, "New Forms of Revolt," *Journal of French and Francophone Philosophy* XXII, no. 2 (2014): 1–19, 2.

80 See, for example, Kristeva's contribution to the UNESCO publication *Taking Action for Human Rights in the Twenty-First Century* (New York: UNESCO Publishing, 1998).

81 Julia Kristeva, *Lettre ouverte à Harlem Désir* (Paris: Rivages, 1990). Translated as *Nations Without Nationalism*, trans. Leon S. Roudiez (New York: Columbia University Press, 1993).

82 Kristeva, *Lettre ouverte à Harlem désir*, 10.

83 Julia Kristeva, *Contre la dépression nationale*, interview by Philippe Petit (Paris: Éditions Textuels, 1998). Translated as *Revolt, She Said*, trans. Brian O'Keeffe (New York: Semiotext(e) Foreign Agents Series, 2002). There are several new interviews in the English edition.

84 Ibid., 70–1.

85 Ibid., 114.

86 Ibid., 129–30.

87 Julia Kristeva, *Visions capitales: Arts et rituels de la décapitation* (Paris: Éditions de la Réunion des musées nationaux, 1998). This was the

catalogue for the exhibition from April 27 to July 27, 1998 in the Hall
Napoléon of the Louvre. It was re-edited by Fayard/Éditions de La
Martinière in 2013. Translated as *The Severed Head: Capital Visions,*
trans. Jody Gladding (New York: Columbia University Press, 2011). In
this context, it is worth noting that prior to 2002, beheading had been
comfortably assigned by the West to humanity's barbaric past, even
though it continued to happen in some parts of the world. It was the
televised, horrific beheading of the journalist, Daniel Pearl, by Al-Qaeda
in Pakistan in 2002 that brought the terror of beheading into Western
living rooms. Since then, Kristeva has been asked many times by
journalists from all over the world to comment on the practice. She has
always refused and still does to this day. She has argued that she does
not want to contribute to a confusion between, on the one hand, pure
barbarity and, on the other, the complex history of the *representations* of
universal, foundational psychic violence

88 See, for example, Jennifer Nash's intellectual history of "intersectionality"
in the late twentieth century, *Black Feminism Reimagined: After
Intersectionality* (Durham, NC: Duke University Press, 2019).

89 For example, see the dialogue between Kristeva and the American
photographer, Ariane Lopez-Huici: "A Conversation Between Julia Kristeva
and Ariane Lopez-Huici," published on the occasion of Lopez-Huici's
exhibition *Solo Absolu* at the AC Project Room, New York, May 18-June 25,
1994, and collected in *Uncontrollable Beauty: Towards a New Aesthetics*, ed.
Bill Beckley and David Shapiro (New York: Allworth Press, 2001), 325–30.

90 Julia Kristeva and Catherine Clément, *Le Féminin et le sacré* (Paris: Stock,
1998). Translated as *The Feminine and the Sacred,* trans. Jane Marie Todd
(New York: Columbia University Press, 2001).

91 Julia Kristeva, "Préface" to *Le Féminin et le sacré* (Paris: Albin Michel,
2015), 13–20.

92 Ibid., 15.

93 Ibid., 16.

94 Ibid., 17.

95 Ibid., 19.

96 Julia Kristeva, *Le Génie féminin I: Hannah Arendt* (Paris: Fayard, 1999).
Translated as *Hannah Arendt,* trans. Ross Guberman (New York:
Columbia University Press, 2001).

97 See Kristeva, "Is There a Feminine Genius?," *Critical Inquiry* 30, no. 3 (2004): 493–504, 493.

98 Ibid., 493–4.

99 Ibid., 499.

100 Ibid., 498.

101 Ibid., 499.

102 Ibid., 501.

103 Ibid., 503.

104 "Julia Kristeva interviewed by Jonathan Rée," *Talking Liberty Series*, Wall to Wall Television: Films for the Humanities and Sciences, 1998.

105 Kristeva's emphasis on psychoanalytic theory in the 2000s put her out of step with the legacy of French poststructuralism in English, especially across the social sciences where Foucault's influence has remained dominant over Lacan's.

106 See Kristeva's interview with François Caillat, *Éloge de l'étrangeté* [*In Praise of Foreignness*] (INA Editions, 2005), DVD.

107 See Julia Kristeva, "L'Exclusion festive" and "Le Film était muet," in *Chroniques du temps sensible* (Paris: Éditions de l'Aube, 2003), 7–14. Kristeva was no doubt spurred in part to critique Baudrillard (although she does not name him) in her November 21, 2001 broadcast because of his article published on November 3, 2001 in the newspaper *Le Monde*: "L'Esprit du terrorisme." See also his book by the same title (Paris: Galilée, 2002). Baudrillard's "The Spirit of Terrorism" was published in English in *Telos* 2001, no. 121 (2001): 134–42.

108 By 2010, there seemed to be a numbing effect overtaking the citizen-consumers of mass media. Kristeva, predictably, did not seem to get at all numb.

109 On the concept of "financialized capitalism" and its relationship to neoliberalism, see Michel Feher, *Le Temps des investis: Essai sur la nouvelle question sociale* (Paris: La Découverte, 2017).

110 Kristeva, *Je me voyage*, 27.

111 Julia Kristeva, *Murder in Byzantium*, trans. C. Jon Delogu (New York: Columbia University Press, 2006), 183–5. Kristeva's mother's name, Kristina, retained its French transliteration (Christine) in the English translation of the novel. The French original was published as *Meurtre à Byzance* (Paris: Fayard, 2004).

112 Kristeva, *Je me voyage*, 280.

113 Ibid., 279.

114 Kristeva is very careful—respectfully distant—when she is asked in
     interviews to comment on Sollers, on his writing, or on aspects of his
     public or private life not related directly to her. For example, in 2002
     Sollers published a novel, *L'Étoile des amants* [*The Lovers' Star*], where a
     character named Maud accompanies the narrator to an island of great
     beauty and repose—one that closely resembles the Île de Ré. Kristeva has
     only recently and briefly admitted that of all the characters Sollers has
     invented who share qualities with her, it is Maud—with her "density of
     metal"—who comes closest to capturing her. See *Je me voyage*, 128–9.

115 This is the Institut de la Pensée Contemporaine.

116 The French title is Ligue du droit international des femmes.

117 In 2008–11, the prize worth 20,000–30,000 euros was awarded to the
     human rights activists, Taslima Nasreen and Ayaan Hirsi Ali (2008);
     the Campaign of One Million Signatures for the End of Discriminatory
     Laws Against Women in Iran (2009); the activist scholars in China, Ai
     Xiaoming and Guo Jianmei (2010); and the Russian novelist, Lyudmila
     Ulitskaya (2011). Since 2011, the recipients have been the Tunisian
     Association of Democratic Women (2012); the young Pakistani woman
     who received the Nobel Peace Prize in 2014, Malala Yousafzai (2013);
     the French feminist historian, Michelle Perrot (2014); the National
     Museum of Women in the Arts (2015); the Mayor of Lampedusa, Greece,
     Giusi Nicolini (2016); the Polish activist for reproductive freedom,
     Barbara Nowacka and her Collective, "Let's Save Women" (2017); the
     Turkish writer, Aslı Erdoğan (2018); and the Salvadoran abortion rights
     activist, Sara García Gross (2019). As part of her activities with the prize
     committee, in 2009 Kristeva went to China and spoke about Simone de
     Beauvoir's 1955 visit to China and Beauvoir's ensuing book on China, *La
     Longue marche* (Paris: Gallimard, 1957), translated as *The Long March*
     (New York: World Publishing Company, 1958). She also talked about her
     own controversial 1974 trip to China with her *Tel Quel* comrades and
     her ensuing *Des Chinoises* (Paris: Éditions des Femmes, 1974), translated
     as *About Chinese Women*, trans. Anita Barrows (London: Boyars, 1977).
     See Kristeva's "Beauvoir in China," translated by Susan Nicholls, posted
     on Kristeva's website in December 2009. See also Kristeva's 2014 article,

"An Acceleration of History," published in the Chinese communist newspaper, *Renmin Ribao*, on the occasion of the fiftieth anniversary of diplomatic relations between France and China.

118 Kristeva's acceptance speech can be found in French on her website. She is, of course, referring to Madame de Staël's famous essay "Literature Considered in Its Relation to Social Institutions," which was originally published in French in 1800, and which can be found in Morroe Berger, *Politics, Literature, and National Character* (New York: Routledge, 2000).

119 Ibid.

120 See Kristeva, *Je me voyage*, 248–9.

121 See Julia Kristeva, "Thinking About Liberty in Dark Times," posted on her website on December 2, 2004. A different but related piece, "Thinking in Dark Times," was delivered at the 2005 Modern Language Convention and published in *MLA Profession* in 2006. For the French version, see Julia Kristeva, *Prix Holberg* (Paris: Fayard, 2005). In English, see the most recent translation, "Thinking About Liberty in Dark Times," in *Hatred and Forgiveness*, 2–23. The theme of "thinking in dark times" is from Hannah Arendt, *Men in Dark Times* (New York: Harcourt, Brace, and World, 1968).

122 Alain Braconnier, "Entretien avec Julia Kristeva," *Le Carnet Psy* 6, no. 110 (2006): 40–7.

123 For example, in the public sphere Kristeva sometimes explored the Freudian "dead father" at the intersection of religion and psychoanalysis without denying her countertransferential relationship to the concept (her father's murder). Her important emphasis on the "dead father"—while controversial—was almost always filtered through her admiration of her mentor, the psychoanalyst André Green, who was at the end of his career in the early 2000s and passed away in 2012 at the age of eighty-four.

124 See Michel Onfray, *Le Crépuscule d'une idole: L'Affabulation freudienne* (Paris: Grasset, 2010).

125 Kristeva says this in one of my interviews with her. For more details on the relationship between the need to believe and the desire to know, see the discussion below of Kristeva's *Cet incroyable besoin de croire* (Paris: Bayard, 2007). Translated as *This Incredible Need to Believe*, trans. Beverley Bie Brahic (New York: Columbia University Press, 2009).

126 Kristeva, *Je me voyage*, 56–7.

127 For Kristeva's remarks on Karzai and Afghanistan, see her "L'Universel au singulier," *Cahiers Bernard Lazare*, no. 312 (2010). Available on Kristeva's website: http://www.kristeva.fr/l-universel-au-singulier.html. This essay was also collected in *Pulsions du temps*, 679–86.

128 Kristeva, *Pulsions de temps*, 681.

129 See, for example, "Julia Kristeva: The Berlin interview!," *Exberliner*, March 2, 2011.

130 Ibid.

131 See Julia Kristeva-Joyaux, "Le Message culturel de la France et la vocation interculturelle de la francophonie," *Conseil économique, social et environnemental*, no. 19 (2009).

132 Julia Kristeva, "Diversité dans la tempête," *Libération*, January 1, 2000.

133 Julia Kristeva, *Crisis of the European Subject*, trans. Susan Fairfield (New York: Other Press, 2000). The volume includes an excellent introduction by Samir Dayal, the editor of the cultural studies series in which the book appears.

134 Julia Kristeva, *Au risque de la pensée* (Paris: Éditions de l'Aube, 2001).

135 Julia Kristeva, *Micropolitique* (Paris: Éditions de l'Aube, 2001).

136 Julia Kristeva, *Chroniques du temps sensible* (Paris: Éditions de l'Aube, 2003

137 Kristeva, *Je me voyage*, 285.

138 Ibid., 164–5.

139 Tragically, his daughter, Laurence Chirac, committed suicide by throwing herself out of a window in 2016. The Corrèze "Welcome Centers" are well known if limited in scope.

140 Julia Kristeva, *Lettre au président de la République sur les citoyens en situation de handicap: À l'usage de ceux qui le sont et de ceux qui ne le sont pas* (Paris: Fayard, 2003). See also Kristeva's "Liberty, Equality, Fraternity, and . . . Vulnerability," *Women's Studies Quarterly* 38, nos. 1–2 (2010): 251–68. This essay was collected in *Hatred and Forgiveness*, 29–45. See also her "A Tragedy and a Dream: Disability Revisited," *Irish Theological Quarterly* 78, no. 3 (2013): 219–30.

141 Kristeva, "Liberty, Equality, Fraternity, and . . . Vulnerability," in *Hatred and Forgiveness*, 39.

142 Julia Kristeva and Charles Gardou, "Accompagner tous les plus vulnérables," *Le Monde*, September 3, 2003.

143 Julia Kristeva, "Liberty, Equality, Fraternity, and . . . Vulnerability," in *Hatred and Forgiveness*, 42–3.

144 Josyane Savigneau, "Julia Kristeva: L'humanisme ne sait pas accompagner la mortalité," *Le Monde*, April 29, 2011.

145 Julia Kristeva and Jean Vanier, *Leur regard perce nos ombres* (Paris: Fayard, 2011).

146 Kristeva, *Je me voyage*, 169.

147 Two of the best articles I know on the novel are by Miglena Nikolchina, "Byzantium, or Fiction as Inverted Theory" and Frances Restuccia, "Sebastian's Skull: Establishing the 'Society of the Icon,'" both collected in *Kristeva's Fiction*.

148 Ivantcheva-Merjanska and Vialet, "Entretien avec Julia Kristeva," 174–5.

149 "Julia Kristeva: Love Is a Philosophy," *Standard*, May 23, 2005.

150 Julia Kristeva, *Hatred and Forgiveness*, 293–7.

151 Although this text was referenced above, we provide the full reference again, given that some readers might be looking for it under the subheading that names the book: Julia Kristeva, *La Haine et le pardon* (Paris: Fayard, 2005). Translated as *Hatred and Forgiveness*, trans. Jeanine Herman (New York: Columbia University Press, 2010).

152 Julia Kristeva, "Secularism: 'Values' at the Limits of Life," in *Hatred and Forgiveness*, 24–8.

153 Julia Kristeva, "Desire for Law," in *Hatred and Forgiveness*, 170–6.

154 Ibid., 176.

155 Ibid.

156 Julia Kristeva, "For Shoshana Felman: Truth and Art," in *The Claims of Literature: A Shoshana Felman Reader*, ed. Emily Sun, Eyal Peretz, and Ulrich Baer (New York: Fordham University Press, 2007).

157 Ibid., 321.

158 Julia Kristeva, *Le Génie féminin II: Melanie Klein* (Paris: Fayard, 2000). Translated as *Melanie Klein*, trans. Ross Guberman (New York: Columbia University Press, 2001). *Le Génie féminin III: Colette* (Paris: Fayard, 2002). Translated as *Colette*, trans. Jane Marie Todd (New York: Columbia University Press, 2004). *Notre Colette*, ed. Julia Kristeva (Paris: Presses Universitaires de Rennes, 2004). *L'Amour de soi et ses avatars* (Paris: Éditions Pleins Feux, 2005).

159 Julia Kristeva, *Seule, une femme* (Paris: Éditions de l'Aube, 2007).

160 One article in *Seule, une femme*, "La Passion maternelle et son sens aujourd'hui," might be of special interest to readers. It is available in English on Kristeva's website as "Motherhood Today."

161 Kristeva, *Melanie Klein*, 16.

162 Ibid., 43, 12–13.

163 Ibid., 246–7.

164 Kristeva, *Colette*, 5–6.

165 Kristeva, *Notre Colette*, 15.

166 Kristeva, *Colette*, 141–2.

167 Ibid., 170.

168 Ibid., 242–3.

169 Ibid., 425.

170 Julia Kristeva, *Thérèse mon amour: Récit* (Paris: Fayard, 2008). Translated as *Teresa, My Love: An Imagined Life of the Saint of Ávila, A Novel*, trans. Lorna Scott Fox (New York: Columbia University Press, 2015). The English translation received Honorable Mention for the National Translation Prize in Fiction 2015.

171 This is another one of Kristeva's books that has had unforeseen influence in English.

172 For a meditation on the divorce between Western philosophy and theology, see Keren Mock, "The Need to Believe and the Archive: Interview with Julia Kristeva," *DIBUR Literary Journal*, no. 3 (2016): 1–10.

173 See, for example, Julia Kristeva, "N'ayons pas peur du besoin de croire," *Madame Figaro*, December 22, 2017.

174 The fact that sometimes in the 2000s the concerns of Kristeva and the Catholic Church overlapped did not help deflect the critique that Kristeva was "going soft" on Catholicism. For a fascinating collection about the future of dialogue between believers and non-believers, see *Reimagining the Sacred: Richard Kearney Debates God with James Wood, Catherine Keller, Charles Taylor, Julia Kristeva, Gianni Vattimo, et al.*, ed. Richard Kearney and Jens Zimmermann (New York: Columbia University Press, 2015).

175 See Kristeva, "The Need to Believe and the Archive," 3.

176 Kristeva, *Je me voyage*, 30–1.

177 Ibid., 217.

178 In the English edition of *This Incredible Need to Believe*, see Kristeva's interview, "From Jesus to Mozart: Christianity's Difference," 77–86 and her March 19, 2006 lecture "'Suffering': Lenten Lectures, March 19, 2006," 87–98.

179 In "Jerusalem," Kristeva laid out her theory of "the need to believe." The talk is available in English on Kristeva's website.

180 For more on the Montesquieu Project, see the Collège des Bernardins website for the 2013–2014 program, "La construction de l'humain," and for their 2018–2019 program, "Dialoguer pour prévenir la violence."

181 In private correspondence between Kristeva and Altizer during the summer 2012. It is also reported that D. G. Leahy, the well-known American philosophical theologian, taught Kristeva's work with great admiration in his courses at NYU.

182 Kristeva, *This Incredible Need to Believe*, viii. Kristeva focuses on the psychoanalytic and discursive analysis of the link between the adolescent psyche and violent extremism, but she is obviously not the only one who has made this link. Social scientists have been researching this connection for quite some time. See, for example, the discussion of "the causal link between young people and extremism" in Barend Louwrens Prinsloo, "The Etymology of 'Islamic Extremism': A Misunderstood Term?," *Cogent Social Sciences* 4, no. 1 (2018): DOI:10.1080/23311886.20 18.1463815. Almost everyone drawing the link between adolescence and various forms of violent extremism in the current historical climate is at some point accused of Islamophobia. Kristeva is no exception. The best refutation of this accusation can be found in her own writing about the profound social, political, and psychic roots of all forms of extremism, of whatever variety. I am also convinced that Kristeva is not personally Islamophobic.

183 Kristeva, *This Incredible Need to Believe*, 16.

184 See Julia Kristeva, "La vie psychique en temps de détresse," on Kristeva's website.

185 Kristeva, *This Incredible Need to Believe*, 21–2.

186 Ibid., 25–9.

187 Ibid., 22.

188 Ibid., 29.

189 Coblence and Montes de Oca, "Une vie psychique est une vie dans le temps," 351–67.

190 I owe this observation to Emma Zitzow-Childs, "A Labor of Love: Visions of Humanism in Julia Kristeva's *Thérèse, mon amour.*" Unpublished paper.

191 Kristeva, *Je me voyage*, 295.

192 See Carol Mastrangelo Bové, "Kristeva's *Thérèse*: Mysticism and Modernism," *Journal of French and Francophone Philosophy* XXI, no. 1 (2013): 105–15, 106.

193 Kristeva, *Teresa, My Love*, 274.

194 See Kristeva, "The Modernity of a Mystic," *L'Osservatore Romano*, March 2, 2015.

195 See Bové, "Kristeva's *Thérèse*," 107.

196 From Kristeva's short introductory remarks before her performance with Isabella Huppert, "Tandis qu'elle agonise: Thérèse mon amour," recorded at the Odéon-Théâtre de l'Europe on March 17, 2014 and broadcast on France Culture on March 23, 2014.

197 See Julia Kristeva, "Le Livre de la vie," *Le Monde des Religions* (2015): 78–9.

198 Kristeva, *Je me voyage*, 293.

199 Bové, "Kristeva's *Thérèse*," 106.

200 Carlene Bauer, "Imagining a Saintly Life, Some of It Not So Holy," *The New York Times*, December 14, 2014.

201 Maria Margaroni, "Julia Kristeva's Voyage in the Theresian Continent: The Malady of Love and the Enigma of an Incarnated, Shareable, Smiling Imaginary," *Journal of French and Francophone Philosophy* XXI, no. 1 (2013): 83–104, 86.

202 The beginning of this extraordinary event set in the ruins of the Roman Forum can be seen in Alain Monclin's *Julia Kristeva—Une étrangère, citoyenne du monde* (University of Paris-Diderot, 2012). I am very grateful to be able to use this screenshot from the beginning of his film.

203 For the collected papers of the Paris panel in French—including Kristeva's "Oser l'humanisme"—see Julia Kristeva, Jean-Luc Marion, Jean Clair, and Axel Kahn, *Lumières, religions et raison commune* (Paris: Bayard, 2012).

204 A reworking of several ideas at the heart of "Oser l'humanisme," this essay—"Ten Principles for Twenty-First-Century Humanism"— presented at the University of Rome on October 26, 2011, is included in Kristeva's *Pulsions du temps*, 561–7. The shorter version that Kristeva presented with the Pope and other dignitaries the next day, October 27,

2011, is also included there on pages 732–3 and can be found in English on Kristeva's website. I have slightly adapted that English translation here for purposes of clarity.

205 The names and affiliations of most of the other dignitaries can be found on page 732 of *Pulsions du temps*.

206 You can watch the entire event on Kristeva's website: http://www.kristeva. fr/assise2011.html or on *YouTube*.

207 Kristeva, *Je me voyage*, 212.

208 Ibid., 252–3.

209 For example, there are new organizations like the Illiade Institute, where French right-wing intellectuals work to "rewrite" European history. See, for instance, "At the Illiade Institute," The Southern Poverty Law Center website, April 17, 2018.

210 Cécile Daumas, "Julia Kristeva: Des catholiques ont repris le flambeau de Voltaire," *Libération*, May 3, 2015.

211 Julia Kristeva, "Renewing the Education Pact," presentation at the Paris Event Center, November 20, 2016.

212 See, for example, Kristeva's presentation, "The Need to Believe and the Desire to Know," delivered at a conference entitled "The Force of Monotheism—Psychoanalysis and Religions," organized by the Sigmund Freud Foundation, Vienna, October 2009. Available on *YouTube*.

213 Julia Kristeva, "Droits de l'Homme et protection de la diversité culturelle," presentation at UNESCO, Geneva, March 31, 2015. Available on *YouTube*.

214 See, for example, Kristeva's 1997 paper, "L'Europe divisée: politique, éthique, religion," presented at the 36th International Meetings in Geneva, where the theme was "Them and Us: Europe Faced with Its New Unravelings." Available on Sollers's website. Some have argued, and I tend to agree, that Kristeva's sustained support of the European Union may be in part behind the vicious 2018 attacks on her credibility and reputation emanating from behind the former Iron Curtain.

215 Julia Kristeva, "Existe-t-il une culture européene?," in *Pulsions du temps*, 635–58. This chapter is a compilation of two lectures: one delivered in 2007 at the Université européene d'été in 2007 and the other delivered in Oslo in 2009.

216 See Kristeva, *Je me voyage*, 251–2.

217 See my discussion in Part II of Kristeva's foundational relationship with her mentor Lucien Goldmann.

218 For instance, Julia Kristeva, "Dis-moi qui tu cites, je dirai qui tu es," *Radio RCJ*, April 22, 2012; "Le Mot de la semaine," *Radio RCJ*, January–October 2015.

219 Julia Kristeva, "The Impenetrable Power of the Phallic Matron." The French version was published in *Libération*, September 25, 2008 and the English version is available on her website.

220 On the question of the abolition of the death penalty, see, on Kristeva's website, "De l'inviolabilité de la vie humaine," her October 10, 2012, address given in Paris as part of the worldwide mobilization against state-sponsored murder. On the question of the #metoo movement (amusingly referred to in French as #balancetonporc: rat-out-your-pig), see the interview with Kristeva, "La parole libre est encore à venir," *Cahiers Bernard Lazare*, December 29, 2017. Kristeva also waded carefully in the 2010s into the debates about marriage equality in France, supporting it but also cautioning against the unforeseen consequences of the rapid dismantlement of centuries-old models of kinship. Thinking together the multiplication of sexualities, new hybrid forms of family, and technological innovations in the field of reproduction, she called for a Harlequin Quilt of possibility.

221 On Kristeva's support for rethinking the medical humanities, for bringing the concept of *cura* (care) to their heart, see Julia Kristeva et al., "Cultural Crossings of Care: An Appeal to the Medical Humanities," *Medical Humanities* 44, no. 1 (2018): 55–8. On Kristeva's support of psychoanalysts persecuted by totalitarian states, see, for example, Kristeva's defense of the Syrian psychoanalyst, Rafah Nached. Her October 2011 presentation at the Palais des Congrès, Paris, France, "Rafah Nached," can be found on her website. It is collected as "Peut-on être Musulmane et psy?," in *Pulsions du temps*, 697–706.

222 Gohar Homayounpour, *Doing Psychoanalysis in Tehran* (Cambridge: MIT Press, 2012).

223 Julia Kristeva, "Praise for *Doing Psychoanalysis in Tehran*," posted on the MIT Press website on April 18, 2019: https://mitpress.mit.edu/books/doing-psychoanalysis-tehran.

224 Kristeva, "Peut-on être Musulmane et psy?" 701.

225 See, for example, Julia Kristeva, "Louise Bourgeois, *runaway girl*," in *Pulsions du temps*, 71–83 and "La Voie lactée de Jackson Pollock," in *Pulsions du temps*, 55–69. See also her essay on the Algerian-born French artist, Adel Abdessemed, "Le Corps d'Adel," published in both French and English on her website. See also her 2015 conversation in English with the Indian-born British sculptor, Anish Kapoor, "Blood and Light: In Conversation with Julia Kristeva," on Kapoor's website.

226 Jonathan Littell, *Les Bienveillantes* (Paris: Gallimard, 2006). Translated as *The Kindly Ones*, trans. Charlotte Mandell (New York: Harper Collins, 2009).

227 Kristeva's remarks on Littell's *Les Bienveillantes* can be found in her April 24, 2007, talk on the novel at the École normale supérieure on *YouTube*.

228 Julia Kristeva, "Interpreting Radical Evil," a lecture at the 2016 meeting of the Kristeva Circle in Stockholm, available in both French and English on her website (I have changed the English translation slightly here). Also see Kristeva, "Comment peut-on être djihadiste?" *slate.fr*, December 2, 2015.

229 Gianluigi Ricuperati, *100 Global Minds: The Most Daring Cross-Disciplinary Thinkers in the World* (Dublin: Roads Publishing, 2015).

230 "The Kristeva Circle" is going strong, with meetings scheduled around the world.

231 In February 2009, Kristeva gave a talk entitled "Une Européene en Chine" at the Centre Culturel Français de Peking in Beijing and at the University of Tong Ji in Shanghai. It is collected in *Pulsions du temps*, 659–67, along with several other important essays on Chinese culture. In June 2012, she sent a video, "My Encounters with Chinese Women," directed by G. K. Galabov and Sophie Zhang, to a conference on "Feminism and China" at Nanjing University (available in French and English on Kristeva's website). In November 2012, she returned to China to do a series of lectures on subjectivity, psychoanalysis, intertextuality, Proust, and women and genius, at Fudan University in Shanghai. In these talks, she begins to acknowledge that she has never written about "race," mostly because she agrees with geneticists that it does not exist, even though she acknowledges that racism does exist and must be dealt with centrally and directly. The banal forms of racism regarding Chinese culture that Kristeva has encountered in Europe have in part motivated

her to go further in her interventions both on and in China in order to try to dispel that particular form of cultural, social, and political paranoia.

232 For Kristeva's description of that overwhelming moment in Buenos Aires, see her *Je me voyage*, 244–5.

233 A video of her entrance into the cavernous amphitheater in Sofia and her subsequent talk, "New Forms of Revolt," is available on her website.

234 Kristeva suffered a great deal at the loss of her dear friend, the semiotician and novelist Umberto Eco, who died on February 19, 2016. Her interview in homage to him on France Culture on February 21, 2016, is available on her website.

235 Julia Kristeva, *L'Horloge enchantée* (Paris: Fayard, 2015). Translated as *The Enchanted Clock*, trans. Armine Kotin Mortimer (New York: Columbia University Press, 2017), 207.

236 Sollers's most recent novel to date is *Le Nouveau* (Paris: Gallimard, 2019). His most recent collection of essays, besides his letters with Dominique Rolin, is *Une conversation infinie: Sollers, Savigneau* (Paris: Bayard, 2019).

237 Philippe Sollers, *Lettres à Dominique Rolin 1958–1980* (Paris: Gallimard, 2017) and Dominique Rolin, *Lettres à Philippe Sollers 1958–1980* (Paris: Gallimard, 2018). On the question of "fidelity," see Kristeva and Sollers's *Du mariage considéré comme un des beaux-arts* (Paris: Fayard, 2015). Translated as *Marriage as a Fine Art*, trans. Lorna Scott Fox (New York: Columbia University Press, 2016).

238 Quoted from Beauvoir's memoir, *Tout compte fait* (Paris: Gallimard, 1972), in Julia Kristeva, *Beauvoir présente* (Paris: Fayard, 2016), 81.

239 Ibid. Kristeva refers to Beauvoir as an "anthropological revolution," 7.

240 See Jean Birnbaum, "Prière d'insérer. Beauvoir, les déchirements de la liberté," *Le Monde des Livres*, February 5, 2016.

241 Samuel Dock, "Julia Kristeva, un Espoir pour la pensée, une promesse de liberté," *Le Huffington Post*, January 27, 2014.

242 It is fascinating to think about the reverberations between Passemant's clock and the 500-foot clock that Jeff Bezos and amazon.com have recently built inside a mountain in West Texas. Bezos's 10,000-year clock is powered by the earth's thermal cycles (see 10000yearclock.net). In a related vein, "Researchers from the Moscow Institute of Physics and Technology have seemingly just done the impossible, turning back time

with the help of a quantum computer. The so-called 'time machine' has successfully moved small particles a fraction of a second into the past, in a development that appears to go against our understanding of the basic laws of physics" (*Cosmopolitan*, March 13, 2019).

243 Kristeva, *The Enchanted Clock*, 14.

244 Julia Kristeva, "Vivre c'est s'exiler et c'est d'abord s'exiler de la mélancolie," *France Inter*, November 25, 2018.

245 Julia Kristeva, "Tenir tête à la pensée unique," on the occasion of the fiftieth anniversary of the Garnier Flammarion Publishing House in Paris (available on Kristeva's website).

246 Julia Kristeva, "It's Just Not My Life—Julia Kristeva Responds," blog of the *Los Angeles Review of Books*, November 1, 2018. Translated by Patsy Baudoin, this article first appeared in French in *Vanity Fair France*, July 2018.

247 Entitled "Face aux méthodes totalitaires" ("Faced with Totalitarian Methods"), Kristeva's first of many denials can be found on her website.

248 Jennifer Schuessler and Boryana Dzhambazova, "Bulgaria Says French Thinker Was a Secret Agent. She Calls It a 'Barefaced Lie,'" *The New York Times*, April 1, 2018.

249 Tzvetan Stoyanov, *Le Génie et son maître* (Paris: L'Esprit des peninsules, 2000).

250 I am deeply grateful to the scholars and artists in Bulgaria who have helped me understand this saga, especially Professor Miglena Nikolchina, Department for Theory and History of Literature, Sofia University.

251 See Jean-Baptiste Naudet, "Julia Kristeva avait été recrutée par les services secrets communistes bulgares," *Le Nouvel Observateur*, under the *BibliObs* section, March 28, 2018, at 7:04 p.m.

252 See Jean-Baptiste Naudet, "'Quelqu'un veut me nuire': Julia Kristeva dément avoir fait partie des services secrets bulgares," *Le Nouvel Observateur*, under the *BiblioObs* section, March 28, 2018, at 9:13 p.m.

253 Julia Kristeva, "Droit à répondre à 'L'Obs,'" ("Right to Respond to the *Nouvel Observateur*"), April 11, 2018. See Kristeva's website.

254 It is truly disturbing to see all of Kristeva and her parents' letters and postcards spread out, numbered, and indexed in the dossier. I chose this image to reproduce here in part because I do not want to replicate the invasion of Kristeva's privacy by reproducing one of her personal letters.

255 An English reproduction of the document can be found in Appendix 1.

256 See Tzvetan Todorov, "An introduction to verisimilitude," in *The Poetics of Prose* (Ithaca: Cornell University Press, 1977), 89–107.

257 For example, see what can only be described as a diatribe by the conservative commentator for the *National Review*, Kevin D. Williamson, "Agent Kristeva: The Covert and Overt Sins of a Celebrated Scholar," *Commentary*, April 16, 2018; or the still-angry-at-French-poststructuralism diatribe by the academic Richard Wolin: "Was a Renowned Literary Theorist Also a Spy?," *The Chronicle of Higher Education*, June 20, 2018; or the carefully constructed exercise in verisimilitude by the usually intelligent and compelling freelance journalist Dimiter Kenarov, "Was the Philosopher Julia Kristeva a Cold War Collaborator?," *The New Yorker*, September 5, 2018; or the somehow-with-an-ax-to-grind speculation by the also usually intelligent and compelling political philosopher Albena Azmanova, "Agent Sabina: On the Abjection of Julia Kristeva," *Eurozine*, April 20, 2018. I found the article by Azmanova the least predictable and therefore the most disturbing. A Bulgarian-born European intellectual much like Kristeva, Azmanova has an admirable academic career at the University of Kent. The choice to use Kristeva's own theory of abjection, a theoretical tool for understanding fascism, against Kristeva so lightly is mysterious.

258 Julia Kristeva, "La Bulgarie, l'Europe post-totalitaire et moi", *Marianne*, September 7, 2018. Republished in English as "Bulgaria, Post-Totalitarian Europe, and Me," *The Philosophical Salon*, November 26, 2018. Available in English on Kristeva's website.

259 Kristeva, "It's Just Not My Life—Julia Kristeva Responds."

260 See Sonia Combe, "Affaire Kristeva: Lire entre les lignes des archives policières," *Le Monde*, April 5, 2018 (translated by Patsy Baudoin and available in English on Kristeva's website); Maria Dimitrova, "A Jar, A Blouse, A Letter," blog of the *London Review of Books*, April 3, 2018; and Sarah Pines, "Ich, Spionin? Jetzt spricht Julia Kristeva," *Welt*, April 4, 2018. Republished on Kristeva's website as "Me, A Spy? Julia Kristeva Speaks," trans. Ida Hattemer-Higgins.

261 Koprinka Tchervenkova, "Post-scriptum du 'cas Kristeva,'" *Kultura*, no. 13, April 6, 2018. Republished on Kristeva's website as "P.S. to the case of Julia Kristeva".

262 Nina Ivanova, "About the Abomination of the Committee for State Security's Fiction," *Kultura*, April 13, 2018. Other articles of interest include, Tomasz Kitlinski, "Today's Fascists Accuse Julia Kristeva," Transregional Center for Democratic Studies, *The New School Blog*, December 20, 2018; Louise Hermant, "L'incroyable histoire de Julia Kristeva, accusée d'avoir été un 'agent secret' de la Bulgarie," *Les Inrockuptibles*, April 4, 2018; Pascal Ceaux, "Julia Kristeva et le fantôme de 'Sabina,'" *Le Journal du Dimanche*, April 22, 2018; Stuart Schneiderman, "Julia Kristeva Responds to Slander" on his blog; Philippe Sollers, "Affaire Kristeva: Phillipe Sollers contre-attaque," *La Règle du jeu*, April 9, 2018; Samuel Dock, "Affaire Kristeva: L'horreur du vide," *Le Huffington Post*, April 11, 2018; Sara Beardsworth, "Reflections on the Kristeva Affair," *The Philosophical Salon*, September 24, 2018.

263 I would, however, recommend to my reader a 2019 video series by *The New York Times*, "Operation Infektion: Russian Disinformation from Cold War to Kanye," which offers insight into the existence of the Sabina Dossier (*The New York Times* website, November 13, 2018). Consider also the Soviet AIDS conspiracy disinformation campaign in the 1980s, which claimed that the HIV virus was produced by American biological weapons experiments. For a fascinating analysis that uses Kristevian theory to scrutinize the Trumpian era in terms of delusional phantasy, see Noëlle McAfee, "Trump and the Paranoid-Schizoid Politics of Ideality," *Contemporary French and Francophone Studies* 21, no. 5 (2017): 556–63. Also published on Kristeva's website.

264 Personal correspondence from a British friend, James Mason, who has studied aspects of Soviet-era intelligence networks.

265 Andrew Higgins, "4,141 Latvians Were Just Outed as K.G.B. Informants," *The New York Times*, January 18, 2019.

266 Diana Bancheva, "Bulgarian Journalists Search the Files of the Former State Security Services: The Murder of Georgi Markov, the Assassination Attempt on the Pope, and the Communist Regime's Repression," *Unredacted: The National Security Archive Blog*, July 14, 2010.

267 Blurb for Katherine Verdery, *My Life as a Spy: Investigations in a Secret Police File* (Durham, NC: Duke University Press, 2018).

268 Miglena Nikolchina, unpublished manuscript. In a series of readings of the Sabina Dossier, Nikolchina found some comical notes by the police

that led her to write: "And finally, Umberto Eco seems also to have been an informer for the Bulgarian State Security Services: It is too long to translate, totally funny. Eco's ultra-leftist ideas, critical of the Soviet bloc ideas of the left, are presented as a conversation with the author of this info, whoever he was, and the conclusion is that those ideas explain the closeness between Eco and Kristeva."

269 Vladislav Todorov, *Red Square/Black Square: Organon for Revolutionary Imagination* (Albany: SUNY Press, 1995).

270 See Martin Tharp, a doctoral candidate at Charles University, Prague. His comment can be found on the *London Review of Books* website in response to Maria Dimitrova, "A Jar, A Blouse, A Letter."

271 Julia Kristeva, "À quoi bon les poètes en temps de détresse?," lecture at the Théâtre National de la Colline, November 7, 2016. Available on Kristeva's website.

Index

But what does it mean to "be transformed by the renewing of our minds?" Our lives can be changed and wholly transformed by understanding and using the power of thought consciously and intentionally. God has given us the ability to think big or small. And what we dwell on in thought, with feeling, shapes our experience. So when we think our thoughts, we are making a personal investment in what will show up as our experience.

So the plan is this: Invest your thoughts moment by moment, day after day in the life you desire to live. Your ongoing thoughts are the prayers that lead to the life you will get to face. So when you "pray up your life" you are using your thoughts and prayers to invest in the quality of life you want for yourself. The life you'll face in the future is being created today by the conscious thoughts and prayers you hold in your mind. Consciously choose thoughts that will bring returns of happiness and great joy.

Make a commitment today to never again conform to the outer limitations lurking in the day-to-day activities we mistakenly call our lives. When you use the power of your thinking with intention and purpose toward living the best life God created you to live, the will of God, which is good, acceptable, and perfect will surely be your experience.

You can literally pray up the life you desire, pray the life you desire into being, by conscious and intentional use of your thoughts, words and actions. When we think intentionally, we are setting in motion the law of cause and effect which will return results to us as we have initiated. So we make our thoughts loving, our words sweet, and our actions kind. This transformation we seek in the outer first begins with the decision to not conform our way of thinking with the mass human thinking all around us. We practice and train ourselves to use God's gift of thought to override the human tendency toward negative, self-defeating, anxious, worry-thoughts. We reach for Godly thoughts at every turn, in all situations and in every circumstance.

The more we focus our thoughts and words on that which is positive, uplifting, life-affirming, healthy, and prospering, then we have created our lives as a living prayer. We can say with the apostle Paul "Rejoice always, pray without ceasing" (1 Thessalonians 5:16-17).

Prayer Practice

Read the prayer anchor for this chapter daily for 21 days. Become sensitive to the thoughts, words, and actions you take in your normal day-to-day activities. Notice where you are "conforming" to the thinking along with the crowd rather than listening and following your own inner guidance. Reading the scripture will simply help you to stay conscious of your mental choices and decisions.

For each of the 21 days, pray and meditate on any of these affirmative prayers or construct your own. This is the work that will help to transform your mind and your way of thinking.

- *"Through the power of the Holy Spirit in me, I transform my every thought to conform to the will of God for my life."*
- *"I use my God-given power of thought to think of life, love, wisdom, peace, joy, health, and prosperity."*
- *"Divine love, active in me, fills my mind, moment by moment, day by day, with thoughts of peace, harmony, health and prosperity."*
- *"Through the grace of God, active in my mind, my every thought is toward <u>peace.</u>"* (Say this prayer 7 times each time inserting a new truth such as: joy, health, wholeness, love, life, divine order).

Make a commitment to yourself to use every waking moment to think on words that are positive, uplifting and life-affirming. In this way you *Pray Up Your Life*!

Sometimes we must join the light that we are, with the lights of our fellow travelers on life's journey. Together we create a brilliant glow that reaches into the depths of the invisible place called unlimited possibilities.

50
Let Your Light Shine

Prayer Anchor: _"Then God exclaimed: "Let there be light" and there was light. And God saw that the light was good" (Genesis: 1:3)._

According to the allegorical account of the creation in the first Chapter of Genesis, on the very first day God created light. God spoke it into being and there it was. We can understand why light would come first, because according to the story, there was chaos and darkness. So the light was made to dispel the chaos and shed awareness into the mystery called darkness.

As I write these words, I am watching a most gorgeous sunset from an airplane headed home to Miami. As the sun sets, it disappears from my eyesight, but not my insight. The light radiating from it shows colors of orange, yellow, a touch of red, and what seems to be peach. Its beauty is indescribable. And although the sun is not mentioned until the 4th day of creation, my sense is that the light created on the 1st day was like the beauty I now see glowing from this sunset before me. That 1st appearance of light on the first day of creation made its grand entrance with elegance and grace. It set the stage for all good things to follow.

Strangely enough whenever I watch a sunset or a sunrise I sense a connection with the largeness of life itself. I feel small compared to the sun and at the same time I feel larger than I've believed myself to be. It is difficult to witness a sunrise or sunset and feel alone and hopeless. God saw that the light was good, and when I see the carefully crafted beams of light stretching across the sky, I think, "Yes, God is right, the light is good."

In the Book of Matthew, it is reported that we are connected to the light and to each other with the powerful words, "You are the light of the world. A city built on a hill cannot be hid. No one after lighting a lamp puts it under the bushel basket, but on the lampstand, and it gives light to all in the house. In the same way, let your light shine before others, so that they may see your good works and give glory to your Father in heaven" (Matthew 5:14-16).

These words bring to my mind those rays of light that boldly shine forth from the sunrises and sunsets that God created for our delight. I remember an experience I had many years ago, and although it happened some time ago, the experience was so profound that I can remember it vividly. I was driving home from work one day and the sunset caught my eyes. It was so beautiful that I pulled off the road and parked so that I could watch the awesome sight in the sky. I sat there for probably 15-20 minutes. It was such a beautiful view, that it brought tears to my eyes. I had a sense that I was one with the gorgeous light show in the sky. I remember thinking 'Surely God who created such an awesome vision would want someone to notice it.' I could not help but think 'Surely God would find pleasure if we, God's children, would stop for a few moments from our busy schedules to take in the beauty of the sunrises and sunsets so elegantly displayed day after day.'

When I was able to compose myself and get back on the road, I went home deeply affected by the experience in a way I could not put into words. I wanted to tell someone, anyone, everyone but the thought of trying to describe the profound experience I had felt as though it would have been demeaning to the experience itself. There simply was no way to describe something that outstanding, and give it fair description. It was beyond words. There just was no way to describe it, or to define the Sunset I experienced that day – it was that awesome. I know now that any sunrise or sunset I allow myself to experience is just as outstanding.

To be the light of the world, we glow, we shine, we are bold with an artistic flare radiating many colors, but from the one source. The light shines in us, through us, and around us; it lifts and inspires all who witness the light that we are.

The light is not ours to harbor or keep from others, from the world. In fact that light that we are must be shared. We have no right to deny the world our light. To not let the light that we are shine would be like God creating a gorgeous sunrise and hiding the rays of light that naturally express from the sun. We would be missing magnificence that has the capacity to expand across the sky into what seems to be forever and eternity converging into a single moment. Surely our Creator would not hide such beauty from its own creations.

And so it is with us. It is humankind's most earnest, innate desire to be an expression of the light of God - the only light there is. We are not always conscious of this desire, but we can't help but want the connection with our creator that we might share in the beauty, grace, poise and warmth of its all powerful, all knowing, everywhere present, radiant flame. We are the holy sun of God created to show forth the true magnificence of that which our Creator named Light. We are charged with the privilege and the responsibility to let that light shine in and through us. **Sometimes we must join the light that we are, with the lights of our fellow travelers on life's journey. Together we create a brilliant glow that reaches into the depths of the invisible place called unlimited possibilities.**

The light of God expresses as streams of consciousness beaming with unlimited possibilities for Truth, life, love and wisdom to manifest on earth as it is in heaven. In one radiant stream of light, there is pure potential for total illumination for all of creation. We have the capacity to claim our illumined consciousness by fanning the flame of our inner light. As we do, we extend our reach to places where truth and grace are needed - first within ourselves and then to others. We let our light shine on the path within and before us, allowing it to be the way by which we can see the grander potential in ourselves and all humankind.

The true joy of the inner light of Spirit comes when we discover that the light we see in the outer is but a reflection of the light that burns in silence within us. It is patient, and yet always ready to ignite on command to "give light to others in the house." Many will be comforted by the warm glow of the light that we are and see our "good works and give glory to your Father in heaven." As we ignite the fire of God within us, we feel but a smidgen of the power behind the words, "Let there be light." The light burns bright within us, and we harness the power to heal, inspire, encourage, lift, bless and love, beyond what we can ever imagine. Sometimes we are literally the light by which others may see the way of hope before them. In the light of Truth, we grow into the living expression of that which we were created to be from the first day of creation - the light of the world.

Prayer Practice

First assignment: Watch a sunrise or sunset at your next available opportunity. Don't just glance at it while you are driving to and from work. Set an appointment to sit and watch the horizon beginning the hour before so that you get to experience the total event. You're not worshiping the sun but you are enjoying the beauty of what God has created. Remind yourself that the same kind of awesome beauty is within you.

Use the light as a visual in your time of prayer. Let the light illumine your mind and heart, putting you in tune with the goodness of God and that which is all good. This is a great time to burn a candle in the outer as you are working with your inner light.

To develop a consciousness of light expressing as healing, spiritual understanding and divine guidance, use the following prayer practice:

Visualize your body surrounded by a white light.
- Imagine that you are tracing the outer form of your body with this light. Start at the top center of your head going down the left side of your body, under the feet and back up the right side of your body back to the top center of your head. Make this journey of light 3 times completely around your body.
- With each journey, affirm over and over *"Let there be Light."*

Next, continuing to visualize, bring the light from the top of your head down into your heart space, just left of the center of your body.
- Hold the light in your heart space for a few moments in silence.

- Affirm: *"The light of God shines in and through me."*
- If there is any particular prayer that you are working with, shine the light on your desire by thinking on your prayer while continuing to hold the light on your heart space.
- Sit in the silence holding the light and your attention in your heart.
- When you are ready to end your prayer, Affirm: *"I am the light of the world"*,
- When you feel a sense of peace regarding the experience, express your gratitude, and say, *Amen!*

You may use this same prayer practice for specific prayer desires, just change the color of the light as follows:

For healing visualize a green light (or white).

For love visualize a pink light.

For wisdom and creativity visualize a yellow light.

For faith, and peace of mind visualize a blue light.

For prosperity and spiritual power visualize a purple light.

Go forth, dear friend, let there be light shining within you and flowing in abundance all around you. "You are the light of the world!"

Closing Prayer

Dear Friend,

*As you grow in your conscious awareness of God's presence
ever active in you,*

*May you dwell under grace in the secret
place of the Most High;*

*May you abide safely in the shadow
of the Almighty;*

*May all that you think, say and do,
be anchored in divine wisdom;*

*May the cloak of royalty rest gently upon
your shoulders as you prosper in
every way and in accordance with
every good desire.*

*With each prayer that you pray and live,
know that you are indeed creating the life that you
so earnestly desire, and so richly deserve.*

Abundant Blessings Always,
Charline

6-18-12

I loss two Chains gold Chains one
Went down the Sewer. I thought how can
two Chains be lost in the same day? I was
in Church, it seems in the dream their was
some type of Chaos going on, don't remember
the details, don't recall what Church it was

Publisher's Page

Crystal Heart Press, Inc. is a non-profit organization dedicated to teaching on the subjects of spirituality, life skills, personal and professional growth and metaphysics. As one of our commitments, and at the request of the author, a portion of funds from the sale of this book will be awarded in a scholarship to a qualifying high school graduate pursuing a college education.

For more information on the scholarship qualifications, please contact us at crystalheartpress@msn.com.

At Crystal Heart Press, Inc. it is our mission to let our heart of love shine upon the hearts of others making a difference in the lives of those we touch — even if it is one heart at a time.